World Mission People

Daniel V. Runyon, Editor

The Best Of
The Missionary Tidings
1990-95

Saltbox Press
Spring Arbor, Michigan

Dedication

To the thousands of *Missionary Tidings* subscribers whose prayers, gifts, and obedience to God are helping to fulfill the commission Jesus gave to make disciples in all nations.

Cover illustration by Evan Church. Subject is Pastor Comandela of Mozambique. March/April 1994 p. 14

Special thanks to Betty Ellen Cox and M. Renee Runyon for editorial help in preparing this manuscript for publication.

All rights reserved. No part of this publication may be reproduced, stored in a retrieval system, or transmitted in any form or by any means – electronic, mechanical, photocopy, recording, or any other – except for brief quotations in printed reviews, without prior permission.

Distributed by:
> **World Mission People**
> **Free Methodist World Missions**
> **P. O. Box 535002**
> **Indianapolis, IN 46253-5002**

Copyright 1995 by *Daniel V. Runyon*
Published by Saltbox Press
167 Burr Oak Drive, Spring Arbor, MI 49283
Printed in the United States of America
Missions, Missiology, Biography
ISBN: 1-878559-04-4
Price: $15.00

Contents

Page	Section	
7	I.	World Missions
77	II.	Equatorial Africa
135	III.	Southern Africa
183	IV.	Asia
307	V.	Europe
331	VI.	Latin America

I. World Missions

Page	Article
8	Riptide
9	To Catch The Tide [Condensed Book]
27	Getting To Know Doane Bonney
31	Answer The Call
43	On Saying "Hello"
45	Called
46	Bent Wood: Special Applications
48	Take The Cross Cultural Challenge
57	Money With Vision
63	If We Only Tithed
65	Second Grace Of Works
68	Pastors On The Cutting Edge
72	Just Send Money?
75	Missions Prepares People For Freedom

Riptide

M. Doane Bonney
Director, Free Methodist World Missions

When Dr. Byron Lamson wrote *To Catch The Tide* (a condensed form of his book begins on the next page), World Missions of the Free Methodist Church had planted churches in 15 countries world-wide. Membership in those mission churches was around 45,000.

Lamson understood well that new structures were needed so that groups of Free Methodist churches anywhere in the world could aspire to become a General Conference. Free Methodist World Fellowship and Area Fellowships are the result.

I'm convinced it is these new structures that freed mission churches to achieve their greatest potential under the leadership of the Holy Spirit. As a result, these "mission" churches have multiplied more than five-fold to more than 275,000 members found in 28 countries.

And the vision continues. Church leaders in Asia and Latin America have as their goal to plant Free Methodist churches in *every* country of their areas by the year 2000. The Equatorial African Churches are developing church plants on both sides of the equator in a strip 30 degrees wide across that continent. Free Methodists in southern Africa are extending their frontiers by targeting countries like Zambia and Botswana.

A new generation of leaders from every continent now participates with World Missions to plant churches around the globe. Free Methodist World Mission People today come from every quadrant of our planet. We are a mighty army marching!

God has called our church to become a major force for him on a world-wide scale. To succeed, we are partnering with our brothers and sisters on every continent for kingdom building.

The tide Lamson saw is flowing ever stronger. May we grow with overwhelming force toward the year 2000 and beyond on the riptide of God's grace, in the power of the Holy Spirit.

To Catch The Tide

Byron S. Lamson
Condensed by Daniel V. Runyon
July/August 1995

Preface

In 1948, J. W. Haley, retired pioneer missionary to Africa, wrote to Bishop Ormston, chairman of the Commission on Missions:

From time to time a general review and study looking to reorganization is necessary in either church or business and I venture to suggest that time is here in Free Methodist missions. The missions of our church have grown so vastly that they are our major interest.

The young churches are becoming self-conscious. Like the son in the home they should be welcomed into our councils. To delay too long might be costly. We should do something convincing to make these churches feel they are really part of the Free Methodist Church and so weld them into our framework instead of leaving the door open for them, through dissatisfaction, to lose heart in us.

Ten years later the responsible commission and church authority took steps to accomplish the purposes set forth in this long-forgotten letter. A fellowship of churches has been established on a worldwide basis. National church leaders now sit as equals in the highest councils of the church, planning the next venture in evangelistic outreach and Kingdom building.

When the World Fellowship was at last an accomplished fact, the missionary daughter of J. W. Haley said, "Isn't this wonderful? I wish papa could see this."

Somehow I feel that the universe is so arranged that the cloud of witnesses, of which Haley is a member, encompasses us more intimately than we know. Their shadows still hover over us in our highest moments of travail for the new day.

This book tells the story of the four years of worldwide studying, planning, praying, and working that resulted in the establishment of a new relation between all the members of our one worldwide church.

Haley's letter was prophetic. He too caught "the tide."

At Dawn– The Tide

That rising tide is so awful that all other things that go with that tide will also rise, or be deluged if they try to go against it.... It says: "I am coming up, and I will take the hand of anybody who helps me up, and destroy any man who is in my way."
—Frank C. Laubach

Hot, muggy air, filled with malarial mosquitoes, hung over the rambling mission residence like a wet blanket. The oil lantern burned low, blacking its chimney. It was almost midnight [in what today is Mozambique]. Visiting American Board missionaries were sleeping soundly. Harry Agnew was reporting to the newly-elected Missionary Secretary Terrill.

Within two years in relatively safe America, the missionary secretary would be fatally stricken with pneumonia. In dangerous, malarial Africa sturdy Agnew would live the strenuous and difficult life of the pioneer for another 10 years -- long enough to lay the foundations of a strong church with aggressive leadership, evangelistic outreach, and the principle of self-support well established.

Agnew concluded his report, "Praise God. He keeps my soul in glorious peace. Victory is ahead."

His lantern had gone out. Mosquitoes buzzed and stung. Agnew took his quinine and rolled into bed. "For," he added, "I must be off soon after daylight *to catch the tide.*" His little sailboat would carry him across the bay to Inhambane.

The tide -- the real tide -- had already carried this sturdy pioneer far from home. He had been caught up in the purposes of God for the evangelization of the world. He was a part of the struggle between light and darkness where God and man share the cost of redemption.

New Testament Missions

Christianity is a missionary religion. God so loved the world that he gave his Son for its salvation. God had one Son and he was a foreign missionary. However we interpret the death of Christ on the cross, we can never forget that *God was there.* "God was in Christ, reconciling the world unto himself." Here is revealed the missionary heart of God.

A disheartened group of disciples, stunned by the crucifixion tragedy, could hardly believe the story of the resurrection. At last the evidence was irresistible. They believed, they obeyed, they prayed – and in the Upper Room something happened!

Daring Hope

The risen Savior had promised, "You will receive power when the Holy Spirit comes on you; and you will be my witnesses in Jerusalem, and in all Judea and Samaria, and to the ends of the earth."

What a fantastic dream! And he made this commitment to nobodies, backsliders, fearful men, ignorant and unlearned, mostly from the rural areas of Galilee.

Their leader had, by his revolutionary teaching, been branded as a heretic and a blasphemer. A hastily improvised trial was held, his crucifixion effected, and a burial concluded.

It was a hard world. The Roman Empire was a military dictatorship. Three-fourths of the people were slaves. Defective boys and unwanted girl babies were disposed of. Worthless old slaves often were put away by crucifixion.

Something Happened

In the city of Jerusalem, the religious center of the world for the Jews, where the hard core of fanatical resistance had so recently crucified Jesus, thousands of worshipers were gathered for the Feast of Pentecost. The city was filled with visitors from widespread parts of the empire.

Out from the Upper Room once fearful disciples released a spiritual avalanche on the city. The closed doors became highways of holiness to the ends of the earth. A secret prayer meeting was transformed into a main-street evangelistic rally. The great roads of the Roman Empire became rivers of salvation.

This is history. It happened in our world. God-filled men, the body of Christ, the church in that first century, changed the moral climate, transformed the customs, and swung empires off their hinges.

What happened? The early church following in the footsteps of Jesus, filled with his Spirit, went to the ends of the then known world, carrying to all men – Greeks, barbarians, bond and free, Jew and Gentile – the good news of Christ, "the power of God unto salvation."

The New Testament Method

After his conversion and separation to the work of Gentile missions, Paul and his companions traversed the highways of Asia Minor and traveled on up into Europe, preaching first in the synagogues. They concentrated on the larger cities, where they established churches.

After a few weeks or months, Paul pushed on after appointing elders to direct in local affairs. He wrote letters, dispatched messengers, evangelists, and faithful teachers, and when it was possible, revisited these mission churches.

But he never smothered them. On he went in the spirit of him who said, "Let us go into the next towns, that I may preach there also." Within a few years Paul could say, "From Jerusalem, and round about unto Illyricum, I have fully preached the gospel of Christ."

Illyricum was a great area north of Macedonia, loosely defined, probably reaching up into Central Europe! That Paul did reach Rome we are certain. Spain was on his itinerary. Some think he may have gone as far as Britain.

Amazing too is the confidence Paul had in the gospel and its power to make its way in spite of all opposition. The Thessalonian church "received the word in much affliction, with joy of the Holy Ghost." As for Paul, he could testify from a Roman prison that the things which happened to him resulted in the advance of the gospel.

Paul established a permanent organization for his churches. In Asia Minor Paul ordained elders in every church. With prayer and fasting, he commended them to God. He confirmed the souls of the disciples. He exhorted them to faithfulness in the face of certain tribulation.

In Crete, where there were 100 towns and cities, Paul ordered Titus to "ordain elders in every town, as I directed you." This was the purpose of Titus' visit to the island.

Apparently the establishment of a strong local indigenous leadership was Paul's fixed policy. Paul outlines the desired qualities for such appointees. The witness of a godly life and the testimony of an exemplary family are most important. The leaders of the local church must be peacemakers, cooperative, and obedient to directives of the church and the law of Christ.

Messengers and Hosts

The church extended its influence and maintained its character and unity in large measure by the service rendered by two classes of persons, namely, the *messengers* and the *hosts* who offered hospitality, not only to the Apostles and prophets, but to the letter carriers to the churches. The saving truths of the gospel were preserved in the letters and their influence extended by means of the church postal system. Often the church grew up around the home of the host. Philemon was a host, but Paul also sends his greetings "to the church in your house."

Thus the churches of the early Christian centuries were rooted in the home, in family and neighborhood relations, thoroughly indigenous to the local community. It was the church in Thessalonica, Philippi, or Rome — never a mission station of the home church at Jerusalem.

Free Methodist mission policy attempts to follow the New Testament pattern of church expansion in the establishment of its mission fields and churches. The correspondence of missionaries abounds with references to Bible schools, the importance of training evangelists and pastors and sending them out to evangelize their own people.

Africa must be evangelized by Africans. Japan will be won by the Japanese. Missionaries assist with the training of the workers. The church is God working through trained and Spirit-anointed witnesses in each and every land.

"Central in all the activities of a new mission," said J. W. Haley, "is the calling out of the people for Christ to be known as the church who will be able, in turn, to carry the gospel to their own people. This can only be the work of the Holy Spirit, for no words of ours could effect the necessary change in the hearts of men."

Missionary Seminars

It was natural that missionaries employing with various degrees of success the so-called indigenous principle and method should discuss these matters while home on furlough. From 1946 to 1950 this was a prominent topic in our missionary seminar gatherings.

J. W. Haley was most helpful in these deliberations. "It is the right of the people of any country," said Haley, "to carry the gospel to their own people. We go to show them the way. Self-support, self-government, and self-propagation are a unit and indivisible."

James H. Taylor also spoke regarding the aim and objective of missionary work. He said, "The primary aim is the salvation of souls. The ultimate objective is to establish the work in such a way that if the time comes for the missionary to leave, the work can go on."

Only as nationals have responsibility will they grow spiritually as they should. Taylor stressed that missionaries must all be convinced of the necessity of this program and "wholeheartedly and patiently put it into effect." He stressed the importance of the national church depending upon God rather than upon a foreign board for support. He buttressed his position by calling attention to the great gain of the church in Korea under this plan.

American missionaries must not establish institutions on an American scale but on a level where the national church can ultimately take over and support them on standards consistent with the economy of the country. There must be training for leadership and for self support. The national pastors must not live on a level too far above those to whom they minister. Taking students from their home environment for too long a period often spoils them for the best service in their native land.

There must be the teaching of tithing and of holiness of heart. A real revival must accompany this shift in program if it is to succeed!

Growing Churches

A missionary statesman has recently remarked that in his opinion, "The church does not develop self-government, self-support, and self-propagation -- the goals to which the mission long gave lip service -- if it is treated as a child for a hundred years."

A Turning Point

Independent nations look with suspicion upon the missionaries coming from the Western world. They are trying to free themselves of foreign influence. They feel that the Christian church is a foreign import. If there is to be a Christian church in these countries it must be truly indigenous, without paternalistic pressures from the older churches of the West.

If true, this certainly changes the role of the missionary. This means missionaries will go to these fields upon invitation of the mission churches, and will take appointment under the mission conferences, and work as partners and servants of the church. Ultimately the mission itself as a mission will disappear. The missionary will work in and through the national church. The indigenous church is just a step -- an important one -- but a step on the way to the organization of full-fledged churches around the world.

Missions Come To Maturity

Free Methodist missions have been in existence since 1881. There has been considerable success in the extension of the church worldwide. Even more marked than the numerical growth has been the development of strong national leaders. Some of our indigenous churches to all intents and purposes have ceased to be mission churches and have become provisional conferences, and then full-fledged conferences. They have able leaders who are theologically mature men.

We must not forget that these churches have often taken the initiative in evangelistic outreach and missionary activity. The Japan church, for instance, has sent overseas workers to China, southern Asia, to the Pacific Coast, and to Brazil. It has increasingly been felt that overseas churches were as truly the churches of Jesus Christ as was the church in North America. Our polity should be adjusted to recognize this fact.

It is a fact that nationalism has assisted in making possible the successful organization of the world fellowship. There are dangers in extreme nationalism. In some areas, missionaries may not be permitted to continue their work. The church in these areas may be isolated from the worldwide Christian fellowship. This will, of course, be a distinct loss.

However, there is at least one blessing growing out of nationalism. This new emphasis on self-determination and self-government has given to nationals the feeling of their own adequacy for the responsibilities of life. This has helped our church leaders to have more confidence in themselves and to believe that they, too, can take more responsibility in carrying forward the activities of the church. This is a distinct gain.

The final factor that urged definite action to establish a worldwide fellowship was the challenge of the great unevangelized areas of the world. If somehow our national church leaders could take over the present responsibilities of our missionaries, this would release the missionaries to open new fields in unevangelized areas. Also, missionaries could inaugurate new types of service for which national leadership is not yet available.

In view of these considerations, a World Planning Council was established in 1958. Senior Bishop L. R. Marston was made chairman and Hugh A. White was elected secretary.

At this time the main concern seemed to be conserving the essential spirit and genius of Free Methodism, while at the same time giving various areas of the church maximum freedom in organizational matters.

Preliminary Planning

Increasingly during the months of 1959, stress was laid upon the importance of a world fellowship as an instrument for planning the strategy for a worldwide evangelistic advance. The conference should study the opportunities and needs of the world and seek ways and means to extend the witness of the church within the various countries. The conference should seek to adopt measures that would maintain the unity of the faith, plan procedures to enrich and enlarge our mutual understanding and fellowship, and prepare the entire church for decisive action in the fields of education, social reform, and evangelism.

It was decided to have fellowship conferences at separate times for Asia, Latin America, and Africa. Studies were conducted, finances were arranged, and committees met. Meanwhile, reports started coming from various overseas conferences and panels, indicating that we had not been any too soon in catching the tide.

Spirit-guided Panels

The blessings resulting from the studies and discussions leading up to the Asia Conference not only affected the nationals but also the missionaries. Concerning one mission meeting, the superintendent said: "We got to grips with a planned program of educational evangelism and evangelistic educational activity, using the hospital as an evangelistic agency, the teams from the seminary as an evangelistic agency, fitting them into the church program -- all these things were frankly faced and thoroughly discussed on our entire mission-wide area for the first time in my experience. It was a real blessing. We broke down and wept with thanksgiving to God for the day. Coming out of this is the development of a new work in this area. It is the brightest possibility we have had for the last 12 or 15 years."

A meeting of the full panel was held in March 1959. The panel was reminded that overseas delegates to the North American General Conference are not interested in much of the legislation that consumes the attention of the conference. The needs of these overseas churches are so different and are not adequately cared for by such a conference. The panel finally decided that "there is no alternative for face-to-face contact. We can learn from each other."

Two major plans of organization were considered. The first was a loose federation of completely autonomous churches who have full authority in both organization and doctrinal matters. This is the kind usually adopted by the congregational form of church government. The alternative was a close-knit organization with one general conference to which all churches of the denomination send delegates, or with area general conferences whose acts are subject to review by a central judiciary board. The panel tried to keep both emphases in mind as the study of organization was carried forward.

What Is Evangelism?

As plans for the Asia Conference developed, it became clear that this was to be a conference on evangelism first, with only a secondary emphasis on organization. This was in line with the essential genius of the church, which in its early years was more evangelism than nurture; more movement than organization.

In our early history, evangelism was spontaneous and not the result of legislation. Both Methodism and Free Methodism were irregular movements. Early Methodists were denied the sacraments of the Anglican Church. Early founders of Free Methodism were excluded from the Methodist fellowship.

In preparing for this emphasis on evangelism, the question was asked, "What is the formula for evangelistic success? What guiding principles do we have? Generally speaking, the slower-growing churches have the best organization. Rapidly-growing churches that are still losing themselves in evangelistic activity apparently do not seem to have much time for organization. Is organization our compensation for failure?

What's In A Name?

The executive committee was alerted to the fact that the overseas churches do not have the same historical background as we in North America. On at least one field the name "Methodist" is unknown. "Is it a Bible term?" asked one leading pastor. "Why do you use it?"

The usual description of John Wesley and the Holy Club of Oxford was given. Their entire life was ordered according to a schedule. They lived according to a *method* and were finally dubbed "Method-ists."

"Well," he replied, "why don't you call yourselves Wesleyans if you are trying to follow John Wesley? Methodists -- I don't get it."

"Free" is just as difficult. For a European it denotes a sect. Well, try this. One hundred years ago most churches rented their pews to finance their programs. This seemed undemocratic. The provisions of the gospel are for all. God's grace is freely given. All need to hear. A "free" church is one with free seats.

But today all churches have "free seats." so you try again -- freedom for slaves (1860), freedom from fixed forms and ceremonies, free from the spirit of the world, free from the power of sin, free to follow the leading of the Holy Spirit, freedom in worship, free grace for all who will meet the conditions of salvation as set forth in the New Testament.

So the conferences must fill this name full of content and meaning, and do the same for many other terms we use so regularly.

April 19-28, 1960, Japan

Delegates journeyed from Egypt, India, Hong Kong, Taiwan, the Philippines, and North America. This consultation of national leaders was the first of its kind in the history of our Church. Church leaders from each country gathered to consider problems vital to their own lands. Missionaries came not as missionaries but as representatives of the national churches where they served.

It was a genuine consultation, with all freely expressing their deepest needs and highest hopes. There was a fine balance between business, organizational procedure, reports, and resolutions for General Conference action on the one hand, and Bible study, worship, sermons, prayers, and high spiritual moments.

Some called it "Pentecost" — moments when it was easy to believe in the resurrection of Jesus and the life eternal.

Something happened in Japan. A sense of evangelistic **must** gripped us as never before — a humbling sense of a great task barely begun. To do our part in this great task, our Free Methodists must be people of a concerned heart. Nothing less than the evangelization of the entire world in every geographical area, every culture, every kingdom, is the objective of our mission.

We affirmed our faith in the complete adequacy of Jesus Christ for the needs of lost men. We pledged ourselves to prayer and sacrifice and suffering for the redemption of our world.

The Place of the Missionary

Is the day of the missionary gone? Are missionaries still needed? National church leaders expressed their earnest desire for continued missionary assistance. However, they are concerned that missionaries be "of the right type." What sort of missionary do these people want? This is their answer:

"Missionaries must be deeply spiritual above all else. They must be cooperative, broad-minded, impartial, able to see the national point of view, not committed to American ways and methods, sacrificial, simple, willing to be frontier pioneers in opening up new work, both in interior areas and cities, with full and adequate equipment to communicate with the most people in the shortest time and by all means."

These are the qualities the nationals themselves desire in the missionaries today.

Highly educated scholars are needed, who not only understand the "breadth and depth of all theological thinking but who also are able to interpret the Wesleyan position, and who in personal piety, conduct, and powerful witness are enabled by the power of the Holy Spirit to lift up Christ who will draw all men to himself. Such workers will be welcomed."

The Centenary Conference

The year 1960 marked the 100th anniversary of the founding of the Free Methodist Church. It was the responsibility of the North American panel to bring recommendations from Asia to the attention of the General Conference.

The conference recommended the immediate organization of a Free Methodist World Fellowship. They proposed a continuing committee with members from each of the areas of the church, the same to study the organizational needs of worldwide Free Methodism, and to prepare a constitution for a permanent Free Methodist World Assembly in which area and national General Conferences will hold membership. They also requested that a bishop be assigned to the supervision of the overseas churches to help them develop strong indigenous churches and fully recognized conferences in each area.

The Real Tide

The real tide was running in favor of the Asia Conference and its recommendations. North American Free Methodists sensed a new current moving in the work of our missionary program. Naturally some were cautious and viewed the recommendations with suspicion. This was especially true since there had been no time between the Asia Conference and the Centenary Conference to alert all furloughing missionaries regarding what had transpired in Asia.

At their workshop an extended discussion took place. The secretary reported that "although it seems that a majority might have voted in favor, yet no action was taken." Finally the committee, together with the Asia Conference delegates, decided it was too soon to present a plan for a world fellowship. In lieu of this, they submitted five propositions which were debated, amended, and finally overwhelmingly approved.

Big Decision

The General Conference authorized the North American panel to organize itself as a Continuing Committee with authority to affiliate with other panels of continuing committees throughout the world. They approved the holding of fellowship conferences along the lines of the Asia Conference in both Latin America and Africa. They endorsed in principle the ideas and general recommendations with reference to a World Fellowship. The already autonomous Egypt Church was recognized as a general conference. Similar status for the Japan church was approved.

The editor of the *Free Methodist* later affirmed that "the most significant change [resulting from General Conference] was the authorization of a World Free Methodist Fellowship looking ahead to a possible World Assembly of Free Methodist Churches. This means that we recognize the strength and national rights of our churches in all countries. Indeed, we listen with a holy jealousy to the reports of the advancement of God's work beyond North America. May God help us to keep pace with them."

Africa Conference

Proceeding on the authority granted, study panels were organized in Africa and in Latin America. At the meeting in Africa one group from a slowly growing area gave a long list of the problems they faced. This was supposed to explain their static condition.

The delegation from one of the faster growing areas presented its report. They too listed a great number of problems. Then they began to tell the entire conference what they were doing in spite of the conditions and how God was giving them success.

Africans sat across the table from Africans telling one another of their problems and how to overcome these obstacles! African delegates pulled out their notebooks and began to take notes on the success stories of their brethren. This seemed to be the real church, under the leadership of the Holy Spirit, girded and ready for action. We were out on the growing edges where Christianity comes to first-hand grips with the powers of darkness, catching the tide!

It was clear to the delegates who had attended the Asia Conference that this Africa consultation, while different, was in no sense inferior. The Asia gathering was more idealistic, laying greater stress upon theology, organization, and worship. The Africa Conference was more practical, more concerned with the "how to" aspects of the church's work.

This event was a large one in the lives of African delegates, easily the most cosmopolitan gathering they had ever attended, and also their greatest intellectual experience in regard to exchange of ideas and large-

scale planning:
1. It did not spoil them.
2. It greatly widened their horizons.
3. It inspired confidence.
4. It elevated these church leaders in the eyes of the Christians.
5. It raised the standing of the Free Methodist Church in the community of Protestant churches in Ruanda-Urundi.
6. It broadened their sense of purpose.
7. It was a spiritual experience.

Revolutionary Latins

The situation facing the church in Latin America is a peculiar one. The Roman Church, traditionally almost a state church, claims loyalty to the same Jesus Christ and the same gospel as is preached by the evangelicals. But much of the Romanism in Latin America is a distorted and perverted Christianity which seems to inoculate the follower against the real thrust of the gospel message.

The needs of Africa and Asia seemed rather far removed from the immediate problems in Latin America. In fact, the Organization Committee was more concerned with establishing a permanent Fellowship in Latin America than with a world organization. A constitution prepared prior to the conference was radically revised and the new purpose stated as follows:

"The Free Methodist Latin America Fellowship is a representative organization of churches in Latin America whose purpose is to provide opportunity for consultation, planning, and mutual aid between the churches. In harmony with this purpose, it shall arrange for area conferences, establish working committees and facilitate the exchange of information and workers for the strengthening of the member churches to better fulfill their mission in the world."

The conference was characterized by the typical warmth and emotional flavor of the Latin. There was an informal freedom, a natural oratory, an uninhibited singing of choruses, and spontaneous prayer. There seemed to be no barriers to understanding between North Americans and Latin Americans. Perhaps the keenest insights regarding political, social, and economic problems, as well as the religious situation, were exhibited here.

Some of the delegates were perhaps a little over self-confident. They had a sense of power, a feeling for words, and an urge to tell missionaries what to do, and to criticize the methods that had been employed in the past. It would be well for missionaries and church leaders to listen to this conversation. There were superlative expressions of thanks for planning such a conference. Several delegates indicated that it was "long overdue."

There was a genuine exchange of ideas. Representatives from slow-moving areas asked questions and took notes. Delegates from other areas filled with the wine of success were eager to describe their activities. There was real fellowship, and a unity of purpose at the conference. All agreed that more prayer, more of the Holy Spirit, more dedication to Christ, and harder work will bring about success for the gospel in Latin America.

World Parish

The World Fellowship Organizing Conference took place January 9-21, 1962, and was held in five consecutive locations: Greenville, Illinois; Indianapolis and Winona Lake, Indiana; Spring Arbor and Detroit, Michigan. The special purpose of the conference was to present the large number of recommendations from the overseas churches and Area Fellowships, and to refer them to the proper committees for study and recommendation.

The great event took place at 7:35 Friday evening, January 12, 1962, in the conference room of Marston Hall on the campus of Greenville College. The constitution was adopted unanimously. It was declared that approval of the constitution did give the body permission to proceed with further organization and the initial operation of the World Fellowship.

The Church and Its Missionary Enterprise, a committee chaired by Dr. W. J. Stonehouse, reported that the missionary serves in a changing world and must be able to adjust quickly to new situations. He must be an example of New Testament Christianity in prayer, love of the Word, and soul winning. He must be cooperative and understanding, with the ability to see others' points of view. He will be ready for sacrifice and able to demonstrate flexibility, willing to learn of, to understand, and appreciate the culture, history, and background of the country to which he is assigned.

Our missionary work is now moving into a period where the national church and its leaders have assumed more responsibility. The missionary is a co-worker. He must have love and understanding. The missionary's ability will qualify him for the position to which he has been assigned in the work of the conference.

The Free Methodist World Fellowship, as defined in its statement of purpose, is "an organization for the coordination of the worldwide activities of the denomination. In harmony with this purpose it shall endeavor to promote closer fellowship and mutual understanding among all branches of the Free Methodist Church, serve as an agent for joint planning and cooperative action, and carry forward studies helpful to the member conferences."

First Century Pattern

Bishop Marston delivered a carefully prepared message relevant to the work of the World Fellowship Conference in the Spring Arbor College chapel. His subject was, "First Century Pattern for Twentieth Century Missions."

After outlining the marvelous development that has taken place on Free Methodist mission fields in the last 75 years, and calling attention especially to the progress of the overseas conferences along indigenous lines, the Bishop concluded:

"The view of missions I have sought to present does not mean releasing the home church from responsibility for world evangelization. Far from it! It rather increases its responsibility if this 11th-hour crisis is to be met successfully.

"Until blocked by national governments unfriendly to missionary enterprise, missionary supervision and encouragement will be necessary for years to come. But the children must be co-laborers with the parent, sharing the labor and responsibility of evangelizing new nations.

"Most important of all missionary tasks will be the training of nationals as evangelists, pastors, teachers, nurses, doctors, administrators, and economic leaders. Then, when an unfriendly government erects barriers to keep the missionary and his foreign church outside, the church will be established inside the country, and the parent church can say, 'It is now your turn to carry on the fight alone.'

"The task the church now undertakes will not be easy, but will require courage, hard work, continuing financial support, and the prayer of faith. The pattern of the task is not new, but was set by the Christian church's first missionary statesman, the Apostle Paul.

"With Paul's confidence in the inherent power of the gospel; with a continuing dedication of the home church to world evangelism; and with increasing thousands of national Christians prepared to accept the challenge of extending the gospel to new nations, the light of the saving gospel of the Son of God will be extended to multitudes that now sit in darkness."

Fellow Workmen

Before the World Fellowship Conference adjourned in Detroit, Southern Michigan Conference Superintendent [W. Dale] Cryderman concluded the day with a tremendous exhortation. His text was, "For we are fellow workmen, joint promoters, laborers together with and for God" (Phillips). He asked: "Can I ever be the same, can I ever be selfish again? No, not after hearing Professor Chauke express the burden of his heart for the education of his people. Not after catching Reverend Isaac Shembe's desire for revival for South Africa. Not after sensing Reverend Simoni Ndikumazambo's vision for growth and for reaching the people of his country.

"No, I can't afford these old-fashioned ideas of selfishness, self-centeredness, after listening to Bishop Oda and two of his outstanding young pastors state their dreams for building a strong church in Japan. Reverend Jesse Nathar's burden for India must become my burden. Yes, I am a laborer together with all these men.

"We labor, preaching the same message; we labor amidst the same opportunities; we labor facing the same problems; but best of all, we labor having the same resources -- we have the empowering of the Holy Spirit for the great task that is ours."

The next day delegates were off to the far corners of the earth to carry in their warm hearts the inspiration of the Conference and to take up again their tasks for Christ and his kingdom. They carried with them a new sense of the unity of the church. They returned with an added sense of responsibility and better understanding of the task. We think also that all came close to the real source of power for the church -- the ever present Holy Spirit.

What a Tide!

Seventy-five years ago pioneer missionary Agnew was expecting the dawn of a new day and a tide that would carry him and his boat to the harbor of Inhambane.

Agnew himself was being carried along by another tide more powerful, more meaningful and enduring -- the tide of God's purposes for

Africa and the world. The tide of a great vision for the extension of the Redeemer's kingdom gripped his mind and heart. He had a large vision. He was full of faith. His young church was learning self support. He wrote: "We had a good service last night. The boys gave us four dollars toward buying lamps. We expect to pay our native evangelist. We hope to support another evangelist...."

What a tide! Agnew was near death. The home board treasury was on the brink of bankruptcy. The prayers of that pioneer missionary were heard -- not only a half mile in Mozambique -- but finally reached the church in America. The "thin and worn" Agnew that returned for a long overdue furlough made a profound impression wherever he traveled. This was the breaking of the new day for Africa, for the world, and for our church in North America.

The tide was right. The method was right. By necessity the pioneers simply were forced to train workers and place heavy responsibility upon them. In this they were going with the current perhaps better than they knew; or are we just catching up with their vision?

Flood Tide

In this field of moral endeavor God works with men. Through prayer, the study of the Bible, by providence, and in the Christian community we call the church, God makes known his will. This is the real "tide in the affairs of men."

In remarkable measure our early missionaries caught the moving current. They lived close to God and the people. Responsibility was placed on the young church for evangelistic outreach and for its major financial support. Inadequately trained, by our standards, national workers performed miracles.

A literature of hymn books, Bibles, and simple theology was produced. Self-supporting and self-propagating mission churches later achieved the status of regular conferences. Some became general conferences. The indigenous church was the real tide that made the World Fellowship possible and necessary.

World Mission People 26

DR DOANE and MRS RUTH BONNEY
General Director of World Missions

Getting To Know Doane Bonney

Interview by Daniel V. Runyon
September/October 1990 pp. 17-18

To understand a man's vision you must know his past. Dr. Doane Bonney's past is colorful, his vision is clear.

What Kind of A Guy is our Director of World Missions? One who goes for broke when playing Monopoly, looks for something familiar on a menu, and who, when lost, is more likely to drive around until he finds it rather than stop and ask directions. His favorite room at home is the living room, where he can stretch out on the floor and read.

Thirty years of hands-on missionary work prepared Doane Bonney for this position, along with a growing faith and a daily walk with God. From 1959 to 1965 the number of students quadrupled while he was director of the Evangelical Institute in Santiago, Dominican Republic. In 1965 he turned the school over to a Dominican director, and in the next few years the school became self-supporting. Bonney then served for five years on the Department of Education faculty at a university in Santiago, and was also active in preparing pastors and lay leaders at the Biblical Seminary.

Since 1979 Bonney has been Area Administrative Assistant for Latin America. Under his guidance the Free Methodist Church has entered four new countries, all under national leadership. "God has been preparing me all along for this challenge as Director of World Missions," he explains, "yet I feel a sense of awe. I have great respect and appreciation for those who have occupied this position. I want to give it my best." His goal is to equip every conference, every local church, and every Free Methodist to fulfill Matthew 28:19-20: *"Go and make disciples of all nations, baptizing them in the name of the Father and of the Son and of the Holy Spirit, and teaching them to obey everything I have commanded you. And surely I am with you always, to the very end of the age."*

Kids Need To Know -- How neat did Doane Bonney keep his bedroom as a child? Fairly neat, considering that he shared everything with his brothers. The bed got made about 70% of the time, but dust balls were seldom cleaned out from under the bed.

Doane lived without electricity until the family moved to Wessington Springs, South Dakota, where he was able to tune in WNAX radio to hear The Lone Ranger, Gang Busters, and the Old Fashioned Revival Hour. Additional culture was gleaned from the "funnies" in the Huron daily newspaper.

When not listening to the radio Doane might be found reading horse stories, mysteries, historical novels, or biographies of people like Abe Lincoln and G. W. Carver -- unless it was chore time. Cows had to be milked and fed regularly, but the worst job was dumping the "slop pail," a relic from days before indoor plumbing. The unpardonable sin was quitting before a job was done.

In 1942 the passion to own a bicycle compelled Doane and his brother to collect iron scrap, sell it for some $20, only to find that no bikes were available due to the war. Finally they got an old one that didn't have a "neutral."

Another coveted possession was an Ingram pocket watch. Doane bought one for $1.00, made a strap for it of braided leather thongs, and tucked it into the pocket on the front of his bib overalls -- blue bibs on weekdays, striped on Sunday.

The youth group at church was active and fun. How important was it to be in church? Very. Once when the car wouldn't start and the horse-drawn jig was out of service, "Mother had a couple of us walk to church in a driving rain. We were soaked," Doane recalls, "so Mother said, 'We'll turn around now and walk home.' She didn't want us to sit around and catch a cold."

Solid Christians, the Bonney parents were practical family raisers who expected the best of their six children. "Make something of yourself," they advised. "Listen for God's call."

Doane's favorite musical group was "the mamas and the papas." That is, about every other Sunday night a neighborhood "sing" was held in a community home. Refreshments were served.

Vacations were unheard of. The equivalent was a family trip four miles away from the farm to go fishing on the 4th of July. Eating is always a priority for boys, and Doane always felt closest to heaven on fried spring chicken with apple pie.

Doane first attended a one room rural school with one teacher for all eight grades – you could take two or three years in one by just listening! Later, the town school he attended was like most schools today.

The Bonney boys are guilty of at least one practical joke – the school teacher agreed to jump out the window if Doane's brother got 100% in spelling. He did, so she jumped. A passing neighbor reported the students had "tossed" her out. What an uproar in the community!

The six Bonney children still keep in touch, and Doane had other pals in the neighborhood: Bud Rhodes, Burt Gillette, Les Patton. "We would go bull-head fishing in the Jim river," Doane reports. "And there was hiking, camping, and swimming in the ditches along the road in spring. When I was five my brother and I spent one summer making mud pies. Christ came into my life at age six."

Important role models set a Christian example for Doane: Bob Short, Earl Dillon, Bob Potts. "I set out to read the Bible through in the fourth grade. A right relationship with Christ has been my most significant aim."

The call for missions service came at age 10. There was no voice from heaven, just a strong feeling in Doane's heart. "A real missionary stayed at our home for a couple of days," Doane remembers. "Miss Thumb made a strong impression on me. Often my parents would say, 'Wouldn't it be great if some of you boys would grow up to be missionaries or pastors?' In that positive atmosphere, it was easy for me to respond with a strong 'yes' when God spoke to my heart about being a missionary."

Doane never doubted this call. Through high school and college it was continually before him. Later, as a school teacher, he had questions about the timing – **when** to go – but the question of going or not going was never the issue.

As a child Doane took deliberate steps to follow through on this call. He shared his feelings with family, pastors, and youth leaders. In high school, "I made known my interest in missionary work to the Missionary Board of our church. Occasional contacts with the Board kept the dream alive in my heart."

As a teen Doane began to narrow in on the kinds of missionary service available. Not until college did he understand the need for educational missionaries: "Missionary Odvar Berg on a visit to Wessington Springs about 1950 was the first to hint to me that a missionary could be a **teacher**," says Doane. This route was confirmed as a result of teaching in the Urbana Free Methodist Church, and in Illinois public schools. Doane concludes, "As an adult I have never been more fulfilled than when teaching some new idea or concept to a class."

"**When I was 10** I first saw Ruth Schantz. My family bought her grandfather's house in Wessington Springs. We began dating when I was a senior in high school. I shared my mission vision with her, and she felt totally satisfied that my call was her call, too. We were married in 1952 between the second and third year of college. I told her I loved her for the first time out in the middle of Lake Mitchell in a rented row boat. We have had a beautiful time ever since. For our honeymoon we spent a week at a rented place on Lake of the Ozarks.

"Ruth enjoys working on details. She brings order, balance, and form into my life. I'm more inclined toward seeing things in broader strokes. We are alike in sharing goals, the way we use our time, and our political and religious convictions. Ruth is the perfect wife for me." Today Doane and Ruth have two daughters, a son, and seven grandchildren.

The now extinct Wessington Springs College conferred on Doane Bonney the A.A. degree, and at Greenville College he received a B.S. in education. His M.A. and Ed.D. are from the University of Illinois.

Specific goals as Director of World Missions include the desire to have 200 career missionaries by the year 2000, 300 VISA workers devoting one, two, or three years to missions, and to open work in 10 new countries, while also cooperating in a major thrust into Europe. And Childcare Ministries should grow from some 5,000 sponsored children to 15,000 or 20,000.

Doane feels his goals are realistic because the world has never been so open or offered so many opportunities for Christian witness as it is today: "The whole Eastern European situation has changed overnight. We must cooperate with others to win this area for Christ. There are opening doors for us in Korea, Bolivia, Kenya, Argentina and Central America. We must help where we can."

A further goal is to equip a new generation for missions leadership. "It is absolutely imperative that we cultivate a corps of younger leaders ready to take over."

And when Doane is done cultivating people -- he would like to cultivate a garden. "I enjoy gardening. When I have less traveling to do, I want a large garden. But traveling and gardening don't mix, so I **wait** to garden."

Answer The Call!

Survey by Heidi Campbell
May/June 1991 pp. 1-7

What does it mean to be "called by God?" When God calls, what is he likely to want? How should we respond? What happens to those who obey? To find out, college sophomore Heidi Campbell (majoring in international journalism) sent a survey to Free Methodist career missionaries. Her findings are summarized below.

God spoke to Moses from a burning bush. There could be little doubt about what God wanted him to do. How does God speak to you?

God called Dean Smidderks (South Africa) into the ministry "directly as a voice I could hear." But generally, God is more subtle. Carolyn Cranston (Philippines) says God calls "through his Word and in my devotional times." William Bicksler (Hong Kong) adds that God generally speaks "through the Word uttered by an anointed servant of God."

Margaret Nelson (Hong Kong) says, "God usually speaks to me through Scripture, reading Christian books, counsel from other Christians, and by directing my thoughts." Jim Nelson adds, "God helps me understand his views through the Bible. My part is to listen, pray, and obey -- and that enables me to hear God more clearly."

Jim Stillman (Zaire) feels God speaks "mostly through my good sense about what is right and proper to do, in conjunction with my obedience to the Holy Spirit. The Holy Spirit gives insight, and insight about God is exciting and filling."

Gordon and Martha Evoy (Hong Kong) elaborate: "God speaks through his Holy Spirit. The Spirit uses various means, such as his Word, Spirit-filled Christians, a sensitive and sanctified conscience, worship experiences, life experiences such as VISA and other cross cultural opportunities."

"The way God chooses to speak fits the spiritual, emotional, psychological maturity, and make-up of an individual," says Philip Gilmore (Dominican Republic). "Once God spoke to me in a distinct inner voice, on other occasions, through other Christians, Scripture, or circumstances. Each time it fit the situation."

Loren Van Tassel (Hong Kong) says God's call usually is seen "through what needs to be done next. Only very rarely does God speak through a burning bush or Damascus Road experience, but when it comes I must be careful to heed. And I must not seek this kind of call – if I do I'll create it myself and that will be false."

David Roller (Mexico) reacts to the basic assumptions behind the question: "A better example of how God calls is Timothy in the New Testament. Paul called him."

"God didn't specifically call Isaiah," adds Gordon Evoy. "God expressed a concern, to which Isaiah responded. The call came out of Isaiah's recognition of who God is."

Garry Cruce (Paraguay) says, "God has spoken to me through the still small voice in which I sense the Lord leading. This is coupled with an 'open door' policy. If the door opens, that is a confirmation of the Lord's will. This is tempered by the counsel of other Christians."

In regard to his missionary service, Dan Parry (Japan) notes, "God spoke to me through a great sense of the need and an inner conviction that I would go." Dale Bidwell (Japan) adds, "I can sense the Peace of God when I am taking the right way."

Carol Watson (Rwanda) usually senses God's "voice" as she quietly goes about her everyday business, and "Sometimes a word from a respected Christian friend gives me confirmation, 'Yes, that God's idea,' and I act on it."

God generally speaks to Carmena Capp (South Africa) "with a quiet 'knowing.' Sometimes He speaks clearly (but never audibly), emphatically and directively."

"God speaks to me through allowing circumstances to point in one direction," observes Ruth Winslow (Hong Kong). "I wasn't sure I should keep teaching last year in China. Then I said, 'Okay God, if you want me to teach show me something that points in that direction.' The next week at least three incidents happened which showed me I was needed there."

When did you first feel God's call on your life? How did you respond?

"I felt God called me to be a missionary from the age of 12," says Carolyn Cranston. "Missionary Mary Schlosser influenced me. I responded, and followed through by getting teaching credentials after earning an AB from Greenville College."

Margaret Nelson attended a missions convention when in junior high school. She went forward to indicate that she was available to God. Jim Nelson was 16 when "I felt God's call to accept him as my Savior. At 18 I felt called to Christian service. At 21 I felt a call to sanctification and total willingness to obey him in all things. As God calls to me daily to trust and follow him I ask for his grace to respond, and he has led me faithfully."

Jim Stillman reports, "When I was quite young I remember thinking I could use my skills on the mission field. It was presented as a privilege, so **not** being a missionary was something I struggled with."

When Michael Henry (Mexico) was 13, "I turned my life over to the Lord's service. Since then it has been a matter of willingness and obedience."

Philip Gilmore felt called to missions "shortly after I committed my life to Christ. After working as a camp counselor one summer I began to want to do full time Christian ministry. I changed my major to fit that desire."

Loren Van Tassel says, "My call came while I was teaching nursing students at the University of Washington. I quit the job and went to seminary."

Gordon Evoy reports, "At age 17, I responded to an invitation to go forward at a family camp missionary service. I committed myself to be a missionary, if God should call me. I visualized Africa, likely due to our friend Gertrude Haight, the missionary at the camp."

But today you will find Evoys in Hong Kong, not Africa. Gordon explains: "In 1988, God called my wife and myself as we listened to a TV pastor share from Isaiah 6:1-6 about 'Those Whom God Sends.' God clearly spoke to both of us. We see how God stamped the image of the Chinese upon our hearts. During 10 years of pastoral ministry (after a two-year stint in Hong Kong), we felt we would return one day, but in God's time. We marvel at God's timing!"

Bob Cranston, the reluctant prophet, admits, "In those early days my concept of the ministry was quite negative. I hesitated to make a lifetime commitment of poverty and miss what I felt were the good things in life."

Dan Parry affirms the step by step process: "I could not have said when I was a teen that I was going to be a missionary, but God led me. One step led to the next."

Often there is a vagueness between steps. Says Dale Bidwell, "When I was 14, I felt the call to preach. I went to a Christian college and later seminary to prepare to fulfill that calling, though there were times when that call grew pretty dim."

Philip Gilmore confirms this process: "God's call was progressive. He took me a step at a time. Each step was only as big as my maturity would allow me to take."

Carol Watson's experience was more abrupt: "I was 25, had a fulfilling job, and felt God's blessing on my work. Then one day, in a flash of insight, God made it clear that he had a big change ahead for me. I immediately sought counsel from my pastor and began a search for God's specific will. I prayed much and knocked on doors. After six months of watching, waiting and working, a VISA short term opportunity came up -- two years of evangelism through informal adult English classes in Japan. Perfect for me."

Dean Smidderks felt the call "at a youth camp when 12 years old, to be willing to do full time service. Later as a college freshman, to prepare for pastoral ministry. I responded both times in submission to what I understood to be God's will."

William Bicksler was in college when "I was asked to take a service in place of an MK, and in that service a mother and daughter received Christ. God's call for missions came my senior year in college. From these points I've never turned back."

Wilma Kasten (Taiwan) feels that "by the time I was 12, I think I knew I was to be a missionary. The call to China was settled in my freshman year of college. My first reaction before I was saved was that I could not do it -- only a very common, ordinary person. After I knew the call to China, I always wanted to come."

How would you respond differently if you had it to do over again?

To this question many said they would do it the same way over again. Others suggested these refinements:

-- "The church should have run a 'Barnabas' program to draw me into a training program." David Roller

-- "I would have talked to my parents or Sunday School teacher, and I would have read missionary books." Dorothy Raber

-- "Listen to God's voice and his timing. It may take years, but it's better than responding to need alone or a false sense of guilt." Michael Henry

-- "I would have been more receptive to God's leading. I would have been saved sooner. I would have paid more attention to the things of God and spent more time with God's people." David Hill

– "Be willing to take advantage of whatever opportunity for service that God makes available." Philip Gilmore

– "Whatever the call to future service may be, day-to-day obedience to God in the meantime is the only way to be ready to follow that future call." Jim Nelson

– "I would have walked more confidently. Only occasionally do we know early on what God has for us. Be content to obey for today. Tomorrow will take care of itself." Daniel Parry, Japan

What steps should a person take who has felt God's call?

"If you feel the slightest interest, plunge right ahead in preparation," recommends Ruth Winslow. "I must say, I wish I'd taken accounting and computers, since I do mission books and am totally unprepared."

"God had to work slowly on me over the years," Beth Stewart (South Africa) confesses. "At age 21 I completely surrendered my life to the Holy Spirit and became an available, usable person. Then He was able to guide me."

Garry Cruce points out, "Our call is not to a place or a position, but rather to the Lord. Cultivate your relationship with God and let him lead. Be active in your local church. If you cannot make it there, you will not make it on the mission field."

Dale Bidwell recommends that you "consult with pastors and Christian leaders about what they feel your gifts are, but don't let them make the final decision for you – only you and the Lord can do that."

Gordon Evoy says the secret is this: "SEEK TO KNOW GOD! Spend time quietly in prayer and with the Word (Psalm 46:10). Allow his Spirit to fill you with himself. Choose to be fully obedient to God. Recognize that there is only one motivation for entering full-time Christian service: to exalt Jesus Christ and glorify God (Col. 1:28, 29).

"In order to be close to others, one must be close to God, focused upon him, and ready to obey him at all costs. Our DOING must always come from out of our BEING. A wise pastor once said to prospective ministers, 'Get out of it if you can.' He meant that if you can get out of it, you shouldn't be in it."

Carol Watson recommends that you "Pray, tell a few trusted friends, act (don't sit around and wait), and continue in the way you're going until new insight directs you elsewhere."

Dean Smidderks has this advice: "**A.** Seek to know and follow God's will for you with patience — it takes time! **B.** Recognize needs or a particular need for workers that may burden you to prayer, whether or not it ultimately involves you. **C.** Make an honest evaluation of your gifts or talents to meet that need. **D.** Wait for God to give you a 'divine sense of oughtness' that you should be involved, and ought not to do otherwise."

Gordon Evoy points out: "The ability and power to do anything for God is his alone. The only thing you can offer to God is your capacity to be filled with his Spirit." He adds that you should "be involved in ethnic ministries through VISA, work teams to other countries, or in your own area. Read biographies of missionaries and other men and women of God. Be in a position to hear!"

Loren Van Tassel advises you to "be open to God in the interior hidden life. Be obedient to God in the outward life. Get involved in knowing, loving, and serving people, then lead them to Christ and help them get established in Christ."

Bob Cranston says, "Some questions you might ask yourself are: Do I have a real sense of the Holiness of God, awe of God? Do I have a sense of the destructiveness of sin? Is there an anticipation of joy when I think of surrendering and following him?" Bob believes that "there is a need to begin to share your faith where you are, not in the sweet bye and bye, but now!"

Dale Bidwell feels you should "Ask lots of questions of those involved in the field you plan to enter. And plan to meet minimal educational requirements. Practical experience in your mission work is very important. Missionaries starting churches overseas often make basic mistakes that could have been prevented with pastoral experience. Of course, you're going to make a lot of mistakes anyway in a foreign culture."

Says Dan Parry, "Keep a journal of God's dealing with you. It will be handy to look back at later when questions arise."

Wilma Kasten adds, "Prepare for one specific area of service, but have a second field of interest and preparation, too. Contact the Department of World Missions and keep them aware of you and your progress."

Then too, says Garry Cruce, you should "Sharpen the gifts God has given you by experience in the local church. Learn how to work with people. And get as much cross-cultural experience as possible."

Other Recommendations:
– Learn to know God's voice by consistent, meaningful times of prayer and Bible reading. Read Christian classics and learn from saints of other generations.

– Hang around godly people. Make your goal to *be*, not to *do*.

– Don't consider any service for God as a "sacrifice." It is a privilege and will only bring fulfillment and satisfaction.

– Do the tasks at hand: teach Sunday School or take a training program, and do the best you can. When the time comes to move on, God will show you. Learn everything you can about everything – welding, agriculture, bookkeeping, computers, engine repair, anthropology, sociology, psychology, literature, history, car repair, engineering, *everything*.

– Be obedient to **all** God asks of you in both big things and small things. Realize that God usually only reveals one step at a time. You have to obey and follow through on that step before he will reveal the next step.

– Don't tell God there are things you won't do.

How do you know it is God calling, not your own idea?
Dan Parry responds, "Your ideas fade over time, but God's call is persistent. Also, as you seek God about it earnestly, you will know in your heart."

Dean Smidderks affirms, "God does not make mistakes. As we pursue his will, we must trust him to open doors and close others. We must proceed in the confidence that God will direct us in his path, before moving beyond or outside his will, through the prompting of his Spirit."

Gordon and Martha Evoy believe that some decisions can be made without great deliberation, such as the choice to go on a short-term mission trip. They say, "We can't imagine one needing to spend agonizing days in prayer if it appears feasible and you are interested in missions. God is persistent. He doesn't push, he leads. Satan tends to push, even into good things that we should not attempt." Evoys add a practical warning: "If you have a desire to leave a difficult situation, it is not hard to feel that 'God is calling you' to do something else. God will keep you honest if you desire a thorough soul-searching."

The flip-side insight comes from Garry Cruce. "If there is peace during the difficult times (and there will be discouraging times), that is a confirmation of the Lord's will."

Another clue comes from Wilma Kasten. "To me, God's calling is a steady feeling (knowing in my heart) that if I don't do this thing, I will be causing God's heart to be sad."

"When there is confusion, you can count on it that it is not of God," advises Martha Kirkpatrick (Rwanda). Rather, says Ruth Winslow, "There is a *rightness*, a feeling that this is right in his call. If you have a lot of doubts, I'd think you aren't really hearing the call. You should also have peace."

Dorothy Raber (Taiwan) concurs: "If the call is persistent, the call keeps coming back to you, you cannot escape it." Carmena Capp says, "Only time spent with God in prayer and fellowship can separate impulse from guidance."

William Bicksler adds this common sense observation: "I've been in Taiwan 32 years. There are killings, demonstrations, disorderly conduct daily. It takes over an hour to get home from work in heavy traffic with gun-carrying, irate drivers. Over 600 cars are stolen in Taipei daily. The air is terrible, the smell, the pollution, the garbage. But I rejoice that because of (and in spite) of these things, God wants me here. Why would I choose it?"

Anyway, distinguishing between God's calling and your own idea may not be necessary. Says Philip Gilmore, "God is able to plant an idea in your head. A personal desire can in fact be God's call. I believe a desire will persist if it is from God and that God will provide opportunities to put that desire into action."

David Roller agrees. "If it's a good idea, who cares? Check it out with someone who loves God and see if the idea makes sense."

Follow this advice and you can't miss. As Jim Nelson says, "God wants you to know his will for your life even more than you want it."

What is the difference between being called and being commissioned?

"God calls, the church commissions," observes William Bicksler. Carmena Capp agrees: "Any individual call should be confirmed by the body of Christ – the church, which commissions on the basis of their confirmation of the person whom God has called." Garry Cruce adds,

"They are definitely not the same. The commissioning is to be a confirmation of the call, not the other way around. The call has to come first."

Carol Watson makes this distinction: "Being called is an inner assurance; being commissioned is the confirmation from the church body. Both are terribly important. In times of great stress or frustration my first term, I would look back to that 'sending' ceremony by the church and I'd also remember that the God who called me here will enable me – real, true comfort in such times."

To put it another way, David Roller says, "Being called is when the ability and the disposition meet the need. Being commissioned is when the church catapults you out with a stout rope tied around your waist and the church's ankle."

Jim Nelson adds, "A call to missions is God's part. Our part is to prepare to go. Commissioning is the church's role in confirming that one is truly ready to go, and in pledging their prayer, financial, and personal support to the missionary going out."

Further insight comes from Dorothy Raber: "Called into missions is the direction God leads you for your life service. Commissioning is done by the Holy Spirit, giving power to serve effectively. This power of the Holy Spirit should be dwelling in the missionary at the time of any commissioning service. The commissioning service does not automatically fill people with the Holy Spirit."

Wilma Kasten makes this interesting distinction: "Being called is a lifetime thing. Being commissioned is being sent by a missions group and could be for a shorter time. In another sense they are both the same. That is, the call and the commission (Matthew 28) both come from God."

Gordon Evoy draws an analogy with marriage: "The difference between being called into missions and being commissioned is much like the difference between a marriage and a wedding. One typically begins in the heart, often quietly, but effects continue for a lifetime. The other is planned well and publicly observed and may last only a few moments."

Are some missionaries never called by God? If so, describe their work.

This question drew mixed responses. Garry Cruce says, "Perhaps, but I believe the sovereignty of God is so great that God can work through our mistakes for his glory."

Wilma Kasten believes some work who are not called, and says, "Their work is more of a social order and does not have the spiritual impact it should have. I feel a call is essential for missionary work."

Martha Kirkpatrick sees the opposite situation: "There are more people called than go. I think all who go are called. Be sure it is God's will to *stay home.*"

Philip Gilmore notes, "God doesn't let me in on his call for others. My gut feeling is that a person who is called will stay on the field. Those who quit after a short while either are not called or lack patience for God to mold them."

David Hill (South Africa) agrees with Philip: "It is not for me to question the call of others." Yet Dorothy Raber is pretty sure that "some missionary dropouts were not clear about their call. The difficulties of missionary life, trouble learning the language, or the customs of native people cause them to became discouraged and gave up."

Ruth Winslow isn't so sure. "I've been on the mission field since I was seven years old. Now I'm 52. I haven't met people who were never called. Maybe everyone doesn't use that particular word 'called.' One close friend said, 'No, I've never really felt called — I'm not sure I should be here.' But this person is here and has been doing a great job for 20 years."

Carolyn Cranston agrees. "I don't know of any missionaries I felt were not called."

Margaret Nelson puts it this way: "I think most of the 'non-called' drop out before they ever get to the field, in language study or during the first term on the field. I don't think many of them ever get to the point of doing any work."

Says Dale Bidwell, "If we have a strong sense of being called we'll have extra endurance when the going gets tough. Those with a weak sense of calling will be the first to pack it in."

Says Jim Nelson, "Some people may have misunderstood their concern for missions, feeling that anyone who loves God and people should also go out to another culture. They may even have a sense of guilt or duty that motivates them. They need to be set free from these misunderstandings. This is important, or their work is likely to be based on human effort, lacking real spiritual power. Others may be called by God to specific types of service and temporarily carry out that ministry on a mission field. That's wonderful. God can use them anywhere, whether they are called to lifetime missionary service or not."

Loren Van Tassel feels that confusion about a clear call has broad consequences. "Some people serving as pastors were called to be active laymen but they mistook it as a call to pastoral ministry. Their work is sincere but they don't 'fit' well and have a hard time leading. I suppose the same is true of missionaries."

Then again, Carmena Capp reminds us that "people are different, some are more effective than others. Some people grow weary in well doing -- but I would never presume to pronounce that they were not called of God. Who am I to say that?"

Jim Stillman concludes, "We are all called to obey. Some are disobedient before and after they arrive on the mission field. Some who are not missionaries are disobedient. A disobedient church will end up sending disobedient missionaries."

Does being "called" make any difference in your decision-making process?

Dale Bidwell believes, "Sorting out selfish goals from God's goals gives perspective to any decision. Put God first in any decision, then give him the opportunity to fulfill his promises in Matt. 6:33 and Prov. 3:5-7."

Henry Church (Malawi) says, "Being called means you can't back out when the going gets tough, when you're not wanted, when you are frustrated. You fulfill your call. Other choices demand prayer, counsel, and discussions with your spouse."

Martha Kirkpatrick has this simple solution: "If I don't know what to do, I do nothing. I follow the path of peace, the way that will not hurt my co-workers, and the way that will be a good example to the national church."

Garry Cruce trys to remember to ask himself, "What would Jesus do?" Then he ponders how this decision will affect the church. He doesn't feel being "called" makes any difference.

David Roller recommends that you "use the brain the good Lord gave you, the gifts and graces he has entrusted you with, and jump into opportunities he opens up."

Carol Watson tries to look at all the angles. She asks herself, "What best reflects my priorities (which I trust are God's priorities for me)?" She may think of a plan of attack, but keeps herself from acting until sleeping on it. Often new insight comes in the morning.

"When I have a decision to make," says Carolyn Cranston, "I try to marshall all the facts and study both the pros and cons of the decision, prayerfully, asking for the Lord's guidance and direction. Being 'called' has vital significance."

"Your call makes **all** the difference," believes Carmena Capp. "If you don't know you are called you are liable to be tossed around on all kinds of uncertainties. You are a sitting duck for an indecisive life pattern, and for discouragement."

Wilma Kasten notes, "My first action in making decisions is to pray and ask God to let me know his will. I do not have my own will in the matter. Maybe I'd prefer one thing or the other, but I put it in God's hands to work out. If he opens the way, I can peacefully and gladly follow without fear. Being 'called' has a great deal to do with this process because since I am now where I feel God has called me, I can trust him with all the decisions that it falls my lot to make -- I am endeavoring to obey him completely."

What would you like to add that can help readers listen for and respond to God's calling.

-- "Remember, if God calls you, he will supply all needs (not wants) and help you to do what he called you to do. It's a good life!" Wilma Kasten

-- "Respond by simply obeying God's call. Jesus said, 'I love to do the will of my Father.' We should all strive to be like that." Carmena Capp

-- "Do ordinary work for God faithfully. Don't try to create a dramatic call." Loren Van Tassel

-- "Just be open to the Lord, let him surprise you! The Christian life is an adventure!" Garry Cruce

-- "Voices are calling recruits to other occupations -- why not recruit and **call** our young people -- there is an awful lot of excitement and work to be done for God." Ruth Winslow

-- "Instead of crying, 'Oh God, guide me,' it is better to pray, 'Oh God, make me a guidable person. Have your way in my life.'" Beth Stewart

-- "Do mention the rewards of following God's call: unity, peace, harmony with oneself and God -- a sense of working together with the Creator of the Universe; purpose and fulfillment in life. It's thrilling to live on the cutting edge of Kingdom building, to be out on a limb with the God of the Universe. I can't imagine living any other way!" Carol Watson

-- Donald Grey Barnhouse once said, "If I knew that I had five years to work for the Lord, I would spend the first two years in preparation." Gordon and Martha Evoy

On Saying "Hello"

Dr. John Gilmore
May/June 1991 p. 2

Jesus' call to his disciples was to follow him. He never told them where they would go or what they would do. He called them to himself, not to a place, position or profession.

The disciples responded to the call by leaving all -- parents, occupation, business, position and many other responsibilities to follow a "stranger." We don't know whether the disciples had ever met Jesus before or knew much about him except through prophecy.

Jesus did not offer much in security for the future or remuneration for the present. There didn't seem to be any pension program and the only health insurance was faith in Jesus.

Answering the call was always a choice -- no obligation -- more of an invitation. The call was always the highest -- to a relationship with Jesus, to a growing, developing experience, to participation in the greatest ministry of all.

There were some who wanted to follow, and Jesus encouraged them to go back home and tell family, friends and community what had happened. Those who did follow were challenged and trained as they saw Jesus in ministry and heard him speak. They felt some of his heartbreak as they worked with him in meeting the needs of the multitudes and individuals.

Risk

Jesus took quite a risk in calling those to follow him who came from different geographic regions. There was quite a chemistry mix of personalities. How could Jesus ever even hope that they would get along well together? They didn't, yet Jesus called them!

Answering the call today is still the response to a close relationship with the person Jesus. He is the one who calls, not an individual, church, conference, mission board, need or country. Although Jesus may work through one or more of these, it is Jesus himself who calls us to follow him. He goes before giving us the direction.

To answer with a whole heart may still mean leaving parents, vocation or occupation, and stepping out in faith not knowing where the road may lead. There may be no climbing of the success ladder, no comfortable home, no stable living situation. Realities may mean living in a hostile environment, rejection, suspicion, political upheaval, loss of possessions, harassment by authorities, revolution, sending children off to school, and the inability to be with sick and aging parents.

As was true of the disciples, it may mean seeing many come to Jesus who have never heard of him before, going into new areas among new people to become a part of their lives; helping train others to become disciples of Jesus.

Commitment

Answering the call means making a commitment to a Person and to a task. The one following does not place limits, or set the time period. The Leader defines these.

Answering the call, then and now, means placing oneself in the hands of those who also are following Jesus in leadership roles. It may not always be pleasant to be subject to the decisions and counsel of others. It is necessary, however, to become a good follower before being able to lead others to Christ.

The Lord affirms his call in our lives through the body of believers. There is this awareness through the presence of the Spirit, gifts for service, and effectiveness in ministry.

When answering the call we should never fear that we will be alone. Donald Frazer has stated, "God never sent a man alone to do His work." He always goes before us.

Called

May/June 1991 p.8

We know that God causes all things to work together for good to those who love God, to those who are called according to his purpose.

For whom he foreknew, he also predestined to be conformed to the image of his Son, that he might be the firstborn among many brethren.

And whom he predestined, these he also called; and whom he called, these he also justified; and whom he justified, these he also glorified.

What then shall we say to these things? If God is for us, who is against us?

He who did not spare his own Son, but delivered him up for us all, how will he not also with him freely give us all things?

Who shall separate us from the love of Christ? Shall tribulation, or distress, or persecution, or famine, or nakedness, or peril, or sword? In all these things we overwhelmingly conquer through him who loved us.

For I am convinced that neither death, nor life, nor angels, nor principalities, nor things present, nor things to come, nor powers,

Nor height, nor depth, nor any other created thing, shall be able to separate us from the love of God, which is in Christ Jesus our Lord.

(for complete text see Romans 8:28-39)

Bent Wood: Special Applications

Daniel V. Runyon
September/October 1990, p. 37

This morning I was cutting up a thick branch of a cherry tree that reached 30 feet into the field.

One straight branch could have been made into nice lumber. Then I came to a sharp dog-leg to the right, where the tree had branched toward the sun.

That crooked piece would be hard to split, hard to get into the stove, and was also worthless as building lumber. Yet, ship-builders of ancient times searched the forests for just such a sturdy, graceful, naturally grown curve like this one. Builders would form the bow and backbone of a boat with it --the source of strength to which many ribs were fastened.

Bent branches have their place, but this one was clearly a misfit.

Misfits

In the animated movie of "Rudolph, the Red-Nosed Reindeer" (I watched it on TV with my kids), the unhappy elf Hermie wants to become a dentist. A grouchy head elf chides him with these words, "Why can't you just make toys like everyone else?"

The misfit elf and the red-nosed deer meet in the forest and sing this sad lament, the elf taking the lead on verse one, the deer on verse two:

Why am I such a misfit,
I am not just a nitwit,
You can't fire me, I quit!
Why don't I fit in?

Why am I such a misfit,
I am not just a nitwit,
Just because my nose glows,
Why don't I fit in?

I often felt this way as a self-employed writer with many unpublished manuscripts in the files and 14 years' worth of rejection slips stacked to the ceiling of my psyche. There were occasional successes, but there was also quiet desperation as I cranked out marketing propaganda and ad agency brochures. Not the stuff of greatness, but the stuff of survival.

At one time or another (perhaps right now), you have felt the same. There you sat, remembering the evangelistic flyer claiming that "God has a wonderful plan for your life." You may have sarcastically replied, "Give me a break! Maybe God has a plan for **your** life, but not mine: I'm damaged goods."

God In The Dumpster

Missions is a salvage operation. The four summers I spent working on a garbage route was perhaps the best preparation for this job. I came to see value in what others abandoned and purpose for what others destroyed.

Satan is like those materialistic Americans who filled the many garbage cans I emptied. He will use you briefly, then fling you away in disgust, flushing down your self-esteem along with the wasted hours.

Hold Everything

Hop on the back of the truck, here with me. Hear the huge tires squawk on pavement as the big rig wheels around and backs in toward you. "Whoa!" we yell, hanging on the back of the truck.

"Sppssssst," go the air brakes. "Clang" goes the winch. Up goes the dumpster. All of Satan's abandoned humanity slides on maggots into the --

"Hold everything! This is **good stuff**!" you yell, still hanging there on the side of the truck. "I can use this. With a little cleaning up, this is perfect for...."

In the same way, God grabbed me in the form of an invitation to edit this magazine. I accepted, not based on my ability, but on the understanding that God chose the foolish things of the world to shame the wise, the weak to shame the strong, the lowly and despised to bring down those the world considers great.

In my journal the day I agreed to take this job I scribbled: "I am just a weak, foolish, despised country kid, yet perhaps God will use me to bring **His Word** to many."

You and me. We are all bent wood. Damaged goods. Stones which the builder rejected. Petros. And on this garbage God will build his church, and all the powers of hell will not prevail against us.

Take The Cross Cultural Challenge

F. Douglas Pennoyer
March/April 1991 pp. 3-7

The gladiator grabbed the rope and swung across the gap into the shield of his waiting enemy. He knocked the man out of position and continued on to the small wooden beam. With the grace of a ballet dancer he managed to avoid all the swinging canvas bags.

Crouched low in a combat position, he continued running, climbing, leaping, and weaving through the remaining obstacles.

Bursting through a doorway, he dislodged the final opponent with a powerful shoulder block. His momentum carried him across the finish line of the T.V. show "American Gladiators." The challenger was a survivor, and a new champion.

As unreal as this program seems, there is an interesting parallel between T.V. gladiators and missionaries. The course is the unfamiliar world of another culture. It's full of surprises. Lurking in the shadows of a strange culture is the unexpected, the unusual.

Both courses require training and preparation, speed and strength, alertness and adroit footwork through a maze.

Few of us will ever put on a gladiator's outfit and compete on T.V. However we may at sometime in our lives take the cross cultural challenge.

To find out what we would need to know on our cross cultural challenge trek, we surveyed our veteran Free Methodist missionaries. These astute survivors gave a variety of tips on culture shock, cultural adaptation, language, family, national teamwork, and reentry.

Culture Shock

Culture shock is the trauma and mental disorientation that result from handling unfamiliar cues and expectations in a new culture. It can be heightened by lack of knowledge, limited prior experience, and personal rigidity.

One of our experts says it's like "a low voltage buzz that puts a little tension in everyday life." But what happens when the voltage is turned up and your hair stands on end?

Imagine going next door to introduce yourself to your new neighbors. When you walk into their living room, an elderly housewife grabs you by the arm, pushes you outside and angrily points at your shoes. You can't speak the language to apologize for violating the "no shoes in the house" rule and she won't let you back in. It may be weeks or months before you take that cross cultural challenge again.

One of our missionaries who suffered this cultural *faux pas* says, "fortunately for me, she later forgave me and we became good friends of the family."

You come from quiet, clean, rural America and land in one of Asia's busiest cities. Culture shock is "noise, day and night noise, from never ending traffic that screams past our apartment building. It's dirt, grit, air pollution. It's the stress of living in an extremely fast-paced, highly motivated society where making money is the end goal. It's living in a society that looks western but thinks, reacts, and has priorities that are often unexpected and confusing, even after 19 years of life here."

Differences in diet can be traumatic. A missionary in Africa tells of eating fish -- heads, eyes, brains and all. "How I thanked the Lord it was dark so I couldn't see what I was eating. Yet those ladies had used their meager allowance to buy and prepare the very best food they could for us. My friend says where she comes from caterpillars are the staple diet."

Others talk about a profound loss of privacy. American culture is more individualistic and privacy is highly valued. Yet, most of the world is more open and communal. The westerner may feel the new life is like being in a fish bowl. People peek in windows and enter without knocking, assuming you have a door at all.

Loss of privacy is coupled with loss of individual time alone. "I'm an avid book reader," confesses one field worker. "Not being able to read was the hardest at first."

Leaving one world for the other means separation from family and friends. The memories of familiar ties and social occasions produce a yearning to be back home in your chair, around your table, in your house. Our missionaries singled out Christmas as a hard time. Missing funerals, weddings, and the birth of relatives is difficult also. New friends and an adopted, extended family help to ease the pain.

Our cross cultural challengers have these words of advice on culture shock:
1. Realize that each new situation is like being a newborn baby.
2. Be observant and willing to learn.

3. Be patient.
4. Appreciate reasons for doing things their way. Your habits are not necessarily the right or best way.
5. Tackle the language, even if it's difficult.

Cultural Adaptation

One wise veteran tells us, "the process of becoming culturally adjusted is on-going." Many missionaries emphasized that even after years and years of service in a country they still feel like outsiders. A deep statement came from one cross cultural philosopher: "The difficulty in bicultural living is that you have to give up part of yourself to take on a new part of yourself. You can try to take on the good of both cultures but you end up being neither one or the other."

Ah! The cross cultural challenger is always slowed down by the weight of carrying two cultures.

To find out how our missionaries felt about cultural adaptation, we asked their opinion on "going native." In some countries the nationals expect the missionaries to live at a higher standard and may even point with pride to the well dressed worker, and the fine home. One couple who was married on the field say, "They would not want us to go native. When we were married there, they said, 'Please go western.'"

Another says, "We can lose their respect by going totally native because they are not proud of some of their living standards and want to change."

The degree of cultural adaptation is one every missionary struggles with daily. And it depends on where you live and the level of society you want to impact.

"There are so many degrees of living," explains one missionary. "Do you mean native like our landlord who lives in a mansion, drives an expensive car, and has so much money he refused to sell our house? Do you mean like our pastors who live in one or two rooms with no bathroom, stove, refrigerator, beds, or floors? Do you mean like families who live in six by eight-foot shacks? Does it mean we give up our workers and learn to cook over an open fire? When I buy candy bars for the family, I know my cook could feed his family for a week on that amount of money. So do I give up an occasional candy bar? Give up our cars and airplanes and only work in places we can reach by foot? What about birthday parties and Christmas? Books and typewriters?

"And where do the children fit into this? Do we put them in a local school and then expect them to function in an American school on furlough? Do we tell them no toys, books, jeans? Must they all sleep in one tiny bed or on the floor so we will be like the community around us? Do we deny them good medical care because we couldn't get to a hospital on foot?"

There are no easy answers to these questions that can keep tension levels high on the field. One missionary couple reports that inflation has eroded their salary to the level of a senior nurse in the country. They also support local pastors. Thus their salary shrank and their "family" increased, forcing them to adopt more of a local lifestyle.

A joyous tale comes from a couple who tell that "church people helped us find housing for a lower rent than they pay. They are pleased to help and happy for us."

Many of those surveyed talk about maintaining a balance in their cultural adaptation. "Basically, we adapt to the new culture as much as it helps in our ministry," offers a missionary. "We have tried to maintain a balance between the old and new culture in a way that doesn't offend those around us and helps us keep in touch with both worlds we now belong to."

Cultural Baggage

How much baggage should a cross cultural worker take into the field to ease the cultural adaptation? While things from home can lessen adjustment problems, there are disadvantages to too much baggage, such as preoccupation with equipment, economic distance from the poor, and people wanting your things. "If I could do it all over again," writes one missionary, "I would only bring what I could carry. We were without our eight barrels of shipped goods for four months and hardly missed them."

An urban ministries couple were given a computer and microwave just before returning to the field. It was included in their baggage. They had great visions of saving time and increased ministry effectiveness. "Our microwave and computer are two of our biggest time savers, but we often apologize for them. They put us in a different financial bracket."

The people often confirm the level of the missionary's adjustment. A national pastor introduced a missionary at a remote farm church by saying, "You don't have to be afraid of this white person. He drinks our tea and eats our bread."

How do you know you blend in and not stick out like a sore thumb? Missionaries have heard comments like, "You look like us," "You have our heart," and, "Isn't our house (the missionary's) beautiful."

Recommendations

Here are some recommendations from Free Methodist missionaries on cultural adaptation:

1. Immerse yourself in the culture. Get as near to the people as possible, yet be comfortable and efficient. Use whatever helps to get the work done on time and keeps you healthy.
2. Modesty is different in each culture. Accommodate to their dress code.
3. Dress adaptation must be done sincerely. They expect you to be you, mature in your own culture, before you leap into theirs.
4. The more you have, the greater the probability of misunderstanding the message. Abandon, and leave behind as much as possible.
5. Take a good course in cultural anthropology or cross cultural communications.
6. Communicate love through your actions. Go on a VISA experience.
7. Work with another culture in the United States.
8. Eat it. You'll eventually learn to like it.

Language

The ability to communicate in the people's language is an essential part of cross cultural survival. The frustrations of learning another language can often be overwhelming. Also, some individuals have more linguistic ability than others to learn the language faster, mimic the sounds and intonation patterns, and keep the grammar straight. Yet most people understand language learning problems. It is not the biggest factor in rejection by the people. Many of them may be experiencing the same difficulties in learning English.

A missionary with years of experience offers this insight: "The biggest problem I face is language. I wish I were more fluent. I speak it but not as well as I need to. This does create some gaps. Yet we feel the people here like and accept us. Perhaps I accept myself more now and don't have to prove something to them. They accept me the way I am, with my occasional stupid mistakes due to inadequate language."

Family

"Mommy isn't going to leave you, darling," sang a two-year-old M.K. as she rocked with her doll. The setting around her was strange, a new house in a new country. But she rocked comfortably in a familiar rocking chair. It felt right and comfortable.

"I knew I'd done the right thing," her mother muses. "When we left for the field I disassembled her rocking chair and brought it. When it was unpacked and assembled, she sat for hours with her dolly, singing 'Mommy isn't going to leave you, darling.' Whatever I could do to make the children feel at home, and able to cope, I felt it was important to do."

Mommies and daddies do leave their darlings sometimes — at school. It can be a painful separation. The other options are the local schools, or home schooling. "We felt strongly that the children needed the American cultural environment that they found at the M.K. school. This was important to help them in the later return adjustment to college and early adult life."

Selecting the proper educational experience for children is one of the toughest decisions a missionary parent faces. Short term considerations loom large: "Can we stand this separation?" Long term implications must also be weighed: "Is this the best education or cultural and social setting available?"

Away from parents in an American or international enclave, the children may grow up with little understanding of the host culture, and no ability to speak the language. A missionary mother shares this dilemma: "The most difficult decision has been to put all our children through the British education system, which has meant our children have grown up not learning the local language. The local system is extremely pressured and would require children to begin studies in earnest by age three or four.

"We know of only two or three families who have put their children through this route, and some of those children have become neurotic, others rebellious. Probably some are doing well. This has meant that our children have had contact with children of many nationalities, whose parents are business professionals, hold government positions or do missionary work.

"About one-third to one-half of the children in this system are local kids whose English level was high even in first grade. They tend to be from families who were educated abroad. Our children loved school, have many friends, and consider their education superior to an average American education."

National Teamwork

The goal of missions is self-sufficient churches with national leadership. Teamwork with nationals is an essential part of the process. Missionaries described their working relationships as "partnerships," "working with," "working under," or "working alongside." Learning and adjustment takes place on both sides. The missionary must resist the temptation to be domineering, and the national must guard against rejecting ideas simply because they are the missionary's.

Here's one missionary's recollection of this learning experience: "Sometimes we have to hold ourselves back and walk on eggs in order not to be domineering. Once we wrongfully tried to take things in hand and straighten out some things we thought were not working. We failed, thank the Lord. I'll never forget the absolute graciousness, but firmness, with which the local pastor dealt with us."

Another missionary responds, "It is very tempting to barge ahead and do ourselves what we see needs to be done, instead of working with national leaders to help them see the needs and do the work themselves."

Many missionaries recounted the joyful experience of casually dropping new ideas and then watching these concepts go through the "improvement mill of indigenization." Months (often years) later, the new ideas emerge as standard operating procedure.

Teamwork often requires role reversal. The missionary may begin as the leader, training national leaders. Once they are in place, the missionary may respond to their leadership. One who has experienced this notes, "I see no disadvantages in this arrangement. Probably the greatest advantage is that we already know and love each other."

Veteran missionaries suggest that constant dialogue with nationals is essential and that communication should be an outgrowth of solid personal relationships. Missionaries see themselves as counselors, catalysts, church planters, and technical advisors. One says, "The missionary should be on the cutting edge, move on, and leave conference leadership to local leaders."

About participation in the decision-making process another writes, "When they see that I want to be a team player, they include me in the decision process."

The need on the field is always greater than the available resources. "Dealing with the disappointed expectations of nationals can be traumatic," reports a couple. "The demands on us for our time, things and money are unbelievable. They cannot accept 'no' for an answer, or they make us feel guilty. We always felt pressured that we had not done enough."

Problems between nationals and missionaries do, of course, occur. Differences of opinion, varying personality types and cultural miscommunication can cause tension. These situations occur on any team, in any church. Keeping the team together and moving ahead smoothly for the sake of the gospel is a firm commitment made by all.

This is beautifully expressed by the missionary who said, "Kingdom building is an exciting task today and the issue of who works under whom, is relatively unimportant. The issue is learning and using the best techniques available for church growth. Missionary and national worker alike share in this challenge."

Reentry

"After 26 years of missionary service, we face greater culture shock coming home," cries a missionary. Indeed, for veterans, home is the mission field — the place where they've invested their lives, talents, and financial resources. A generation or two of Christian children honor and respect them like patriarchs and matriarchs of a large extended family. They have watched churches spring up like wells in a dry land, sustaining new life.

Excitement for the veteran is not owning the latest piece of technology or adding a new wing to the house, it is contributing to an on-going process of growth in believers and planting new churches.

Returning to America involves a whole set of structured activities that only happen every few years — travel around the country, endless meetings with friends, relatives and supporters, new schooling experiences for the children, and a host of everyday details that are not present on the field calendar. An automatic clock ticks inside each furloughed missionary: "RE-TURN, RE-TURN, RE-TURN," and the alarm sounds after nine to 12 months.

"It's a shock to return to materialistic America," echoes another missionary who has reentered many times. Others talk about deprogramming the family from the host country's culture and bracing for the bumpy reorientation into American culture.

I experienced this as an M.K. Later, as an adult, I became a part of my parents' reorientation. Just off the plane from tribal Philippine settings, my mother visited a large shopping mall. I listened to her relate the shopping mall trip to a friend. "I took the elevator up several floors, and they even had... what's the word? You know, walking stairs...."

"It's *escalator*, mother, *escalator*," I replied in a tone I had just used that morning with my three-year-old daughter.

Recovering vocabulary is a simple exercise. Missionaries worry about more substantive issues like the best way to describe the ministry. It can be difficult for workers in non-traditional mission fields.

"I can't talk about grass huts because we live in a gorgeous apartment building," laments an urban missionary. "We can't speak about long jungle hikes because our city has one of the world's finest subway systems. How can we uphold the idea that we are suffering for Jesus when our biggest complaints are no snow at Christmas and only six kinds of pop to choose from?"

    Yes, the field today is the concrete and steel of bustling cities, the grass of rural villages, and the forests of upland tribes. Missionaries are not like T.V. gladiators in several respects. The gladiator functions on his own strength. Christians who take the cross cultural challenge have a Guide, The Spirit of Truth, the Comforter. They have partners, the nationals who lend a helping hand, and the praying folks at home.
    Gladiators fight human opponents. Cross cultural workers are on a spiritual battlefield where often the enemy is unseen. World Christians win these spiritual battles because an all powerful God does the protecting and the fighting.
    Taking the cross cultural challenge does involve shock, trauma, surprises, and no small sacrifice. The prize is not an earthly title, but rewards in the heavenlies.
    Given the spiritual resources at the believer's disposal, and the educational training and experiential advice readily available, any Christian can step forward with confidence and take the cross cultural challenge.

Money With Vision

Daniel V. Runyon
November/December 1991 p. 1-6

The average Free Methodist *church* in North America gives only 3.34% of its income to missions; the average *Free Methodist* gives only 65 cents a week to missions. To help you explore this situation I have interviewed three key leaders in our world missions program so that you will know better how to support missions with your prayers and giving.

Glenn White is chairman of the Commission on Missions. *Dr. M. Doane Bonney* is general director of World Missions. *Rev. William Fox* is director of administration for World Missions.

How long have you been involved in Free Methodist Missions?

Glenn: Because of my parents' great interest in missions, I have very early memories and impressions of the partnership between laymen and missionaries that is necessary to reach around the world to present Christ.

Doane: I have been a missionary since 1957.

Bill: In 1986 I began my responsibilities with the World Missions department. The previous 10 years I served as conference superintendent of the Oil City Conference.

Why is missions a priority with you?

Glenn: It's an opportunity to be part of an exciting and important operation where dedicated people using a minimum of money accomplish great things of eternal value.

Doane: Because Jesus said to go into all the world and make disciples. That world means the globe, all 360°. Our tendency is to stay in Jerusalem.

Bill: My local church emphasized missions, my grandparents were deeply committed to missions, and at least once each year General Missionary Secretary F. L. Baker visited in their home. My parents demonstrated missions commitment by giving above their tithe to spread the gospel, and my sister, Sylvia Fox, went as a missionary to Burundi.

All these were important influences, but greatest of all is the personal realization that the great commission is much more than just an option on a spiritual smorgasbord. Christ placed a mandate upon the church, and therefore, upon me, to go into all the world and preach the gospel to every creature.

Describe your fundamental role in our missions program.
Glenn: I'm an excited, dedicated believer in missions who wants to help others get involved as givers, short-term workers, or full-time missionaries.
Doane: As an exhorter and as a connector. When persons realize the need for evangelization world-wide, they'll want to do something about it. I'm here to facilitate that connection. The exhortation part comes into play in bringing people to realize they have a personal responsibility to the world that is lost close to home but also far away.
Bill: I plan and control the budget. This involves maximizing every dollar for effective ministry. The funds channeled through the missions department now total nearly five million dollars annually.

What is the most rewarding aspect of this work for you?
Glenn: I enjoy seeing what getting involved with missions does for people. And it's rewarding to see what is being accomplished on the field. We were at Kibogora mission station in Rwanda, Africa, and attended a Sunday morning church service.
As we brought greetings to the church, I looked out at about 250 young Africans who were studying to be medical technicians. It was an awesome sight. They all wore white shirts or blouses, with dark pants or skirts and wonderful, friendly faces.
You couldn't stand there looking at those students, all of whom were learning about Christianity as well as about medicine, without understanding the benefits of missions.
Doane: I'm a firm believer that changes for the good in families, towns, countries and the world as a whole come when there are radical changes in the hearts of individuals. This happens when persons accept the pardon and forgiveness offered by Christ and begin to live under his Lordship.
Missionary work is so very rewarding because often we find ourselves on the cutting edge where the gospel has scarcely been heard. With a handful of new born-again Christians living under the Lordship of Christ whole communities change for the better.
An example of this principle happened in Nagua in the

Dominican Republic as born-again Christians began filling the administrative posts in public works, the hospitals, and town boards. Suddenly the funds going to these institutions began flowing to actual road and bridge building. The hospital began having sheets available to put on the beds.

Bill: The rewards are diverse. It is to have a nine-year-old girl share that God called her to missionary service during a camp meeting message. It is being able to say to a couple in England, "You **can** go as VISA missionaries," and then visiting them later in their Africa home. It is changing your message at the last moment because of God's prompting, then later hearing a young couple say, "God spoke to us through your message today to call us into missionary service."

As the budget manager, it is also rewarding for me to report that our current budget is set up so that every penny of every dollar you contribute to the Department of World Missions will go directly for ministry. The entire home operations and promotion budgets are funded from other sources.

Tell about our mission's financial struggles. What has happened in both our giving and in our program?

Glenn: We have not successfully expanded the giving base for missions. We need to develop more understanding of the thrill and importance of being involved in missions as a giver, or a "go-er," or both!

Doane: World Missions giving has never rebounded from the double digit inflationary period of the late 1970s. This coupled with endemic inflation in many parts of the world means we actually have had to severely cut personnel overseas. From a high of 202 career missionaries in 1960, we've dropped to 117 in 1991.

Total giving for all purposes through local FM churches has increased significantly over the past two decades. But the proportion going for World Missions has dropped. As a church we are giving more in dollar amounts, but a disproportionate part of the increase is being spent on ourselves. If we had maintained the same percentage level of 1970, we would have more than $1 million each year in additional resources for World Missions.

Bill: In 1970 Free Methodist *churches* gave 5.05% of their total income to world missions. In 1980 the percentage slipped to 3.79% By 1990 our churches gave only 3.34% of their income to missions. Our concern is that Free Methodists are taking the great commission less seriously.

We have also made a study of the effects of overseas inflation on the purchasing power of UMC-World Missions income. Beginning with our base year in 1970, overseas inflation has significantly decreased the purchasing power of the missionary dollar. The 1990 cost of buying the same goods and services that were purchased in 1970 would be over four million dollars — or one-and-one-half million more than was actually given in 1990.

In spite of the decline in purchasing power, our overseas church has grown significantly. In fact, our church overseas grew more in the past three years than it did in the first 60 years of Free Methodist missions! Can you imagine what our growth *might have been* if we had funded more missionaries and expanded programs? Our target for overseas membership is 500,000 by the year 2,000. Reaching this goal will take a renewed concentration of resources.

I have made projections of Free Methodist giving for missions through the year 2000. Assuming that each church increases its giving by 5% per year, the projected overseas inflation rate of 9% will erode our purchasing power to just 70% of its present level. Unless our giving improves significantly, and soon, there will be even more serious negative implications for missions.

Do you get angry or frustrated about this situation?

Glenn: I don't get angry, just more determined to work harder and smarter to get more people involved. The new *Missionary Tidings* is a wonderful means to expand our reach.

Doane: My frustration is that the answer is so simple yet seemingly so hard to communicate. We have a grand total membership of 83,886 (*1990 Yearbook*) in North American and United Kingdom churches. By every member giving a minimum of $1.00 per week for World Missions, more than 4 million dollars would be available in 1992. This would be enough to send out the 11 new missionaries we are ready to send in 1992. It would replace a half a dozen mission vehicles that are ready for the chop shop.

It would allow us to continue all the essential and productive ministries we now have. In addition, giving at that level would allow us to enter new areas in Brazil, get on with the Eastern Europe opportunity and enter other opening doors. All of this for a couple of cans of pop per week, per member!

Bill: I am more grieved than angry over the fact that the average Free Methodist gives less than 65 cents a week for missions. I am grieved because we are losing our vision. We stand on the edge of the greatest harvest opportunities ever. Can we not see that the fields are white unto harvest?

We now face the need to cut a million dollars out of the legitimate budget requests for 1992. What will I say to our missionaries and national leaders when they ask why their budgets must be cut so dramatically?

The Lord seems to accomplish a great deal with very little money in many places where we minister. And the North American church has grown only slightly on the vast amounts we spend on ourselves. What's the issue here?

Glenn: Money is not the critical issue. People's interest and involvement is what we need to address. Then their money will follow. When people are exposed to missions and missionaries, things begin to happen. We shouldn't have a missionary service and make everyone feel good about our mission program without helping *each* person to get personally involved. When we do, they get excited and appreciate being made part of an important program, and the needed money will be given.

Doane: I think money *is* the issue. Money and its management have always been indicators of our priorities and level of commitment. I believe we need to regain the belief that we are our brothers' keepers. Some of these brothers live far from us!

Bill: I think *tithing* is the issue. Most financial problems in the church would be solved if God's people would tithe faithfully. Tithing is also a spiritual answer to the temptation to selfishness and greed. It becomes a good indicator as to whether we seek first the kingdom of God and his righteousness. We are asking people to be faithful in tithing to the church and then to give one more dollar per week for world evangelization. Truly, our God is worthy of at least this much.

Is it possible that God's work has not been hampered by our lack of giving, since the "poor" church is growing faster than the "rich" church? If so, then why should we give more?

Glenn: Rich church/poor church isn't the point. People are the issue. Get them to pray, to participate, to read, to learn, and then their money will be given to support the programs they are interested in, without a hard sell being required. Missions is worthwhile. Missions is exciting. Missions is worthy of our personal commitment. Results are eternal!

Doane: More than half the population in the world has no chance of even hearing the gospel. The "poor" overseas churches have a responsibility in this outreach, too. There has to be a correlation between ability and responsibility. The more the ability, the more the responsibility. God has blessed the Free Methodist church. That blessing has to be shared. And the greatest gift anyone can give is the gift of the good news. That is what missions is all about!

What I'm aiming at is that everyone be equal in the level of effort. The poor barrio church in the slums of a megacity can do *something* about world evangelization. Obviously a church with a $100,000 budget can do much more. I want both to be on the stretch for carrying the gospel to the world.

Bill: It would be easy to get into a question of "Whose responsibility is it to send out missionaries?" Should a larger church bear a greater responsibility than a small church? I think the answer is simply that God has called his church to go into all the world. This is not a responsibility given to the Department of World Missions or just to a larger church. We are all responsible before God to obey the great commission, with whatever means we have.

If We Only Tithed...

Clyde E. Van Valin
November/December 1991 p. 2

Why does the church struggle for funds when we live in one of the most affluent societies of all history? The sufficiency of resources in all God's ventures recorded in the Bible contrasts painfully with our cash flow crisis. Why was there enough wood and pitch for the ark? Where did all that money come from? Why did they lavish tons of gold on the temple at God's command? Why was Abraham so wealthy?

How could Jesus afford to travel without steady employment but no apparent lack of resources? Why did Paul move so readily across the middle east without support of United Ministries For Christ–Home Ministries income?

The Book of *Acts* points out that post-Pentecost believers worked from one inspired center. They were "all filled with the Holy Spirit." As a result, "No one *claimed* that any of his possessions was his own but shared everything." No wonder "...there were no needy persons among them...."

The early Christians arrived at simple yet profound conclusions. The Holy Spirit was in charge from the heavenly perspective. The Apostles were in charge from the earthly side. The ability and authority of the leaders of the new church replaced the ancient temple treasury. The people trusted them with the proceeds of the sale of possessions, houses and lands. Apparently tithes and offerings were given to trusted leaders for equitable distribution. Christians gave out of grateful hearts.

How fascinating that the first business meeting after Pentecost dealt with the age-old issue of equitable distributing of goods! This question has forever divided families, filled court rooms, defeated nations and caused international conflict.

They handled it well. Stephen, chosen to lead the program, was so effective that his sermon sparked a revival. The resulting persecution scattered the church until the gospel leaped to the Gentiles and the whole world. *Imagine that! The implementation of the great missionary movement of the Christian era began at a "general conference" called to deal with the issue of finance!*

New Levels of Conviction

Studying the Old and New Testaments and reflecting on our stewardship history bring new levels of conviction about church finances. The church should still lead the way in the generosity and trustworthiness required in handling public funds. And our giving must come from Spirit-filled hearts that recognize God's ownership. Otherwise we merely select objects of philanthropy from among competing promoters who "raise" money.

Our terms of "giving to missions" or "giving to evangelism" may have created the myth that we exercise good stewardship when we respond to appeals for this or that need. Do we actually give to programs and to ministries, or to God? All is his. We give a portion back to him. His servants are then responsible for its equitable distribution for the good of his kingdom.

Tithing to the church is the time-proven, biblical basis for regular, proportionate giving. In the full blessings of God's covenant, offerings and faith promise giving then go beyond the tithe. *If every Free Methodist tithed, total income would increase between $30 and $40 million annually. We would meet our financial needs within six months.*

One church planter in Alabama took home from annual conference a supply of the book, *Tithing, God's Plan for the Church* and preached on the subject. Offerings which averaged $175 per week rose sharply, then leveled off at about $600. In another new church, offerings increased by $500 to $700 per month. Offerings in an established church in Oklahoma have doubled.

The simple, biblical remedy for our financial needs today is a commitment by every Free Methodist to tithe to the church. We can then give joyfully with Spirit-led discretion to additional opportunities for spreading the gospel. Do this, and God promises blessings so immense that we cannot contain them.

Second Grace Of Works

Daniel V. Runyon
November/December 1991 p. 39

Christians who are born and raised in the church tend to speak in code. Non-Christians can't understand us. We often damage God's reputation by failing to talk about him with words that communicate.

Where I came from it was understood that people who had experienced the "second work of grace" were fully tuned in to God. These people were wired-in with a direct cable-link to heaven. Their spiritual satellite dish picked up every heaven-sent transmission.

There was no problem with the language until new or pre-Christians wandered into earshot. Upon hearing, "second work of grace," they would scratch behind the ear in thoughtful silence, then ask, "Grace who?"

These people have not experienced the first work of grace. When they hear of the need for a second work, they suspect the job was poorly done the first go around. "What good is Grace," they ask, "if she has to be called in for a second work, like a second-rate plumber?"

The First Grace

Put simply, when Jesus died on the cross, it wasn't a freak accident of history. It was God in the flesh giving his life in exchange for yours. God made the world and everything in it. His long-range plan called for you to have the opportunity to be forgiven.

You don't deserve either heaven or a right relationship with God. God offers these to you anyway. It cost him a lot, so we call it "work." It is a generous gift, happily offered, so we call it "grace."

The easy part is up to you. Simply thank God for his work, reach out and accept his grace, and start living each day in friendship with him. For more instructions on doing this, find a Bible, look in the table of contents for the "Gospel of John," and read the good news printed there.

The Second Grace

Some things you simply can't get enough of. People who live for money are never content and keep striving for more. *It is the same way with people who live for God. The more they get to know him, the more they want to know, and the more they discover.*

What joy to personally know God and to be in partnership with the One who charts history! What comfort to be loved by the author of love himself!

Is it any wonder that a time comes when you want to experience a "second work of grace?" You want all you can get of God, and you discover there is only one possible way -- God must first have all of you.

A Moving Story

Moving from a house you have lived in for 20 years is easier than giving God all there is of you. You have no idea how much junk has accumulated until it comes time to sort and move it all. Give God all of yourself and make the same discovery -- much of you is mere pack-rat clutter that really should be trashed. What's left will be the good stuff. This He will clean up, fix where necessary, and put to good use.

Until you allow God to do this in your life, you cannot comprehend how clean, simple, efficient, happy, and meaningful life can be. And now you're ready for the "second grace of works."

Wrong Works

Many religions of the world teach that it is possible to work your way to heaven. People who try this are the thieves and robbers Jesus mentioned who try to climb over the wall instead of going in through the door. Their works have nothing to do with grace. They are motivated by selfishness and the self-preservation instinct. They serve themselves, not God. Pray for them.

However, not all works are bad. Some folks daily experience the "second grace of works." They joyfully offer themselves to do any work God might have in mind for them, never keeping track of the cost, always aware that they have been bought at a greater cost. They give glory to God in all they do. These people are the answer to Jesus' prayer: "Thy kingdom come, thy will be done, on earth as it is in heaven."

Of course, the kingdom comes in quiet, unassuming ways, like the two sisters my father told me about. One got a job, lived on half her salary, and supported her missionary sister with the other half. No fund raising campaigns, no fanfare, just two obedient women doing more to revolutionize the world for God than the entire congregation of many Free Methodist churches today.

These are the workers Jesus, the Lord of the harvest, was looking for when he noticed that the harvest was ripe, but the laborers were few.

Think about your life. Do you hope to get in on any of the harvest? Could your life be cleaned up in such a way that more resources could go to do God's work? Would you rather stand by the window clutching your bag of coins, or would you rather join the singing reapers in the fields?

How long will it be until you experience this second grace of works?

Pastors On The Cutting Edge

by Schneider, Bonney, and Phiri
January/February 1992 pp. 1-4

Pastors with a heart for missions foster congregations with greater impact on the home front and around our planet. Wayne Schneider, Harry Bonney, and Alufasi Phiri are three such pastors. Wayne is pastor at Warm Beach, Stanwood, WA. Harry is a retired superintendent and now associate pastor at Chelsea, MI. Alufasi pastors 11 churches in Malawi and Mozambique, Southern Africa.

Hindsight
by Rev. Wayne Schneider

Hindsight is a wonderful tool, if used. I like to think that my three trips to Haiti have already effected leadership changes in my present church. While I cannot do anything regarding the past churches I have served, I can make a difference in my present one.

However, if I could turn back the clock a decade I certainly would have had a radically different ministry. Missions would be a high priority for my ministry and that would impact my teaching as well as my preaching.

I would emphasize to a higher degree the responsibility each church member has for missionary efforts. I would make our Missions Commission co-equal with our executive committee (formerly the official board) in power and influence.

I would do a far better job of both modeling and training our youth. I would ensure that a major pillar of the youth ministry in my churches would be missions participation and education.

I would call all of my adults (regardless of age) to prayerful consideration of missionary involvement beyond prayer and finances. I would establish at least an annual retiree missions ministry, where as many as possible of our retired members would have a hands-on experience in missions.

A Richer Church

If I had a decade of missionary emphasis to look back on, I suspect that my churches would be richer in spiritual growth. There certainly would be more joy as they see first hand the result of their efforts. Since love is an attitude rather than a feeling, my people would probably be a more loving flock. The more you give the easier it is to love.

I would like to believe that worship at the churches I served *was* sincere. However, the worship experience should become more meaningful as our people focus on the spiritually important matters, rather than the externals. I cannot help but believe that a church which thrusts herself into missionary work (foreign and domestic) is going to grow.

A church which has a true concept of the place of missions will not build a "glass cathedral." Rather, it will expend its resources in areas which produce the greatest harvest in regard to eternal values. I would like to think that the local budgets of these churches would reflect a duality: 50% of the church budget would go for local operation and 50% would go for outreach locally and abroad.

One Last Regret

I have found that it is impossible for me to communicate to my spouse (of 25+ years) how Haiti has affected me. Words can never replace experience. My three trips to Haiti are areas where our usual deep level of sharing and communication are not possible. I have experienced something that is unique for me and foreign to her. Because of my missions experience, I have had a paradigm shift in many of my attitudes and my wife has not. I am now convinced (contrary to my original opinion) that a pastor and his spouse need to experience short-term missionary ministry together.

Balancing The Costs *by Rev. Harry Bonney*

Our recent trip to Rwanda, Burundi, and Zaire left Marilyn and me amazed: Amazed at the moving of God's Holy Spirit, amazed at how much is done for kingdom building in Central Africa with comparatively little, amazed at our love for all the conveniences of home, amazed at how much many of us take our great missions program for granted, amazed at our intrepid missionaries, amazed that God trusted us enough to give us this great experience.

We have always promoted missions since our first trip to the Dominican Republic some 30 years ago. Now, however, there is a fresh realism about the cost of missions. There is a financial cost, of course. There is also the cost of personal dislocation and inconvenience, the cost of time in prayer, the cost of action in behalf of missionaries, and the cost of loneliness across separating miles.

Another cost is that many interesting and profitable activities will get brushed off when mission vision is sharp.

But these costs must be balanced against the cost of disobedience. Who can measure the cost we pay when individuals and churches resist God's call? And there is the cost of souls lost without hearing the good news.

Forget The Romance

A person or church heavily and healthfully involved in missions will not have time, money, and energy for non-essentials. There will of necessity be a concentration of activity and resources in mission-related activity. A certain toughness will emerge -- a selectivity which chooses for eternal values.

At the same time it is possible to succumb to fascination with the romantic aspects of missions from afar. This is not healthy. It is not a realistic perception of life the way it is on the field.

Money and bandages are relatively easy to give when the recipients are far away and do not impinge on my comforts or time. In this mode it is easier to be "concerned for the dear Africans" than it is to care for desperately needy persons close by. Especially is this true when neighbors get drunk, fight audibly, or drive on my lawn.

My deep concern is that the impressions we gained in Central Africa will not fade with time. We want God to keep us sensitive and responsive to what we experienced. We want these attitudes constantly to be translated into actions. We want to faithfully report what we saw God doing in Africa.

National Model   *by Henry Church and Rev. A. Alufasi Phiri*

Alufasi was one of the quietest students in the Malawi Bible School. You scarcely knew he was there. But put him in front of his congregation and he comes alive! He is a dynamic, purposeful, visionary leader.

Alufasi planted so many churches his circuit had to be divided and he still has 11 preaching points. He lives on the Mozambique border, pastors four churches in refugee camps, four inside Mozambique and three "regular" churches.

In May 1991, our mission gave Pastor Alufasi 1,000 Portuguese

New Testaments for free distribution to refugees. July 1 he was graduated from Bible School and on the same day ordained deacon. It was a special day.

Though Alufasi finished his course, he has not relaxed his efforts. Listen to excerpts from his recent letter dated five weeks after his graduation:

> *I write to inform you about the work of God which is now grown. From the month of July to this August I have planted six churches. I think God is working miracles here at Nsanje. Now I have a vision to plant many churches to cover new parts of our district, even in Mozambique, without fear, because of God's power through your prayers.*
>
> *Please continue to pray for me and my ministry here. Because of your gift of Portuguese Bibles which we share with these people, now I have a chance to enter Mozambique to preach to the people of this country, and even to the soldiers. Now, I am reaching unreached people with the Word of God.*
>
> *Please pray for me because I have a big job.*

Just Send Money?

Larry Winckles
November/December 1994 pp. 10-11

Should Free Methodists go to the expense of sending work teams, or should we just send the money? The issues involved are complex, but I believe the most important aspect of a work team is the interaction between team members and members of the host church and community. Completing the project is of secondary importance.

Some of my best memories are of time spent with Dominican Free Methodists in the villages of Jaibon and Navarrete. The Dominican youth played our team members in soccer and basketball. We played dominoes by the light of an oil lamp, struggled to communicate, and laughed at each other's broken English and broken Spanish. We showed family pictures, shared dreams and problems, and talked together about our common faith in Jesus Christ.

Economically, we were worlds apart. Spiritually we were peers. Both sides benefited and matured because of the experience. The work projects became the means of bringing together two groups of believers from different cultures and bonding them together, strengthening their faith, broadening their horizons, and equipping them for more effective ministry.

The Friendship Factor

If completing the project is the *only* goal, then it would be better to just send the money. Capable contractors and construction workers are available in most countries, many from our own Free Methodist churches, who could complete the project if financing was available, and who would also be very grateful for the employment.

More than once I have seen American builders stand in amazement at how Paraguayans use clamps made out of reinforcement rod to build forms for windows and doors. Likewise, I have seen a Dominican cement contractor stand amazed at the eight-foot-wide darby that an American concrete finisher made to smooth out concrete after it was poured. Both sides can learn from each other.

VISA team members who seek out interaction with the host

church and community are invariably changed from such experiences. Their ways of thinking change. Their values change. Their perspective on wants versus needs changes. They are empowered for effective prayer. They are able to put faces to their prayers. They have better insight into the work of missions. They will be different people when they get home, and the people of their home churches will know it.

Embarrassing Exceptions

All work teams, however, are not like this. Some have a "fortress mentality." They may travel from the mission compound to the work project and back almost as if they were under armed guard. They interact only with North Americans and gain neither insight about nor respect for the very people they have come to serve.

Their behavior implies an attitude that says: *This is American money, and we will do it the American way! We paid good money to come here, and we don't want anyone coming in and messing up our work. We don't want national workers to help us. We can build it better, faster, and stronger with one hand tied behind our backs!*

People with this attitude are bound to come away frustrated, bitter, and disappointed. They may feel good about having done something for those "poor" people, but they have gained no appreciation of who those "poor" people are. Life change has not taken place and a tarnished image of North American Christianity has been presented. In cases like this, it would have been better to just send the money.

Can You Risk This?

You have to be willing to risk a great deal to be part of an effective Action Team. These risks are seldom related to physical well-being. The real risks are internal and deeply personal. They deal with attitudes and beliefs that have developed over a lifetime.

You may risk losing your preconceptions and stereotypes, or find out that you do not have all the answers. You may risk discovering that the world doesn't revolve around North America, that the word "poor" doesn't mean "stupid," and that "happiness" is not the same as "wealth." Most importantly, you must take the risk that God will move in your heart and that you will be forever changed.

If you and your church are willing to risk all that and more, then send a team. You won't ever regret that you did!

Who is wise and understanding among you? Let him show it by his good life, by deeds done in the humility that comes from wisdom.

The wisdom that comes from heaven is first of all pure; then peaceloving, considerate, submissive, full of mercy and good fruit, impartial and sincere. Peacemakers who sow in peace raise a harvest of righteousness (James 3:13, 17-18).

Missions Prepares People For Freedom

Edward Coleson, Ph.D.
July/August 1994 p. 32

Freedom can be frightening, even fatal. Many people have found it so. *Liberty, equality and fraternity*, the slogan of the French Revolution of 1789, led to the guillotine, not to Utopia.

A couple years later the slaves of Haiti, a French colony in the Caribbean, were beginning to realize that French freedom didn't include them, so one night they arose in wrath and burned the sugar mills, the cane fields, and their masters' homes. They also killed every man, woman, and child they could get their hands on.

Haiti had been the richest little country in the world – but since then their poverty has been proverbial. Freedom has led to disaster as when *In those days Israel had no king; everyone did as he saw fit* (Judges 21:25).

Given the tragedy in Haiti, imagine what the sugar planters from the British West Indies said when English abolitionists, led by William Wilberforce in Parliament, began to try to do something about slavery!

Wilberforce was young when he started his campaign against the ancient evil of slavery. The aged John Wesley sought to encourage him, knowing it would be a long and difficult battle.

Wesley had written a popular pamphlet against slavery several years earlier, so now it pleased him to see a young man with great political ability take up the fight. In fact, he wrote the young statesman a letter just before he died in 1791, the last letter he ever wrote:

My Dear Sir, Unless the Divine Power... has raised you up for this very thing you will be worn out by the opposition of men and devils; but "if God be with you who can be against you?" Are all of them together stronger than God? Oh, be not weary in well doing. Go on, and in the... power of His might, till even American slavery, the vilest that ever saw the sun, shall vanish away....

– Your affectionate servant, **John Wesley**

William needed all the encouragement he got, because it would be years before his efforts would begin to bear fruit. The first victory was a law forbidding British ships to engage in the slave trade, passed in 1807 when England was fighting for her very life against Napoleon.

The thinking of the time was very interesting. They believed they could not ask for the Lord's help while the blood of Africa was on their hands. Yet passing the law, difficult as that had been, was easier than enforcing it.

After Waterloo the British navy took responsibility to police the African coast and the "Middle Passage" between there and the Americas. The task was expensive in men and money, but the Christians saw to it that the government kept at the job.

Wilberforce and other abolitionists saw from the beginning that they must get the slaves freed on the sugar islands of the British West Indies, but victory was long in coming. By that time Wilberforce lay dying as the Emancipation Bill made its way through Parliament in 1833, but he lived long enough to know it would pass. He rejoiced in his final hours, knowing that the cause for which he gave his life would triumph.

But in the days that followed many people remembered Haiti. They were not so sure that liberating slaves was wise. They had to wait a year for the answer, but missionaries on the islands had done their work well. Freedom was what Wilberforce had prayed it would be, as Ralph Waldo Emerson told the American people before our Civil War:

On the night of the 31st of July, they met everywhere at their churches and chapels, and at midnight, when the clock struck 12, on their knees, the silent, weeping assembly became men; they rose and embraced each other; they cried, they sang, they prayed, they were wild with joy, but there was no riot.... The first of August came on Friday, and a release was proclaimed from all work until the next Monday. The day was chiefly spent by the great mass of the negroes in the churches and chapels. The clergy and missionaries throughout the island were actively engaged, seizing the opportunity to enlighten the people on all the duties and responsibilities of their new relation, and urging them to the attainment of that higher liberty with which Christ maketh His children free.

II. Equatorial Africa

Page   **Article**

79   Meet Jim & Martha
86   In Search Of Umuganda
92   J. W. Haley: Central Africa Pioneer
97   Central Africa: 55 Years Of Progress
103   Sub-Sahara Lingo
106   Lamentations Of A Medical Missionary
110   Rwanda Diary
133   A Coming Kingdom

World Mission People 78

THE KIRKPATRICKS
Virgil (Jim) and Martha
Missionaries to Equitorial Africa

Meet Jim & Martha

Martha Kirkpatrick
May/June 1991 pp. 27-29

Jim and Martha Kirkpatrick have been missionaries to Central Africa since 1964. Their leisure activities these days include playing with grandchildren, reading, learning to use the computer, and each furlough Jim works on a Doctorate in Missiology at Trinity Evangelical Divinity School. Here is their autobiography in brief.

I am the oldest of eight children of a farmer in northwestern Ohio. When I was six, my parents bought the farm they still live on. From early childhood I drove tractor, milked cows, fed hogs, and worked in the garden. At strawberry picking time we received five cents for every quart we picked. If God had not called me to missions, I would have been happy to live on the farm in the same house all my life.

Summer vacation was defined by rain. When the soil was too wet to work we would go to Lake Erie for the day and wade along the shore. Along the way we stopped at a store to buy bologna, bread, potato chips, and chocolate bit cookies: food that farm people did not often get.

My parents belonged to the Church of the Brethren, but every summer took us to an interdenominational holiness camp meeting in Findlay, Ohio. They faithfully observed family worship every morning before breakfast. Father followed the daily Scripture readings in the Union Gospel Press Sunday school quarterly. We always knelt to pray.

Breakfast was an important meal. In the summer when young hens started to lay we could eat as many small eggs as we wanted for breakfast. We often raced to eat a dozen each.

My parents advised us to set high goals, work hard, and stick with whatever we started. Because of the great depression, they themselves were not able to go to college. Very few of our school mates went on for further training, but our parents saw to it that we all went to college and we all worked our way through.

Our family included seven girls and one boy. The fourth daughter was born blind on Valentine's Day in 1945 and died in 1949. She shared my bedroom, and losing her was the first grief I remember feeling. Her death made a gap of nine years between us first three children and the younger four. Each of us older girls took a younger sister to care for. Mine was Becky (Riemenschneider) who now works in the mission office. She and husband Dan have helped our family in extraordinary ways, even moving into an apartment during one of our home assignments and letting us live in their house!

Jim, From Kenya

My husband Jim was born in Kenya, Africa, on a site that is now a tea plantation. His father owned the land until the tea company offered to trade for another tract of land, which is now the site of Kenya Highlands Bible College.

When Jim was 18 months old, his parents, missionaries with World Gospel Mission (WGM), moved from Kenya to Burundi and started many WGM stations. Later they served for 25 years as inter-denominational evangelists under the Africa Revival Fellowship.

Jim is second of four brothers. A sister died in South Africa when one year old. The family was on its way to the States for their first furlough when the baby became ill on board ship. They got off and entered her in the hospital where she died. Jim's mother died on her 80th birthday in 1984. His father is 89 and lives with Jim's brother at Upland, Indiana.

The Way God Worked

At camp meeting when I was five I first felt that I needed Jesus. I went forward to pray and asked Jesus to be my Savior. At home while sitting on the back steps with my parents, I told them I had become a Christian and that I wanted to be a missionary to Africa.

Every year a speaker came to our little country church from the Kentucky Mountain Holiness Association (KMHA) to receive donations from farmers for the schools there. In grade school I prayed that my parents would consider me mature enough to go to Mt. Carmel High School of KMHA (300 miles away) when I was 14. I felt I needed to go there for training for the mission field, and two of my childhood girl friends went with me to that school.

After my Freshman year I went home for the summer. In special revival services I felt powerless and bound and that I needed more from God if I were to be a missionary. After a week of praying and confessing and surrendering, my dad advised that when I had done all I could, I needed to trust God to accept me. From that day on I professed the experience of "entire sanctification." The Bible became alive as I read it and Jesus was near.

My future husband Jim was saved when he was 10 years old as the result of a dream in which his brothers were going to heaven and he was not. He woke up and asked Jesus to be his Savior. At a later time when seeking the baptism with the Holy Spirit, Jim had to be willing to stay in the States. That was his consecration. Then the Lord let him know that he would be a missionary to Africa after all.

Kentucky Mountain "Friends"

When I was a junior in high school, we heard about two brothers, missionary kids, coming from Africa to attend our boarding school. We students gathered at a classroom window to watch them trudge up the hill carrying their suitcases. But these two boys did not seem to know I existed. Besides, the rules were very strict. Boys and girls could not date in high school.

Upon graduation I moved up the road a mile to attend Kentucky Mountain Bible Institute (KMBI). Just after Christmas one of those boys from Africa asked me for a date. A girl was expected to pray about it before she gave her answer, and the dean of women asked me if I knew that this fellow was going to ask me. When I replied that I didn't realize he knew me, she said, "That's the way it's supposed to be!"

I prayed about it for a week, so excited I couldn't eat or concentrate. Then I gave him an affirmative answer. After a few dates and getting acquainted, Jim Kirkpatrick asked me to be his friend.

All through school I professed a call to missions in Africa. So did a lot of other people, and it was considered improper to go with anyone not called to the same mission field. I had promised God I would only go out with someone called to Africa. If God did not give me someone special to go with, I was willing to go to Africa alone.

After graduating from three years at KMBI, Jim went to Asbury College, Wilmore, KY. The following year I graduated and went to Marion College, Marion, IN. I had a job with World Gospel Mission. In the summer I travelled to interdenominational camp meetings representing their prayer band department. During the school year I worked in their office. After two summers and one school year Jim asked me to marry him, so I transferred to Asbury and majored in Jim, now in Asbury Seminary.

In college I cared for a Methodist evangelist's invalid wife while he was away in meetings and worked in the registrar's office. Jim worked as night watchman and on the maintenance crew. After we were married we also had a student pastorate.

We took two weeks off in June 1960 to get married in the little country church I attended as a child. The brother that came home from Africa with Jim was his best man. I said all the best man had to do was get Jim to the church on time, and they raced a train across the tracks to keep that promise. Jim's parents were on furlough from Africa and his dad performed the ceremony.

Jim's uncle had a cabin on the edge of Mohican State Park in central Ohio. We went there for our honeymoon – good preparation for what we thought Africa would be like -- no indoor facilities.

I am thankful God gave me Jim. We have opposite temperaments. I think I have helped him be more assertive, and I know he has helped me to be more laid back and easier to get along with. On the field Jim is known as the greatest optimist. I need that side of him, too.

Free Methodist Encounters

When Jim was in his last year of seminary we received a phone call from Clyde Van Valin, then Free Methodist pastor in Wilmore, KY, where we lived. The Free Methodist Mission Board asked him to see if we would be interested in going to Africa under their board. They knew about our desire through Gerald Bates, at that time a missionary living in an apartment next to Jim's parents in Africa. We had applied to other boards but nothing seemed to click or be God's will.

Within two weeks we had joined the Free Methodist Church and felt peaceful in making arrangements to serve on a Free Methodist mission field. In those days a person signed up "for life."

The mission board felt we needed to get acquainted with the church and the church should get to know us, so they gave us to Southern Michigan Conference for two years. W. Dale Cryderman was our superintendent as we pastored the Pulaski church. During those years Jim did substitute teaching to augment our salary of $55 a week. I stayed home with Beth, born while Jim was in seminary. Margi was born while we lived at Pulaski.

On Our Way

Some of the most difficult hours of my life were when we said good-bye to loved ones at the train at Toledo to go to New York Harbor to board the SS Maasdam for Amsterdam. I was strongly tempted to turn back. Four years away from parents and brother and sisters seemed like a long time. Also, taking our little girls into the unknown seemed like such a big ordeal.

When we arrived, Jim could immediately communicate with the Africans, and I didn't understand a word! I was motivated to work hard to learn the language so I could communicate with somebody. And I arrived in Africa without a job description, so I always had to figure out what I would do and where I would fit in wherever we were assigned.

Life Out Of Death

Our oldest daughter, Elizabeth Faye (Beth), was born in 1961 and died as the result of a fall in 1976, at Nyakarago in Burundi, Africa. This place had no church, school, or medical facility. Two weeks before she died I had asked my sister, a missionary with Christian radio station CORDAC, what would it take to get a church started there? Government regulations required that we build a permanent building before we could evangelize the people.

Beth's death challenged people to give to build a church acceptable to the government authorities. God impressed me with Genesis 50:20-21 where Joseph said to his brothers, "You intended to harm me, but God intended it for good to accomplish what is now being done, the saving of many lives. So then, don't be afraid. I will provide for you and your children."

Satan intended this experience to do us in. God intended it for good to accomplish what is now being done, the saving of many lives. The first words that came to my mind when my husband told me Beth was gone were "Well, she's safe in the arms of Jesus!" Beth awaits the resurrection day at Kibuye in Burundi.

Margaret Alice (Margi), our second child, was born at Jackson, Michigan, in 1963. She is married to Rick Kendall, a youth pastor in the Pacific Northwest Conference. Our second grandson, Philip Mark, was born to them on April 3, 1990. Margi and Rick have a goal to be missionaries in Africa.

Our son Virgil Edwin (Ed) was born at Kibuye in Burundi in 1967. Now a student at Taylor University in Upland, Indiana, he loves Africa and hopes to return some day.

Leonard Wayne (Len), our youngest, was born in Jackson, Michigan, while we were on our first furlough in 1968. His wife Juli, daughter of former missionaries Jim and Jane Rea, was born at Kibuye in Burundi. Juli claims she is more African than Len because she was born in Africa and he in the States. Our first grandson, Joel Craig, was born to them in 1987. Last year Len graduated from Oakland City College in southern Indiana, was ordained deacon, and pastors the Tunnel Hill Free Methodist Church in Wabash Conference.

What I like most about being a parent is the joy of seeing our children follow the Lord.

About Our Africa Home

Of all the places we have lived, I prefer our current home in Butare, Rwanda. This is the first time in our missionary career that we have returned to the same house after furlough.

They call Rwanda "the land of eternal spring." We have ideal temperatures year round. Because of good weather and adequate water, we also have fresh vegetables all year. My favorite native food is the fruit: papaya, pineapple, bananas, loquats, mangoes, guavas, avocados. Our children like the palm oil and little fish and manioc bread which I find very hard to digest.

Burundi and Rwanda are also called "the Switzerland of Africa" because they are landlocked and because the natural beauty of the many hills is breath-taking and awesome. You need to see our rain forest and parks and mountains to understand.

The People We Love

The people in Rwanda and Burundi are very stoic in temperament. Almost the worst sin you can commit is to show your anger. People in Zaire are much more emotional.

Our official language in Burundi, Rwanda and Zaire is French. Every missionary who wants to get next to the people must also learn the local language. Africans cannot understand why a person would not learn their local language.

My best African friends are Anonciate and Laetitia. I have discipled them. Anonciate is sensitive to the impressions of the Holy Spirit to pray for me. Laetitia is like a sister and can see what I need done without my saying anything. Both of them are faithful to correct and guide me in the ways of African culture.

Jim's best African friends are Anasthase and John. They were our students and Jim discipled them. They can confide in each other and Jim counts on them to give the African viewpoint in an issue and yet be true to Christian principles.

Willard and Doris Ferguson of the Evangelical Friends are also special friends. We got acquainted in French study and lived together for some years on the same mission station. In all difficult times that either of us have had we have been together. We have fellowship with them and can easily pick up where we left off each time we are together.

Our Greatest Needs

We need experienced, trained pastors from North America to help train leaders in Central Africa. We are also very concerned about what will happen to the church in West Africa if we do not get missionaries there soon.

A second need is for buildings for people to worship in. Many groups are still sitting on the hillsides in rain or sun for their church services. Church buildings we do have are packed and overcrowded.

The national church in Central Africa sets its own goals, and as coworkers and servants, we try to help them reach these goals. Therefore, a third need is to build the Central Africa Free Methodist University in Kigali, a new project that is just getting underway.

Jim and I took as our life verses Proverbs 3:5-6: "Trust in the Lord with all your heart and lean not on your own understanding; in all your ways acknowledge him, and he will make your paths straight." As we have done this, God has answered our prayers and shown us the way.

In Search Of Umuganda

September/October 1990 pp. 1-5

This article is condensed from the "Umuganda" movie script written by committee: Jim Kirkpatrick, Betty Ellen Cox, Irvin Cobb, Dr. Tom Ball, Wally Metts, and Dan Runyon. The three college students are Rochelle Oderman, Christy Peters, and Chad Schneider.

The year was 1990. We were college kids interested in missions. The chance to tramp through central Africa for three weeks with a movie camera on our shoulders in search of Umuganda (Oo-moo-gah-ndah) sounded like the thrill of a lifetime.

Most likely, you don't even know what Umuganda is. Neither did we until we read about it in our video script. First we thought it might refer to a lost city that slipped into the Rift Valley in the heart of Africa. But, as it turns out, Umuganda is not a place.

If Umuganda **were** a place, it belongs here, where the Rift Valley splits the globe from the Dead Sea in Israel to the south of Africa. In this rift we found magnificent Lake Kivu -- formed when lava poured from smoking volcanoes to dam up the rivers. Here pioneer missionary J. W. Haley traveled on Lake Tanganyika, the longest and second-deepest body of fresh water in the world.

Despite the location just 200 miles from the equator, the temperature is moderate, for the elevation is high. In this idyllic land of temperate rain forests, prehistoric ferns still grow -- if you know where to look -- and the Free Methodist Church of today thrives.

There are plenty of people. Both Burundi, the "Switzerland of Africa," and Rwanda, the "Land of Eternal Spring," have 600 to 750 people per square mile. Vast and less populated Zaire (formerly Congo) shares much of their culture and lifestyle.

Is Umuganda At The Market?

Since Umuganda is not a place, we thought it might be found at the open market. In this barter culture all present are both merchant and buyer at this, the social event of the week and the most important economic event in central Africa.

Interesting sights and smells await the visitor, for the market place is full of dust and smells and noise and fleas and dogs and beggars ... even soap box preachers! The people are just like us — busy making a living and caring for their families.

In central Africa apartheid does not exist. Missionaries and Africans work side by side, hand in hand, to bring about a strong faith and better life.

Of course, people are not the same **everywhere.** You see, in Zaire they carry loads on their **backs,** but in Rwanda and Burundi they carry loads on their **heads.** They are known to walk to market and talk a mile a minute while weaving a basket, carrying a baby on their backs, and balancing a bottle (or slippery fish) on their heads!

The young people are like teens everywhere — trying to find their way — earnestly seeking for God and right values. For them, church is music: a way of worship, a way to memorize the Gospel, a place to belong. These turned-on youth will walk all night to a revival meeting.

About 1% of the population holds a cash-paying job. The rest are fully employed in the actual production of food for their own families. To eat, you must first plow the ground, plant the seeds, cultivate the crops, harvest the food, prepare it for human consumption, and then cook and eat it.

If you don't think it's delicious, maybe you missed a step along the way. No matter how it tastes, we found out that **food** is also not Umuganda.

Now Where Should We Look?

"Maybe Umuganda is a game!" one of us proposed, so we went looking for children. You don't have to look far. Kids are everywhere, enjoying their home-made toys — banana bark balls, bottle cap checkers, bike rim and stick, hopscotch and stones, whatever.

We found out that educational needs are the same as anywhere, but opportunity is lacking. In some places only 40% of school-age children are in school. In Rwanda a mere 8% of those who complete elementary education are admitted to high school. Those not in school watch cows, care for small children, hoe a field, or do nothing and look bored. They would give anything to get their hands on our video cameras!

Most schools are run by the churches following government curriculum. High school costs the parent about $600 a year. For them that's a huge pile of money — and we thought we had it tough getting through college in the West!

The Free Methodist Child Care Sponsorship Ministry has made education possible for many. Others could be helped, but more sponsors are needed. It is astonishing what difference just a few dollars a month can make.

Maybe Umuganda is MONEY!?

For those our churches cannot afford to educate, youth cooperatives provide one alternative to high school: projects in farming, fishing, and building. These apprentice-type programs teach a trade such as how to raise rabbits, operate a fishing project, or gain horticultural knowledge which might be used in business such as at a tea plantation, where some of the finest tea in the world is produced.

Churches are also involved in the business world. Communal church gardens bring people together and earn money. But Umuganda is not money.

Maybe It's Medical

It was a joy to discover the ministry of our hospitals as they respond to dire human need. At Kibogora in Rwanda we provide a six-year medical training program, and at Nundu, Zaire, we provide a two-year nursing program.

Physical healing is accompanied by spiritual healing. Chaplain Michael Wakana at Kibogora shares the gospel with hundreds of patients each month. Many become Christians. Chaplain Matthew Rumoka at Kibuye, Burundi has a similar ministry. We bring both health and eternal hope to thousands.

And teachers are equipping thousands more. Central Africa is a land of opportunity -- for where needs are great, opportunity abounds. A new generation must be trained to lead the Kingdom of God, and two out of three Africans are under the age of 20.

In addition to elementary and secondary schools, the Free Methodist Church provides Theological Education by Extension (TEE). This programmed instruction reaches villagers, preparing them for lay leadership and as assistant pastors. About 1500 have graduated from this program since it began some 20 years ago.

Additional training is offered at four Bible schools in Zaire and at Mweya Bible Institute in Burundi, a cooperative effort of the United Methodist, Evangelical Friends, and Free Methodist churches. Pastoral training and high school subjects are provided in this traditional residential program.

Free Methodist schools in central Africa are staffed mostly by Africans, but foreign volunteers and missionary teachers are both welcome and needed.

The Theological School at Butare in Rwanda is a cooperative program of Baptist, Presbyterian, Episcopalian and Free Methodist churches. Four-year graduates earn a college level theological diploma.

Under the guidance of Bishop Aaron and Mr. Butorano, a new University of Central Africa is now being developed by the Central African Fellowship of Free Methodist Churches. It is already approved by the Rwanda government, and will serve all three countries from its location at Kigali.

The university will offer classes in both English and French. The five-year program will lead to a Master of Arts degree in pastoral studies and theology, teacher training, economics, or languages and literature.

Still Not Umuganda!

This is all great news! But it is not Umuganda. We saw that while education will bring future improvements, prayer is bringing immediate change. Bishop Bya'ene of Zaire affirms that "Prayer meetings and volunteer lay evangelism are the reasons for the rapid growth of the church in Zaire."

He is right. Certain cities in Zaire that were once unsafe have seen dramatic improvements. Thugs who once prowled the streets are now in prayer meeting. Most high schools have voluntary prayer groups. The prayer groups result in spiritual victory and fellowship.

In fact, (now that we pause to consider), it seems that **everything** in central Africa is done in groups. We looked at each other in surprise and said together, "THAT'S IT! UMUGANDA MEANS 'GROUP!'"

How To Be A "Groupie"

We asked a few questions and discovered that "Umuganda" is a word used in Rwanda, and it means "group service." In Burundi the word "Umugambwe" (oo-moo-gah-mbgay) means the same. And in Zaire they talk about group service with the word "Salongo" (Sah-loh-ngoh).

The government of Rwanda requires that **everyone** works together for three hours each week on some improvement program. For professional and government employees, Saturday morning is the time for Umuganda. For rural people, Tuesday morning is Umuganda time.

You might see them mulching coffee trees, fixing up a soccer field, or constructing a building. Indeed, the entire excavation for the first level of the administration building at Kibogora Medical School was all done by Umuganda. Students, workers, and teachers moved the mountain together!

Umuganda was introduced in Rwanda in the mid-1970s, when *Time* magazine reported that country as one of the five poorest places in the world. Today Umuganda pervades central Africa. The President of Rwanda, Major General Habyarmana Juvenal, has said that "the first foundation of development for a country is moral development." He has introduced a service system and a Christian work ethic that is transforming his land.

Moral Development

This moral development based on God's Word runs deep in many Free Methodist leaders. Pastor Mark, a national missionary in Rwanda, risked his life in a power encounter with pagan spirit worship. A mob tried to kill him and others when an axe was applied to the root of the Spirit Tree. God spared his life and blessed his ministry, so that today the Spirit Tree has lost its mystique, was cut down in June, 1990, and many have turned from idol worship to Jesus.

Pastor Paul Nzacahayo of Rwanda turned down attractive job offers to accept a paper circuit in 1986. He entered a remote area to do basic evangelism and had to build his own house before he could start. Already he has two churches, a tree planting and agricultural development program, and 1,000 in church on Pentecost Sunday.

And there is Steven, a teacher and business manager who felt the call to preach. In Burundi, he pastored the largest Free Methodist congregation in the world -- until it was deliberately divided into many smaller congregations and satellite churches. He later stepped down from this secure position to do itinerant evangelism in Burundi.

Another key Free Methodist leader was offered the Ambassadorship to an English-speaking country, and government officials wanted him to go into business with them. He turned down these opportunities to serve the Free Methodist Church -- a shining example of moral development in central Africa.

Simeon, a well-paid nurse at Kibogora, also felt called to preach. After four years of seminary he went to Gisenyi, and within four years planted 40 churches organized into four zones for training and problem-solving purposes.

More Than Just A Group

As we began to catch the vision, we weren't surprised to learn that Umuganda means more than "group service." It also means "sacrifice." The Gospel of Jesus Christ is transforming central Africa through the sacrificial giving of its own people. The group service called "Umuganda" is pervasive – so pervasive that it may even catch on in your own church.

Picture yourself making a contribution in Africa. Through the Free Methodist Child Care Sponsorship Ministry you can help one of the 60% of the population who cannot afford an education.

Although Simeon has started 40 churches, most of them meet under a tree or crowd into a home. It takes only $500 to $1000 per church to buy the metal roof for a new building – the labor provided free by the church members. How many churches could **your church** build in central Africa this year? At least one?

Teachers who speak English and French are needed in many of our educational institutions. Through the VISA program or perhaps as a career missionary, you can join the Umuganda effort that is bringing about a moral revolution in central Africa.

Our three hospitals in central Africa have a continual need for bandages and medical supplies. Perhaps you could start your own Umuganda group to roll these bandages, buy these supplies, and ship them to the hospitals – a direct healing ministry.

Umuganda Is Up To You

In central Africa, Umuganda is mandatory for three hours every week. In the Kingdom of God, Umuganda is voluntary. You may want to begin by giving three hours of your weekly wages to Free Methodist Missions. Or, devote three hours each week in your own Umuganda group, advancing the cause of missions at home.

You might spend three hours each week in prayer, or in writing to missionaries, or in sharing this issue of *Missionary Tidings* with others.

Yes, in the beginning, you may want to give just three hours a week. But as you experience the joy, the fellowship, and the growth and progress that is Umuganda – you may soon want to follow the example of leaders in central Africa by volunteering your entire life for the cause of Christ.

J. W. Haley: Central Africa Pioneer
September/October 1990 p. 7-8

J. W. Haley established Free Methodist missions in central Africa in the last 10 years of his career. His story below is condensed from <u>Soul Afire</u>, by Gerald Bates, Light and Life Press, 1981.

May 16, 1932: North America is caught in the great depression. John Wesley Haley at Fairview mission station in South Africa wrote, "I am deadly in earnest for the salvation of those who have never heard.... Jesus calls me and I am going where He opens up the way. We can live in a mud house and if we let the young church do its part we will not need much more money than we get now, my soul is afire and I am making all preparations...."

It All Started In Canada

Haley was born in Bracebridge, Ontario in 1878 to immigrant farmers from the United Kingdom, one of seven boys and one girl. Two years after becoming a Christian at age 20, Haley helped W. H. Wilson in pioneer church work in western Canada, where 18 converts in Caron, West Ontario, formed the nucleus of the Westview circuit.

In 1902 Haley sailed for Africa, to be joined in 1905 by Esther Hamilton who, by previous arrangement, soon became Mrs. Haley. Haley began language study and work at Inhambane, Mozambique. Within three years close to 1,000 decisions for Christ are reported, and Haley gained experience in teaching and living under primitive conditions.

For health and family reasons the Haleys returned to Canada from 1909 to 1917, then again sailed for South Africa. The mission prospered, but by 1923 Haley felt, "In my own heart the Holy Spirit burned the words of Deuteronomy 2:3, 'Ye have compassed this mountain long enough: Turn you northward.'"

In Nairobi, Kenya, on his way home in 1926, Haley was given the name of a Foreign Bible Society agent who was to be in London on the only day the Haleys would be there. They had only five minutes to talk, long enough for the man to say, "Why don't you go to Urundi? There is no missionary there. There are 2,500,000 people."

"That day I accepted responsibility for Urundi," Haley wrote, but political formalities followed by the great depression shelved the project for eight years.

Preparations

In 1931, with permission for a visit to central Africa, Haley deposited his life insurance policy as security for the 180 pounds sterling ($900) necessary for visas to enter Belgian territory. He waterproofed the tent and received from his brother an instrument for taking altitudes and a compass. Dr. Backenstoe gave him medicines and a hypodermic thermometer.

"Today, May 24th, '32 Miss Gunsolus handed me $50 for the trip," Haley wrote in his journal. "It means her savings, I fear, and I told her I could not take it but I saw she would be disappointed if not grieved, so I accepted it thankfully.... Of course we are in the midst of the greatest financial collapse the world ever knew but that is not my matter. I am preparing and He will open the way."

On May 31 Haley, his son Blake, and Missionary Frank Adamson left for Urundi in Adamson's vehicle, a "Willys six." Each night was spent in a small tent fastened to the car. Haley took only passing notice of lions and leopards, but Adamson recalled this nightly prayer: "May there be no rude awakenings during the night." They were not encouraged by reports from settlers that "Leopards are as thick as bats." Upon arrival at Likasi, the car with Adamson and Blake was sent home and Haley continued the journey alone, traveling by train and then steamer to the head of Lake Tanganyika.

Kindly received at the Swedish Pentecostal mission in Congo, Haley wrote: "While I was regretting not being able to get through with my own car, the Lord had two cars waiting for me with missionary drivers who spoke English, French, and the native language." After two weeks in Urundi Haley returned by train and boat to South Africa. Struck by the dire need of the people, he also wrote, "I fell in love with the country and feel we must open work there."

Go

At conference in 1934 the Haleys and Ila Gunsolus, on the instructions of the missionary secretary, were "separated" at a special service for the work in Urundi. Fund raising and government red tape finally brought him to Urundi, where he searched for a suitable mission site. While waiting for permission to occupy the site, Haley traveled, studied the language, and "made up two beds, five window frames, two door frames and a food safe. We have to make sashes for the windows also and two doors."

Night overtook Haley during one excursion in search of appropriate mission sites, so an African chief gave them shelter. Haley wrote, "The hut was small and had to accommodate, besides we two, about 10 people, 4 or 5 calves, two dogs and a cock. They made up a bed of grass on the floor, put a new mat over it and gave us a good blanket. The fire dried our clothes. They kept it going all night. A little naked lad roasted nice ears of mealies for us which made up our supper, and although the dogs snarled at each other, scratched fleas and the cock crew, we had quite a good night."

At Easter in 1935 when a guest at a Baptist station, Haley preached on "Except a corn of wheat fall into the ground and die..." He shelled two ears of corn as the product of one grain and then challenged them to open 40 new places that year.

Muyebe

On May 2, 1935, Haley arrived at Muyebe, first station of the Free Methodist Mission in central Africa, and hub from which a chain of other mission centers and hundreds of churches would spring. Haley was 56 years old. What would he say to these poor, half-naked people who had gathered to observe the strange behavior of this white man?

"I told them I had come to live with them. We were ready to start school any time they wanted to learn. They should tell us and we would all stop a day and build a little grass school. My houses are mine and I pay for them. The school is theirs. I will not eat or sleep in it. They must build it. This is the beginning of self support or the mission doing the things they ought to do, so it is vital."

Haley was a veteran of many battles around the issue of national churches dependent on mission resources. He urged self-reliance and trust in God. Haley knew if the expansion of the church depended on foreign funds, then it would be limited by the same. But if the church became part of the local society, including the economic structure, then there were no limits as to where it could go.

Within three months Haley's wife and two of four children joined him. After five months of teaching and preaching he felt it was time to issue an invitation to those who wanted to follow Jesus. Haley describes the scene:

"I asked those who wanted to pray for Jesus to take away their bad hearts to stand and a number of men rose. Then we had each pray for himself. It was perhaps the first time they had ever prayed to Jesus." After 1900 years, the drama witnessed by the Apostle Paul was repeated in central Africa.

Fanning Out

In a few months a sub-chief nearby asked for a school to be built near his place. Haley measured out a site, obtained government authority for registry, and expansion was underway. New Christians and workers from Muyebe went to help. In line with his principles of self-support, Haley observed, "It was all unpaid labor, for the building is for them not us." At Haley's urging the class planned an offering in which men would give one franc a month, women and young men one-half a franc, children 30 centimes. This money was saved to pay an evangelist or catechist at the new outschool. Within weeks a second and third outschool site were surveyed and thatched shelters put up.

Unsatisfied with mere local expansion around Muyebe, in 1936 Haley made an exploratory trip into southeastern Burundi. Here he began to lay out a strategy for placing mission outposts, taking into consideration population densities, so as to assure reaching the area. Out of these early plans grew the missions of Kibuye and Rwintare.

By 1940 Mweya mission was established, later to become a tri-mission station in cooperation with the National Holiness Association and the Friends Africa Gospel Mission, both holiness groups with whom several projects were carried out. Another mission, Kayero, was established by Haley and later turned over to the National Holiness Missionary Society (now World Gospel Mission).

In 1941 Haley traveled north up the Ruzizi valley from Lake Tanganyika, to scout out yet another mission site. A year later, with barely enough funds and a World War in progress, Frank and Hazel Adamson moved to the new mission at Kibogora. Haley noted, "It is planned to build a hospital there, as the people are very needy and medical work helps definitely to introduce the Gospel."

Under Haley, Free Methodist missions were established in Muyebe, Kibuye, Rwintare, and Kibogora. In 1943 he reported that nationals "pay all the workers at their 79 outstations and are building brick church-schools at the main centers. They represent 911 members... and 8,629 pupils...."

To What Effect?

The stubborn vision and godly energy of this missionary pioneer to central Africa affected tens of thousands of African Christians and resulted in three of the most vigorous and growing conferences in the Free Methodist Church.

The religious dynamic, message, and devotion of Haley was first a novelty, then a revolutionizing force among those contacted by it. This sense of wonder is still evident after half a century as early converts share the transformation brought about by this invasion of the gospel, starting for them from a modest "grain of corn" at a remote spot in the heart of central Africa called Muyebe.

HALEY COMMENTS:
by *Byron S. Lamson,* Missionary Secretary, 1944-1964

"J. W. Haley moved with resolution, speed, and dispatch, in tackling any assignment."

"He seemed to have an almost unlimited faith in God. His dependence on prayer was very great."

"He presented to the Commission on Missions a plan for opening a new field.... It seemed that every argument was against such a move; but when J. W. Haley finished telling the Board how God had opened the doors to the Congo... no one on the Commission wanted to say 'no' to God and J. W. Haley."

"Try to believe me when I say there were 3,000 seated on the ground in the patio between the two wings of the school building. Eleven years ago there were no Christians here. Then came a man sent from God, and his name was J. W. Haley. Today there are these hundreds of humble followers of Jesus Christ."

Central Africa: 55 Years of Progress

Betty Ellen Cox
November/December 1990 p. 19-21

J.W. Haley opened Free Methodist missionary work at Muyebe in Burundi in 1935. His goal was to develop a fully indigenous church. At that time the country was known as Ruanda-Urundi, and was governed by Belgium as a trusteeship of the League of Nations (and later of the United Nations). When independence was granted in 1962, the country became the two separate nations of Rwanda and Burundi.

Four New Stations

Within a few years, other missionaries joined the Haleys: Ron and Margaret Collett, Frank and Hazel Adamson, Ila Gunsolus, Margaret Holton. Four new mission stations were opened within seven years: Kayero (later turned over to the World Gospel Mission), Kibuye and Rwintare in Burundi, and Kibogora in Rwanda.

Elementary schools and medical work were a part of the ministry from the very beginning. These were greatly used of the Lord to win people to Himself and to the church, as everyone needed teaching and medical care. Virtually all of the church leaders today first came to the church through the elementary schools. At Kibuye, the dispensary expanded into a hospital when Dr. Esther Kuhn came in 1948.

About 1941 a mighty revival, which began among Anglicans in Rwanda, swept into Burundi. Hundreds came to Christ. Great conferences were held where thousands of Africans from all the churches met together, many walking several days to get to the meeting. Confessions were made, fetishes burned, lives transformed. This gave an impetus to the work that never really stopped. Since then the growth of the churches in Burundi and Rwanda has been phenomenal.

An African writer, Jean-Claude Kabera, gives six reasons for the remarkable growth of the church during those years:
1) The revival of 1941;
2) An existing belief in God among the nationals;
3) Missionaries' efforts to learn the national languages;
4) Teaching in the schools;

5) Fighting disease;
6) Teaching the nationals to help themselves.
   Other reasons, such as systematic evangelism, could be added.

Getting Organized
   Regular business meetings had always been held by the missionaries to plan for the work. In 1943 national delegates, both ministerial and lay (though none were yet ordained) from the various pastorates were invited to participate in these meetings.
   This was an initial step toward the organizing of a conference. The number of churches and preaching points was increasing. These were led by young men, most of whom had only an elementary school education, which at that time comprised just five years. They preached and also taught literacy classes.
   When Dr. Byron Lamson visited the field in 1946, the first national pastors were ordained deacons: Daniel Ntahomereye, Matthew Myiruko and Joseph Rudagaza. Daniel and Matthew are still in the ministry today, but Joseph has retired.
   The church also began sending out their own missionaries, some to Rwanda when that work was begun in 1942, others to new areas in Burundi. They were supported mainly by contributions of the churches, given especially for this purpose in a fund called the "Let's-go-on" box.
   In 1949 the Belgian government agreed to subsidize Protestant education, as was already done for Catholics. This provided great advancement to the educational program, but also required better training for teachers in order to meet the requirements for subsidized schools.
   The Alliance of Protestant Missions, organized in Haley's day, agreed to open a four-year Teacher Training School on the high school level at Kibimba, a Friends' mission station. All of the participating missions would contribute personnel. This became the source of teachers and principals for the elementary schools.
   A year later a Bible School was begun at Mweya, sponsored by the Free Methodists, World Gospel Mission and Friends. The educational level of this school has steadily risen, and this institution has trained most of our pastors in Burundi, as well as some for Rwanda and Zaire. A junior seminary has been added for advanced theological training, in addition to the Bible School.
   It was a great day when the Ruanda-Urundi provisional annual conference was organized in 1954. Eight young pastors were ordained deacon at this time. The church was marching forward.

More Education Needed

In the capital of Usumbura (now Bujumbura) a large group of people was looking for a mission to provide them with government-recognized schools. About the same time the Belgian government was building a residential section of the city for Africans, to be called Ngagara. They included a Protestant church and school center which the Protestant Alliance decided the Free Methodists should have.

In 1956 the Bergs and Orcutts assumed responsibility there. Along with this work in the city, a large number of outstations in the surrounding area joined our church. This work has prospered and countless numbers have come to know Christ.

The need was felt for some advanced education for girls, as increasing numbers of them were completing elementary schools. So in 1959 a Home Economics School was begun at Muyebe on the post-primary level. Many young women trained there and became pastors' wives, or went on for higher education. Their contribution to the church has been significant. Eventually the government phased out this type of school, and a co-educational high school was begun there in 1976, which still continues.

Through these years, the church was developing and growing. Africans were capably carrying more and more responsibility. In 1961 the full Ruanda-Urundi annual conference was formed. The same three men first ordained deacons were now ordained elders. Samuel Simbare was elected as the first national Legal Representative to serve as liaison with the government.

Independence Brings Separation

The following year the United Nations granted full independence to this area, and Rwanda and Burundi became two separate countries. The conference remained united until 1964 when problems of transportation and communication resulted in Rwanda becoming a separate, full conference. Aaron Ruhumuriza became their elected Legal Representative. During this period, advanced students were being given scholarships for studies in other countries: some to Union Biblical Seminary in India, others to Kinshasa in Zaire, one to Belgium, some to the United States. Bishop Aaron Ruhumuriza is a graduate of India's Union Biblical Seminary and has done further studies at Trinity Evangelical Divinity School in Deerfield, Illinois.

The hospital at Kibogora was developed with the arrival of Dr. Kuhn in 1963. There had been a dispensary from the beginning, but now the medical ministry was expanding. The first ward building was completed three years after her arrival. Later, under Dr. Al Snyder, this institution became one of the best in the country, with a 150-bed capacity.

One Thousand Free Methodists Killed

Tragedy struck the Burundi conference in 1972, when ethnic conflict erupted in the country. Many thousands of people were killed, particularly those with leadership capabilities. Our church lost about a thousand people at that time, among them pastors, school principals and teachers, lay evangelists, and high school students. The situation seemed dark indeed. But God raised up new leaders, men who loved Him and were devoted to the church. The church has continued its remarkable growth pattern.

The church saw the importance of evangelizing the capital city in Rwanda, so in 1975 a pastor with a burden to reach the lost was sent to Kigali. Gradually the church began to grow, and now there is a large, thriving congregation, desperately in need of an adequate sanctuary.

Fifteen Year Plan Achieved -- In Five Years

As the church matured, leadership was increasingly in the hands of Africans. Missionaries served as medical personnel, teachers and church planters, and performed other needed services. In 1979 for the first time, the presiding officer of the annual conferences was a national, nominated by his own conference and then designated by the American bishop in charge of the area.

Rwanda prepared a 15-year plan for the development of their conference, which envisaged planting Free Methodist churches in all 10 provinces. Within five years this plan had been fulfilled. It was necessary to make a new plan.

The two conferences were looking ahead and preparing for General Conference status. One of the important steps was to have the *Free Methodist Book of Discipline* in their own languages, with the necessary adaptations to their cultures and structures. These were prepared in the early 1980s, then refined for approval by the 1985 General Conference in North America.

The momentous decision was made at the 1985 General Conference to grant Burundi's request for Provisional General Conference status, and Rwanda's request for full General Conference status. The conferences had made nominations for their bishops: Noah Nzeyimana for Burundi, and Aaron Ruhumuriza for Rwanda. Great were the celebrations in these two countries when the new status was inaugurated and their own bishops installed!

Come Over Into Congo And Help Us

At the time of organizing the first Annual Conference in 1961, some representatives of a group of churches in eastern Congo (now Zaire) were present and made an earnest plea for Free Methodist missionaries and other help for their churches.

They represented about 7000 members, mostly of the Babembe tribe. Many of their fellow tribesmen were living in Burundi and had become Free Methodists. They appreciated the way Free Methodist missions emphasized medical and educational development along with evangelism. Their desire was for this to happen in their country.

A survey trip was made into Congo the next year, and it was decided to enter this field. In 1963 the first missionaries were stationed there, but stayed only a few months, as severe fighting broke out in the area. For a long time rebels controlled that district. Some people were killed, thousands fled to hide in the hills, and mission houses were looted and damaged. As last in 1967, the central government gained control of the area, and people were able to return to their devastated homes and fields.

By mid-1968 Gerald and Marlene Bates were able to travel to Baraka, the main mission station, and hold annual conference. That year the Bible School opened at Baraka under African leadership. Deacons and elders had been ordained, membership was growing. Elementary schools were reopened. Plans were made for a hospital building at Nundu, the second mission station. In 1972 Rev. Al Nelson and his wife arrived to begin construction.

Progress was evident in many ways. A clinic opened at Baraka that year, and a high school started. Women's classes began as well as classes in Theological Education by Extension. Churches organized in the cities of Bukavu and Uvira. Amazing growth took place, not only in the areas close to Baraka, Nundu and Bukavu, but in distant places as well. Four Bible Schools have been started to train leaders in various areas.

When a student went to study in the capital city of Kinshasa, on the western side of the vast country of Zaire, he was distressed to see the scarcity of evangelical groups. Before long, he had started several home churches in the city. Today there are more than 20 of these. Four groups have a church building.

As the church has grown and expanded, Zaire, too, became ready for a Provisional General Conference. The North American General Conference approved this step in 1989 and elected as bishop the man who had been nominated in Zaire, Rev. Bya'ene Ilangyi. They now have three annual conferences.

110,000 Strong

These central Africa churches are moving ahead with vision and purpose. Their total membership now exceeds 110 thousand! And they're not standing still! In Rwanda, some government authorities say that wherever the church starts, social and physical progress follows.

One of the latest developments is a plan of the Central Africa Fellowship to start a Free Methodist university in Rwanda's capital, Kigali, by 1992, which will serve all of central Africa and perhaps more. There is much enthusiasm for this project. Of course, it will be costly.

As we see what God has done in this part of the world in the past 55 years, we can only marvel and praise, and pray that the same spirit of determination and purpose that has characterized the work thus far will continue to motivate and challenge the church of tomorrow.

Sub-Sahara Lingo

Betty Ellen Cox
March/April 1991 p. 32

"Go to the garden and get a buffalo," may not be what you want, but very likely it is what you said: **Imbogo** means buffalo; **Imboga** means lettuce.

The only difference between the words "chicken" and "basket" is a high or low tone on the middle syllable. So don't be surprised when, at the market, you find yourself with an empty basket for the price of a chicken.

These are examples of the problems in learning African languages, which are totally unlike any European language.

Each of the 52 nations comprising the continent of Africa has its own languages, for most nations are composed of several tribes, each with a particular language. There may also be a "trade" language for communication between language groups, as well as an "official" language, usually European, determined by the country which governed in pre-independence days.

In Zaire, Rwanda, and Burundi the official language is French, for these countries were formerly governed by Belgium. French is used for government communication and in schools above the elementary level.

Bantu

Much of sub-Sahara Africa is made up of a family of peoples known as the Bantu (bah-ntoo) peoples with their Bantu languages. In the dim ages of history these languages undoubtedly have a common origin, possibly in West Africa.

In most cases the various Bantu languages are not mutually understandable. However, they share a grammatical structure and some similarity of vocabulary. Thus I have found words in Zulu, used in South Africa, that are identical in sound and meaning to words used in Burundi, though the two peoples are 3,000 miles apart.

A Zulu would not understand much of what a Murundi said. However, Kirundi (kee-roo-ndee), spoken in Burundi, and Kinyarwanda (kee-nya-rwah-ndah), spoken in Rwanda, are mutually understandable despite confusing differences. When I moved from Burundi to Rwanda, I learned that the word I had always used for "wait" now meant "stop."

My Uncle In Heaven...

Certain characteristics of Bantu languages make it difficult to translate literature. When missionaries first began to work in Burundi they wanted to translate the Lord's Prayer. Now, in Kirundi, the word **data** means either "my father" or "our father." Likewise, **se** means "his, her, or their father." The possessive adjective is not used.

The missionaries wanted to be sure the people understood it to be "our" Father, not "my," for when people together call God "our Father," that makes them brothers and sisters -- too precious a thought to lose!

So the translator thought, "If we put **wacu,** which means "our" with **data**, the people will surely understand that we want to say "**our** Father." He didn't know these two words put together do not mean "our Father" at all, but rather "my uncle."

For a short time the people prayed, "My uncle who is in heaven." Of course, the translator soon discovered his error, and settled the matter by saying, "Father of us all."

Why God Clears His Throat

Often an object or concept in one culture does not exist in another culture. Translating "Behold I stand at the door and knock" (Rev. 3:20) presents a problem. In those early days, most homes in Burundi were made of grass and had no door, only a doorway. Of course, no one "knocked," and there was no word in the language for these ideas.

Missionaries learned that when visiting a neighbor it was customary to stand outside the entrance, or gate, and clear your throat or call out a word of greeting. There is a word for this behavior, so in the Kirundi Bible Rev. 3:20 reads, "Behold, I stand outside the gate and clear my throat," or "call out."

Gobbledygook

One of the trials for a new missionary is the longing to communicate with people, yet be unable to comprehend a language which at first seems like a lot of gobbledygook. Generally the first technique you learn is to stand and smile and wish you could say something.

That experience pushed me to work hard to learn at a time when there was no grammar book of the language to study. Each new phrase and bit of knowledge was a triumph. Even now, when people ask how long it took me to learn the language, I reply, "I don't know, because I'm still learning it."

Learning a language may be a slow, frustrating process. It is also fun and challenging, like solving a puzzle. In Rwanda, just when I learn that **gushaka** means "to want," I discover it also means "to look for." And then I find that, without the addition of another word, it may mean "to look for a wife!"

Not Just In Africa...

"N'goh yiu saam jeuhng," Martha Evoy in Hong Kong said clearly to the young man in one of our church offices. She wanted three copies of a program outline.

"Do you really want three elephants?" the young man laughingly replied.

The wrong tone tripped her up again. She said "jeuhng" in a low tone rather than in a high tone.

Our missionaries need courage, God's grace, and a sense of humor as they plunge into the language of their people. Pray that they will be given facility in learning, and steadfastness to learn well.

Lamentations Of A Medical Missionary

Tim Kratzer, M.D.
July/August 1991 pp. 29-30

In 1974 my wife and I traveled with two small boys to Rwanda to live out my boyhood dream and call to serve the Lord as a doctor. I suppose, now that we have served three terms, that we may qualify as veteran missionaries. You would think we should be ready to return to Zaire, our home since 1981.

I must tell you that we have not been all that excited about returning. We now have the responsibility of sending our two oldest boys to college. How will we meet our financial obligations for college expenses? Who will meet their personal needs as we head off to Zaire?

Then, there is the reality that our two younger sons will go to boarding school, just as the others have. Will we be able to manage the empty nest syndrome? We are still young-at-heart parents and not quite ready to give up our last born.

Our experiences in medical missions also make me stop and think -- the financial burden on the church is considerable. The hospital that is calling us back is nearly bankrupt and lacks trained leadership. Where will we find the financial resources needed to continue? How can we find or train nationals or missionaries to fill the ranks?

If You Are Willing

As my mind was burdened with these problems, I came across some notes I made as a young doctor. These notes reminded me of why we became involved in medical missions. "We have the means to help and a message to communicate," reads the note. The reality of these words are seen in the life of Christ and are not just the ideas of an idealistic young doctor.

We have the means to help. In Matthew 8 Jesus had just come down from the mountainside where he was teaching his disciples. A large crowd followed him and in that crowd was a man with leprosy. He knelt before Jesus and said, "Lord, if you are willing, you can make me clean."

Then Jesus, knowing that he had the power to heal, reached out his hand and touched the man. "I am willing," he said, "Be thou clean!"

This reminded me of a 14-year-old boy who came to Nundu Hospital with an open, infected leg fracture. While playing on the soccer field, he dove with both feet for the ball. The left foot got tangled with that of a defender and snapped. The shattered bone of the upper leg tore through the skin.

His family took the boy to a traditional healer who applied the necessary stone to prevent infection and heal the bone. A week later, when the flesh started to putrefy, the boy was brought to me. I was afraid he would lose his leg. We put it in traction, debrided the dead and infected tissue each day, and gave antibiotics. What a relief to see him finally leave the hospital in a cast, and back on the soccer field before a year was out.

Many came to me with pneumonia and malaria, near to death, who went home cured. Others with chronic, slowly killing diseases like tuberculosis and leprosy returned home with treatment that arrested their disease and gave them strength.

These Zaire friends have been touched by people who care and who shared their financial resources, medical knowledge, and technical expertise in a healing ministry. Countless others in desperate physical need have no hope of relief from suffering unless someone says to them, "I am willing. Come and be healed." Jesus gave us the example which we are to follow as we share from the means that he has provided.

How To Heal Sin

In the very next chapter of Matthew, some men bring to Jesus a man paralyzed, perhaps from polio. Impressed by their faith, Jesus saw both the physical suffering of the patient and his spiritual brokenness. He said to the man, "Your sins are forgiven."

Teachers of the law took exception to this. Then Jesus went on to say, "Why do you entertain evil thoughts in your hearts? Which is easier to say, 'Your sins are forgiven,' or to say, 'Get up and walk'? But so that you may know that the Son of Man has authority on earth to forgive sins...." Then he said to the paralytic, "Get up, take your mat and go home."

When we look at those around us with physical needs it's easy to think, *if only they could walk again, or be free of pain, or have better homes — then all would be well.* But we know there are also spiritual needs which leave them broken in their relationships and unable to cope.

They are separated from God because of sin.

The example of Jesus is that as we heal in his name, we give witness in word and deed that Jesus has power to forgive sins. God works in our lives so that we will know that he is God and that he wants to be involved with us. Do we want to share our faith with the world? Then we must heal in the name of Jesus so that they will believe and understand.

Not Allowed To Die

One young man came to me with a large abscess in his leg. Just as one abscess cleared up, another would appear. We soon discovered he had diabetes. The man gave up hope and stopped eating. When I realized how much weight he was losing, I quite firmly told him that he was not going to be allowed to die. I insisted that he eat. He got the message, started to eat, his diabetes came under control, and -- he now faced an enormous hospital bill.

One day as he left the hospital, I learned that he was selling his home to pay the medical bills. My heart was broken. My response was to forgive his debt. Why? Because his healing would not have been complete without forgiveness of this material debt, and yes, his spiritual debt.

The young man with diabetes heard our message that there is forgiveness of sin and the possibility of becoming whole in his spirit because Jesus has authority on earth given to him by the Father to forgive sin.

But the sobering reality is that the needs of the world are overwhelming. Medical missionary work is proving to cost more than local populations can afford. I sometimes see no hope and, like the diabetic, just want to give up. But here is how Jesus responded in the same situation:

When he saw the crowds, he had compassion on them, because they were harassed and helpless, like sheep without a shepherd. Then he said to his disciples, "The harvest is plentiful but the workers are few. Ask the Lord of the harvest, therefore, to send out workers into his harvest" (Matthew 9:36-38).

Jesus had compassion. We are to follow his example, even though the needs are overwhelming and the workers are too few. I don't understand, but the need is clear and I am privileged to be part of our team.

When Nundu Hospital was opened, I heard this story: "The Free Methodist Church of Zaire has prayed for a decade that a doctor would come to help them develop a medical program." *I was the answer to their prayers,* and I understand very clearly the mandate to serve the Lord through medical missions.

No Pat Answers

I still don't know in what way the needs of my own family will be met as we separate in three directions. I don't know where the financial resources will come from to keep the medical work going. And I don't know how we will have a large enough staff to keep up with the growing demand. But by the example of Jesus we know that as we obey his will, he will provide the means to help.

Because of Jesus' death and resurrection we have a message to communicate – there is forgiveness of sins. And yes, there is a mandate to serve as we remember that Jesus had compassion.

Rwanda Diary

C. Albert Snyder, M.D.
July/August 1994 pp. 17-31

No Threat Of Malpractice

Louise and I thought our medical missionary career ended when we retired in 1990, but now Kibogora Hospital in Rwanda, Africa, had no surgeon. On April 25, 1993, we headed for Africa to fill that post. In our absence, Rwanda had been invaded by the Tutsi-organized Rwanda Patriotic Front (RPF). Things were different now. People were scared. Friends told us this was not the type of retirement we should consider.

We had reservations about going back. Yet it seemed God was calling us, so we prayed like Peter, *Lord, if it's you, tell me to come to you on the water* (Matthew 14:28). But (also like Peter) we have never had much success with walking on the water.

April 26, 1993: We reached Paris at 6:00 a.m. and took a day-room at Hotel Ibis -- rather spartan but in keeping with a missionary's budget. I bought ice cream and cake to celebrate Louise's birthday (I had *promised* to take her to Paris for her birthday).

We flew from Paris at midnight, sharing a three-row seat with Frere Gabriel, a Catholic brother coming back from two months leave in Montreal. He said that on Christmas eve in Kigali, the capital of Rwanda, a bomb went off in a nightclub 50 meters from where he lived. In November, one close friend was robbed and killed. This may have been politically motivated since that brother was rather outspoken on politics. Frere Gabriel seemed to be under great stress.

I quietly slipped off my lapel button which indicated I had received a medal *Chevalier de la Revolution Nationale* (Knight of the National Revolution) from the present Rwanda government. I feared to be identified with one party or another. Oh the glories of multi-partyism!

Tuesday, April 27, 1993: We arrived in Kigali at 10:00 a.m. French military were everywhere with their automatic weapons. I had never seen this before. Bishop Aaron and his wife, Edith, met us and managed to talk our way through customs without any lying or deception on our part.

That afternoon we went shopping and saw where the post office and our box 861 were blown out last week by a bomb. Broken glass was everywhere, clear out into the street. Our mail had now to be obtained from the wicket inside.

The town bustled with activity. Stores were full. People walked around with children, going about with an air of *whatever will be, will be* — a kind of continual living Russian roulette.

Louise and I went to bed dog-tired at Vernon and Susan DeMille's place in Kigali. I noticed the Scripture written on our quilt sent by the Women's Missionary Society: "But I have prayed for you that your faith fail not."

Wednesday, April 28, 1993: We reached Kibogora just before dark and were excited to find the dirt road was being resurfaced and much easier riding, not to mention it would now be more difficult to plant land mines.

At dinner with Tim and Muriel Teusink the conversation kept drifting back to war, political instability and attendant problems. However, I was as uneasy about doing surgery again after a hiatus of almost three years as I was about anything. I would have four days getting back into it with Dr. Tim, and then it would be me and the Lord for it as Teusinks went off on furlough.

Well, that's why I came. At least I left the threat of malpractice behind.

Ethnic Conflict
Friday, February 25, 1994: We have been back in Rwanda almost a year now, and I am beginning to piece together what seems to have happened with the impasse between the various government factions. Last Monday when the Transitional Government was to have been installed, the Minister of Public Function, who was sympathetic to the Tutsis, was killed.

Tuesday, in retaliation, the president of a radical Hutu splinter group was killed along with his brother. The Hutu response was to burn 12 Tutsi houses and injure many people. The sister of our professor Azarias received a laceration on the scalp and a broken clavicle.

Philemoni, our Tutsi watchman, asked if his family could stay with us tonight for protection. We arranged for his wife and niece to stay on cots in our store-room and told Philemoni he could circulate on the mission with the night watchmen. We felt if they were truly scared this would be a relief, but if they were trying to manipulate us they would refuse such humble accommodations.

Now starts our dilemma. How far do we go in getting involved in this ethnic conflict? I have given jobs to people of both groups. Many times I haven't known what ethnic origin workers have. Anyway, many of them are so inter-mixed that their official classification is somewhat meaningless.

When I asked Pastor Wakana for advice, he said, "If they ask for refuge I take them in."

To clarify what we as Christians might have to do, I asked, "What if the killers come after them and attack your house?"

Pastor Wakana replied, "I guess I would die with them."

Saturday, February 26: I learned today from Sheila Etherington, our missionary nurse from England, that last night the residence of our national nurse mid-wives was crowded out with Tutsi mothers and children from Tyazo, the hill just behind the mission compound. I talked to one of our national doctors about contacting local authorities to help these people, but he said the Tutsis would not trust them.

Dr. Roy Winslow called from the United States tonight asking about travel plans for coming out on short-term assignment with his family. I told him to phone next weekend and we would hope to give him better news.

The DeMilles report that Benjamin, Philemoni's son, has gone into hiding. There are 70 or 80 Tutsis staying in our Kigali church every night. One political figure who was killed had his home near our Kigali mission and church, so at his death revenge was unleashed on the Talls (Tutsis).

Sunday, February 27: I have been waking up depressed each morning over conditions in this country, but still have found much to be thankful for. Today 1 Samuel 30:6 came to mind: "But David strengthened himself in the Lord his God." I am trying to do that also.

Monday, February 28: I left for Kigali at 7:30 a.m. to deliver colleagues to the airport. It was a relief to get them out of the war zone. Outside the supermarket I met my old friend Colonel Rwabarinda. He gave me a warm Kinyarwanda embrace and I asked about his father with the broken hip, whom we flew by helicopter out from Kibogora two months ago. He said things were going well and "all we need now is a government."

I asked when that might be. He said, "Maybe in two weeks."

"Yes," I said, "maybe."

"We must pray hard," he replied. "Yes, we need much prayer."

We left Kigali about 6:30 p.m. to get back to Gikondo before curfew at 7:00 p.m. Gikondo is the section of Kigali where our church and mission are located. I don't like these evening trips to the airport -- couldn't help remembering last summer that Tim Auchen and his father-in-law ran into a road-block coming home in similar circumstances and Tim got shot in the hand and his father-in-law in the leg.

I spent the rest of the evening reading and quieting my soul. Louise visited with Vern and Sue DeMille and heard all the grizzly details of the terror that reigned in Gikondo the past week. All was quiet when we went to bed. I left the windows closed in order to not hear any disturbing sounds in the night.

Psalm 37
Wednesday, March 2: Jim Kirkpatrick, Area Director of our mission program in central Africa, came today, on his way back from Burundi and Zaire. He says Zaire soldiers are not getting paid, so they are selling their guns to the Hutus in Burundi who in turn attack the Tutsi dominated military.

Thursday, March 3: We did 19 gastroscopies today and identified four or five surgical cases, two of them stomach cancers. The rest were chronic duodenal ulcers. I continue to be amazed at the amount of gastric problems out here. I wish I knew why there is so much stomach cancer. It doesn't seem to be related to AIDS. We've checked that out. The ulcers are old stuff out here.

I guess we would have ulcers too if we went hungry like they do, and endured the stress they live under. If things don't change in this country we're all going to have ulcers.

We had good rains yesterday and today -- a relief after several days of hot sun. One more bad bean crop will finish the people off.

Friday, March 4: I phoned Vernon DeMille in Kigali to get his opinion on what to tell Roy Winslow about coming to Rwanda. He said, "Yes, come, but be aware that things are touch and go." It bothered me that he seemed more uncertain than usual.

Martha Kirkpatrick reported on a recent meeting with David Rawson, United States Ambassador to Rwanda. In a meeting with embassy staff plus missionaries and other expatriots, Rawson commented on the plight of Rwanda and then read the 37th Psalm as if it were a government document:

Do not fret because of evil men or be envious of those who do wrong; for like the grass they will soon wither, like green plants they will soon die away.

Trust in the Lord and do good; dwell in the land and enjoy safe pasture. Delight yourself in the Lord and he will give you the desires of your heart.

Commit your way to the Lord; trust in him and he will do this: He will make your righteousness shine like the dawn, the justice of your cause like the noonday sun.

Be still before the Lord and wait patiently for him; do not fret when men succeed in their ways, when they carry out their wicked schemes.

Refrain from anger and turn from wrath; do not fret -- it leads only to evil. For evil men will be cut off, but those who hope in the Lord will inherit the land.

The Relinquished Life
Saturday, March 5: I keep wrestling with what to tell Winslows, but I didn't discourage my own kids from coming last June at the time of grenade explosions at the market. So I think I'll just tell them that it's pretty much business as usual for us. Still, one doesn't really know what will happen. How I pray for wisdom!

Roy Winslow phoned about 8:00 p.m. He doesn't seem frightened off by the situation. They plan to arrive 7:10 p.m., March 14, and to stay for five weeks. It is amazing how we can talk by phone with ease from central Africa to the United States.

Today I realized just how much I let my hopes for a political solution go up and down with the daily news. I had to really battle my thinking to pull out of an anxiety-depressive reaction today.

Sunday, March 6: *Jesus knowing that God had given all things into his hands...* (John 13:3). This verse caught my attention this morning. Is there anything about my day that God doesn't know? It indicates his foreknowledge and control over my day, my plans, my walk with him. How carefully I should walk, yet how carefree I should be! I, like Jesus, can be assured that I "came from God and am going to God."

In light of this, my struggles yesterday concerning Winslows were needless. If we are fully aware of our adoption as sons and know our

World Mission People

relationship to God as sons, no service will be menial and beneath us, or too large and frightening.

I made hospital rounds this morning, then went to the students' 9:00 a.m. service in French. Also took some videos today. We need to get to work with picture taking as we only have eight more weeks left here before our volunteer assignment ends.

Monday, March 7: Today Bishop Aaron said the new government is to be installed by the 15th. I will have to see it to believe it. The news tonight tells of more than 100 killed in a section of Bujumbura, Burundi, where Carl Johnson and Dr. Dwight Hedgepath live -- said to be the military trying to disarm civilians.

Tuesday, March 8: Early morning is the worst time for me. I kept going around and around about my son Dan and his family making a trip to Kigali to meet Winslows at the airport at night. I remind myself of Jacob and how he arranged his family when worrying about meeting Esau.

Today's reading in Oswald Chambers is on the "Relinquished Life." He asks, *Am I willing to relinquish my hold on all I possess, my hold on my affections, on everything, to be identified with the death of Christ? Go through the crises, relinquish all, and God will make you fit for all that he requires of you.* Dear Jesus, help me to cast everything on you. Thank you for this test of faith. Help me to pass the test.

Wednesday, March 9: I operated with Dr. Misago this morning. He is our new doctor, and I believe he's going to be okay. I hope we can keep him.

Thursday, March 10: I read in Oswald Chambers today, *When we come up against the barriers of natural relationship, where is Jesus Christ? Most of us desert him.... The test of abandonment is always over the neck of natural devotion. Go over it, and God's own abandonment will embrace all those you had to hurt in abandoning. Beware of stopping short of abandonment to God. Most of us know abandonment in vision only.*

Also, I was reading in *Knowing God* by J. I. Packer about "cheerful self-abandonment" to the adequacy of God. I'm sure it is the only way to happiness in Christ, and peace of mind.

Doing Surgery

We did about 14 gastroscopies today, and identified more cases needing surgery. I plan to help Dan do a vagotomy and gastro-enterostomy tomorrow. He can do them after I leave if he picks cases wisely until he gets more experience.

News from Burundi is of more ethnic violence -- against Hutus in the Bujumbura area and against Tutsis in the north near Ngozi. It seems that the military, by government order, is cracking down.

Friday, March 11: I helped Dan do a vagotomy this a.m. on a thin 66-year-old man near starving from beginning pyloric obstruction from duodenal ulcer. The procedure went very well and we found two large anterior and posterior vagal nerve trunks. I was happy for Dan that it went so well. It was sort of my swan song as Roy will soon be here and I'm going to turn to something more suitable to retirement living.

Saturday, March 12: We watched a video of the Winter Olympics tonight. What amazing perfection and discipline of the athletes! This evening I spent time trying to compose my speech in French for the dedication of our new hospital building on March 23. What a joy that new two story building is to work in!

Sunday, March 13: Fideli, our cook Ruhigira's son, is having fever again. He almost died from malaria and black water fever complications last month. I suggested he enter the hospital but he didn't want to. This resistant malaria is scary. Without quinine we wouldn't have a chance.

Our worker Haki's son was sick one day and the next unconscious from cerebral malaria. He was just a breath or two from "answering God" as the Africans say.

Resistant malaria, antibiotic resistant bacillary dysentery, AIDS, chronic hunger and malnutrition, terrorism, when will it all end? I think of what one Tutsi school boy said to me some years ago, "I wonder if God knows we are people."

Monday, March 14: I have a linear fracture of the proximal phalanx in my toe from accidently kicking the bed last night, but have managed to walk on it by strapping it to its mate.

We operated on an indirect hernia this morning. I let Dr. Misago do a lot of it. Of all our African doctors, none have started out any better than he. I hope the government assigns him to Kibogora. He likes surgery and seems to like it here.

Dr. Elizabeth Fries came from Bujumbura today and tells of a lot of killings in Kamenge section, and Melli (Andrews) Johnson writes of gunfire back and forth across the mission requiring their missionaries to lie on the floor at times.

BBC (British Broadcasting Corporation) told tonight of an assassination attempt on one political figure at his home in Gitarama, Rwanda. Grenades were tossed into his house but he escaped.

I phoned Kigali at 9:00 p.m. and talked to Dan, who went in to pick up the Winslows at the airport. They had no problems and are safely back to Gikondo. The electricity was off so they used candlelight at the mission. Praise the Lord for his watch-care.

Wednesday, March 16: Dan brought in the Winslows about 5:15 p.m. today. They met with no special problems except for a skid on the wet blacktop road on the mountain in the rainforest. The Daihatsu van is bad about that. It can make your heart skip a beat. It's great to have Roy, Bev, and Josh safely here. Lots of surgery is awaiting Roy.

Thursday, March 17: Busy day at the hospital, with four major operations. I helped Dr. Laurent do a tubal ligation and Dan scrubbed with Roy.

Today Bishop Aaron said we should go ahead with dedicating our new building. We can't postpone it forever. If something blows up this time, I guess we'll dedicate it with local people present only.

Building Snyder-White
Friday, March 18: U.S. Ambassador Dave Rawson phoned. He will not be able to attend the building dedication. We are disappointed, but now it will be more relaxed and low key.

Today the nurses came to say that the boy whose leg we amputated last week steals from other patients, collaborating with a group of bandits who are behind it all. Yesterday I arranged to pay for a prosthesis for him. Now I don't know what to do. He's an orphan who has learned to survive by his wits.

Saturday, March 19: Today in my devotions I was thinking about John 12:21 "Sir, we would see Jesus." I guess that sums up every reason why I came back to this country and these people. If at the end of my days or along the way I can see Jesus, then it is worth all we're enduring.

Sunday, March 20: Louise and I took our two-mile walk -- slowly -- due to my fractured toe. We took 10 kilos of beans to the hungry family (five kids) along the road. One of the girls was sick. People just stay home these days, since they can't afford medical care. Fortunately, the rains are good and crops are coming great so far. How I pray that it continues. People are so hungry.

Word is that the Transitional Government is to go in place tomorrow but no one really expects it to come off. VOA reports the Burundi president now has an elite corp of 1000 soldiers answerable only to him to guarantee his safety. They also reported many Hutu-Tutsi killings over the weekend.

Monday, March 21: Sue DeMille said on the phone today that things are very tense in Kigali. We plan to go ahead with our building dedication even if no dignitaries make it.

Tuesday, March 22: Bishop Aaron and other church dignitaries arrived tonight for the dedication, and local government officials will probably come tomorrow. We're getting everything polished up for the occasion. Missionaries from Kigali are also here. Vern and Sue are beginning to sound "spooky" about living in Kigali. Now and then something sets off gangs that tear down the street attacking anyone in their way. Shopkeepers close up shop. Cars take a detour. DeMilles are a real comfort to all of us by staying in Kigali and keeping in touch with the embassy.

Wednesday, March 23: Well, we finally got the "Building Snyder-White" dedicated. The church chose that name as a memorial to my parents and Hugh and Edna White. Their Foundations were the principle donors who made this dream possible. Numerous others also helped bring it to completion and these were all mentioned and honored today.

This has been a miracle building. It cost about $200,000 and has $60,000 of new equipment. This two story facility is in the center of the hospital campus. There's nothing quite like it in the Kibogora area.

Much praise and commendation were heaped on me and it was embarrassing. At the same time, to be honest, I did enjoy having my ego stroked. God forgive my prideful heart.

Many political, medical, and church dignitaries were present for the dedication. The Banyarwanda (people of Rwanda) do love a big "bash," especially when it involves killing a cow, which is essentially what we did to feed everyone.

Dying Daily

Thursday, March 24: The news says 1,000 more were killed in Burundi. A U.N. observer says the reports are widely exaggerated. A defense spokesman says the government is in control and working well with the military. Others report a coup has taken place. In any case, one pastor from a bad area of Burundi has arrived here as a refugee.

Friday, March 25: There's a good lesson today in Oswald Chambers on "The Friend of the Bridegroom." How easy it is in our Christian walk to play the role of the bridegroom rather than the friend of the Bridegroom. But God said he will share his glory with no man. I think that is the reason Billy Graham is so effective. He presents Christ in a straightforward, simple way, and doesn't present himself.

Today Rwanda's president and most important parties were all assembled for the swearing in ceremonies to install the Transitional Government. All the radios here were blaring with minute-by-minute commentaries, alternatively in French, Kinyarwanda, Swahili, and English.

Then a snag was reported. One group hadn't arrived and was still trying to thrash out some details concerning the role of the radical Hutu party. Eventually, the President just left and radios returned to programming. Once again the installation was aborted and our hopes dashed.

Saturday, March 26: Kratzers leave for Kigali Monday to pick up their kids coming from Rift Valley Academy in Kenya. We're all concerned about roadblocks and political demonstrations. I have to admire the courage and faith they have shown for the past two years.

Sunday, March 27: Dan, Deedee, and kids went to Cyangugu today (about 50 miles west of here). After they left I learned of political demonstrations yesterday in Cyangugu. It gave me a panic to have my family members on the road, but I regained my composure and have been at peace the rest of the day. Seems like I die daily these days.

It is hard to keep one's "abandonment" to God in place. I guess I put my all on the altar and then pick it up and take it back. I spend much of my spare time in reading and meditation. That's the only way I seem to survive. I have been reading both Frank Laubach and Brother Lawrence on the techniques of practicing the presence of God. I do it for awhile but don't think I do it minute by minute.

On rounds I learned the toddler with cerebral malaria died. A 32-

year-old man is unconscious with cerebral malaria and doesn't look like he will survive. I also came across a seven-year-old with an abdominal mass. Tim Kratzer was on call so he and Roy operated on it and reduced an ileo-cecalcolic invagination, a rare condition at home but common here.

I read in the January 1994 *Reader's Digest* that Jeanne Kirkpatrick, former U.S. Ambassador to the United Nations, decries the U.S. getting involved with the U.N., as in Somalia, in the "same kind of ill-defined peace-keeping mission in war-torn Rwanda, a tiny landlocked nation in the heart of Africa." She doesn't want anything to do with "vague global interests." I suppose U.S. government's policies are based on what's good for the U.S., not on what is right or humanitarian or least of all Christian.

Keeping Up
Tuesday, March 29: Today is Ashley's 9th birthday. She is very excited. Grandma Louise is going all out with preparations for supper and her party.

At the hospital, I helped Roy on a difficult perineal repair of injuries which resulted from massive hematoma during a home delivery. I had done a colostomy on her earlier. The husband said he would not take her home with a colostomy. If she didn't get it fixed she could go back to her father's rugo (home). I asked the staff if he had pledged to love her in sickness and in health until death do them part. But no, he had just had a pagan wedding.

Wednesday, March 30: Several bright spots today warmed my heart. The young man with cerebral malaria, unconscious for three days, finally responded to quinine and doxycycline and was talking, sitting up and asking to eat.

I helped the shop crew put down new linoleum in our kitchen which will be nice for Dan and Deedee when they move in our house in May.

The day was sunny and beautiful. Dan's and Roy's families had a nice afternoon at Kumbya swimming in Lake Kivu. Kratzers got in safely with their boys this evening and brought a lot of mail.

VOA tonight brought an interview with a spokesman for the CDR (radical Hutu party) in Rwanda. They insist on being included in the Transitional Government. RPF balked at that but now says they have no objections as long as CDR agrees to a code of ethics and conduct as set up by the Arusha Peace Accord. At least they are still talking.

Thursday, March 31: Last night a youth leader of a political party was assassinated. Things are tense in Kigali and people have a self-imposed curfew.

Our phones in the entire Kirambo commune have been out since being zapped by lightning last Friday. Tim could find no glucose anywhere in Kigali. This is serious. We need glucose to make intravenous solutions. We can't do gastric surgery without glucose to nourish patients for a few days until they can eat.

Friday, April 1: No one pulled any April Fool jokes. Strange. Lately, after a rain we can see the volcanoes at the north end of Lake Kivu, always awe inspiring.

Today we had Martin Suhr, a German builder, and his African helper, for three meals. They are working for a Swiss aid project to build a permanent market structure with concrete floors, booths, and roof covering. Such a structure might have prevented the disaster last May when the grenades were planted in the market area.

While helping Roy resect a chondroma from the chest wall by removing a rib today, we discovered we weren't given any blood administration sets with our last order of blood. That plus no glucose makes one feel a bit frustrated. The total disintegration of this country is more and more apparent.

A young man was transferred in today whose lower leg was destroyed by someone tossing a grenade into a bar last Tuesday. So it seems terrorism is still going on. Crazy world we live in.

Saturday, April 2: BBC recently commented on near-famine conditions in Rwanda. Makes me wonder what more we as a mission should be doing. Louise regularly feeds our orphans Topfy, Martin, and Shime with a roll each evening. Sheila and the hospital have some feeding programs going and we take a bag of beans to the family beside the road every now and then when I can't stand it anymore to live in our white man's affluence.

I told Roy and Dan today that I was really getting tired and I remembered how the Masai do when the old man can't keep up with the nomadic life. The oldest son takes grandpa out and gives him all the beer he can drink and then walks away to let the wild animals finish him off. I think I should get out of here before they get any ideas. My tendinitis in the right shoulder, my partial knee cartilage tear, and my broken toe make it hard to keep up with the hunt.

Easter Sunday, April 3: We had a wonderful sunrise service in Sheila's front yard, followed by breakfast. Some of us attended service at the hospital with the patients as it was crowded out at the church. We doctors on call were busy.

Monday, April 4: Easter Monday is a holiday here but we kept busy anyway. I counted the hospital beds and we have 162 but have 24 coming in the containers so we'll be up to 186 eventually. We often have two in a bed and people on the floor, so what does a bed count mean anyway?

Tuesday, April 5: We had steady rain all morning which was a marvelous answer to prayer. The beans couldn't take the hot sun too much longer. Tonight the highest volcano, Karisimbi, on the Zaire-Rwanda border and the area where mountain gorillas live, had snow visible on top. We could see all four volcanoes today, a good reminder that God is also changeless and constant -- always there even when the clouds obscure our view.

Little James isn't feeling well. He was fine before coffee time. Then, while playing he started crying that his neck hurt, and he kept holding his head to the left. Everything else seems normal. No fever. So we're thinking he strained the muscles some way. None of us have ever seen that in a toddler, however, and I can find nothing about it in *Nelson's Pediatrics*. I have my usual battle to commit him to the Lord and know "He does all things well."

Wednesday, April 6: James was much improved this morning and by evening was jumping and playing as usual. What a relief!

News today on VOA and BBC tells of a summit meeting in Dar es Salaam of heads of state from East African countries, dealing specifically with problems in Rwanda and Burundi. Also, the U.N. has extended their peacekeeping mission four more months here in Rwanda. They plan to reevaluate in six weeks. That is great news for us here.

A Plane Crash
Thursday, April 7: Psalm 46 came to me this morning: "God is our refuge and strength. A very present help in trouble."

At 5:30 a.m. there was a knock on the door. The watchman delivered a note from head nurse, Eraste, saying the plane carrying

President Habyarimana and the president of Burundi had crashed coming into Kigali from Dar es Salaam last night about 8:15 p.m. There were no survivors. Sabotage is suspected.

Kigali was said to be full of "fireworks" all night. We have Lois Meredith -- Canadian, Daniel Roland -- Belgian, Martin Suhr -- German, and now Girard Vandenberg -- Dutch with his Rwandan wife and baby all here on the mission, in addition to our normal missionary staff. Lois, Daniel, and Martin are all here on business but Girard came asking us to take them in as I think her family are Tutsi.

We closed the hospital this afternoon out of respect for the president and of course the flag was at half mast. No one knows what will happen now.

The late evening news says Kigali is in chaos. The Presidential Guard has refused access to the crash site of the plane for investigation. This makes people think the army had something to do with it.

Some Belgian U.N. peace-keepers were killed, also the Prime Minister and some African priests and nuns. RPF is fighting back in Kigali. Missionaries in the mid-week prayer time discussed evacuation plans. French troops in Bangui, Central African Republic, are on alert for evacuating French nationals.

Friday, April 8: BBC reports that 11 U.N. peacekeepers have been killed. Meanwhile, we worked fairly normally today. Roy and I operated on Yohani once again for his recurrent jejuno-gastric reverse invagination. This time we did it up right, I hope. We converted to a Roux-en-Y and reanastomosed to the stomach with a smaller opening.

Tim Kratzer and Martin Suhr went to the Sous-Prefecture (local government post) and phoned Vernon DeMille. What a time to have our telephone down and our shortwave radio not working either!

News from the U.S. Embassy is that we should prepare to evacuate with one bag per person. During the day at the hospital it was learned that the government doctor over our area was killed yesterday while driving into Bushenge Hospital. I guess he was a member of the PR (liberal party).

Today a Danish Baptist couple on vacation at Kumbya decided to come to Kibogora. So they with their two children are now here. So we have Dan's three children, Winslow's one, Kratzer's two, and the Dane's two. Great environment for kids. We all try to act calm around them. Poor Martin is here without his wife and two children who are at home in Gitarama.

At 5:00 p.m. Tim, Martin, Gerard, and Olaf went to make phone calls at the S/Prefecture. At 8:00 p.m. they were still not back. We were getting uneasy and decided to try and contact Gasigwa to see if the Bourgemestre (local official) could get some news.

The minute we walked off the mission station we saw Kayigema and others running around with clubs, spears, and machetes, and very alarmed. They said Azarias' house had been attacked. He seems always to be the most prominent Tutsi they go after.

We saw it was impossible to venture further so we returned to the station. About 8:15 here came the car back under escort by the S/Prefet and his military. We felt great relief to know these guys were back, but they said, "Four people have been murdered up there behind the church." Tim Kratzer reported that we were to evacuate tomorrow at 6:00 a.m.

I felt this was not wise. Every missionary catastrophe I ever read about was when they decided to cut and run. Better to sit tight among people who know us and whom we trust. Tim said he would hold a mission meeting at 9:00 p.m. to discuss it.

Sheila and I went down to the hospital to see who might come in. Two Tutsi women stood with their little children begging for a place to hide. A car arrived with the injured, and then mobs of people started showing up.

Four small children had head wounds and were either unconscious or too stunned to respond. We began emergency procedures and Dr. Marie-Grâce, a Hutu, came from her house near the hospital. Our surgical person on call, Suzanne, came immediately as did most of the maternity girls on duty, and others from the nurses' quarters. These midwives were all Tutsis and my heart bled for them. I knew how scared they must be for their own lives.

We then learned that Suzanne's sister, Evelyna, was killed near her home in Cyangugu that very day.

Louise came down from the house and informed me that the consensus seemed to be that we should evacuate. I said there was just no way we could do that.

Next they brought in Azarias' wife. She was dead. The side of her face and head were crushed in. Also her oldest boy, about 8 or 9 years old, arrived dead. All had been clubbed behind the ears. Most wounds were with a blunt weapon.

Time To Cut And Run

I went up to talk to Tim and learned that the U.S. Embassy was going to close down! DeMilles, who had resisted all previous advice to evacuate from Kigali, had now decided to leave. The Embassy said we should convene a convoy at Butare in the morning. "Get out the best way you can," was their advice. They had all they could do to evacuate Kigali people. In fact, our friend the Ambassador was at his house blocked from leaving, at that time, by gunfire.

A thousand things rushed through my brain. But my gut level conviction was that we should all leave. Sheila, working through the same struggles as I, said, "Well, we've been rehearsing this for three years."

I thought, *We're fortunate to have four African doctors here for this moment. There will never be a more logical time to turn things over to them. And its true we have been doing all we could to nationalize all departments.*

Kibogora was in a cul de sac of the country, without phones, without radio contact, and no access to supplies. The one way out was to the South-East via Butare and into Burundi, a country in nearly the same situation as Rwanda. Happily, for about 10 days there had been relative calm in the capital, Bujumbura.

Back at the hospital I found two more of the children had died and Roy was working with the last two. We don't know if they made it or not.

Suzanne, a Tutsi and our beloved worker for more than 25 years, asked Sheila if we were leaving. When Sheila answered, Suzanne put her head down and began to sing a dirge.

Tim Kratzer, as director, met with Dr. Marie-Grâce, the director-adjoint. He informed her of our plans and gave instructions both verbally and written. Meanwhile, Dan wrote letters to the other three national doctors.

I wrote Dr. Marie-Grâce and told her what pain I had in leaving, that our government had told us to get out, and that we hoped it would only be temporary. I left my keys with her and told her of some private drug supplies in my desk drawer. I also wrote to the hospital chaplains, Pastor Michel Wakana, and Pastor Epayeneto Rwamunyana. I asked if they could come to the Mission at 5:30 in the morning. I asked the night watchman to deliver my letters to them at 4:30 in the morning.

I met Marie-Grâce in the hall and we were both so emotionally down that I could only say, "I've written this letter explaining some things," and I handed it to her.

It was already midnight. I went to the Intensive Care Unit to check all our post-op patients and write orders on their charts for IV fluids, when to pull naso-gastric tubes, when to pull drains, and when and what to eat. The night nurse looked on quizzically, as I had never appeared at midnight before to write post-op orders for the next week or more.

Finally, I went home. Like zombies, Louise and I went about final details -- houseboy's wages, keys to be left with Aaroni the maintenance man, and so on. At 1:00 a.m. I took a sleeping pill, set the alarm for 4:30 a.m. and went to bed.

Angel In A Red Toyota
Saturday, April 9: This day seemed surreal. It didn't seem possible that we were actually leaving. This thing had blown up so fast. Here we were, 48 hours after hearing that the President had been killed, on our way out of Rwanda, a country literally going to hell before our eyes, with civil war and ethnic purge in overdrive.

We arrived at the garage with our baggage at 5:30 a.m. Louise and I had only one carry-on bag apiece, leaving space for the families who would need to take much more. Aaroni had already had his 15-minute briefing from Tim. I gave him a hug and said I would go back to the U.S. since we were due to leave in a couple weeks anyway. I hoped Dan and the others would be back soon.

My voice cracked. Tears flowed down his cheeks. Our friendship went deep and long -- I first started him in the garage over 25 years ago. Now he was a middle-aged man, an ace mechanic who knew more about maintaining the mission station than anyone. Still, he had not anticipated so much responsibility so suddenly. A large sum of money was turned over to him along with all the keys to the houses and many instructions. It was a worry also that his right hand man was a Tutsi.

Pastor Wakana was not back from Cyangugu to see us off. He would have been well aware of how we felt as he himself fled the bloodletting in Burundi in 1972. Pastor Rwamunyana, an old man now, was his usual serene self, his faith entirely in the God he served. He prayed for us all and we drove out.

Our five vehicles contained three Winslows, five of the Dan Snyder family, Eddie Rogers the teacher, four Kratzers, Sheila Etherington, Elaine Williamson, Harriet Bolodar, Lois Meredith -- Canadian caught at Kibogora while auditing, Daniel Roland -- Belgian, Martin Suhr -- German plus his national helper, Girard Vandenberg – Dutch with his Rwandan wife and their child, four Danes – Olaf and wife and children, Louise and myself.

Sheila had the misfortune to be without her British passport which was in Kigali awaiting a new visa. Daniel Roland lamented not having his second passport which was Swiss, because the Belgians were being blamed for shooting down the President's plane.

As we left at 6:00 a.m. we saw Hesironi our Tutsi head nurse in the surgical building. He lives next to Azarias and could well have spent the night in hiding since they almost killed him last year. I waved.

Dan asked, "Aren't you going to stop?"

I replied, "What could we say?" and continued. Dan remarked that he was haunted by the look on Hesironi's face.

We stopped at Nyamasheke, the Catholic Mission, where a Belgian couple and their visitors joined us. A short distance from that mission we stopped again and the Sous-Prefet's chauffeur came to explain about another murder during the night.

The S/Prefet decided to escort us to the main road in the rainforest 15 miles away. After about five miles we came to our first roadblock set up by thugs and local militia. The S/Prefet made short work of them. He took one of them off to jail after taking away his machete. One other ran off and the S/Prefet's guard raised his rifle but decided against shooting.

The S/Prefet, a Baptist, was very good to us. At the main road he waved good-bye. We continued on and soon met up with a bunch of other cars making a convoy of 13 in all.

I don't know how the S/Prefet knew we would have no trouble in the rainforest, but for the next hour we saw nothing but beautiful scenery, its peacefulness not in keeping with the mood of the rest of the country.

Our only snag was when we first met the other cars. One car had three Dutch tourists who were camping for the week-end. One of them had gone off on a morning hike to see the monkeys and birds. They had already been waiting for 30 minutes and asked us all to wait.

Should we go on and let them come when he arrived? Should we wait and maybe jeopardize our meeting the convoy in Butare on time? What if he was lost? What if he was hurt? What if? What if? We kept agreeing to wait 15 more minutes, and then 15 more minutes, until an hour had passed.

African scouts who knew the forest were looking for him. Then we all tried honking the car horns at the same time. When he finally did show up I wondered if he knew how much danger he was in from "friendly fire." There's one in every group I guess.

After the rainforest we encountered a road block at Musebeya with fairly large trees across the road. We all sat calmly in our cars as if we expected them to just let us go by. Thugs and local militia walked up and down beside our cars. Most were armed with clubs and machetes. Louise had along some things to do in the car to entertain Ashley, Rachel, and James for just such an occasion.

It started to pour down rain. People around the cars retreated to shelter on the porches of the local shops. Then a red Toyota pick-up pulled out of a side road with some local official and a couple of soldiers. They drove to the head of the line and asked why we weren't traveling with an escort.

Someone replied, "Why don't you be our escort?" So that's just what they did. Like Peter being led out of prison by an angel, we all followed the red Toyota for the several miles until we met another roadblock.

Again, like the waves being rolled back in the Red Sea for the children of Israel, we went through on "dry ground" following our friendly guide. A little later they pulled off and waved us on, apparently thinking there would be no further problems between there and Butare. They were right.

Various Life Rafts

We drove into the little university town of Butare to discover the military out in full strength. It was fortunate that the troubles exploded while students were on Easter vacation. We were especially happy that our 1300 students at Kibogora were not caught in this madness.

A convoy that grew to 72 vehicles was lining up down the main drag. In front were two jeeps with big Red Cross flags flying. We were happy to see that Carol Watson of our mission had made it through from Gitarama and that Martin Suhr's wife and little ones were also there, having joined the convoy from Kigali. Carol had seen Benjamini, our watchman's son, who had been in hiding for the past couple of weeks. He was now with some Tutsi friends in Butare.

I saw Dr. Eva, a German Catholic lay-sister. She was seeing off some volunteers. I asked, "Are you going too?"

"No, I rest," she replied in her accented English-French mixture.

That reply sort of stabbed me but I thought, *Well she is single, she is in a Catholic sisters community, and her hospital is near Butare and not shut up in a corner like we were in Kibogora.* I wondered how long before she would have to follow us, and I greatly admired this brave lady.

It was about a 45-minute drive to the Burundi border where we were met by Burundi military escorts. They were very courteous.

At the first rest stop on the five-hour drive to the capital we were surprised to meet news media people with their giant cameras and microphones. Dan and Deedee with their little family were especially in demand for pictures and interviews. We hadn't realized what a big deal this was to the whole world.

We descended from the mountains overlooking Bujumbura, Lake Tanganyika, and the Ruzizi plains just as the sun was setting across the lake behind the Zaire mountains. A gorgeous sight.

The convoy stopped at the first big intersection in town and many officials from various embassies went from car to car making contact with their respective citizens. We entered the U.S. Embassy and saw Marine officers and enlisted men arriving with their backpacks.

Our Burundi missionaries, Wayne and Barb Vibbert, left word where we were to stay. We also heard that Vernon and Sue DeMille were in the next convoy that would arrive in the night. Louise and I went to stay with my cousin Melli Johnson and her husband Ken. They fed us and gave up their waterbed and slept on the floor.

We went to sleep in peace thinking all our missionaries were safe and accounted for. We felt very grateful to God for bringing us safely out. In the morning I expressed my appreciation for the waterbed. I had never slept on one before. It was a case of fleeing all day and being on a life raft all night.

Operation Distant Runner
Sunday, April 10: Our son Steve phoned first thing in the morning. It was midnight his time. We asked him to let the rest of the family know we were all safe and sound in Burundi.

A bit later our son Glenn phoned and said in a grave tone of voice, "Dad, DeMilles didn't make it out from Kigali. They are at the U.S. Embassy and Vern has just left to go across town to locate six families that aren't accounted for. Sue has phoned home to ask for special prayer." Down went our spirits once more. Not only for DeMilles but for our friends the Fergusons, Bennets, Shears, Pences, and Randolfs.

We arrived at the Bujumbura airport about 10:00 a.m. and saw large Marine transport planes and about 300 Marines. We all let out cheers and nearly cried when the Marines walked in.

A transport plane rolled in from Kigali and we watched carefully for our people. Someone spotted the Muellers of the Conservative Baptists but we couldn't get any word about DeMilles and the others.

We hadn't anticipated leaving Burundi immediately, but the Embassy was on alert to start evacuating their personnel that week. They said unless we had compelling reasons to stay and places to go, we should go on to Nairobi, Kenya.

In the airport the marines passed out bottled water and complete dinners in olive drab plastic wrappers. They were cold but much improved over the K rations and C rations of my army days. Since Bujumbura is very hot, a cold lunch was fine. We spread out on the floor with blankets for picnic lunch and had a great dinner. As I bowed my head to thank the Lord the words from Psalm 78:19 came to mind, "Can God spread a table in the wilderness?"

We were on board when the big Hercules C-130 took off at 2:00 p.m. Baggage was stacked in the middle and we sat along the sides on webbed seats. There were 80 people on that first flight.

Arriving in Nairobi we couldn't believe the number of media people wanting to talk to anyone. Mostly they wanted to know, "Did you see any bodies, killings, or massacres?"

I tried to avoid them, fearing some ghastly statement would get attributed to me. I simply modified what the Marines had suggested, "I'm grateful for the kindness of the Burundi government and to the U.S. military for their help." That was an understatement! I remarked to an embassy officer that I would not mind paying my taxes this year. I couldn't imagine what *Operation Distant Runner,* the code name for our evacuation, had cost.

In the airport were planes from various countries preparing flights to Kigali for their citizens. There were contingents of Belgian paratroopers and Dutch paratroopers. Wow, this must be a big deal.

We were taken to the new Grand Regency Hotel where the U.S. Embassy arranged a special price for us. It was still a hefty sum for missionaries, but most of us elected to live it up for one night. But in spite of many fine restaurants, many of our missionaries ate on the porch by candlelight. Candlelight and eating outdoors wasn't unusual for us though. We wondered why we had made that choice.

We went to our rooms and followed the news on CNN and on Kenya radio and shortwave. It was awful. Each time we hoped for good news, and each time it would only be worse. The U.N. Commander,

Gen. Dallaire, said he was seeing what seemed like watching demons in human form. He once caught himself saying of one incident that "there were *only 46 bodies*." Then he thought, "What am I saying?" Forty-six bodies had become only incidental among the other things he was seeing.

During one interview on the BBC with a U.N. officer in Kigali the interviewer asked, "Are you afraid? Doesn't all this frighten you?" The reply came back, "No comment." This reminded me of 10-year-old Josh Winslow asking his mom if she were afraid. She said, "Yes, how about you, Josh?" He replied, "I'd rather not talk about it." He was old enough to have a pretty good idea of the gravity of the past few days.

We went to bed Sunday night tired and happy to be safe. But still, there was that lingering doubt about DeMilles, Fergusons, and the rest.

The DeMilles' Story

Monday, April 11: This morning I went directly to Menno Travel to see about getting reservations and tickets for the U.S. Dr. Doane Bonney, director of World Missions, was on his way out to meet with us. But he wouldn't need Louise and me to be there. We were only volunteers and now our job was done.

Another planeload of evacuees arrived in the early afternoon. We were overjoyed to see Vernon and Sue DeMille, but no Fergusons or others. After all the hugs and cheers and many flowing tears we got around to hearing Vernon's story.

The DeMilles were confined to their house in Kigali and not sure they could get out. Finally an Embassy vehicle came by and got them. At one point Vernon saw 70 bodies within a half mile of our mission.

At the Embassy they showed Vernon a list of six families. He knew where they lived, and it seemed they expected him to volunteer to look for them. So with an embassy vehicle and two gendarmes (policemen) they set out. From one house to the next they found no one. Finally, someone along the road told Vernon they were all up at the John Bosco Technical School. Vernon went there and found everyone under protection of the Belgian contingent of the U.N. They had actually been fired upon one time.

The Belgians assured them they could leave with the Belgians via the airport and they felt safer doing that. So after a few minutes of consultation they signed a release of responsibility for the Embassy.

Vernon worked his way back across the terror-infested town to the Embassy. They evacuated Sunday morning with a convoy of 151 cars. Sue had some hair-raising stories about the trip out:

As the DeMilles left their home in Kigali, a beautiful little girl of about seven years looked through the fence, smiling and waving goodbye. They knew by the time they arrived on the road outside the mission they might see her body lying dead beside the road.

In the convoy were many Asians, some in tears, saying they had been born in Rwanda and had never experienced anything like this.

At various roadblocks the cars were scrutinized for any Tutsi-looking people inside. One Kenyan lady was told to get out, but Ambassador Rawson intervened. When she was safe he told her, "Today God gave you your life. Now you should give your life to God."

It was a great relief to see the DeMilles alive. They experienced far more danger and stress than the rest of us. We are deeply grateful to them for hanging in there until the last, and for their bravery and trust in the Lord. And God did not forsake them.

We had Hoped

At 7:00 p.m. the group from the Belgian military plane arrived. They were delayed by the refusal of the Rwandan government to allow their plane to land in Kigali. That flight was turned back several times before receiving landing clearance.

There were our friends the Fergusons! And there were the others we had wondered about. What rejoicing! All the missionary family that we worked with had made it out safely. Not one hair of their head had been harmed. The circle was unbroken.

Then we thought of those we left behind. Our hospital staff. Our station workers. Bishop Aaron and his extended family of 52 in his house. Also our dear Tutsi friends, from houseworkers to hospital staff.

We felt like the disciples on the road to Emmaus after Jesus was crucified. They said, "We had hoped...."

Like them, we had hoped, and hoped against all logic that everything would work out. For months we tried to overlook each act of terrorism, each setback. We tried to explain things away, but there were no explanations that made sense. I could only hope that it was like that African American's Easter sermon reported by Tony Campolo, "Today's Friday, but Sunday's comin'."

A Coming Kingdom

M. Doane Bonney
July/August 1994 p. 33

"Thy Kingdom Come..." We all recognize these words from Luke 11:2. Worldwide, our Lord's prayer is repeated by millions week in and week out. Children lisp it. Old men and women find strength and comfort in it. But when Jesus taught us to pray, "Thy kingdom come," he was issuing a direct challenge to Satan. War was declared.

Missionary work, evangelism, healing, digging wells, and planting churches are all about kingdoms. Chuck Coleson had it right when he entitled his book *Kingdoms in Conflict*. The battle is on to release people from Satan's kingdom and his fortresses and move them to God's kingdom.

Paul understood perfectly this ongoing struggle when he wrote, "For our struggle is not against flesh and blood, but against the rulers, against the authorities, against the powers of this dark world and against the spiritual forces of evil in the heavenly realms" (Ephesians 6:12).

This spiritual struggle is raging around the globe but especially in areas where the church is growing rapidly. Satan does not give up territory easily!

All Out Warfare

I'm convinced that the chaos in such places as Rwanda and Haiti is the visible evidence of a deeper struggle for the very soul of those nations. Jesus prayed, "Thy kingdom come," and that is exactly what is happening in both countries.

In Rwanda, for example, the evangelical community now makes up 20 percent of the total population. Most of the growth has occurred in the past 30 years. The traditional religious belief in that area was animistic. The female goddess Nyabingi was often the focus of this worship. The people were in Satan's kingdom. It was his territory. They belonged to him.

Haiti is said to have been dedicated to Satan in 1791, and Voodooism continues as a pervasive evil that affects every level of society. The 1993 edition of *Operation World* notes, "The registration of the National Association of Voodoo Practitioners and nationalistic spirit has led to intimidation of Christians – especially those who speak out against Voodooism."

In 1991 Haiti's president-in-exile Aristide rededicated the country to Voodooism as its cultural heritage. Shortly afterward, he was deposed, yet the United States and the United Nations impose severe sanctions to restore him to power!

God's kingdom is coming to Haiti in spite of strong resistance. Estimates for the number of Haitian Evangelicals range from 14 to 30 percent. This is the result of widespread evangelism, Christian commitment to social development, and the power of Jesus over Satan.

Join The Battle

The front lines of battle move steadily from country to country as the church of Jesus Christ challenges the kingdom of Satan. We are proud to be on the front lines, yet we are bound to fail unless the supply lines are intact.

Your prayers *are* the supply line! Prayer is the key available to us to participate in this spiritual struggle. I'm asking you to join in this battle currently being fought in central Africa and in Haiti. May God's kingdom truly come to these suffering countries!

III. Southern Africa

Page **Article**

137 Conversation Around A Cooking Pot
146 A Taste Of African Imagination
154 The News From Zimbabwe
156 Doing To Learn
159 Malawi Secrets
162 What Makes It Grow?
165 Mozambique: The Aftermath Of War
170 Uanela: Mozambique's Bishop
172 Francisco Goes Home
174 From Edwaleni To Inner City
175 The Roots Of Apartheid
177 Proof Of The Gospel

HENRY and BONNIE CHURCH
Southern Africa

Conversation Around A Cooking Pot

An Interview With Henry and Bonnie Church
by Daniel V. Runyon
May/June 1994 pp. 1-7

Did you two meet out here in Africa, or did you come here together?
Henry: I met Bonnie at a Free Methodist Youth Camp in California. She was a sweet gal, but so was her friend -- so I dated her friend! A few months later my family moved to Modesto, where Bonnie attended church. We got better acquainted -- and I proposed to her at a stop sign on the way to her house just before I left for Seattle Pacific College. We were married on Tuesday, July 3, 1962, in the Modesto church.

That was fast...
Bonnie: No, we went together two and one-half years before we were married. Our dates revolved around church and Youth for Christ -- Saturday night rallies and weekly Bible Clubs. I had finished one year of college and was just a few weeks shy of 19. Henry had three years of college and was 20. That meant his father had to sign before we could get a marriage license. I was old enough to sign for myself. We didn't have time for a honeymoon.

Henry: Our honeymoon was a drive from Modesto to Seattle. I had one week off work to drive to California, wreck my car on the way, get another car, get married, and drive back again.

You are from California?
Henry: I was born in Los Angeles. Father was a Free Methodist preacher back when you had to move every two years, so I lived all over California.

Bonnie: I was born in Williamsport, Pennsylvania, but I don't remember the place and have never been back. My dad worked for Curtis Wright and I traveled all over the U.S. before I went to school. We moved to California the summer after I completed second grade and my parents have lived ever since in a small town, Hughson.

Were you an only child?
Henry: I have one brother three years younger. He married Bonnie's sister. Bonnie is the oldest of five -- three girls and two boys. My brother's wife is second in Bonnie's family.

Did anything about your early years prepare you for this African lifestyle?
Bonnie: My father had many hobbies -- one was lapidary work. For several years our entire family went to the desert the holiday week before Easter to hunt for rocks. We would find a place in the middle of the desert and set up camp. We had only the water we carried with us. There were no people around. During the day we looked for rocks. All of us learned what to look for. An ugly rock on the outside can be beautiful on the inside.

Sometimes we got the car stuck in the sand but eventually Dad would get us out. I thought my dad could do anything. I never worried when we got stuck. One time we didn't get home in time for Easter, so my sister and I hid jelly beans in our car for our younger sister and brothers to find on Easter morning.

Dad also used to take me fishing. We hiked a long way to some of his fishing places. I was prepared for Africa by knowing how to rough it. You can live without running water and a toilet. You can get yourself out of places when you get stuck. You can do most anything you put your mind to. New places and experiences are good and fun. Not scary.

If you like camping, that makes you a good missionary?
Henry: It doesn't hurt.

Good! What about sports?
Henry: I was never interested in sports. I preferred music. I played trumpet in the Ripon, California, high school band, achieving drum major my senior year.

Bonnie: I played clarinet all through high school.

So music is key?
Henry: Leadership training is key. I was very active in Youth for Christ, Conference FMY and other youth activities. In junior college I worked part time for YFC as a club director.

Bonnie: Being an obedient Christian is key. I heard the Lord speak to me as a teenager one day as I walked home from school. I knew he wanted me to live for him. Before this I was not interested in church or anything to do with the Lord, but from then on my values changed. I became active in Youth for Christ at school and our church youth group. Before I gave my life to the Lord I thought the worst thing to be would be a pastor's wife. When I married Henry the Lord changed my outlook.

And you, Henry?
Henry: Sister Bertha McCally was the evangelist on November third, 1954, in a tiny church in rural Ione, California. The Lord got hold of me and that night made a difference. I have had ups and downs since, but that faith has been the center of my life.

I didn't want to be a preacher. I wanted to be a high school music teacher. But I knew the Lord was calling me to preach. I didn't like it, but I knew.

I first majored in music at college, hoping the Lord would let me off the hook. After junior college, with an AA degree in Music, I transferred to Seattle Pacific College and began a Biblical Literature major. It took me 10 years to graduate because I worked full time as a driver/salesman for the Pepsi Cola Bottling Company, and later for Frito-Lay Inc.

Somewhere in there you and Bonnie were married --
Henry: Yes, during my second year at SPC. During my third year I began pastoring Delridge Chapel, a small church in West Seattle. We stayed three years, pastoring, working full-time, and going to school when time permitted. The church grew from 25 to 100, acquired more property, remodeled, and had their first full-time pastor when I left.

Bonnie: Then we pastored a church for the deaf that met in Demaray Chapel of First Church -- a fascinating year of "cross-cultural" ministry.

What got you moving in the direction of Africa?
Henry: Later in our lives we had a big missions convention while pastoring in Corralitos, California. I was interested in missions -- as a supporter. I knew that a growing church is a missions-minded church. When we are self-centered, we cannot grow.

Bishop Paul Ellis visited. I didn't know him well, but he invited me to travel with him to Southern Africa for three Annual Conferences. In

April 1972 I flew to South Africa and met him at Edwaleni Mission. We traveled from there to Mozambique, and later to Lundi Mission in what was then Rhodesia. At Lundi, Eldon Sayre asked me to preach the evening messages at the conference. The Lord blessed and relationships began. After that month I wanted to return to Africa to work with pastors.

Bonnie: After that we applied to the General Missionary Board (GMB) to go to Rhodesia for two years under VISA to work with pastors.

Henry: It turned out that GMB wanted us, not under VISA, but as "career" missionaries on salary. But this was not a "two year time out." This called for commitment. We accepted and in September 1974 we and our two young sons joined the Lundi family.

Wait, where did these two sons come from?
Bonnie: Eric and Evan were born in 1969 and 1971 while we were pastoring in Corralitos.

How was your experience at Lundi?
Henry: We learned language and culture, held pastors' workshops, did some evangelism, and shared leadership in a six-week evangelistic foray into Malawi. After two years the independence war broke out in our area of Rhodesia and we were advised to leave. We pastored the Sacramento Church in California for two years. Then Dr. Kirkpatrick offered me a position as Director of Church Relations for World Missions.

Bonnie: I worked in Childcare Ministries.

Henry: Then something very unusual happened. In September 1980 I was planning activities, but every time I planned anything for 1981 the thought came to me, "There's no use planning that – you will be in Africa next year."

Bonnie: It was strange –

Henry: I asked Elmore Clyde what was going on in Africa and told him what was happening in my mind and how I felt. Within a few days a letter came from Zimbabwe asking for missionaries. Dr. Kirkpatrick asked me to consider it, and within three months we were back in Rhodesia (now Zimbabwe).

So, you were finally where you wanted to be!
Bonnie: I never wanted to be a missionary. When Henry first came up with the idea I thought it would go away. We were building a new parsonage and happy in our church. So I tried to dismiss the idea that night. But when I awoke the next morning I heard the Lord say, "Wouldn't you go to Africa for me?" I couldn't answer him no. So I said, "If that is what you really want, I'll go."

I have never been sorry. I have had many unique experiences and have grown through it all. My advice is to follow the Lord and you'll be surprised at the things you'll do and how much you'll enjoy it.

Whatever became of the two young sons you hauled off to Africa with you?
Henry: Eric graduated in 1992 from Spring Arbor College and is working for an advertising firm in Chicago. Evan is a senior at Spring Arbor this year.

Bonnie: I feel we are friends with our sons. We have an openness and mutual respect, and share freely.

Henry: They are gifted young men, and we feel they were God's gift to us.

Was it easy raising them in Africa?
Bonnie: We did everything together. When we went into the bush the boys went along. Children and adults did things together. This is very positive – no situations of parents going one way and children another. When we had a birthday party at Chikombedzi everyone came. If it was a child's birthday, all of us played the children's games. While the children didn't see their grandparents, they had many Aunties and Uncles whom they grew very close to. I don't remember parenting being hard.

Henry: Bonnie is a certified teacher so she had a "school in a box" when our boys were younger. We were on the road a lot, but they had school every day, regardless of where we were. When they reached high school level, we offered them the choice of attending Rift Valley Academy in Kenya. Separation was not easy, but their choice to go was a good one. The school prepared them well for the U.S. college system and gave them relationships which span the globe.

Bonnie: We always had our evenings free to be together. No one comes to the door after dark. When the boys were young we had no TV, so we played games in the evenings --

Henry: -- Until we were tired of that. Then, we read all kinds of books -- classics, biography, fantasy, humor. I read the books aloud to the family.

Bonnie: It gave us good family togetherness. And if we wanted something, we didn't go out and buy it, we made it.

The hard part came when the boys went to the U.S. for college. There was no "home" to go to during holiday and summer breaks.

Henry: This was especially hard on Mom, I think, as she wants to be there when needed, but the distance is too great.

You seem pretty happy here, sitting by this cooking pot. What makes for happiness?
Henry: I don't know where I'd be today, without Christ. Possibly a teacher. I would be an unhappy person. My spiritual journey has led my entire life.

Bonnie: *Where* you live is not what makes for happiness. I have liked everywhere we've lived. We have friends in those places. There is beauty, things to do, and places to go.

Henry: During the last General Conference I went to Seattle for the first time in years. I thought, "I'd like to come back and live here." I'll be happy no matter where we end up, but when we eventually leave Africa we will miss it terribly. Africa gets into your system in ways that are indescribable.

Feels a little lonesome to me. Do you have any special friends?
Bonnie: I talk everything over with Henry, so he is a best friend. Faith Smidderks is also a close friend, and I am close to my sister.

Henry: Phil Capp was my mentor when I came to Africa and he tolerated a lot of nonsense. I value his counsel and advice. I will miss him when he retires.

What do you do for excitement around here?
Henry: The Malawi Bible School is exciting. It started out while we lived in Zimbabwe. The first resident missionaries in Malawi had a school going with four students. A family emergency called the missionaries back to the States.

Bonnie: We expected them to return, but time passed and we were desperate to finish training the four men. The Malawi church was growing -- they had 3,000 members and only five pastors!

Henry: As Area Director, I asked Phil Capp to brainstorm with me on how best to finish these four men. Out of that brainstorming session evolved a whole new program -- one of the most exciting ministerial training programs *anywhere*.

We opened the program in September of 1983 with the four students and eight new ones. We have now graduated 34 students, and our church has grown to more than 10,000 members. We have about 40 circuits and more than 200 preaching points. Our ministry is spilling over into Tanzania, northern Mozambique, and Zambia.

Bonnie: The explosive growth is exciting and challenging. We are thrilled to be part of it. We have a lovely campus here in Lilongwe, the capital city. It is used for school and conference activities. Guest teachers from North America and England lend their expertise to the program. And Malawi has developed into a creative conference finding new ways to administer their work.

Give me an example.
Henry: They do not have a conference superintendent. That approach simply does not work here. Instead, the Malawi pastors have found that a "committee on the superintendency" works far more effectively.

With all this excitement and success, you probably don't know the meaning of discouragement...
Bonnie: I get discouraged. Some people don't seem to change and always want a handout. I believe strongly that people need to *do* for themselves. Giving handouts is usually not helpful. I favor teaching people through development projects how to do for themselves.

Henry: My big disappointments have to do with people. Luke Klemo was a brilliant preacher, fine teacher, and good friend. But he went astray and is lost today. My heart grieves over him. Moses Phiri, founder of the Malawi Free Methodist Church, has also gone his own way. Today some dissidents in Mozambique are causing great trouble and leading many down the wrong path. These are great disappointments.

Bonnie: When we catch a ministerial student cheating or misusing funds we are discouraged.

Henry: But the scriptures are full of people who failed. Some came back and went on to victory. Others were lost.

Still, I can tell you really like this place...
Bonnie: Missionaries have the best of both worlds. I enjoy going out to the villages. It's so restful and quiet. True there are pit toilets and no running water. But the people are friendly, life is slow, and it gives you a chance to relax. You would be surprised at how good a bath you can get with a bucket of warm water, a reed enclosure (no roof) and a cup. But after a couple weeks of that it is great to go home to a hot shower and have some ice cream and cake!

Mmmm! Is that a typical African dish?
Bonnie: It's *possible,* but not typical. My favorite African food is greens with peanut gravy eaten with the thick cornmeal porridge. The first time I ate the porridge we were out with the Zimbabwe Bible School students and we had very little to dip the porridge in. My stomach said, "What is this?" But I have grown to like it very much.

Henry: The cornmeal porridge has a different name in each language. In Mozambique it is *wuswa* and you dip it in a gravy of chicken in coconut oil. In Zimbabwe you dip your *sadza* in a gravy of greens mixed with peanut butter. Afrikaners like their *meilie pap* dipped in a gravy made by cooking onions and tomatoes together with a little sugar. Malawians dip their *nsima* in sauce made of boiled fresh chambo (perch-like fish).

Is the weather as reliable as the food?
Henry: Mozambique is almost always hot. The Drakensberg mountains in South Africa are cold. Around Lundi and Chikombedzi in Zimbabwe it is usually hot, but can frost in winter. Malawi is temperate, not overly hot in summer, not cold in winter.

Bonnie: In Malawi we enjoy sunshine almost year round. Even on rainy days the sun shines part of every day. It's great.

With your nice cooking pot full of nsima and your lovely weather, what more could you possibly need?
Bonnie: We need people who are called by God to the mission field. People who are creative, flexible, not afraid of hard work, who can get along with people at home, and who want to serve others. We need people with commitment who are willing to stay when the going gets tough.

Henry: We need a leader to direct our creative new Bible school program in Zimbabwe, which last year was remodeled on the Malawi model and has the potential of starting the Zimbabwe Church on a great movement to urban areas.

Bonnie: We need someone to take over a multi-racial, multi-cultural church planting project in Pietermaritzburg, South Africa. This is a great opportunity to show South Africans how all races can work together.

Henry: We need a full time couple to come to Malawi to operate the Bible school. And we have a great opportunity in Tanzania and need a missionary couple to live in northern Malawi and reach across the border. We have two churches in Tanzania now and could have dozens.

Bonnie: We need encouragement. That comes through letters, care packages and telephone calls.

Henry: We need prayer, lots of prayer. Pray the Lord of the Harvest to send workers into the harvest field.

A Taste Of African Imagination

September/October 1993 pp. 4-8

Monkey Heart   Gerald E. Bates

      Once upon a time, along a large river in Africa, there was a tree. In the tree lived a monkey.

      In the water beneath the tree a crocodile slept away the lazy days and dreamed about how delicious it would be to have a monkey sandwich. But he couldn't climb trees so he thought hard about what to do.

      One day he said to the monkey who lived in the tree, "We both have a friend on the other side of the river. He needs our help. How about if you and I go over there and help him?"

      "But I can't swim across the river," said the monkey. "You will have to go alone."

      "Oh no," replied the crocodile -- "It is not suitable for me to go alone. How about if we go together? I will swim across the river and you can ride on my back."

      The monkey thought about that for a while. *Crocodiles are good swimmers,* he thought. Finally he said, "Okay, fine. That is a good plan. We will go tomorrow."

      The next day the crocodile came to the tree. The monkey dropped down on his back, and they started out across the river. When they got half way across the rushing water the crocodile said, "Oh! There is one thing I forgot to tell you."

      "What is that?" asked the monkey.

      "Well, there is only one thing that can help our friend, and that is the heart of a monkey."

      This news was very distressing to the monkey. He looked back and saw that it was a long way to the safety of his tree. He ran up and down, up and down, and up and down the back of the crocodile, wondering what to do.

      But, you know, when a monkey is in trouble he can think quickly. So this monkey ran right up to the front end of the crocodile and spoke directly into it's ear. "Oh dear," said the monkey. "We have a terrible problem!"

"And what might that be?" grinned the crocodile.

"I forgot to tell you-- I have left my heart back there in my tree!"

"Is that so?" asked the surprised crocodile.

"Oh yes indeed! We monkeys never travel with our hearts. We must go back and get it."

The disappointed crocodile made a u-turn and swam in under a low branch of the tree. The monkey leaped for the branch and scrambled up.

When he was safely on a high branch the monkey called down to the crocodile, "I have found my heart, but I have also changed my mind. I think I'll just stay up here in my tree, where my heart is."

There is a moral to this story and it is this -- we Christians must guard our hearts. Monkeys, when they stay in trees, are safe. And we, when we stay close to Jesus Christ, are also safe.

A Taste Of African Preaching *Eldon Sayre*

Folktales play a big part in sermons by African preachers. Pastor Langbouy Banda of our Muloza church in Malawi gave the following story as he preached on John 16:1-18 on a Sunday when I was worshipping with his congregation:

A Father's Gift *Langbouy Banda*

When Jesus was preparing his disciples for his departure, he explained that even though he would not be with them, he would send the Holy Spirit to be with them. The Holy Spirit would be his departing gift. The disciples did not want him to go. They could not understand how the Messiah would suffer and die.

Jesus explained that the Holy Spirit would meet all their needs and would be their teacher. The Spirit would instruct them in all they needed to know. He would be their Comforter. Whenever they would be troubled or hurt, he would be there to strengthen them. When they lacked strength, the Spirit would be there to lift them up and give them strength.

The disciples did not understand what a great and priceless gift the Holy Spirit would be. They wanted Jesus to stay with them. They were like a certain young boy called Mabhuto.

Mabhuto lived in a very poor family. His father worked hard, but there never seemed to be enough money. His father and mother tried their best, but it seemed there was never enough food. Or, if they managed to sell a goat, the money was never sufficient to buy the clothes needed for the children.

When Mabhuto grew big, he also worked hard. He became a man and began his own family. But again the needs were many and his own family was also poor.

By this time Mabhuto's father was getting old and weak. He realized that soon he was going to die. So he called Mabhuto to talk to him. He told his son that he felt he would not live much longer and would soon die. Mabhuto objected to this thought. His father told him he was very sorry that he did not have any wealth to leave for his son -- no money, no cattle, no goats.

Then the father went to a little box under his bed and took out a small wooden doll and handed it to Mabhuto. This was his inheritance.

Mabhuto could not understand why his father was carefully giving him this child's doll. He could not see that he would have use for it. In his eyes it was a small thing to receive in place of his father.

However, his father said, "Possibly this is the most valuable thing you have ever had. Receive it and keep it carefully. It is the best thing I have to give you. It may be able to do more for you than I can ever do."

Mabhuto was disappointed. He could not understand how this old doll could help him. He wanted his father to continue to live to guide and teach him.

Soon Mabhuto's father died. Because he deeply loved and respected his father, Mabhuto took the doll to his house and carefully tied it up under his bed so it would be safe from animals and his children would not play with it or break it.

Now, in Mabhuto's country there lived a very rich and powerful chief. He had a large house, many cattle and goats, much money and jewels, and many servants, soldiers and policemen. He also had a daughter whom he loved very much. He played with her every chance he got. She was the most important person to him in his whole area. However, one day she became sick and the chief was troubled.

The chief and his wife tried to give the girl the best care they knew of, but she did not improve. He called the doctors of his region to come and try to make the girl well. Many doctors came. They tried many cures, working both separately and together, but they did not succeed.

Then the chief called the herbalists and the witch doctors. He promised that anyone who would make his daughter well would be rewarded by receiving half of his area to rule as well as half of all his other wealth, money, jewels, cattle, goats and all.

Oh, how they all tried! The doctors worked hard, but failed to make the chief's daughter well. The witch doctors worked hard, but their ceremonies did not succeed. The herbalists brewed their best drink, but the daughter did not improve. The chief and *all* his people were very sad and troubled.

One night Mabhuto had a dream. His father came to him and said, "Mabhuto, take the wooden doll I left you and go to the chief. Tell him you can make his daughter well. Ask if you may try. When he gives permission, take your knife and scrape some of the wooden side of the doll into a cup of water. Stir the scrapings and water carefully, then have the girl drink it all."

When Mabhuto woke up and thought about the dream he was very afraid. He was just a poor man, not a doctor, herbalist or witch doctor. He was afraid that the powerful chief would punish him for being so bold. However, because he was an obedient son, and his father had told him to go, he decided that he would try.

He carefully took the doll from its hiding place under the bed and went to the great chief. Very fearfully he approached the chief and told him that he would like to try to make the daughter well. He was only a poor man under the chief but his father had given him a present which would make the daughter well. The chief looked at him and thought of his daughter who was getting sicker each day. He had already tried all the people who should have made the girl well and they had failed. He figured this poor man could not do less than the others, so he welcomed Mabhuto into his house.

Mabhuto asked for a cup of water. He then took the little wooden doll out of his pocket, scraped some of the side of the doll into the water and stirred it well. Then he gave it to the girl to drink.

The chief's daughter was very weak from being sick for many days. With great effort she managed to drink the whole cupful of medicine and thanked Mabhuto for trying to help her. Mabhuto was afraid because the medicine had been only an old wooden doll his father had given him. But he had done what his father told him to do.

Soon the daughter began to smile. She moved around. Then she tried to sit up. She told her father that she was feeling some better. A few minutes later she stood up. A little while later she was playing around as if she had never been sick!

The great chief was very happy when he saw his daughter

looking so well. He remembered his promise and quickly divided his chieftainship, giving half to Mabhuto. He also divided all his riches, money, jewels, cattle, goats and everything he had, and gave half to Mabhuto. Mabhuto was never poor again, and his family had a very good life.

Mabhuto now realized that his father had told him the truth when he said the little wooden doll was the best thing he could give his son when he died. Just so, Jesus left the Holy Spirit to us as the greatest gift he could leave to us, his brothers and sisters in the faith. Let us receive him gladly and let the Holy Spirit do his work in us, a work that only he is able to do.

Mr. Hyena's Choice *by Leonard Banda*

Leonard Banda is an older student who leads the Chiqwila church in Malawi. Pastor Banda chose the text of Luke 9:57-62 for his sermon and was bringing out the point that when Christ calls us to follow him, it requires a change in our lives. If we follow Christ and become a member of the family of God, there will be changes in our living and our thinking.

One day a farmer was walking along the road and met Mr. Hyena. The hyena was trying to behave like a person. As it was a long trip from town to his home, the farmer visited with the hyena a long time and they became good friends.

Mr. Hyena seemed to be much like the farmer, so the farmer generously invited the hyena to come to dinner at his house the following week. He promised that his wife was a good cook and would prepare them a wonderful feast.

When the appointed day came, Mr. Hyena got ready and came to the farmer's house to enjoy the feast he had been promised. He did not know what to expect as he had never eaten with a human before. But since the farmer was so healthy and so friendly, he was sure that the food would be very good.

When he arrived at the farmer's house he found preparations in full swing. The wife and older girls were busy cooking the food, the table had been set and all was nearly ready. The farmer met him at the front gate and welcomed him warmly. He told his oldest son to take Mr. Hyena into the house and get him a cool drink while he went to tell his wife the guest had arrived.

The son opened the door and brought the visitor into the house. As they came in, Mr. Hyena spotted the skin of a calf lying on the floor as a rug in front of a fine comfortable chair. His mind immediately went back to the last time he had killed and eaten a calf. Oh, how his mouth watered when he thought how delicious that calf and its skin had tasted.

The boy invited Mr. Hyena to sit and relax in that chair, but all the hyena could think of was the skin on the floor. He just kept walking around looking at the skin.

The boy urged him to sit down and rest while he went to get him a cool orange drink. Yet the hyena just kept walking around looking at the skin.

Finally the boy went to the kitchen to get the drink. As soon as the boy was out of sight, the hyena's appetite for the skin got the best of him. He forgot all about the delicious feast the farmer's family was preparing for him. He forgot about the wonderful smells coming from the cooking pots. His old nature was still in control, so he grabbed the calfskin in his teeth and ran out the door with it.

Mr. Hyena ran as hard as he could to steal away with the old skin. He ran toward the road to make his escape. Because he was running so fast, the skin flew this way and that, and finally blew right across his eyes. The hyena did not seem to worry though, as he was thinking only about eating that old dry calfskin. He did not see the big truck racing down the road toward him. He did not jump out of the way, so the truck hit the hyena and killed him.

The hyena was trying to act like a human, but his old nature had not been changed. He still had the same behavior and the same old desires of a hyena. These desires led to his death.

If we want to be part of the family of God and enjoy the good things God has prepared for us, we must truly be changed to act and feel like one of his children. Otherwise our old habits and feelings will lead us to our spiritual death while we gain nothing more than an old dry skin.

White Egrets And God's Kingdom *by Henry Nonde*

African sermons are often picturesque as preachers work into their sermons stories from their folklore. The congregation can relate very well to these. An African audience catches the implications of the illustrations better than we do.

Here is part of a sermon by Henry Nonde, a Malawi Bible

School student and pastor from the Ngaba church. He was speaking about the final rewards of Christians when God prepares to receive those who have been cleansed and made white in the blood of Jesus.

God is well able to judge all who come before him. Those who are cleansed and made white by the blood of Jesus Christ will enter into their reward. Those who are not made white will be cast out. Those who are of the family of God will enter into the feasting and joy of the Lord. Others who have not really been born again or truly cleansed will also want to enter in, but they will be found out and cast away.

It will be similar to the time the king of the white egrets decided to have a great banquet for his faithful followers. He had his workers prepare a wide variety of the most delicious and special things that white egrets like to eat. A great auditorium was decorated for the event. Special musicians and singers were selected to perform. When the king saw that all the plans were laid, he invited all the white egrets to come to his feast.

Mr. Raven heard about this wonderful dinner party the king of white egrets was giving. He told his wife and family about it in great detail. The more they talked about it, the more they wanted to attend. But they knew that only white egrets would be allowed into the party. So they devised a plan.

Mr. Raven went to the store and purchased some white paint and a brush. Then he had his wife stand very still and he painted her all over, until she looked as white as an egret. He painted all his children the same way. Finally, his wife painted him also. Mr. Raven looked at the entire family with great satisfaction as they made their way to the egrets' party.

At the party the Ravens went in with the white egrets and found a place. Oh, what a feast they had! How the egrets rejoiced with what their king had done for them. They began to sing and dance for joy. They would hop on one foot and then the other. As they hopped around, they raised one wing and then the other. What a good time they were having!

In order to be like the egrets, Mr. and Mrs. Raven and their children joined in the singing and dancing. Soon they were having a most enjoyable time. They hopped and threw their wings up and down in rhythm with the music.

The king of the white egrets was watching the crowd as they danced and enjoyed themselves. Suddenly he began to see some flashes of black among the white crowd in front of him. This puzzled him.

The king called his officers and told them to bring to him the dancers who seemed to be the cause of the black flashes. When they came to the king, he asked if they enjoyed dancing with all the egrets, and he began to hop back and forth and alternately raise his wings.

The ravens assured him they truly were enjoying the party, and to prove it they began to hop and raise their wings in rhythm with the king. As they did so, everyone could see the black feathers under their wings. They were quickly seized by the guards, beaten nearly to death and thrown out of the banquet hall.

In the same way, many people try to deceive God into thinking they have been cleansed and made white. However, they only deceive themselves. God will find out their deceptions and know that they have not been cleansed or born again to become the children of God. In the judgement they will be found and cast out.

The News From Zimbabwe

Daniel V. Runyon
November/December 1993 pp. 1-4

Zimbabwe's worst drought in memory turned the land to dust, destroying crops and most livestock. Free Methodists countered the effects by sending more than $43,500 in relief food supplies, thanks to those who participate in *Operation Hope*. "Because of your help, more than 4,000 people were fed monthly," reports Superintendent Phineas Majoko.

World Relief brought additional food stuffs to Zimbabwe, using Free Methodist churches for distribution points and working closely with our national and missionary personnel. "None of our Free Methodists starved to death in the Lundi area," Elesinah Chauke reported, "but it was a very difficult time. Many people suffered greatly, but the relief arrived in time to save us. We are very, very thankful."

Maybe our prayers had a bigger impact -- rain began to fall last November, "Probably the best rains in 12 years," says Area Director Henry Church. Because of our seed corn and God's rain, people are again able to grow enough food to feed their families.

But there are limits to what can be accomplished by hand. The need now is for teams of oxen to replace those that died in the drought. Proverbs 14:4 describes the situation exactly: *Where there are no oxen, the manger is empty, but from the strength of an ox comes an abundant harvest.*

There are 17 Free Methodist churches in Zimbabwe, an additional 50 preaching points, and a 1993 membership of 3,425. The administration of all churches, clinics, schools and hospitals is handled by national leaders.

The school at Lundi Mission has capacity for 660 boarding students, and steady growth in facilities and programs. A new kitchen, dining hall, and dormitories will service the A-level education program (equivalent to college freshman level in North America) slated to begin in January 1994.

The church at Lundi averaged 464 in attendance last year. Pastor Phineas Maluléke of the Lundi church also has six additional places of ministry — preaching points and small church plants.

"Water has *always* been a problem for us," the Chikombedzi Hospital administrator reported at annual conference. "We used to tell patients when they came that they had to be like camels, bringing their own water."

Now there is good water, thanks to three new "bore holes" and accompanying pumps, installed with the guidance and resources of Dr. Ferrer, recently arrived from Switzerland.

Zimbabwe church leaders are pleased by developments at Chikombedzi Hospital, saying that "Every morning we have prayer, and our new doctor from Switzerland encourages everyone to be at morning prayer meeting. Our doctor helps us when we are sick and also teaches us, as well as bringing a new administration that is very good."

The medical clinic at Lundi treats some 60 patients a day, offering vaccinations, immunizations, and public health and home visitation services via a mobile clinic. Staff salaries and payment for drugs come from the Zimbabwe Ministry of Health. Free Methodist World Missions also provides a subsidy, and packages of bandages and medical supplies sent from North America are essential for their continued work.

Income from patient fees defrays some expenses as well. Under the watchful care of Mrs. Joyce Harangoni, who has been director of this clinic since 1977, a woman can have her baby for just three Zimbabwe dollars — currently worth about 50¢ in U. S. funds. Comfortable beds for recovery are available in the postnatal care area, but many patients prefer the cool and spotless cement floor.

Masvingo is a city of 55,000. Pastor Samuel Maluleke came here in 1991 with a burden for urban ministry after working 24 years in the Soweto district of Johannesburg, South Africa. The fledgling Wesley Bible College is located here, and Pastor Maluleke works closely with the students. Evangelism, church planting, and leadership training are priorities.

Aggressive church expansion plans are in place and enthusiasm abounds. National leaders dream of a dynamic Free Methodist Church in Zimbabwe. The dream may indeed be realized, but success will likely hinge on a practical and high quality training program at Wesley Bible College.

Doing To Learn

Donald Crider
November/December 1993 pp. 8-10

As a teenager in rural Minnesota I participated in Future Farmers of America (FFA). Our motto was *learning to do and doing to learn*. It meant that in class we learned principles of cattle judging, then we went to farms and judged cattle on the hoof.

Wesley Bible College in Zimbabwe has both the learning and the doing. Students are expected to gain certain ministry principles in the classroom, then go into the field to practice those principles in actual ministry situations.

Into The Fire

Just four blocks from the Bible College is Victoria Junior school. Several hundred vivacious primary school children are learning there. Scripture is in the curriculum of Zimbabwe schools. In Masvingo the ministers' fraternal has accepted the challenge to care for the Scripture lessons.

Several months before the Bible College opened I was approached by the coordinator of Scripture teaching. She requested that I supply some teachers for teaching Scripture in the many schools of Masvingo.

I cautioned that we were still to open and I couldn't be sure what strengths our students had. I pled, "Please let them teach for several weeks under the tutelage of an experienced teacher before they are given a class of 40 or 50 active youngsters!"

But the need was great. Our students were thrust into the fire immediately! Fortunately, we scheduled them to teach in teams of two. One would give the lesson while the other circulated among the students, assisting them and keeping order.

It is quite a fire. The room is packed with children. Some come from Christian homes, others have Moslem, Hindu, or traditional African religion background. The children are lively, often giving a real challenge for the young Bible College students. Questions fly. What is the best day to worship? What color was Jesus? Which church is the best? To whom should I pray?

The teacher must be very wise. He or she must have scriptural integrity, and must not be offensive to other religions. The fire is hot. One unwise answer or improper attitude could jeopardize this ministry with school authorities.

God is walking with them into the fire. One day a team leader reported that 23 grade-five pupils committed themselves to Christ. He and his teaching partner went to each of the 23 and prayed with them.

Mrs. Faith Smidderks has held two Christian education courses with the Bible College students. One was on the use of simple visual aids. These courses were of great help.

The Killing Place

Teaming with the local pastor, students helped plant a church in Bulawayo, Zimbabwe's second largest city. *Bulawayo* means "Place of killing," or "a place which is being killed." It comes out of a turbulent past.

For the young Free Methodist Church it is a place of life and peace. Last October the pastor and conference superintendent, along with two Bible College students and Caroline and myself, participated in the formal organization of the Bulawayo Free Methodist Church. Ten charter members were received and two lay leaders installed.

As yet they have no resident pastor. The Masvingo pastor, Rev. Samuel Maluleke, travels to Bulawayo about once a month on the bus, and two students go about once a month. We endeavor to have someone on hand every other weekend.

There are dangers – not from warfare but from road accidents. Buses are frequently involved in serious accidents. One of our students narrowly escaped serious injury when a taxi and bus intersected at a rather high rate of speed. He was miraculously spared, checked over at the local hospital, and released.

The experience of planting a new urban church under the loving guidance of a seasoned pastor is a valuable learning experience for our students. A vibrant Free Methodist Church can help transform the killing place of Zimbabwe into a place of life.

Youth Work

One of our students is a district youth president. Others are area representatives of youth ministry in the conference. In these capacities they travel to various parts of the conference for district and circuit meetings.

Youth revivals are a vital youth ministry. Two, three, four or even five students go to a place for a weekend to conduct services, Bible studies and counseling sessions with young people with special problems. They come back with reports of conversions, deliverance from evil spirits, and progress in the spiritual life of individual young people.

The youth of the area where our students minister take offerings to defray travel expenses. When there is a shortfall, the field ministry budget of Wesley Bible College chips in.

Students are also given responsibilities by their local pastor in preaching, worship leading, and teaching. He also guides them in visitation and home meetings.

Field ministry is very important at Wesley Bible College. Our students are learning to do, and they are doing to learn.

Malawi Secrets

Henry Church
January/February 1994 pp. 1-5

The fastest church growth in Free Methodism took place last year in Malawi, where our church spurted forward at the astonishing rate of 43.94 percent.

Ten years ago there were five pastors serving a membership of 3,000. Today there are 39 pastors, five full-time evangelists, 40 circuits, 196 preaching points, and more than 10,000 members. What is the secret of this remarkable progress? Malawi is tolerant of Christians, even though many of its population are Muslim or animistic. Malawi is still a rural society with 90 percent of its population living in villages. Malawi has been at peace politically for almost three decades with a consistent, generally stable government.

Malawi is poor but not starving. In recent years it took in a million refugees from war-torn Mozambique. Incidently, most of the refugees have now returned home. Many are new Christians thanks to encounters with Malawi Free Methodists, and probably 12 new Free Methodist churches are being planted in Mozambique as these individuals return home.

No question about it, conditions have been favorable in Malawi for the spread of the gospel -- yet our church is growing faster than others. How do we account for that? Certainly the Holy Spirit is moving and God is blessing -- but **how?** Equally important, what can the North American church learn from our brothers in Malawi?

Avoiding Mistakes

September 1993 marked the 10th anniversary of the Free Methodist Bible School in Lilongwe, the capital of Malawi. South Africa missionary Phil Capp and I designed this Bible school to precisely match the needs of our Malawi church.

We were discouraged by the high cost and the low success rate of taking future African pastors away from their families and sending them overseas for college and seminary training. We noticed no correlation between high academic achievement and success in ministry. We suspected any head knowledge gained in a classroom has little relevance unless students continually have the opportunity to teach, preach, and minister *while* they learn.

Phil and I were aware of many pitfalls to avoid in training pastors. What we lacked was a successful model to follow in building a theologically sound, economically viable, and immediately useful training program for pastors.

Who Ever Heard?

Who ever heard of a Bible school that you attend for one month at a time in three- to four-month intervals? These month-long modules are tucked between times of planting and harvesting so students can continue to care for their families and need not be away from their villages for extended time periods.

Who ever heard of a Bible school that required each *student* to plant three churches during the course of his education? Few of the *teachers* in most Bible colleges and seminaries have done this, so our requirement was a radical departure from tradition when implemented 10 years ago.

Who ever heard of a Bible school that takes a minimum of five years to graduate? After taking the two or three courses taught in a given module, students must return home and teach to others what they have just learned, usually in the context of the churches they are planting or pastoring.

Who ever heard of a Bible training program that costs little more than the price of a round trip bus ride to the capital city once every few months?

Secret Is Out

Well, after Phil Capp and I finished laying these radical new plans for our Malawi Bible School, quite a few people heard! Five of them were transfer students from an earlier program, and eight were new students. These 13 comprised the opening student body.

Today, a decade later, it is time to evaluate. Has this drastic and revolutionary method of training pastors worked?

✓ 33 students have graduated and now serve as ordained ministers in the Malawi Provisional Conference.

✓ 3 graduates are ministerial candidates and serve as appointed pastors.

✓ 32 students are currently enrolled and are already planting churches and planning for graduation.

If Phil and I could go back 10 years, would we do it over again? We definitely would! In fact, we already are. The Bible school in Zimbabwe is being restructured along similar lines.

Side Benefits

Frankly, some of our hopes and dreams have not been realized. In their place, other happy surprises that we could not have imagined have come our way. For example, our graduates have invented a whole new method of church administration that uniquely suits Malawi. Instead of electing one man as superintendent, they have developed a *Committee On The Superintendency* made up of nine men elected to alternating three-year terms. The chairman cannot serve more than two consecutive years. This method of shared leadership is so successful that the Transvaal Conference in South Africa is experimenting with the same approach.

We knew the modular structure of our school would benefit students, but did not anticipate the impact it would have on teachers. Malawi Bible School students receive an excellent, well-rounded education. How is this possible in such a small school? Scores of volunteers make the difference. Pastors, teachers and church leaders with a wide variety of experiences bring a unique flavor to the school.

In 10 years, 47 different teachers gave students a broad education. As expected, these teachers made a profound impact on the lives of our students. Less expected was the profound impact our students and program tend to have on their teachers! These teachers have both shaped and been shaped by the Malawi Bible School.

What Makes It Grow?

Eldon Sayre
January/February 1994 pp. 10-11

The Malawi mission started because of a war 17 years ago. From a membership of zero in 1977 it has grown to about 10,000, and last year the Free Methodist Church grew at approximately 44%. I wanted to see what made it grow like that, so when Henry Church invited Florence and me to teach a module at the Bible school in Lilongwe, our hearts jumped at the prospect.

Ethics From Scratch

Our hearts said "Go," but my brain said "You can't do it," when Henry suggested that I teach an ethics course as part of the load. After all, we are retired. We left Africa 15 years ago. Governments have changed. People have changed. Ways of living have changed. Countries now have independence. It is a different situation than we knew.

Yet we felt God's call. We had a personal stake in the church in Malawi. We helped train the first pioneer preachers of the work. They came to our Bible school at Lundi mission in Zimbabwe (then Rhodesia). During the war our school had to be closed and the students sent away. I remember our fears that they might not make it safely home. God not only saw them home, he set them aflame, endued them with power, and built a growing church. What made it grow? I wanted to find out.

We spent many hours in preparation. I asked my friends, "How would you teach ethics to African preachers?" Some had good ideas; others turned blank. I could find no books or previous material on the subject. One friend blissfully said, "I guess you will have to start from scratch." Well, it wasn't quite from scratch, as I turned to the teacher Jesus promised to all Christians. The Holy Spirit developed one thought after another. The day before we flew, the lesson plans were typed and in my suitcase.

On the first day of class I found out my 27 students came from 10 languages and two family life cultures. Some were from matriarchal societies where Mother is the central figure, others were patriarchal where Father is head of the home. They also come from a wide geographic area.

Some come from just a few miles of the southern border, about 600 miles from their colleagues, who serve near the northern border. One man has a preaching point inside the next country.

Unity

With such differences, I wondered what unifying forces there might be. To begin with, English is one of two official languages of the country and has been the medium of instruction in schools. I also found unity of the best Christian kind -- genuine Christian brotherhood. They were all away from their families for over a month. Whenever one person received a letter telling of sickness or trouble at home, he was immediately surrounded and uplifted by 27 others of us. Time was taken each day for united prayer until we felt that needs were being met.

A Singing Church

It did not take me long to fall in love with their singing. Before the first class, about 10 of us were waiting for the rest to arrive when someone started a chorus. They all joined in. And how they sang! Beautiful tenors, deep resonant basses, and all the parts in between. Translations soon showed me that the songs were full of meaning. Nearly all Africans sing and love music. They enter into it with heart, mind and body. The second reason for church growth is that we have a singing church in a culture that loves music.

Joy

Every Christian I met was openly enjoying being a Christian. They were happy and smiling. In testimonies and music I always sensed a sparkle of joy. There was lots of hand clapping, and every once in a while the song leader would do a little dance. Their joy is contagious.

Normal Activity

Our leaders in Malawi take it for granted that they will reach out to the unreached. They feel it is a normal Christian activity to go where there is no church and start one. The only thing our early pastors knew to do was to visit in villages and homes around them, tell the good news of the gospel, and thereby start new churches. So that is what they did, and continue to do. Today it is a conference requirement for graduation that each student plant three new churches. Even if all course work is successfully completed, there is no graduation until that third church is alive and well.

Perhaps In America

If we were truly united in the bonds of Christian love, sang joyously from the heart, showed radiant faces when we go about our lives, and took it for granted that normal Christian behavior is to go everywhere spreading the good news and making disciples, then perhaps Malawi-style church growth would happen here in America.

Oh yes, the ethics course went beautifully. With the students I had, what else would you expect?

Mozambique: The Aftermath Of War

Dan Runyon interviews Dean Smidderks in Mozambique
March/April 1994 p. 6-8

To see most of the places in southern Africa where our church is working requires long drives in VW vans in the company of missionaries. What do you talk about after several days of bumping along, kilometer after kilometer? In Mozambique, you talk mainly about the aftermath of 17 years of civil war.

Have any Free Methodists died of starvation in recent years?
In early 1984 two Free Methodist pastors in northern Mozambique were in dire circumstances and malnourished. We sent food and our people transported it as far as Massinga, about 100km south of them.
That district had five churches (circuits) and they could not get food through because of combat activities between Massinga and Vilanculos. After three or four weeks we got the food through, but it was too late -- the two pastors had died from starvation. They were middle-aged men. One was Manuel Xitlhango, the other was Lazarus Massinge.

Was drought the cause of the food shortage?
Those were not severe drought years. It was more because terrorists carried off people's food at gun point to help themselves. Also, in the early years of independence the government was following a hard-line communist policy. A certain amount of crops had to be turned in to the government. People could only keep a ration, so it was a very difficult time.

So, more people died from violence than from starving?
Definitely. The war lasted 17 years and officially ended in October, 1992. From direct combat and from atrocities and terrorist activities, about a *million* people died over that 17-year period -- almost one in 10 of the population.

Were there any Free Methodists among them?

Yes. We had a pastor on the Zunguze district, Nhachengo circuit, who was killed by the terrorists. There were also instances where God miraculously saved our people. Alda is one example of a woman who risked her life and managed to save others.

Did the terrorists pretty much take over the entire country?

Except for certain regions in the very center of Mozambique up in the Sofala and Monica Provinces, and a little bit in Zambezia, there was very little territory that the terrorists held continuously over an extended period. Sometimes they would hold towns and cities for a month or two, then move on.

Was religious persecution part of this civil war?

Religious persecution was pretty much limited to the first few years after independence in 1975. The government was pursuing a hard-line communist policy. They issued an edict that no one was permitted to conduct activities for children or youth except under the auspices of the government. This policy had a detrimental effect on our church youth programs.

Fortunately, some local administrators in different areas were not prepared to enforce this policy. In a few areas our church had difficulty for a year or two in 1976-78. At the end of that period virtually all geographic areas relaxed enforcement of this policy.

The other difficulty was that the government took control of some of our medical and educational facilities. Overnight the buildings and their contents became government property.

The government also told us that the Inhamachafo church was too close to the primary school and therefore we couldn't have our church any more. But about five years ago the church was returned to us, and now they are returning all the rest of our confiscated property.

Who was fighting whom?

A resistance movement was fighting the communist government. The communist government was led by President Samora M. Machel [Mish-éll], who was the son of a Free Methodist lay evangelist named Moses Machel.

President Machel's political organization was called the FRELIMO Party (The Front For the Liberation of Mozambique). It was the original liberation movement that had sprung up before Portugal granted independence, and remains in power to this day. Machel was President of Mozambique from the time of independence on June 26, 1975, until he was killed in an airplane crash in 1986.

Two or three years after independence from Portugal in 1975, there began a resistance movement against the hard-line communist government.

The resistance was known as the RENAMO (National Resistance of Mozambique). RENAMO wanted a free trade system, a free political system, and it also had some tribal overtones. In the early years it did not draw much of a following among Shangaan people in the central and southern areas. But it drew a following among people in central and northern Mozambique from the Ndau and Macua tribes.

Alfonso Dlakama is the leader of that movement. He is an Ndau man from the Sofala province. Dlakama apparently managed to draw support during all the long years of this war from conservative Portuguese people in South Africa and Brazil who had fled Mozambique and were angry at what had been done with the communist takeover.

Dlakama may also have received some support under the table from the South African government. However, by the early 1980s the South African government moved into a more neutral position.

Who won?

The war was never really won. It was merely terminated in October 1992 with the signing of a cease fire agreement between the two parties in full-scale negotiations in Rome.

Before President Machel's death in that plane crash, he had become more moderate and was beginning to soft pedal hard-line communism.

Any theories as to why?

For two reasons in my opinion: First, he never received the level of financial and material aid envisioned from communist bloc countries. Second, he was expecting some massive infusions of medical and technical personnel. It happened only on a very small scale. When aid didn't come, Machel began to have misgivings about how wonderful the communist world really was.

The president today, Mr. Joaquim Chissano *[Shee-san-o]*, the foreign minister (secretary of state) under Machel, is even more moderate. Today they don't use the word "communism" at all. They talk about their program as a "modified socialism."

Do you see prospects of a more peaceful and democratic future for Mozambique?

One of the agreements in the 1992 cease fire is that there will be a nationwide, multi-party election (to be held in March 1994). My own feeling is that President Chissano's FRELIMO Party may win any free election in the near future. Many people feel that the majority of the war atrocities can be attributed to RENAMO or unidentified 3rd force bandits rather than the FRELIMO government.

What was Mozambique like before this long civil war that recently just ended?

The Portuguese controlled Mozambique for more than 400 years. They believed they had a divine mandate to evangelize and civilize their African territories with the Holy Roman faith, and to educate the primitive people. The idea was that culturally the African people were in great poverty and should be given a rich culture, such as the Portuguese culture.

Upon achieving a certain level of education and fluency in Portuguese, the Africans were "assimilated" into Portuguese society, could be given better employment, and received the right to vote.

No vernacular instruction was allowed in schools, and educated African children learned Portuguese from the first grade.

The last 20 or so years have certainly brought many, many changes to Mozambique.

Yes, and you can believe the next 20 will bring more changes still.

A Life Is Spared   *Dean Smidderks*

During the war in Mozambique, Alda made a visit from her home in Maputo up to Zavala to see her mother, a crippled woman unable to walk. One day when her father was away, and while Alda was there with her mother, terrorists came to the family village.

"We will give you 30 minutes to leave this area and then we're coming back," they warned. "Anybody we find still here 30 minutes from now we will kill. You are not to remain here."

But Alda's mother did not have a wheelchair and there was no way they could escape in just 30 minutes. So the mother said, "Alda, you leave. Go. There is no use for two people to die. I'll stay here and take the consequences."

All the other people hastily made preparations to get out, but Alda said, "No, mother, I will not leave you. Come what will, if they have to kill us both, I am staying to take care of you."

Then they knelt down and prayed for the Lord's help. They told God they were ready to meet him if indeed they were to be killed soon.

At the end of 30 minutes the terrorists did come back, apparently with the idea of plundering the homes and taking everything they could lay their hands on. When they found the two women they were very angry and asked, "Why didn't you leave? Didn't you hear our orders?"

Alda spoke to them, "Yes. We understood very well, but my mother is crippled, we don't have a wheelchair, and I had no way to get her out. I will not leave my mother alone no matter what the consequences."

The terrorists turned and did what they wanted in the rest of the village and then simply left, sparing the two women. The pastor, his crippled wife, and Alda are all still witnesses of that deliverance today.

Alda and her husband have two children. Alda is the daughter of Pastor Simão Nhanombe of the Zavala district, who is now secretary of the Central Mozambique conference.

Running Like Elijah Dan Runyon

I asked Superintendent Titus Sonia (with Faith Smidderks translating) if he was ever bothered by terrorists during the war:

Oh yes! Many times they came and took away everything we had. One day, they stopped my 26-year-old son on his motor cycle, tied him up, and mutilated his genitals. Many other Mozambicans also had their ears, nose, or lips cut off by terrorists.

One Sunday after church -- it was March 30, 1985, terrorists came into our church building, stole the offering, and made me go with them. We walked all day and then walked all night. The next day we reached a camp and were allowed to rest.

While resting, the FRELIMO (government forces) came to the camp and all the terrorists ran away. The FRELIMO soldiers began to abuse us prisoners, suspecting us to be sympathizers of the terrorists. Suddenly they began shooting and killing everyone in the area.

I just began to run away just as fast as I could run. I was too afraid to stop running. So I just kept on running and kept on running until I was all the way home.

Uanela: Mozambique's Bishop

Daniel V. Runyon
March/April 1994 pp. 3-5

On March 14, 1993, the Reverend Luis Uanela Nhaphale was installed as the first Bishop of the Free Methodist Church of Mozambique.

The installation service began at 5:30 p.m. when about 50 superintendents, pastors, family members, missionaries and visitors gathered in the conference room of Hotel Escola Andalucia in Maputo, Mozambique's capital city.

After a time of singing, Southern Africa Area Director Henry Church led in prayer, followed by the presentation of a biographical sketch of Bishop Uanela.

It was 5:58 p.m. when presiding Bishop Gerald E. Bates led in a prayer of dedication for both Uanela and our church in Mozambique. Supt. Elias Matsinye of the Maxixe area of Mozambique then read Acts 20, and Supt. Thomas Malemane read Matthew 28.

The sacred duties of the office of Bishop are many. As Bishop Bates read the questions, Uanela answered in the affirmative, and after the elders and missionaries laid their hands on him in fervent prayer, Uanela rose to his feet and received the robe symbolizing his new role as Bishop. A Bible was presented to him, and he also received a *Book of Discipline* as well as a copy of the bylaws of the Mozambique Church.

We Have A Bishop

It was 6:31 p.m. when Bishop Bates announced, "Ladies and gentlemen, I present to you the new Bishop of the Free Methodist Church of Mozambique, Luis Uanela."

Before turning the program over to others, Bishop Bates exhorted the congregation and the new bishop to "run the race." From his text of Hebrews 12, Bates reminded them that *the race requires sacrifice, the race must be run following the rules, and winning the race requires peace and forgiveness.*

Congratulatory messages were extended to Uanela from other areas of Africa as well as from the United States and Latin America. Many gifts were presented and words of encouragement offered, including an elaborate presentation from Mr. Chambal, Head of the Ministry of Justice, Department of Religious Affairs of the Government of Mozambique.

It was 8:15 p.m. before Bishop Uanela himself was given opportunity to speak! But instead he led in singing, with his wife at his side. He thanked those present for their great kindness and then began the task of leading the church.

Francisco Goes Home

Henry Church
March/April 1994 p. 12

In December 1990 I was allowed to return home to Mozambique.

With these words, Francisco Javinete began his report to the Malawi Annual Conference. He had been a refugee in Malawi for several years, due to the brutal war raging in his homeland.

While in Malawi, Francisco became a Christian in a church planted in a refugee camp by one of our Bible school students. Javinete soon became a lay leader in the refugee church.

When government forces freed his home town, Milanje, from the grip of rebels, Francisco wanted to go home. Through Red Cross efforts he was repatriated in 1990.

It took three weeks for Francisco to get government and traditional permission to open a new church in his home area, but he persisted. Eighteen months later he stood as a specially invited guest to report to the Malawi Conference.

Milanje is just two kilometers from the Malawi border. The work of the Mozambique Conference is hundreds of miles away across war-ravaged countryside. Therefore, the Malawi Conference Board of Administration made Francisco's new church part of the Luchenza Circuit of the Malawi Conference.

A few Bibles and hymn books were sent to the new church for encouragement. A roll of plastic was donated to help keep the roof from leaking. Pastor Chimombo of Malawi went to Milanje every few weeks to check on the work and to encourage Francisco. It was Pastor Chimombo who asked permission for Francisco to report at conference.

Francisco stood quietly before the conference and began his five minute report. He described how there are now five preaching points in Milanje District, one as far as 90 kilometers away! He went on foot, alert at all times for military action -- but now, thanks to a gift from friends in America, there is a new bicycle to assist Francisco in his church planting and pastoral ministry. Francisco reported that in his district in Mozambique the Free Methodist Church grew to more than 850 members over an 18 month period. His report was received with no fanfare, shouting, or clapping, just a few quiet "Praise the Lord" comments from delegates.

I visited Milanje to see this new work and to preach in one of Francisco's churches. His report is true. The people are there. The churches are there. The Lord is there.

Growth is normal in our church. It is expected. And God meets our expectations.

From Edwaleni To Inner City

Gerald E. Bates
July/August 1994 p. 1-2

A century ago Free Methodist missionaries started our church among the rural blacks in a carefully segregated South Africa. Today the church scrambles to adapt in a society threatened by racial violence and changing political and geographic boundaries. South Africa is moving from racial segregation to racial equality. The population is moving from rural to urban. The church is moving from missionary leadership to national autonomy.

Strategic action was taken at the 28th annual session of the Transvaal Conference to split off the northern and eastern districts into a provisional annual conference. This action reduces the amount of travel necessary for church leaders and should result in the development of stronger regional church leaders. Nearly all pastoral leadership is bi-vocational. Full-time pastors are needed.

The 89th annual session of the Natal-Transkei conference met at Edwaleni March 24-27. As a result of venturesome planning, Zululand and Pondoland are being divided off as provisional annual conferences with the remainder of Natal continuing as a full annual conference.

As the three conferences plan to meet and organize separately next year, they approved a draft copy of a provisional general conference constitution and nominated Robert Nxumalo bishop to the 1995 North American General Conference. Nxumalo received 26 out of 32 ballots cast.

This year a common Natal-Transkei Board of Administration is caring for business with a common budget. The newly developing Boards of Administration (Zululand and Pondoland) will prepare constitutions, budgets, and nominations for next year.

In a dramatic influx of leadership, they took in one ministerial candidate and ordained one elder and seven deacons. Four of the new deacons are women, all experienced church workers and soul winners. These timely developments bode well for new life, youth and vigor in the South Africa Free Methodist Church. The church saw a net growth of 570 members in 1993.

The Roots Of Apartheid

Edward Coleson, Ph.D.
July/August 1994 pp. 8-9

Most everyone in America believes that South African politics has been dominated by the Dutch for centuries. Actually, the Dutch did not get to South Africa first. The Portuguese, who were exploring the African coast long before Columbus was born, reached the Cape of Good Hope five years before 1492.

The Portuguese failed to make a settlement at Cape Town, but the Dutch did a century and a half later, in 1652. The Dutch found some Africans at this location and enslaved them, but did not find any very formidable foes until they started moving northward a century or so later. Then the *Boers* (the Dutch word for *farmers*) met up with tribes moving south. A series of hard-fought wars resulted. This was the beginning of racial animosity.

In their considerable contact with Africans over the years, the Dutch, although good Calvinists themselves, did not try to evangelize black Africans. Indeed, when a Moravian missionary, Georg Schmidt, came to South Africa in 1737 and won a few converts among the slaves, he was driven from the country.

Later in that century the Dutch Reformed Church began missionary work with the Africans, but such efforts were still regarded with suspicion. When Robert Moffat tried to publish his translation of the Gospel of Luke in 1830, he found the printers in Cape Town unwilling to print it! They felt it might give the "inferior" race the notion that they were equal to the white man.

Great Trek

Although the colony in South Africa was far from Europe, the Napoleonic Wars brought trouble. The British took over South Africa. They not only ruled the country, but even insisted that English should be the official language. They also abolished slavery in all the British colonies in 1834, and of course this included South Africa.

This was the last straw. The Boers packed up and moved north in the so-called Great Trek. They just wanted to be left alone, but this privilege was denied them also.

Much of the plateau where the Dutch settled was semi-arid, so they might have been left in peace. In particular, they hoped gold would never be found there, for they didn't want a gold rush. When a former "Forty-niner" from California appeared and started poking around, the Boers warned him not to let the world know if he did find gold or they would execute him. Fortunately, he did not find much and soon wandered off.

The beginning of trouble was the discovery of diamonds. The big strike came in 1871. Now foreigners came in droves, including that famous Englishman Cecil Rhodes. If this were not trouble enough, in 1886 the incredibly rich gold field of the Rand was discovered. Johannesburg became a great city and the Boers' peace and quiet were gone forever.

The Boers were brushed aside and empire building became the fashion. This was a game that Cecil Rhodes, with his vast fortune, was fond of playing. His dream of a Cape-to-Cairo railroad was never built, but he did get a couple colonies named for him, Northern Rhodesia (now Zambia) and Southern Rhodesia (now Zimbabwe).

The Boer War

Boer-English relations continued to deteriorate until the conflict came to blows in the Boer War, beginning in 1899. The war was an utter disaster for the Boers and impoverished them seriously. The English will assure you the peace of 1902 was a generous one and that they later continued their charitable policy. Indeed, the Boers recovered and have made good use of their political power since.

Today the white population in South Africa remains a small and divided minority. A third of the whites are English who simply don't agree with the Afrikaners, as the Boers are now called, on racial policy. And with the official end of apartheid in 1990, the vast differences between the tribes that constitute the majority black population are coming to a head.

It has been accurately said that the country of South Africa is a time bomb. Can it hang together, or will the country disintegrate into smaller nations like Lesotho and Swaziland?

Recognizing the great diversity of South Africa sheds light on the roots of apartheid, and underscores the need for the missionary's message of hope.

Proof Of The Gospel

Carl Rice
July/August 1994 pp. 45-48

More than a century ago the Free Methodist Church sent missionaries to southern Africa. With this summary of that pioneer effort we hope to inspire a new generation of trailblazers who will carry the gospel to new locations well into the next century.

In the margin of my father's *Nave's Topical Bible* is a note dated February 14, 1910. It reads, "God's promises to me," and refers to Isaiah 43:1-3. *I have redeemed thee. I have called thee by thy name [James Silas Rice]. I will be with thee. I am the Holy One of Israel.* This promise was given to my Dad three and a half years before he sailed to Edwaleni, South Africa, as a missionary.

An only boy with four sisters, Dad was raised Catholic in Cortland, New York. Altar boy for the priest, he knew nothing of a personal salvation experience until age 21. His alcoholic father died young, and James went to work at age 12 in a factory to provide for his mother and sisters.

When converted while praying by his bedside in the middle of the night, James soon began to search for a church. He walked into the Free Methodist Church in Cortland and listened to the message intently. At the close the pastor said, "I feel led to open the doors of the church. Is there any one here who would like to join?" Dad stepped forward, gave his testimony about peace in his soul, and joined the church the very first time within its doors. He was 21 years of age but had passed only the sixth grade.

In the Cortland Church was a businessman, C. A. Lowell (father of Dr. LeRoy Lowell). He managed a shop that manufactured forge welding flux. Through Lowell and the church, my father went to Mechanics Institute, Rochester, NY, and Greenville, IL, where the college had a prep school.

Working at Mr. Andrews' Model Glove plant, selling Nave's Topical Bibles, and other jobs such as carrying wood up Hogue Hall stairs to the girl's dorm, he made his own way. It was while listening to

Clara Leffingwell preach that he felt called to missionary work and first applied to go to China. Heavily downhearted from not being accepted, he pressed on in Bible training.

An African herd boy and converted son of a renowned warrior came to Greenville. His name was Simbini M'Komo and he and Dad were roommates. Another influence in Dad's missionary call was the fact he boarded with the widow of Vivian A. Dake, Ida Mae Dake Parsons (Vivian died in Monrovia, Africa in 1891). Dad loved to sing the song composed by the Dakes, "We'll Girdle the Globe with Salvation," and fell under the same influence that God used on G. Harry Agnew some 20 years earlier. Again he applied to the Missionary Board and this time was accepted to go to Edwaleni, South Africa -- if he could find a bride....

The Plot Heats Up

Mabel Kidney was from Pardeeville, Wisconsin. High school friends invited her to attend the church where Rev. R. H. Warren took a personal interest in the young people. During the next revival she was converted. The parsonage became her spiritual home since her parents and five siblings were unfamiliar with her new-found peace in the Lord.

The next pastor at Pardeeville was B. J. Vincent, who within two years was asked to become assistant principal of Evansville Seminary, Indiana. Aware of Mabel's need to continue her education, the Vincents asked her to move with them and care for the children in their home. They, in turn, would see to her education at the seminary.

Meantime, at Greenville College, word was received of a serious boiler malfunction at Evansville Seminary. Could any experienced men at the college help get the furnace operating?

Mr. and Mrs. Ralph Jacobs and James Rice traveled to Evansville to restore heat. After prayer meeting, the Jacobs were walking Mabel home with James along. Ralph and Ethel Jacobs turned off to their abode, leaving James to walk Mabel on home. And so the romance began....

Sailing For Africa

In 1913 James Rice and Mabel Kidney were married in Cortland, and sailed for South Africa within a few weeks of their wedding.

Dad taught manual training at the Bible School with Brother Ghormley. On Sunday afternoons Dad would take with him an African interpreter named Phillip to home meetings. They took the Sunday school picture cards and enlarged picture poster to illustrate the Bible lesson. As a boy I used to go along to carry the scroll of pictures, rolled up for protection in a 30 inch piece of downspout.

Once in Dad's early house-meeting experience he noticed the people talking seriously among themselves while he was explaining the way of salvation. Thinking this was related to their thoughts on salvation, he pressed home more urgently the way of repentance. However, there was no response to his invitation to repent.

Walking back to the mission station Dad asked his interpreter, "Phillip, the people were very serious about repenting today, were they not?"

"No, no...."

"But they were talking so seriously, were they not?"

"You see," Phillip replied with a bit of a grin, "they were discussing how old you are. Some said you are an old man. Others contend you are but a young man." Dad, being Irish, had turned gray at age 36, whereas to the Africans gray hair occurs only in much later years!

G. Harry Agnew

James Rice was by no means the first Free Methodist missionary to southern Africa. One of the first such individuals was G. Harry Agnew, a teenage stowaway on a ship that sailed from England to Canada. He worked his way to Boston, New York, and on to Duluth, Minnesota.

As he tells it, "One day a tall, sober-looking man came into the store to see me. He talked about my soul and eternal matters until my heart fell in love with him. This man was Vivian A. Dake, at that time a district chairman in the Minnesota and North Iowa Conference of the Free Methodist Church."

A year later, 1885, at the age of 21, Harry Agnew joined two couples (Kelley and Shemeld) and sailed for Durban, South Africa. Upon arrival at Durban, a difference of opinion arose as to where to locate.

Shemelds decided to stay in Natal while Agnew and the Kelleys went on up the east coast. Here they established the mission work first known as Inhambane in what is now Mozambique.

Within a year Agnew was left alone, battling the dreaded African malaria. He suffered untold loneliness and illness. Reinforcements that came three years later did not last long. The entire Lincoln family died within the first year. Others had to leave due to ill health.

Agnew returned to the United States in 1889 in poor health and discouraged. He came in touch again with Vivian Dake, this time in Greenville, Illinois. The Pentecost Bands under Dake's leadership were evangelizing through camp meetings. During this time God gave Agnew, now 26, purity of heart and new zeal to return to Africa.

He labored in Africa almost alone for another five years, then returned to attend the General Conference at Greenville, Illinois. Back in Africa, he labored another 14 years. He was married to Miss Susie Sherman shortly after his return, only to see his bride die in less than a year. Two years later he married Miss Lillie Smith.

Help From Mr. Baker

Success in missionary work for Agnew came through the help of Mr. A. W. Baker, a lawyer, philanthropist and earnest Christian. Baker had started his own outreach in the gold reef area to bring the gospel to the thousands of mine workers living in compounds near Johannesburg, South Africa.

Mine administrators were very supportive of missions due to the changed lives of mine workers. One of these workers returned to his home in Mozambique where he told Agnew about Baker and his work.

Struggling alone as he was without home church support, Agnew contacted Baker. In turn Baker offered land for a mission chapel and home near the Johannesburg compounds. This is now the Primrose location of our Transvaal mission headquarters, and the tin house (now gone) is where I lived with the Ryffs and my brother, Lowell, 40 years later.

Harry and Lillie Agnew had a boy, Harry, and a girl, Susie. Work at the compound was going great with many converts. Agnew also translated the New Testament and hymns into Zulu.

With tickets in hand and trunks packed, ready to sail to the States, Mr. Agnew was stricken again with malaria and died in 1903. He was buried behind the chapel on mission property.

A Parting Of Ways

J. W. Haley first went to South Africa in 1902. By 1923 he felt ready to start a new work in central Africa. He finally made the move 12 years later, in 1935, with his wife, Jennie, and two daughters, Peace and Dorothy.

Haley lived at Edwaleni before sensing the call to go north. The Bible School and Industrial School were both in operation at Edwaleni. While my Dad was strong for evangelism through schools for lay leadership, Haley was strong for evangelism through pastoral training and preaching. I remember, as a boy, hearing their differences! The history of Free Methodist missions testifies that God certainly uses both.

Three years after Haley moved to central Africa, Mr. and Mrs. Ralph Jacobs left South Africa where they had already served 23 years to start the work in what is now Zimbabwe. I was a high school student in Durban when they came to stay a few weeks at Concord Missionary Home. What a privilege to have worked with Ralph after school to help build their only home, a camper pickup truck, for their pioneer mission outreach.

They were not young folks – they were the same Brother and Sister Jacobs who, at Evansville Seminary 26 years earlier, had left the walk home from prayer meeting so Dad could walk Mom home alone for the first time. Now they would start a new mission while living in a truck. Mrs. Jacobs was a large lady while he was the opposite. I wondered how she would ever live crawling in and out of that pickup truck home.

Proof Of The Gospel

I have lived long enough to see the proof of the gospel. God has placed an assurance upon my heart that some youthful reader will feel the call to carry on the work. I believe it is God's plan that every generation that follows will accomplish more for the kingdom than the preceding one. Thank the Lord for each new one who is obedient to the heart tugs of God to serve anywhere he calls.

IV. Asia

Page	Article
185	Bury Me In Florida
194	By Love Compelled [Condensed Book]
226	Nomads To India
229	A Visit To Egypt
230	Sketches Of Japan
232	DeShazer [Condensed Book]
278	Land Of The Rising Sun
280	Welcome To Taiwan!
282	Six Pieces Of Wood
284	40 Years In Hong Kong
286	Leo Gives A Tour
291	Leprosy Care In China
294	The Amazing God Of China

DR. ROBERT & CAROLYN CRANSTON
The Philippines

Bury Me In Florida

*Interview with Bob and Carolyn Cranston
by Daniel V. Runyon
May/June 1993 p. 1-7*

Have you been Christians long?
Bob: I was brought to church in a baby blanket. Later we boys slept on a seat with our head on a book. A lady once said to Dad, "When will your boys be big enough to stay awake in church?" Dad just laughed at her.

If we slept through the message, we woke up during the invitation. Even today when I hear *Almost Persuaded* I feel like going to the altar. The sermon would be on **Judgment Day** or the **Second Coming**. We boys would be scared to death. All four of us would go forward. We wanted to do the right thing. But with four boys in the home it **was** hard. It didn't help when a few days later Mom would be frustrated with our behavior and exclaim, "I thought you boys went to the altar Sunday night!"

These experiences continued through school and a short U.S. Navy career, where I lived a clean life. I met with other men in the stern engine room of the ship for Bible study, prayer, and singing, and was ridiculed for reading my Bible and praying. But I also attended the movie in the evening -- and thus felt I was not a Christian. There was no drinking, no smoking, no shacking-up on leave, no gambling, but also no real peace in my heart.

I think my final commitment came when I arrived back in the States in the summer of 1946. I went forward at a meeting and decided that this was for keeps. I've been going in that direction ever since -- sometimes faltering, but always attempting to be God's child and to serve him.

Carolyn: I gave my heart to the Lord when I was four years old. Dr. Curry Mavis was our conference superintendent. When he gave the invitation to the communion one Sunday, I began to cry and asked Mother if I could go forward to pray with others taking communion. She led me to a conversion experience.

I never forsook that decision, although for a time in high school I dreamed of being a great fashion designer or home economics expert. And I determined *not to be a pastor's wife!* But when I said "Yes," to Bob's proposal for marriage, I knew he was a philosophy-religion major.

Anything else you want to mention about your roots?
Bob: I arrived as the first of four boys into the John Cranston home in Florida. Mother gave direction and admonition. Dad gave never-faltering hope for the future during tough times.

And times were tough. The bank reclaimed our farm, gave us $1.00, and let us keep our cow. Social services gave us mattresses on which was written *cannot be sold.* The cow hooked my brother Ralph and we took him to the doctor to sew up his face. Frank fell out of a tree and broke his arm. He broke it again when he fell from the top of the barn and landed in the manure pile. We had to bathe him under the big artesian well before taking him to the doctor (the outside well was our bathing place).

Another disaster came when Dad waited for the price to get just right before selling his field of escarole. One night the weather report told of a freeze, we built bonfires all around the field, and grandma prayed. Next morning, dad broke a leaf to discover it was solid with ice. We turned the field over to our cow, but dad said, "Just wait for next year, it will be better, somehow the Lord will work it out...."

In spite of these things, ours was a happy, Christian home. Church and sports were the center of my life, and I liked to sing. We sang in church, in the car, around the piano. None of us could read music, but sing we did!

Rules at home were strict, but I learned to live by (and around) them. I got my first prize in grade one for having the *smallest* kite, a medal in fourth grade on the relay team, and set a high jump record in the ninth grade. I played tennis, basketball and football in high school (and got two front teeth knocked out when I missed a tackle).

I craved recognition and got it, so school was fun. It didn't matter how poor you were, if you could excel in sports you were noticed. I received my first athletic letter in Sanford, Florida -- a big orange "S" on a white sweater.

Carolyn: I was born in Fillmore, Minnesota, about 30 miles from Rochester. Grandfather was a pastor in the Dakota Conference. He also had a farm to support his 13 children. Grandfather died in the flu epidemic following World War One, leaving Grandmother with the youngest child less than a year old.

My father, Franklin B. Shaw, was the seventh in the family. He had two years of high school at Wessington Springs in South Dakota, but had to leave school at age 14 when his father died. He was farming the family land when I was born, but shortly after that started his more than 35 years of ministry for the Free Methodist Church.

My early memories are of our first parsonage in Fillmore, Minnesota. As the oldest of four boys and three girls, I carried heavily my role as **big sister**. I learned to sew, cook, and clean house. I loved school, was active in basketball, the school newspaper, and made good grades. I graduated from Greenville College in 1948.

There were very few men in my classes the first two years of college because of World War Two, but the next year enrollment swelled with many G.I.s returning from war. I met a sailor from the South who stole my heart, and we were married September 12, 1947.

He *stole* your heart?

Yes, in the summer before my junior year. I went to college early to prepare the dorms, and to earn a few shekels. There were maybe 15 of us at Greenville that summer. A young man from Florida named Ralph Cranston was in our group that met for fellowship, games, singing, and maybe apple cider and doughnuts. Ralph kept talking about his big brother, Bob, who would be coming to Greenville in September.

After a year of laughing, joking, attending sports events, and singing in a mixed quartet together, Bob and I were married. Our wedding was in Fillmore, Minnesota, in the church my Grandfather Shaw started. We had lots to learn in coordinating the assertive ways of two who grew up as oldest in the family, and in channeling our lives into obedience to the Lord. But the journey has been one of ever increasing love and closeness. In the last 10 years we have been involved in Marriage Encounters, getting leaders who can train teams of pastors in the Philippines. It is a great source of satisfaction to see Filipino couples learn and grow in leadership with Marriage Encounter. But these years also helped us personally to improve communication and growth in married love with each other.

Why are you missionaries?
Bob: I probably didn't have a very good *call*. You see, Mom says when I was born the doctor held me up by the feet and said, "He's going to be a preacher!"

"How do you know?" Mom asked.

"He has such long fingers to take good offerings."

While I was still in the cradle, a sainted lady looked at me and said, "Our little Free Methodist bishop." All I can say is, thank the Lord all the prophecies didn't come true!

Later, when we four boys would go to the altar or give our standard testimony (*I'm saved and sanctified and need your prayers*), someone would call out to my father, "Thank God, brother John, four Free Methodist preachers!" So, the problem wasn't how to accept the call, but how to *get out of* it!

After seminary, my drive was to just be a good pastor and build a successful congregation. I feel we accomplished this our first three years in Lake Worth, Florida. The stationing committee considered us for the largest church in the conference. But I prayed, "Oh Lord, don't let them send us to St. Pete!"

My Lake Worth delegate was on the stationing committee. He put his foot down and said I was not available anywhere but back to Lake Worth. It was a good pastorate. Two of our children, Bob and John, were born there, and the saints of Lake Worth prayed us into becoming good pastors.

The confirmation of God's call comes in a sense of his presence as I serve him -- the change in the lives of people, the training of national leaders, the growth of the church under our leadership, and the overall planning and development of a strong national church. Objective confirmation comes from the increased responsibilities granted to us by our church. We've never felt adequate for the responsibilities, but even at times with much surprise I have seen God work through me.

Carolyn: In our parsonage we often had missionaries as guests. I was enthralled with their stories and messages. When I was 12 I told my mother I wanted to be a missionary, after the Willoughby sisters from China were our children's workers at camp meeting. Two years later John Schlosser's mother spoke at our church. In her positive, exciting way, she encouraged me by saying, "You prepared a lovely dinner!" (Mother was sick with pneumonia.) She also sat down at the piano and played a hymn, then said, "You must spend lots of time practicing piano. It is very important for a missionary to be able to play." Her assumptions sent a message to my young heart that I never forgot.

When Bob and I pastored in Florida, it seemed the ads which Dr. Lamson ran in *Light and Life* and *The Missionary Tidings* for missionary applicants were for us. I used to leave these magazines on Bob's desk, open to the ads, sometimes even pointing them out to him, hopefully.

After three years on the pastorate, Bob was asked to be evangelist for the Tampa Spanish Mission Church in Ybor City, Florida. He came back from there excited about the numbers who knelt at the altar. The altar in Lake Worth seemed barren by contrast, and when we were asked to meet Dr. Lamson for an interview about going to Tampa Spanish Mission, our hearts were open and ready. Six years later we were appointed to the Philippines.

Of all the places you have been, where would you like to live?
Bob: That depends on where my work is. For 25 years it was the city of Butuan. We often played tennis with the mayor and leading professionals, we waved hello to the governor, and we spoke at most of the civic clubs. We enjoyed the food, the people, the climate, the beaches, but most of all the many friends we made over the years.

But that was another day. Today, here in Manila we are building the conference to prepare for the first Filipino bishop in 1994 – then pointing to the USA and the pleasant pastures of our home in Lakeland, Florida. We have already purchased two three-wheel bikes.... The pace will be leisurely, the friends great, and it will be **home** at last. In Florida I was born and will be buried.

Carolyn: We have lived in many beautiful and exciting places, but we feel most at home in Butuan City.

Are you willing to share about disappointments in your lives?
Bob: Most of those came in my early ministry. More recently, my heart attack in 1991 was a major setback. The situation following the heart problem also stopped me in my tracks. I was recuperating in the States in September of 1991. Part of my work is to evaluate, approve, or cut the submitted 13 budgets from my area. When the mission budget came from the Philippines I was shocked to find that no request was made for our house rent for 1992!

When we arrived in Manila in 1992 and went to the annual mission meeting, it all began to seep into my head – *the Philippine mission did not expect us to return!* I couldn't believe it. I looked at the present missionaries as very inexperienced. And who was prepared to be Area Director? Yet I felt I was no longer the leader. I found myself groping for a place to fit in.

Later, I rushed to the ad hoc meeting leading to the Provisional General Conference that will become reality in 1994. I had been the architect of this schedule, but during the first meeting I was in the States waiting for heart surgery. Now, with major legislation being developed, I rose to speak. But it seemed that no one listened. The committee debated a budget that would tax each church some 20% of their income. My chest tightened with emotion. It was unreasonable. Impractical. Impossible! I debated with all my might, but they didn't agree. The vote was taken. The budget passed. We are moving on a graduated scale toward the 20%. Even now less than 2% is coming in. By 1994 it will become evident that a change must be made. But for now, I felt totally defeated.

I wrote to Dr. Doane Bonney, Director of World Missions, telling him of the incident. Here are excerpts from that letter: Can you take time for an old story? *The favorite dog, a real pet, died and the children were in mourning. The father suggested they have a funeral for the dog. So, they built a small casket and decorated their bikes for a parade around the block. They came back to have the funeral, their sorrow now turning to joy. But then they looked in the box and the dog began to wag his tail. In disgust one little boy yelled, "Stay dead!"*

As I offered my advice in the Philippines I could almost hear them saying, "Stay dead!" Times change and our roles change (How many times have I told this to other missionaries!). Now I'm trying hard to find just the place where I'm supposed to fit.

Carolyn: It disappointed me when I realized our boys *wanted* to stay at Faith Academy. I thought I could home school them, but they wanted to live in the dorms instead! I had a real struggle sending them off to school each year, but now I am convinced they received a much better education this way.

Another disappointment came when the librarian who took my place made it clear she did not want my assistance. It was hard to leave a library I had built from 2,000 to 12,000 volumes. But the Lord helped me focus on other areas of service, such as the new Graduate School of Theology, and the opportunity to work more closely in supporting and assisting Bob.

We are torn between how much Bob should do since his heart surgery, and how much I should protect him from stresses of his work. There is a delicate balance between succumbing to invalidism and working to the point of a second heart attack.

But it hasn't *all* been discouragement, right?
Bob: The Philippine church has moved from one conference in 1980 to four full conferences today. The Light and Life Graduate School of Theology, organized in 1985, has turned out 43 Master of Ministry graduates, and 25 students are attending John Wesley Bible College in Manila. These leaders are the foundation for the future general conference. LLBC continues to provide pastors, with about 100 now enrolled, and another outreach Bible college began classes this year in Davao City. So we have leadership and we have fertile soil for evangelism and church planting. About 200 pastors minister to 11,000 members. The horizon has never been brighter. Our dreams are becoming realities.

On the personal level, my most exciting experiences come in preaching. Runners speak of a *runner's high*. I feel that at times a minister hits these highs. He is preaching with intensity, urgency, it seems he is outside of his planned course, and the Holy Spirit takes complete charge. This happened to me one Sunday in Yavatmal, India. I was preaching on the in-filling of the Holy Spirit. People started coming forward to pray. Maybe they were praying in Hindi or in Marathi, but the Holy Spirit was working. I just stepped back and the Holy Spirit took charge.

This experience is beyond preparation, study, or planning. Maybe it is like what Peter experienced in the House of Cornelius. This is a great confirmation for one at times filled with doubts about if God has really called him.

Many things have come my way: awards, degrees, positions, garlands, and accolades. But what means the most to me are words of encouragement from family members. Recently my oldest son, Steve, wrote to us when one of my nephews committed suicide. Steve had played many happy hours with this cousin and wondered how one family could be so different from another. He wrote, "I'm not sure what the difference is or what you did, but our family is special." These words exceed all other recognition.

Carolyn: Last summer at the World Fellowship Young Leaders Missions Congress, as I walked into the auditorium, several pastors from Butuan stopped me. They asked, "We miss you in Butuan, Ma'am. When are you coming back?" Such expressions keep us feeling rewarded.

Perhaps more rewarding is to sit back and watch events such as that Congress move ahead with very little input from us. It is a thrill to see young leaders take the initiative to win Asia for Christ. The present interest in missionaries *from* Asia *for Asia* is thrilling beyond words.

Do you make time for hobbies?
Bob: I enjoy all sports. Since my heart attack I walk a mile each evening to get the heartbeat up. I'm gradually digressing into table games – a new commitment. And using the computer is a sport in itself as Carolyn and I learn together and vie for time on the keyboard.

Carolyn: Sewing, cooking, and other homemaking skills have increased instead of diminished in importance, as one of my functions these days is to keep rooms available for guests. I find this very rewarding and enjoyable. Reading is another hobby we find helpful as we grow older.

Tell about foods you've encountered, places you've been, and adventures we might otherwise not hear about.
Bob: In India I am consistently served curry. They will say, "Dr. Cranston, we prepared this just for you, how do you like it?" By the time they finish the statement the curry is in my mouth and it is starting to burn. It begins on the outside of the lips, then into the mouth, and on down the throat. It sets me on fire. I begin to perspire, and this leads on to the hiccups. I mutter words of thanks and look for water. But alas, the water does not put out the fire! So, the last time I was in India I told the cook I liked eggplant (I meant the way Carolyn fixes them – eggplant omelette). The next meal and each succeeding meal I got eggplant – just boiled.

Carolyn: Singapore is my favorite city. It is litter-free, a veritable garden. Orchids grow everywhere, and the city has a synthesis of all the delightful cultural patterns in Asia. India, with its monuments, gateways, British architecture, the Taj Mahal, and most unique culture is another favorite. And Medan, Indonesia, Hong Kong, Tai Jeung, Taiwan, and Osaka, Japan, are all lovely. But our family most enjoys the beaches and cities and scenery of the Philippines. The weather is hot and hotter, except in the typhoon or monsoon season, so we learned to love the rain.

Tropical paradises all, these are places God has let us work. We are fortunate to live and work in Asia.

What is the greatest need you are aware of today?
Bob: Hong Kong, Taiwan, and Japan are all fighting the syndrome of materialism. It is difficult to get men and women to leave the prospects of

accumulating houses and lands to take up the call to ministry. Hong Kong also faces the anxieties of 1997. No one knows what the future holds. In Hong Kong we also do not have our own theological training institution. Without this it is difficult to build a lasting and loyal church. As soon as a pastor is trained he is tempted to move to a better paying church in another denomination or leave for a country with better prospects.

Japan has a training institution, fine supporting churches, and educated pastors, but lacks the zeal for evangelism. India is crippled with poverty, lack of church buildings, and a limited number of people training for the ministry. But India has the excitement of church planting with William John in Bombay. In the Philippines the biggest problem today is providing funds for church building, especially in the cities. Once we get a center church built in a major city, daughter churches can spring up quickly. But in Manila alone, to build the center church in combination with a Bible College will cost in the vicinity of $200,000.

Carolyn: Our large cities in Asia need adequate church centers and buildings so new converts and pioneer churches have a place to look for leadership. This was achieved in Bombay several years ago. It is now a critical need for Manila. There is no way the 10 struggling, young churches can raise enough funds to do this on their own.

By Love Compelled

Carolyn Winslow
Condensed by Daniel V. Runyon
November/December 1991 p. 15-26

First published in 1981 by Light and Life Press, *By Love Compelled* is the autobiography of Carolyn Winslow, Free Methodist missionary to China and Taiwan. This carefully edited and condensed version faithfully captures the spirit, style, and content of the original. Special thanks to Harry and Ruth Winslow for editorial guidance.

Section 1 – God's Lane

"For ye shall not go out with haste, nor go by flight: For the Lord will go before you; and the God of Israel will be your rear guard." – Isaiah 52:12

I. More Than One Turning

"Sweetheart!" I looked up from my little Skyrite typewriter. "Aren't you glad we're *called?*" Harold asked.

We were in the mission home in Kihsien, Honan Province, China, and the city was being bombed by the Japanese Imperial Army. That day I had run from room to room with our nine-month-old baby Harry as bullets came through an upstairs window. Three-year-old Paul stayed very close to his daddy. The bursting of heavy artillery, the sharp rattling of the windows, the snapping of machine guns, and the danger and tension made our call come back bright and clear.

Harold was called to the ministry as a young man. After graduation from Greenville College (Illinois) he attended Biblical Seminary in New York. There he realized clearly his call to the mission field.

I received my call to be a missionary as a 10-year-old when I knelt on a little red rug in the clothes closet and prayed. When my father [Clyde Van Valin] came home I called, "Papa!"

"What is it, Carolyn?"

"Jesus wants me to be a missionary!" I said joyfully.

"That's nice."

"But I'll have to go right away," I exclaimed. I felt so strongly a compassion for those who had never heard of Jesus, it just overwhelmed me.

"You'll have to grow up," he answered. "You'll have to be educated, and some day the Missionary Board may accept you."

So I began to prepare. I cut out stories I thought would be suitable for children. I diligently read my Bible and memorized Scripture verses.

Throughout my childhood, the prayers of my father and mother were my "sun and shield." As a toddler at camp meeting in central Pennsylvania, I had wandered away from the tent, found a discarded can, and ate the leftover contents. Soon I was in convulsions.

"Get Papa, quick," Mother said.

Papa hurried from the tabernacle, looked at his little girl in the throes of death, and said quietly, "We will do as the Bible says," and he called for the elders of the church. They laid their hands on my little head and prayed with faith. Mother said that in half an hour I was playing about the tent.

Then, at age five, I had pneumonia. Papa went to the cellar for a bucket of coal. There he knelt in the coal bin and promised the Lord he could have his little girl for Africa, India, China, Japan, or any place he wanted. I recovered.

When I was seven I gave my heart to Jesus. During a revival meeting I sat by my father on the front seat in the Free Methodist Church. As the invitation was sung, I went out slowly toward the altar. Then I turned and looked at my father. He smiled! I dashed the rest of the way, and God really saved me that night.

When I was in the lower grades at school a few girls sometimes made fun of prayer, of salvation, and of me. One day when I went home crying, Mother said, "Carolyn, it's a long lane that has no turning. You will not be in this school much longer. You will go on to high school and maybe even to college." Yes, God's love has more than one turning. How little did I know then that I would go not only across the ocean but around the world!

Missionaries often visited in our home. Once the Reverend John P. Brodhead of Fairview, South Africa, was there. Looking at me, he said to my mother, "I'd like to take this girl to Africa."

Tears came to mother's eyes. Then she smiled and said, "Well, the Lord can have her anywhere he wants her."

Turning to Reverend Brodhead, I asked, "What course would you advise me to take in high school?" He recommended the Household Arts course, saying I would probably be at Fairview Girls' School. Well, I took the Household Arts course, but never worked in South Africa. Many years later in Taiwan when the mission asked me to draw plans for a new building, I did, and the only thing the contractor changed was the porch roof, thanks to Household Arts!

In high school I read the New Testament during noon hour and tried to witness to my classmates and neighbors. Nearly half of our town, including our family doctor, were Hixite Friends who did not believe Christ was divine nor that the Bible was God's Word. One evening I tried to study but was strongly impressed that I should call on the doctor. Afraid of his mammoth dog Duke, I finally prayed for courage, went to his home, and opened the gate.

The doctor was not home, but his wife and her sister received me graciously. I gave them Sunday school papers, visited, and finally asked, "May I pray?" They agreed, and I prayed. Dr. Russell died two weeks later. I didn't understand all about the incident, but felt that since I had tried to witness, I could meet the doctor on Judgment Day without guilt. And I learned that God protects us when we do what we believe to be his will, and that we need not be defeated by fear.

I was a plodder in high school and had to study hard. But I sincerely tried to put Jesus first, and he helped me. At Commencement I received the history prize, the Household Arts department gold piece, and I was given the essay prize in gold money. My brother Francis matched each prize, and after tithing it, I put it in the bank to prepare for Greenville College. How beautifully God prepares his children for the future.

II. Love Found and Lost

The following year I attended Dickinson Seminary in Williamsport to complete college entrance requirements. My cousin, Eloise Smith, was also in Williamsport and had previously attended Greenville College. One day Eloise and I sat together in Brandon Park and ate our lunch. "Brownie is wonderful," she said, and told me about a popular, handsome, fine Christian student at Greenville. Although I had never met him, I felt admiration springing up in my heart....

One day I went home from Dickinson and found Mother in bed. The doctor had ordered bed rest because of her heart. Her condition worsened. The day we took her to the hospital she cried, but explained, "These are tears of joy, for I have lived to see every one of you saved." We were all home except Ernest, who was away teaching. When he arrived and stood at her bed, she looked up and said, "Ernest, boy!" Those were her last words.

As the 10 of us stood around her bed my father said, "She's so precious!" When she took her last breath he added, "Sweeping through the gates into the city!"

So that my sister Helen could continue her college work at Greenville, I dropped out of school to cook, wash, clean, iron, and sew for the seven of us at home. After some time my father remarried. One afternoon when I stepped into his dental office I saw him holding a coat for a patient – a stately, smiling, beautiful lady who was to become our "Mother Estella." Our lovely new mother and her talented daughter, Etelka, became part of our family, and Etelka and I shared a bedroom.

....At last, plans were made for me to go to Greenville College. It was a long train trip to Illinois, but the water tower was finally in sight, and Helen and I knew we had arrived. That evening long lines of students in the gym waited to go for refreshments at the college opening reception.

"There's Brownie," my roommate whispered. All the girls liked Brownie. I took a quick glance as he came through the door. I noticed his radiant smile, then I looked straight ahead. I must not reveal anything of my excitement! In a few moments I realized someone was beside me.

"Hello, Carolyn." It was Brownie! Why does he call me by my first name, and I have not even met him? I learned later that my sister's friend had told him about me. In two weeks he asked to take me home from church.

Professor Holtwick made his annual speech in chapel about the Lyceum Course. The fellows began to get their dates for Lyceum. It came to the last day. Nobody had asked me, and I was embarrassed. After the last class was over and I was going to the basement of Hogue Hall, Brownie met me.

"Has anyone asked you to go to the Lyceum?" he asked. Why doesn't he just ask me, and not embarrass me, I wondered. Then he said, "May I take you?"

With joy I answered, "With pleasure."

As the weeks and months slipped by and we had many strolls in the gullies and went to various programs, I found that I really cared. Brownie came to Greenville to prepare to go to Africa as a missionary. But a crisis came. There was a Student Volunteers organization on campus. Should I join? Was I *really* called, or was it a childhood commitment to do God's will which I had misinterpreted as a missionary call?

I prayed about it, but no answer came, so I decided to fast and pray about it. I locked myself in my room and did not go to breakfast or dinner. I wept and prayed and walked the floor, but no answer came. I was not used to God's seemingly turning his ear away. At three o'clock there was a knock at the door. It was Edna.

"What did God tell you?" she asked after I told her my problem.

"He didn't tell me anything."

"Well," she replied, "If he has not told you to do something different, go on doing what you were doing." What wise counsel!

I was proud of Brownie. He was class president and deeply spiritual. When he was at church he was radiant. Sometimes he shouted under the blessing of the Lord until the whole audience was showered with blessing. And he was a man of prayer, even dropping one subject in order to have more time to pray.

Brownie and I tripped through the gullies with happy hearts. Finally we sat down under a tree, and he asked me! I threw my arms around his neck and said a happy "yes." I felt clear to do so. He took my hand, and we fairly flew back to Burritt Hall, hearts light as a feather and happy beyond words.

Brownie got a teaching position at Mulberry Grove, Illinois. I returned to Pennsylvania to prepare for the great event and make my own wedding dress. Brother Will Barkas, our district elder, married us.

Brownie's real name was LeRoy. That summer LeRoy and I represented Greenville College at 11 camp meetings in different states. At the last camp I was ill, but improved enough to attend my senior classes the first week of school. Before long I became terribly sick and went to bed. The doctor suspected typhoid fever. The tests came back negative, yet I continued to get worse.

One night LeRoy sat up all night with me, not expecting me to live until morning. One afternoon I said to him, "Do you see that wonderful light?" It came through the door and enveloped the lower half of my bed. Jesus appeared in the doorway. Oh, the glorious Presence and beauty of the brilliance surrounding Him! It seemed I left my body and went about two feet above it. My body, except my head, seemed like stone. Then my spirit came back to my body. I thought Jesus did not want to take me yet.

The next day LeRoy was advised to go to the doctor and have a typhoid shot himself. But it was too late. That evening he was down with an unusually high fever. Our home became like a little hospital. A double bed was put in the living room for LeRoy. The dining room table was stacked with bottles and various medicines and utensils. Rugs and curtains were taken out. Mother Estella came from Pennsylvania to help us. Warren Chase dropped his teaching at the college and came to care for his pal. "Don't bite that!" he said firmly as he put the thermometer in LeRoy's mouth. But LeRoy did bite, and swallowed a piece of broken thermometer.

    LeRoy got worse. Nurses wrapped me up and slid me to his bedside on a chair. He moaned with every breath. I laid my hand on his and said, "Darling, Jesus will be with you." To the nurses I urged, "Can't you do *something?*" They took me back to my bed and decided on a starch enema for LeRoy. Before long I heard a deep thud, and the nurses were using towels to mop up his blood. The swallowed piece of broken thermometer had done its work. I heard his every breath — then his last.

    It seemed I almost went part way to Glory with LeRoy. There was neither agony nor tears. I fell asleep and did not waken until three o'clock in the morning. God was very near. I reached my hand up in the darkness, and a great, strong hand grasped mine!

    Brother Sanderson came when LeRoy was brought home in his casket. They helped me into the living room, and I stroked the waves in LeRoy's brown hair. Then they sealed his casket because of the fever. The next evening President Burritt and the ministerial student quartet came and had a little service for me, for I could not go to the funeral at the church. My father told me about the beautiful flowers and lovely tributes. About 200 students walked to LeRoy's grave at the cemetery and sang his favorite hymn, *There is a fountain filled with blood,* closing with the stanza, "Then in a nobler, sweeter song, I'll sing Thy power to save, When this poor lisping, stammering tongue, Lies silent in the grave."

    They took me to an excellent doctor back home in Williamsport, Pennsylvania. "You must be careful of an acute heart attack any time," he said as he snapped his fingers. I was 23, and LeRoy had gone to be with Jesus just three and a half months after our wedding day.

III. Healing of Hearts

    Summer came and I went to Mill Hall camp meeting. After six days I had such a longing to be in a service that I ventured slowly and cautiously toward a chair at the edge of the tabernacle. They were about to have a healing service. *I am so sick it would be presumptuous for me to go,* I thought. *I should pray and read the Word and find His will.* Others went and knelt at the altar. As I knelt quietly by my chair, I felt an unutterable pull to go, so I did. When the pastors laid their hands on my head that Thursday, it was as if I had hold of a battery (I had played with batteries with my brothers years before).

On Sunday my brother Ernest helped me in to the service and took a cushion for me. I testified to my obedience in being anointed, and that I was trusting God to guide. As I sat and listened to others, a strong impression came to me -- *Carolyn, get up and go to the other end of the altar.* I was surprised and perplexed. What would I do at the other end of the altar? I began to feel troubled and could not enjoy the testimonies. Was this of God? I feared doing anything in the flesh. Finally, with tears running down my cheeks, I turned to Sister Haskins.

"My child, do what the Lord tells you," she said. I did, and as I went toward the altar I felt as light as a feather. I began to run, and when I got back to my chair, I just couldn't stop running. Sister Haskins went to the platform, spread both hands out, bowed, and kept repeating, "Come and dine." Every time her arms went down, it seemed the mighty power of God was present.

I finally felt I should sit down and quietly did so. Others were still praising the Lord. Brother Barkas, the district elder, came to me and said, "Carolyn, I noticed when you sat down you were not out of breath." It dawned on me. I was healed! If I had run like that before the healing service, I would have dropped dead.

The next day we returned to the same doctor in Williamsport. After examining me he said with surprise, "Your heart is all right."

"Doctor," I said, "I was anointed at camp meeting, and the Lord healed me." That fall of 1927 I went back to Greenville to again start my senior year. That year, the six seniors with the highest grades were required to take a course in oration. The orations were to be given on commencement day because they did not have special speakers then.

I was especially interested in Muslims, so I chose as my oration topic, "The Cross and the Crescent." I did not expect first prize, but when my name was called President Marston reached his hand into the pocket of his striped trousers and pulled out a 10 dollar gold piece and handed it to me.

That summer I began to think I might go to the mission field alone. I took my stationery and pen to my bedroom, knelt, and prayed for God to guide me about writing to the Missionary Board. *Carolyn, if you do this, you do it of yourself,* seemed to be whispered so clearly in my ear. I was startled. Goose flesh came out on my arms. With a sense of awe I rose and put the stationery away.

Just what should I do? Perhaps I could teach. I had college majors in history, English literature, and secondary education, with minors in science and languages. So I applied to 12 schools but did not get a job.

Josephine was going to marry my brother Ernest and asked if I would come to her home in the Catskills in New York and make her wedding clothes. I was working on her navy "going away" dress when her father came in with a telegram for me! I was asked to teach first, second, and third-year Latin and first-year Bible in the high school and world history and religious education in Spring Arbor Junior College in Michigan.

I roomed at Hilliard House with my stepsister, Etelka, who taught at Parma. The school was facing a financial crisis and Dr. Merlin Smith called us to prayer. He could not give us regular salaries, so we had faculty fast prayer meetings.

As Mother had said when I was a child, it had indeed been a "lane" of life with many turnings. I found that Jesus was at every turn. In my heart I could say, "Lead on, O King Eternal, and I will follow thee!"

Section 2 – God's Tapestry

"So he fed them according to the integrity of his
heart; and guided them by the skillfulness of his hands."
– Psalm 78:72

IV. Love Reborn

Orin Winslow had a booming sawmill in Orin, Washington. He took ill, returned to Pennsylvania, and was in bed for more than 10 years with heart trouble. "He takes enough strychnine to kill a horse," the doctor said.

The family lived on a small farm at the edge of Brockport. There were two sets of twins. The twin boys divided the work. Harry taught during the day and cared for the farm. Harold taught and cared for his father at night, to relieve his mother. He had been called to the ministry but felt he could not follow it as long as his father needed his care; nor did he feel free to marry.

My father and Orin Winslow were good friends. At family worship my father usually added to his prayer: "And Lord, heal Brother Winslow." I heard it so many times as a child that I too incorporated it in my prayers.

One day at family worship the Winslows were reading Job 5. When they came to verse 26, "Thou shalt come to thy grave in a full age, like as a shock of corn cometh in his season," faith sprang up in his heart and gripped God's promise, and he was healed. "I went into his room in the morning to see how he was," Harold said, "and Father was up and out. He even went deer hunting with us boys."

The summer of 1926, when LeRoy and I represented Greenville College at Pleasantville Camp, we talked with Harold about going to Greenville. He decided to go. When I returned to campus that fall President Marston asked me, "Knowing Harold Winslow, do you think he would be good as a proctor for the men?"

"I think so," I replied. I had met him just once, and admired his princely ways, fine stature, and solid faith in Christ. The yearbook, *Vista*, described him: "Sturdy as an oak on a mountaintop."

During my first year teaching at Spring Arbor, the new Greenville *Vista* came. On a back page I saw an excellent picture of Harold at his desk in the proctor's office. I found myself often looking at it. One day I pressed a beautiful yellow rose at that place. When I went to Greenville for commencement, Harold talked to me in the hall while we waited for lunch. He seemed very gentlemanly.

Monday afternoon of commencement Harold left to travel for the college during the summer. That fall he entered Biblical Seminary in New York. He was given Greenville's first scholarship to the seminary -- two thousand dollars.

I took a religious psychology class that summer and the professor asked for my definition of sin. I gave Wesley's -- a willful transgression of God's law. He replied, "Sin is not a thing!" I said there is also inbred, inherited sin. I knew from personal experience that God had saved me from my sins, and I was just as sure that He later cleansed me from inbred sin. It was at the Mill Hall camp meeting when I hastened to the altar expecting to pray for greater power in my life and to be filled with the Holy Spirit. But the Lord reminded me of traits of character I had not been aware of. In response to his gentle but definite probing I said "yes." I neither cried nor shouted, but I felt wonderfully *clean*. Great peace flooded my soul. The Lord cleansed my heart and filled me with the Holy Spirit and I knew it.

Later that summer I went to YPMS conference in Pennsylvania. I thought, *Harold is not far away. If he cares he will try to attend, for a time at least.* But he did not, so I told myself that he did not care. After camp I visited Ernest and Josephine in the Catskills. I spoke at their church Sunday night on Abraham offering up Isaac. It *burned* in my heart. Just as I was going to church, Josephine's father said, "Did you know Harold Winslow is going to be married?" And he named the girl. I turned cold. I gave my message, and God surely helped me. I felt I really was offering up my Isaac that night.

At the close of summer a scenic card came from Harold! I sent a card in return, so excited I made a blot of ink on it, and my father teased me. Later I received a letter from Harold, asking if I would correspond with him. I learned afterwards that he wrote it two weeks before but hesitated to send it. He highly esteemed LeRoy and did not want to be in too big a hurry. Also he feared I might turn him down. He prayed much about it, and the Lord told him to be patient.

My four years at Spring Arbor Junior College were crowded with busy teaching and many interests. During summer vacations I did children's work at Manton and Detroit camp meetings (Bishop Dale Cryderman was a little boy in my Detroit camp DVBS). Some of the boys started their own prayer meeting. They took tabernacle side curtains that were not being used and made a place to pray.

How pleasing – or hurting – letters can be! A friend wrote that a girl whom Harold dated in college had gone to visit Biblical Seminary. About that time I received a letter from Harold suggesting that we had better terminate our friendship. My heart felt like stone. I went to the church and there, alone in the prayer room, wept and prayed in agony. Was this God's will? I truly wanted only his will. I tarried in prayer and tears until dusk.

Suddenly I felt inspired with the thought, *call him.* I had never done such a thing. I got him on the phone. "Hello, sweetheart," he said. "It is good to hear your voice." How wonderful that sounded to me. In his next letter he explained that he thought I wanted to quit writing because my letters were coming irregularly. So he was trying to make it easier for me, but had decided that if I turned him down, he would never marry. The letters kept coming, and I numbered them – 386!

One night Harold and I made a covenant of our love with one another and with God that if he would open our way, we would go to the mission field. Harold had been called early to the ministry and while in seminary received his missionary call. It all seemed like a miracle. Our wedding was in Spring Arbor on August 16, 1932. Harold's twin was best man, and my sister Myra was my maid of honor. Dr. Smith gave me away at the lovely rose arbor where Bishop Pearce married us.

We honeymooned in Indiana. The second day we went to Winona Lake (this was before our publishing house moved there). One evening out on the lake I played my auto harp and sang. Harold liked this love song my uncle Will Van Valin taught me when he came back from Alaska:

When the rose of today has faded away, and the years leave their trace on your brow, in your heart fond and true, love will always be new, like the love I bear you now. When your hair turns to gray, I will think of the day, when you were my own village queen. You'll be nearer to me, and dearer you'll be, when you're five times sweet sixteen.

V. Chalices of Gold

The month Harold graduated from seminary, Greenville College wired him to come to his alma mater to teach. We went to Chicago to offer ourselves to the Missionary Board for service, but they had a heavy debt and could not send us. So we went to Greenville and rented four rooms on Spruce Street. Later we rented the Gaddis house on North Elm. We got along on simple things, for we wanted to be free if the way opened to go to the mission field.

Harold loved to teach. He taught every book in the Bible in a three-year cycle. He also taught Greek exegesis, church history, and world missions, and studied Hebrew. When Grace Murray, a nurse from China, passed away, we stood by her casket at Donnell Home, and God spoke to us. If we could fill a little of the gap she left, we were willing. China was beginning to fill our horizon.

Word came that the Missionary Board was appointing missionaries, two each to the Dominican Republic, India, and China. One noon Harold came home and said, "Sweetheart, don't get lunch today. Let's pray this through."

When we finally arose from our knees, I said, "Harold, I believe we are going to China as much as if we were on our way." A letter soon came asking us to go to the *Dominican Republic!* Harold wrote in reply, "I am willing to go anywhere, but unless the Lord makes me to feel otherwise than I do now, I feel it will have to be China."

In Harold's fourth year of teaching a letter came stating that Missionary Secretary Harry F. Johnson was coming to Greenville and wished to interview us. Brother Johnson came down with malaria and had to interview us from the president's bedroom. He asked us to meet the Board in May. When he introduced us to the Commission on Missions he said, "These are *called ones.*"

Soon we were busy packing. Our little son, Paul, was 14 months old, and he was such a joy to us. He took his first steps before we left. One Sunday Dr. Marston took him in his arms as we stood by the altar in the Greenville Church and beautifully dedicated our child to the Lord.

We were commissioned by Secretary Harry F. Johnson at Oil City Conference held at New Castle, Pennsylvania. He had us kneel at the altar as he laid his hands on our heads. What a precious prayer he prayed! Then we left for faraway China, by way of Seattle.

It was an unusual privilege to call on the Reverend Ernest F. Ward before we sailed. Our veteran missionary to India, he seemed like a patriarch of faith, with his hoary head and white beard. God seemed very near as he prayed.

A telegram arrived from the Missionary Board: "Don't go. Too dangerous." Mattie Peterson, returning to China on the same ship, asked Harold, "Are you afraid?"

"No," he replied. I was glad she did not ask me.

"What do you say we send a telegram saying, 'May we?'" Mattie suggested. We did, and the Board approved.

The day came for us to leave on the *Hikawa Maru*. There were about 150 friends on shore to see us off. Friends on shore threw rolls of colorful streamers to us. What a sight — all colors of the rainbow tying us to the homeland. As our ship began to gently move, the crowd on the wharf began to sing: "Jesus never fails, Jesus never fails, Heaven and earth may pass away, but Jesus never fails."

A tiny tugboat was leading our great ocean liner out of the sound to the Pacific Ocean. One, then another streamer broke, and finally the last one snapped. There was a tug at my heart and a lump in my throat and yet a great happiness that at last we were on our way to China, where God had called us. The tears poured down my cheeks, and I praised the Lord as I stood there alone on the deck. The chalices of God's will were now opening.

Harold took little Paul for a ride around the long deck in the little red wagon given to him by the Junior Missionary Society at Greenville.

VI. China - Center of Our Universe

Our ship began to rock on the waves. Water leaped and splashed furiously as high as the second deck. We nearly rolled out of bed. "Two typhoons are going to meet," Captain told Miss Peterson, "but I will lower the speed of the vessel and take it as easily as I can."

"There are 19 missionaries on board," Miss Peterson told him, "and we will pray." The wind blew fiercely. Waves mounted higher and higher. There was little sleep. Even to stay on the bunk was a feat.

After a couple days of this, one morning as I was making the bed, Harold came in. "Come to the deck, Carolyn," he said with excitement. "I'll take Paul." I looked out the porthole and saw that the storm had ended. The sea was calm like glass. Waves were gone except those in the frothy wake of the ship. We arrived in Yokohama Harbor the night *before* we were due!

We went by train to Osaka and were welcomed by Ruth Mylander of the Nipponbashi Church. She showed us the compound, we visited the seminary, and we saw kindergarten children put their wooden clogs neatly in rows as they came in from play. When a faculty member invited us home for supper, we sat on cushions on a matted floor. "I want to show you our garden," said the host, and slid back the paper doors. Before I knew it, curious little Paul punched his boyish finger through the paper door. I was very embarrassed!

We then took ship at Kobe for China. Paul seemed very quiet. I didn't think he was feeling well, so we put him down on his bunk. Soon I heard a gurgle, his eyes rolled back in his head, and he was in convulsions. I ran for the ship doctor or nurse. Both were ashore. Miss Peterson's room was locked. Back at the cabin, I dropped on my knees. *Will we have to bury our boy at sea before reaching China?* I wondered. What a price!

But our calling stood. In my broken heart I told the Lord, "Even if it costs this, we are sure of our call to China."

Harold went to the cabin medicine cabinet and took out a bottle. "I went to the drugstore before we left the States and asked what would be good for this and that," he said. Then thoughtfully, "I don't think this will hurt him." And he gave Paul some worm medicine. That evening as I held Paul in my arms, he screamed with spasms of pain and dug his little fingers into my arm until I could hardly stand it. But we kept praying. Gradually he recovered.

Because of the "Shanghai Incident" which took place during our three weeks at sea, we did not know where we could land. A few minutes after eight o'clock one morning we pulled into Shanghai Harbor between warships of different nations. Workmen on the wharf were fascinated by Paul's little red wagon.

We took a taxi to the China Inland Mission guest house, where my eyes fell on a wall motto: "And Jesus himself drew near, and went with them" (Luke 24:15). How precious those words were that day!

In two days we took the new Green Express — just brought from Belgium. At stops, vendors called their wares at our train windows. On shallow, big boxes slung from their necks I saw boiled eggs, fruit, and Chinese pastries. I was thankful I had Pablum and canned milk for Paul. After two days we reached Kaifeng, capital of Honan Province, where our headquarters were located. Thirteen missionaries came to meet us that night. Oh, what joy there was!

We all gathered at the home of James Taylor, Sr., and they soon had some delicious hot chocolate for us. What a happy missionary family we all were — the Taylors, Silvas, Greens, Bernice Wood, Mattie Peterson, Bessie and Pearl Reid, Brother Ashcraft, Kate Leininger, and Brother I. S. W. Ryding. They welcomed us with warm open hearts.

We were to stay in the "cottage," robbed by bandits only two weeks before. They took Miss Wood's clothing, and articles were strewn all the way to the southern end of the city. Alice Taylor thoughtfully placed a hot water bottle in each of our single beds. Mine leaked! I crawled in with my husband.

A teacher was secured for us to begin language school. Then, early in January 1937, we went to Peking for language study at the College of Chinese Studies. We took with us our amah, Chia Ta Sao, to watch little Paul while we were in class. He loved to play in the snow on the campus. Chai Ta Sao had been demon possessed, but Alice Taylor brought her to the Lord. She was a lovely amah. How she adored Paul, and he just loved her.

Not a word of English was allowed in our classroom. The fascinating language was spoken in tones. We had inspiring lectures on Chinese history and culture. We were excited to learn that China was a civilized nation in the time of King David and even back to Abraham's day. We were warned that if we found Chinese characters hanging in the air, we were studying too hard. One day I saw them right above our bed.

After I learned to ride a bicycle on the school tennis courts, Harold and I rode 10 miles out of Peking to the Altar of Heaven. Made of beautiful white marble, it is in tiers, but the top is in circles. The very center is believed to be the center of the universe. Indeed, when you say "China" you say "Chung Kuo" (Middle Kingdom or Middle Country). Harold and I stood on the center of the universe! The curious Whispering Wall was such a perfect circle that Harold, on one far side, spoke in a whisper very quietly, "Sweetheart," and I heard him perfectly.

We also rode our bicycles to the British Embassy Sunday afternoons to attend Christian services. Harold conducted an English Bible class at National University. I joined the Apollo Club at Peking Union Medical College and rode my bicycle there each Wednesday evening.

A missionary doctor at school warned us to lie down after lunch, in the heat of the day. "The difference between the missionaries who have to go home and those who stay," he asserted, "is decided by those who rest after lunch and those who don't." One recess we went to our room and lay down for a few minutes. When time came to go back to class, we just could not get up. We did not hurt anywhere, not even a headache, but our strength was gone. We missed the next class.

One day Harold suggested, "Let's go out on the roof." It was the Chinese New Year and people were changing their kitchen gods. Looking down into the neighbor's courtyard, we saw the family gathered to burn the paper god. He had honey on his lips, so he would report only the good things about the household in the next world.

VII. War Clouds

The mission sent us to Kikungshan (Rooster Crest Mountain) for the summer to escape severe heat on the plains. Our mission had six cottages there in the lovely mountains. There were 412 missionaries and children of different denominations in Kikungshan that summer. We had services in a church at the top of the hill.

One Sunday morning, July 4, 1937, as we approached the church, we saw a momentous sign on the outside bulletin board stating that the Sino-Japanese War had broken out. All British subjects were ordered to evacuate, and Americans were advised to do so.

A Lutheran missionary stepped to the platform. "Let us sing *A Mighty Fortress Is Our God*," he said. What a hymn! And for such a time as this. "A bulwark never failing." Then we came to "Let goods and kindred go, This mortal life also; The body they may kill; God's truth abideth still; His kingdom is forever." Oh, how relevant those words were, and how deeply we felt them.

The Chinese government subsidized a train to evacuate foreigners from Kikungshan. It was to leave from Hsin Tien, five miles down the mountain, at seven o'clock in the morning. I was expecting little Harry in three months. "If you stay, you will not have a doctor or nurse, foreign or Chinese," I was told.

While on our knees for evening prayers the Lord gave me Isaiah 52:12, "For ye shall not go out with haste, nor go by flight; for the Lord will go before you; and the God of Israel will be your rear guard." When we rose from our knees, I said, "Harold, I believe we should stay." The Lord directed him likewise. Of the 412 missionaries, only 16 of us stayed. It seemed foolhardy because the Chinese troops had retreated, Japanese troops had not yet come, and bandits were active in the area.

Before the American school evacuated, the staff lent me a sterilizer and a hospital bed. Dr. Green gave me hospital sterile pads. Without my knowledge, Dr. Mary Taylor from England received permission from her board to stay until Harry was born. Miss Hunt, a missionary from Australia, and Mrs. Danielson, a nurse from Norway, also got permission. Think of it – a doctor and two nurses! Harry was born March 31. The enemy troops had not yet come.

We had planned to be in the mountains three months, but the mission decided we should stay a year and a half and study, and not come into the combat area. It was very cold. We did not have enough bedding. Harold took a severe cold that developed into pneumonia. I made a tent of newspapers and improvised a way for him to breathe easier. He recovered.

Brother Ashcraft and Harold started an English Bible class at the Ashcraft house for students from the University of Kaifeng who were trekking west from the enemy, but who tarried for a time in Kikungshan. One of the faculty, Professor Ho, came and taught us in the language until he moved farther west. While with us, he tenderly held our baby in his arms and named him Han-Fu, Han for China and Fu for resurrection as he was born about Easter time. Professor Ho said reverently, "May the Lord use this child to bring about a revival in China." Today Harry is a missionary to the Chinese.

One day a group of 60 were at our house when we heard the drone of enemy bombers coming. We all ran out into the yard and hid under trees. President Chiang Kai-shek had rented two of our Free Methodist cottages. The United States consul had ordered us to have American flags painted on our roofs. Would the Japanese airmen know? The planes went over so low we could see the emblem of Japan on the wings. They roared on and dropped their bombs on a fuel dump at Hsin Tien, and we saw it burning all day.

We enjoyed our stay in the mountains. I shall not forget the motto on the wall at Ashcrafts: "He is silently planning for thee in love."

VIII. Moving To Kihsien

We received our first appointment. It was to Kihsien, within enemy lines 35 miles southeast of our mission headquarters in Kaifeng. Harold walked the five miles down the steep mountain, and I rode in a bamboo chair on poles on coolies' shoulders with six-month-old Harry in a basket on my lap. Chai Ta Sao, our amah, rode with Paul in another chair.

Arriving in Hsin Tien, Harold bought our railroad tickets to Hankow, where I had a dental appointment to repair a broken molar. "There may not be a train," the ticket agent said after Harold bought the tickets. "The tracks have been torn up, up north." We waited five hours, then heard a train whistle. The tracks had been repaired. It was a troop train. Soldiers were being rushed to defend Hankow, the "Chicago of China" and the military capital. We arrived in Hankow safely, and after lunch I went to see the dentist. I was only five minutes late for my appointment.

We took a train north to Chengchow. Little did we know those tracks would be torn up in just two weeks, not to be re-laid for seven years. That Thursday of arrival was a cloudy day, and we were glad, for the bombers might not come, as was their habit. Harold applied for a pass to cross the "lines" -- which was the Yellow River.

"We cannot give a pass," said the official. "There are too many spies."

"Well," said Harold, "we will go up to Jungtseh and help Edith Frances Jones." We went, and on Sunday we were taking an afternoon nap when there was a rap at the door.

"Are the Winslows here?" asked a Red Cross nurse. "More than two tons of Red Cross medicines have come. There is no one to take them over the enemy lines. If the Winslows will take them, they will be given a pass." How God makes ways!

The next morning we were at the Baptist Hospital compound ready to start out in their ambulance. We waited five hours, then the driver came. We got almost halfway to the river when he announced, "The sand is so deep I will not have enough gas to get back if I go farther."

Harold walked to a village, and at long last came back, bringing a donkey and a cart pulled by three cows. Chai Ta Sao and I got up in the cart with Paul and baby Harry, and we went at the rate of three miles an hour. Harold rode the donkey, poor thing, for Harold was six feet tall, and his feet nearly scraped the ground. We spent that night in a bandit village, and foreigners would bring good ransom money (Missionary Ryding had been in their hands for 12 days).

Dikes of the Yellow River were broken to forestall the advance of Japanese troops, and it was now four rivers. The next morning we had to cross the first river with the help of farmers turned boatmen, standing and poling the flat-bottom boats.

The second night we got to a village by the second river. It was a bandit village. "You stay with your wife," Brother Ashcraft said to my husband. "I will sleep by the riverbank with the baggage." We slept on a dirt floor. I was so tired that I slept soundly, but the next morning my hips were sore.

After we got over the fourth river, Harold got 14 carts, planning to thus finish the journey. "Oh, no you won't!" a guide said. He had gone ahead and reported that the enemy had reinforced the city with fresh troops. "They will shoot at anything that moves."

"Well," Harold said, "we will stay here by the river for the night."

"Oh, no you won't!" the guide said again. "Missionaries were robbed here two weeks ago." Harold consulted with the drivers. If he gave them more money, they were willing to go. Those 14 wooden carts had solid wooden wheels. What a noise they made! We pulled into the China Inland Mission hospital compound just outside the city of Kaifeng about eleven o'clock that night. I was never so tired, so hungry, nor so happy!

The next day we took rickshas to Kihsien, our appointment just 35 miles away. When we got there that evening after dark, to our surprise there was a mile of water around the city. Japanese troops had ordered everyone to leave, then broke the city dike to let water wipe out the city. Later the Chinese got into boats, went in and retook the city.

When we were halfway across the water, I said, "Oh, listen, Harold, there is singing." The Christians had gathered at an elevated place inside the 40-foot wall and were singing hymns to welcome us. When I got out of the boat I heard, "Hello, Carolyn." There was Bessie Reid, my college mate. She had come to hold a revival at Kihsien.

IX. The Siege

Rumors came that enemy troops were getting closer and would cross the bridge. It was winter and snow was on the ground. I was bathing nine-month-old Harry in our upstairs bedroom, for the stovepipe came up and had what we call a drum, a wider space, so the room was fairly comfortable.

Harry had a new tooth! When Harold came through the door he admired the tooth and then calmly said, "I was over at the police office. While we were drinking tea an officer came in and announced, 'The Japanese have crossed the bridge.'"

"What shall we do?" I asked.

Harold said, "I think we should take the children's beds downstairs." So he did, and put them in the dining room. Before long I heard the first exploding shells, followed by constant fire from machine guns. Suddenly it seemed one side of our living room would surely burst. That was the story for hours. By one o'clock things had died down, and I needed to go outside. On the way a bullet whizzed by my ear, and I dashed back to the house.

Harold read Psalm 91 for family worship: "He that dwelleth in the secret place of the Most High shall abide under the shadow of the Almighty. I will say of the Lord, He is my refuge and my fortress: my God; in him will I trust." Before he got to the third verse, a shell came through the children's bedroom window upstairs, went through the floor, made a big hole, and hit about two inches above a mirror in the room adjoining where we were sitting. I found the shrapnel under my desk.

That day and night more than 5,000 Chinese refugees fled to our church compound where we lived and to our hospital compound two blocks away. Our church, schoolrooms, Sunday school rooms, and even our woodshed were jammed beyond capacity. America was not yet in the war, and the troops promised not to molest Americans, but a couple in language school with us were shot and thrown into a well.

"I am going to the 'front,'" Harold said, "and be there when the troops arrive." I was alone with the children when I heard soldiers yelling at the refugees on our porch. Soon there was a terrific pounding at my front door, so demanding that I knew they would break the door in, or fire. Two soldiers were peering in with their hands at the edge of their helmets.

I opened the first door — and the second. "Wo men yao kan kan!" They wanted to search.

I answered courteously, "Pu hsing" (not proper, must not).

They answered roughly, "Wei shen ma pu hsing?" and, grabbing the gun with the bayonet, pushed it to my face until it nearly touched my nose. What else could I do but let them in? As I turned the doorknob to the living room door, I whispered with trembling breath, "Dear Jesus, help me!" Three-year-old Paul turned white as a sheet and slid behind the studio couch.

I had not seen my husband since before daylight. I learned later they tried to kill him at the front gate. At this very moment the door opened, and in he came. He stood beside me -- so big and tall -- and said, "This is my wife." Paul, hearing his daddy's voice, peeked out from behind the studio couch. Harold said, "That is my child. We are all Americans." The soldiers turned and went out the door.

One day during the siege of Kihsien, Mrs. Liu was sitting on a wooden platform in the main temple building near our house. A shell ripped out the side of the building, and shrapnel went through her head. Mr. Liu, one of our grade school teachers, got a cart and pulled his wife 35 miles to Kaifeng only to find that the missionary doctor had gone on furlough. The nurses were afraid to operate without the doctor, but they took x rays and located the steel in her brain. They wrapped her head with gauze and Mr. Liu pulled her all the way back home on the cart. He then prayed, "Dear Jesus, take the shrapnel out of my wife's head." They found the twisted steel outside her head, inside the gauze. I feared the experience might affect her mentally, but she was all right.

The real strain, though, began when the city of Kihsien was taken the first time, before we lived there. Government officials brought large bags of relief money and put them down in Miss Leininger's living room, saying, "Here, take this," and then they fled for their lives. She took bricks out of the wall in the upstairs hallway, put the money in, and bricked it up again. At the hospital Geneva Sayre dropped "bricks" of money down a chimney on a string.

Was God planning for us about this money trust? The troops would not allow Chinese money used in the city. But outside the city, our pastors in the country dare not have Japanese money. So we took this relief money in money belts, in shoes, and the like, and got it out of the city to pay our pastors. We even bored holes in the legs of the mission cart and stuffed money in there. We still kept our mission money in the bank at Shanghai to pay back when the war would end. How little we knew it would drag on for eight years!

"Carolyn, I think we should invite the Japanese army general to our house for supper some night," Harold suggested one day. I fairly gasped. Would we be considered "pro" by the Chinese? But I understood Harold's reasoning. Our city had been captured, and the weeks and months were going by. Would there be something we could do to bring Christ to those ruling over us?

So one evening the general came with his bodyguard. Harold presented him with a leather Japanese Bible, and he seemed pleased. While we were eating, a Japanese officer appeared in the dining room doorway and briskly asked if he could play the piano. My heart sank. We were at war, and if the Chinese would see an enemy soldier playing our piano we might be in danger as possible spies. The enemy had asked us to give money to help restore Buddhist temple worship, and we had refused. They had asked that our students march in a Buddhist parade, and we declined. Harold was right -- to this we could say yes, even if it was a personal risk.

The little officer played, oh, so loud! He fairly *pounded* the piano. And it was his national anthem. He appeared in the doorway again, politely thanked us, and was gone. Not long after this, soldiers made old Mr. and Mrs. Yang leave their parsonage and stay in the church where it was cold and they had no blankets. The Japanese billeted their soldiers in the parsonage. Word came to us, and Harold rode his bicycle way out there to see what he could do. When he arrived, whom should he meet on the street but the officer who played the piano! "How do you do, Mr. Winslow," he said. "Is there something I can do for you?"

"Yes, there is," and Harold explained the situation.

"Sit down here. I will be back," the officer said. Off he went, and when he came back he promised, "by Wednesday they will be gone." And they were. The next time I saw Mr. Yang he was making arrangements to buy bricks to enlarge his church. How glad I am that we let the sprightly little officer play the piano!

I played and sang hymns for Old Blind Sung, who lived next to us at Kihsien. Old? Blind? Yes, but day after day he took a bamboo stool, a Chinese Bible and his walking stick, and off he went to one of the gates of the city. He sat down on his stool, opened his Bible to choice words that, no doubt, another had marked for him, and listened attentively for the sound of passersby.

"Lai, lai" (Come, come), he would call. When a crowd gathered around he said, "Please read," and then he witnessed for Jesus. Off to another gate the next day, he did the same thing, and he even worked his way through the crowds to another village.

I felt that Old Blind Sung helped in getting our attendance. We often had more than 1,000 in Sunday school and many more for worship service. More than 2,500 attended our last Christmas service in Kihsien.

We started a Junior Missionary Society. The children wanted to meet *every* Sunday, and 225 came! One Sunday afternoon Chi Pei-wen had charge of the service. She told a moving story of how she lost one hand, then exhorted, "You have two hands. Have you given them to Jesus?" Young people filled the altar. What a service followed, and such precious testimonies! Was God preparing them for something in the unknown future?

"Carolyn, what do you say we bike out to the Ti Tzu (outer city wall)?" Harold suggested one Saturday. When we reached there, he helped me to the top of the hard mud wall. What did we see? We were in the great wheat belt, and as far as eye could see, there were ripened fields, just bending with the golden grain.

"This makes me think of China," Harold said with deep emotion. "So white to harvest and not enough reapers!"

X. Hills and Valleys

In 1940 the mission asked us to transfer from Kihsien to the headquarters station at Kaifeng. Chinese men brought our piano on poles on their shoulders — 35 miles in one day! When I opened it up and played for the men, they acted like delighted children. Harold paid them well, and they went away happy.

During this time both boys were seriously ill. Harold too, was ill. A doctor thought it was Harold's heart which was causing the illness. We went to Peking but had to wait for two weeks before we could get a hospital bed for him. He entered Peking Union Medical College Hospital, the best in China. They could not diagnose his case.

Harold seemed to get worse. He could not speak above a whisper. One day a doctor said gravely, "Mrs. Winslow, you must get your husband to the States if he is to live."

But Harold had said in a weak whisper, "I don't want to go home; I'm afraid I can't get back." Must I go against his wishes? If God should heal him, we could stay. If he should die, I would feel responsible for not obeying the doctor. I really sobbed out my prayer. Then Sister Pearl Schaffer prayed. While she was praying, there was a gentle rap at the door. There was a short message from Harold scrawled in weak handwriting. *He* had made the decision to return to the States. Guidance now was clear.

I learned that a riot was planned by the military, so I packed as quickly as I could with the help of the students. On Wednesday I met Harold at the train station. He had sat up only 15 minutes before he was taken from the hospital to the train. We had to leave nearly everything behind to travel on the evacuation boat.

It was a three weeks' journey across the ocean. Harold sat up for meals four times on that voyage. When our ship arrived in San Francisco we were welcomed home by former Missionary Secretary W. B. Olmstead. It was quite an adjustment to be in America. Going over the brilliantly lighted Oakland Bay Bridge, I could not but think of the dark streets of our Chinese cities and only the tiny, smoked lights under our rickshas. I brushed some tears away. The spiritual darkness of the Chinese weighed heavily on my heart.

Harold entered a special hospital in Pittsburgh, but they could not diagnose his case. He soon improved, and the doctor dismissed him. He gained weight, and the color came back to his cheeks. I was sent to the west coast on deputation work. My next assignment was Mansfield, Ohio. Saturday night on the campground I felt such a burden for the service that I prayed almost all night until dawn. I then fell asleep and was wakened by the singing in the dining room below me at breakfast time. Someone came later and told me that Missionary Secretary Harry F. Johnson had passed away. How could I ever speak in that service? World War II was on. I began: "Last night one of the stars in God's 'Service Flag' turned gold."

After a time, a telegram summoned Harold to a Board of Administration meeting. While there, he was elected general missionary secretary. This moved us from Pennsylvania to Winona Lake, Indiana. Once, when Harold was planning to go to Minnesota on missions business I asked, "Will you be near Rochester?"

"Not far away," he replied.

"Why not go to Mayo Clinic? Maybe they can find out the reason for your backaches." He did. They found that he had tuberculosis of the spine. Mayo doctors took about seven inches of bone from Harold's leg and grafted it to his spine, but it did not heal. He decided to resign his position. Dr. Byron S. Lamson, pastor at Greenville College Church, was chosen to take Harold's place. He had no mission field experience, but he had a missionary heart and quickly fitted into the position.

Gradually Harold became worse and had to be hospitalized again. Was my dear Harold leaving me? It was a gray, cold, rainy day.

Could I go on? Could I bring up our boys, then six and eight, without my precious companion? I relied and rested on his judgment.

The Lord gave me a verse: "The meek will he guide in *judgment:* and the meek *will* he teach his way." I prayed that I might qualify for that wonderful promise.

Harold was taken to a larger hospital in another city. He was fed intravenously, and surprisingly, he was able to take food. Sunday evening I was feeding him when suddenly he looked up and, oh, the consciousness of God's presence in that room! I burst into tears and, gently stroking his arm, could only say, "Precious Jesus! Precious Jesus!" I have wondered if he saw Jesus or heard the angels sing.

The next morning after Harold went to be with his loving Lord, Brother Birney Gaddis drove me home. Lines from the poem I had memorized years before rang in my heart:

And, if through patient toil, we reach the land,
Where tired feet, with sandals loosed, may rest,
When we shall clearly see and understand,
I think that we shall say, "God knew the best!"

On one occasion when we were in China we visited a rug factory in Peking. Young people sat on backless benches, tier upon tier, making exquisite Chinese rugs. Harold and I were amazed. The workers saw only the wrong side of those beautiful rugs. They merely used the colors as directed, the somber ones as well as the more delightful ones.

So it is with God's plan for our lives. We let him choose and blend the colors for his tapestry, for he knows best.

Section 3 – God's Sheaves

"In the morning sow thy seed, and in the evening withhold not thine hand: for thou knowest not whether shall prosper, either this or that, or whether they both shall be alike good."
— Ecclesiastes 11:6

XI. In Myriad Ways

The boys and I continued to live in Winona Lake. My right leg began to ache and the doctor diagnosed it as phlebitis. I was in bed for a month and could not step on my foot. Then I was in a Detroit hospital for a time and finally had to do my work by sliding around in a kitchen chair. Paul and Harry took an interest in helping me. They learned to bake desserts, make casseroles, and were good at helping with the housework, but doing dishes — that was not a favorite.

I tried to make the home a cheery place for the boys. I didn't want them to be brought up in sadness. Sometimes we took our lunches in the park and had fun eating and watching the sunset on the lake. Or I took a book and read while they swam in the lake or leaped off the diving board.

My health, however, began to fail, and because of nervous exhaustion I had to rest for almost two years. In doing so my phlebitis cleared up, and I became strong and well again.

[Note: These two years were among the hardest in her life, but she leaves them out. She was admitted to the psychiatric center at Johns Hopkins University for intensive counseling and shock treatments. Her anxiety became so intense she despaired of life itself. Only by the grace of God through medical skill and the loving care of close friend Hattie Yale was she brought back to full strength and ministry.]

One night at church I saw movies of Taiwan and the flag of Free China waving in the breeze. The bamboo curtain had come down on the mainland and all our missionaries had to leave. Was there now a place to work with our dear Chinese in Taiwan? I was deeply moved and went home to pray.

I was asked by the Missionary Board to take a circuit. I did so, fearfully, but God led. We went to Elkhart, Indiana. It was excellent experience for me to prepare the weekly bulletin, for prayer meeting, and the messages for two services on Sunday. Each morning saw me in my study. After working on my messages I studied Chinese, trying to be ready if the way opened to return. At year's end I attended an all-night Watch Service in Winona Lake. I remember testifying and feeling such peace. The next morning I got word by telephone that I had been appointed to Taiwan!

I went in the kitchen, burst into tears, and told the boys of my appointment. They helped me pack. At noon we were so tired we took a mattress and laid it down in the aisle of the church to rest. At that moment a telephone call came.

"Could you leave by the second of June?" asked Missionary Secretary Lamson. In just a few days? I wondered, *could we?* "There is a ship sailing then. This ship has reservations for three."

How we hurried! A train trip to San Francisco and then off to

Taiwan by ship. It was a lovely voyage until one night the ship's boiler blew up and great flames burst into the inky sky. In time the boiler was fixed and we limped along, so disabled that we could not go into Manila Harbor. We finished the trip in small boats. Another ship took us to Taiwan, up past the rugged, rocky east coast to the Keelung port. As the sun was setting, little Chinese sampans with their tiny lights glided about the water like fairies.

When we went ashore and waited to have our passports checked, it seemed wonderful to see Chinese faces. They were my people. I had come home after an absence of 13 years.

XII. God's Sheaves

We lived with Geneva Sayre and Kate Leininger, our first missionaries to Taiwan, for about six months. One day Harry took his accordion outside the fence and began to play. Soon a crowd of children gathered. Wilson Wu was at our house, and he went out and preached to the children. This experience brought joy to Harry.

"At Pingtung," Miss Sayre told me, "we have a street chapel, and I wish you would take my English Bible class there." So I did, and soon we moved there. As I waited for my bus, the children crowded around and asked, "Yao chang ko" (sing). I sang *Jesus Loves Me*. They always watched for me to come.

After an English class in Pingtung, as I waited for my bus, an Air Force officer came up and asked, "Would you tell me how to become a Christian?" I gave him a couple verses such as John 1:12 and I John 1:9, and as the bus came around the corner I quickly taught him a prayer asking forgiveness.

Two weeks later I saw him again and asked, "How are you?"

"I have peace," he replied.

"Where did you get it?"

"In my room." He had sincerely prayed that prayer, and God had saved him. He asked prayer for his roommate, Captain Lai, who also found the Lord and became pastor of a Chinese church in Singapore with 500 members.

When I was appointed to Pingtung I was apprehensive because there was a mile-long bridge, and I was near a big Air Force base. The American consul ordered that we have a bag packed ready to leave on 15 minutes' notice. We were only 100 miles from the mainland of Red China, and they were determined to "liberate" Taiwan.

One afternoon a colonel's wife, Mrs. Wu, came in and sobbed, "they have taken my husband and put him on a train. He didn't have time to take his pajamas or toothbrush or anything."

It happened this way. A soldier who had planned to place a bomb under the mile-long bridge to detonate when the president crossed became frightened and divulged the plan to government headquarters at Taipei. Colonel Wu was held because the soldier was in his detachment.

On a previous Sunday I had presented Christ to the colonel and his wife, but he replied, "I'm so *busy*, I can't go to church. I have 2,000 men under me." But now he was detained for a year and had lots of time. He read and reread the Testament I gave him and finally gave his heart to the Lord. The seed of God's Word had not been sown in vain.

Paul returned to the States for college, and Harry went to Morrison Academy at Taichung for three years. He came home one weekend each month. His Air Force friends came to see him. Harry played the accordion, I played the organ, and we all sang.

James and Alice Taylor joined us in 1953, and he became our superintendent and also started our Bible school in Kaohsiung. He came to Pingtung once a week for Bible study. Our street chapel could nicely seat 16, I was told, but 54 Air Force men jammed in for English Bible class. When we held DVBS, 128 children came. We had to have classes at our outside entrance, and even at the neighbor's place, across the road.

We all agreed that we must have a new church. It was a happy day when we dedicated it in 1955. Shortly after, we had our first wedding. We used heaps of red poinsettias for decoration. You see, in China red is the symbol of love.

It came time for furlough. Since I was just about halfway around the world, I planned to go home by way of India, Egypt, Lebanon, Israel, and Europe. My brother Francis met me in New York City. It was great to be in America – especially to see my two boys, many relatives and friends. I attended commencement at Roberts Wesleyan College and Greenville College. The year of furlough sped by quickly because I was occupied with deputation. Before I realized it, it was time to return to Taiwan.

Not long after my return, Missionary Secretary Lamson was scheduled to visit. This was an *event*. After breakfast at Kiehn's in Taipei we went to President Chiang Kai-shek's church for the Good Friday service and were ushered in by General Wang. President Chiang Kai-shek spoke, and after a solo, Madame went to the pulpit. After about two sentences, it happened. James Taylor, Sr.'s chair collapsed. James, Jr. tried to help his father up, but he swung his hand, Chinese fashion, meaning "no." He did not want to make further disturbance, so he continued to sit on the damaged chair and hung on to the one in front of him. After the service a Presbyterian missionary friend addressed Brother Taylor in his southern drawl, "Brotha Tayla, you are the *only* one God could trust with such an accident."

XIII. New Horizons

In Pingtung, I discovered that mothers, though Buddhist, were happy to have someone pray for their little ones. The interest grew, and in a few years we had 400 children on our local Cradle Roll. On Mother's Day we had Cradle Roll graduation. Each little graduate received a certificate, flowers, and a gift, and each mother received flowers. How that plan did feed our Sunday school! We were always welcome in the homes, and the parents accepted tracts, Gospels, and pastoral calls.

The young people's work grew by leaps and bounds. We felt the need for a youth camp as well as local meetings. The first camp was held in a school down south. One evening Brother Trachsel of the World Gospel Mission preached on Naaman. He made it so real that when Naaman came up cleansed, the whole audience spontaneously clapped heartily.

It was such a joy to work with the Chinese young people. They are the hope of China. The WMS (Women's Spread the Gospel Society) also grew rapidly. At Pingtung Mrs. Tsang, the president, was full of ideas. Each month a different committee visited the Air Force Hospital and gave out tracts and gospels. She also bought tracts and had women go with her to meet the crowds pouring from the trains in the early morning. She started a weekly Friday morning prayer meeting that met in homes and invited unsaved neighbors. This was successful.

I went through copies of the *Missionary Tidings* and typed the highlights, had them translated, mimeographed, cut up, and given to the WMS women, and they gave the "news" in the next meeting. This informed them about our mission work around the world and stimulated them to action. They sent money gifts to Egypt, India, and Africa and often prayed for those countries.

Mrs. Tsang felt we ought to have a WMS annual retreat. We started with a one-day retreat, and soon it was so successful that it became a two-day retreat. She also started a reading circle.

Paul had left for college before James and Alice Taylor arrived in

Taiwan in 1953. He had made a trip to the mountains where we had not started mountain work. "Mother," he said earnestly, "when Brother Taylor comes, *persuade* him to start mountain work." The mountain people were not Chinese but Malaysian. Alice Taylor became an ardent worker with them through an interpreter. This work grew so fast that now we have many churches and two superintendents. All churches are served by mountain tribal pastors who have attended Holy Light Theological College.

When Geneva Sayre first came to Taiwan we did not have one pastor out of Mainland China. Now we have 43 churches, and all are manned by national workers. Eight Chinese delegates came to our 1979 General Conference in Indianapolis. Holy Light Theological College has a national president, and a national makes tapes that are beamed into Mainland China. A post graduate school – China Evangelical Seminary – was started, and we, as a denomination, participate. James Taylor, Jr., has acted as president.

May the horizon stretch farther and farther.

XIV. By Love Compelled

Time sped by, and I began to plan to retire. The last time I spoke to the Pingtung WMS, I saw two stacks of cloth tied with a string on the altar as I went down the aisle. The president said, "This is cloth for the widows of Burundi. We understand you are going home by way of Africa, so we thought you could take it for us." It touched my heart deeply that our Chinese Christians had such a love for God's suffering people in faraway Africa.

Lovely farewells were planned for me. Then the Christians gathered at Kaohsiung International Terminal and prayed and with tears sent me off with their deep love.

In our day, as well as in pioneer days, the urge of the saved soul is to win the lost to Christ. What we do, may it always be by love compelled. His great love for us reminds me of a WMS meeting at Kihsien. "Today I wish to speak of the love of God," said our president, Mrs. Li. "I shall illustrate God's love with a story about my little boy.

"One day, 'Your boy is in the well!' screamed the children. I ran to the well and looked down. Sure enough, there was my little boy down in the water. I yelled for help, but there seemed to be no men nearby. So, not knowing what else to do, I jumped into the well, picked up my precious little boy and held him high above the water. He soon became so heavy that gradually my arms came down lower and lower. All the while I continued calling, 'Help me! Help me!'

"At last something was coming down toward us. Ah! It was a bucket on the end of a rope. Carefully I placed my little son in the bucket and up, up, up he went to the top of the well. He was dripping wet and scared almost to death, but he was safe. I was too big to get into the bucket, so I just stood in that cold water for hours until they found a ladder to lower down to me.

"*Now I will get out,* I thought. I grasped one rung with my hands and was about to lift my foot when I found I could not bend my knees. I had stood in that cold water too long. So I grabbed a rung with one hand, then a higher rung with the other hand. Letting go with the first hand, with my body swinging in the air, I desperately grasped a higher rung with that hand. Slowly I pulled myself up the ladder and finally reached the top. Then some people carried me to my house and laid me on my bed."

And then, rubbing her legs, she said, "Sometimes my legs still hurt me so badly that I have to lie on my bed and cannot attend services." Finally she asked, "Do you think I care? I saved my boy!"

Tears started rolling down her cheeks as she continued earnestly, "Did Jesus just jump into a well to save us? No, he shed his blood for us. He gave his *life* for us!" With outstretched hands and with deep emotion, she pled fervently with more than 300 Chinese women, "We ought to love Him!"

XV. Old Teacher Mother, We Have an *Anchor!*

The Chinese called me Wen Shih Mu, "Winslow Teacher-Mother." I feel unworthy of the title, for it is very significant. The teacher was on a high level in the social scale. Each year they celebrate Teacher's Day in September. Another title they gave me was "Mother." They wished to express not only their respect but their love. In the last few years they added still a third title — "Old" (Wen Lao Shih Mu). One need not be afraid of being old in China. It is an honorable title. God grant that I shall have the maturity, the dependability, and the wisdom that should characterize the old — strong in faith and transparent in Christian character.

One night after English Bible class, all the Chinese Air Force officers had left except Lieutenant Wang. We were sitting in the front seat chatting when down the aisle came a tall major in uniform. "Mrs.

Winslow," he asked, "can you tell me how to become a Christian?"

I told him simply and clearly, giving him just a few scriptures. I urged him to open his heart and receive Christ, and using I John 1:9, I then handed him a card and asked him to write down all his sins. I said, "I do not want to know them, but it helps you to confess them to God."

He was surprised and said, "I have no sins!"

"Did you ever lie, Major?" I asked quietly.

"Oh, lie, everybody lies!"

I showed him the Bible clearly teaches that this is a sin. He took the card and began to write. He wrote, and wrote. He then came over and asked, "Mrs. Winslow, do you have another card?" When he was finished writing, the three of us knelt at the altar. I don't know what he told the Lord but after a short time he turned and said, "I have peace." He is still serving the Lord.

We need dedicated leadership like these men, committed Christians whose values will cause them to respond to the challenging tasks. May the Lord give us workers with vision, self-discipline, humility, who are filled with God's Spirit and a genuine willingness to serve. These times call for heroism, yet in this chaotic world we have the assurance that Christ's cause will win.

Five days before President Chiang Kai-shek passed away, he made his last will. In a land where many believe in idols, this will has great potential for getting out the gospel. It was printed, and posters of it hung in restaurants and public places, and students in the schools are required to learn it:

I am extremely pleased to exhort people to study the Bible, because the Bible is the Holy Spirit's voice to publish abroad God's righteousness and compassion to the world's people, through the sacrifice of the Savior Jesus Christ, who shed his blood to save all who believe. His righteousness enables nations to elevate Christ as the rock foundation of all liberty. His love can cover all transgressions of all who believe. Everyone who believes in Jesus Christ shall be saved.

— *President Chiang Kai-shek*

On one ocean voyage a typhoon near Japan prevented us from entering the harbor. Twelve other ships stayed out, too. I spent much of the night kneeling on my bunk and watching out the portholes. Suddenly we neared a lighted ship. Then the furious waves took us away, but quickly we dashed near another ship. Then all was dark until, oh, here we seemed ready to collide with still another lighted vessel. There was very little sleep that night. At breakfast next morning I was at the captain's table. "We didn't sleep much last night," I ventured. The captain seemed surprised. "We were afraid we would hit one of those ships," I explained.

Calmly he replied, "We have an *anchor,* madam!"

In all of life's changing scenes, its storms and its happiness, God's Word is our stay. "Which hope we have as an anchor of the soul, both sure and steadfast" (Hebrews 6:19). His Word also exhorts us, "But we have this treasure in clay bowls, that the excellency of the power may be of God, and not of us" (II Corinthians 4:7). We cannot but share "for the love of Christ constraineth us" (II Corinthians 5:14).

Nomads To India

Dorothy Bowen
July/August 1992 pp. 24-26

India! Nothing in all of our 25 years in Africa prepared us for what we experienced during our three weeks here. The sights, the sounds, the smells, but especially the people!

All my life I have heard the term *teeming millions*, but our ride from the Bombay airport to our hotel gave me a little insight into the meaning of this phrase. There were times in Kenya when we wondered where all the people came from. However, Kenya has only 112 people per square mile. And both times we visited Nigeria, we thought it surely must be the most densely populated country in the world with 343 persons per square mile and an average of more than five persons per room. India makes even Nigeria seem empty. India has 677 persons per square mile. After our visit, I do not find this difficult to believe.

Although we had been invited by Indian leaders and even though we knew the Lord was directing us in this venture, we made this trip to India with many fears. Could we cope? Would we be accepted by those to whom we had come to minister? Would we be understood? Would our message be relevant? Did we really have something to offer?

However, the greeting we received at our first workshop went a long way towards dispelling those fears. We were greeted by Prema Gnanakan, a beautiful Indian Christian, and her daughter Anupa, and we had no questions about the authenticity of their welcome. From that moment we knew the Lord had gone before us to prepare the way.

There is a very large Indian population in Kenya, and this has influenced the Kenyan food, so we had already acquired a taste for Indian food. In fact, it had become our choice when selecting a meal out in Nairobi. Our gracious Indian hosts were at first unprepared for this and very thoughtfully planned *western* style food for us. However, whenever we could convince them that we enjoyed their food, we were treated to the delicious Indian cuisine. When Prema learned of our preference, she prepared a different dish every meal. What a treat!

Our first workshop on Two-Thirds World learning styles and appropriate teaching methods took place at ACTS Institute in Bangalore.

More than 300 Christian organizations have their headquarters in Bangalore, and we had opportunity to visit several ministries there. A very special highlight was a day at the South Indian Biblical Seminary (SIBS), a school for which we had prayed for many years. Principal Dr. Narendra John and his wife, Jaya, received us so graciously and we enjoyed attending the Christmas program there at the seminary. Narendra and Jaya are Free Methodists and have a significant ministry at SIBS.

Almost everywhere we went in India, we met graduates of the seminary. We learned that a large percentage of the indigenous missionaries of India are graduates of SIBS. We need to pray for Narendra as he leads the seminary and for Jaya as she manages the library.

On our Sunday in Bangalore we ministered in a village service. Many Indian churches worship in western style buildings, but this service was more traditional. Indian musical instruments were used and we all removed our shoes and sat on mats on the floor. Earle preached through an interpreter and we both prayed with 12 to 15 Indian seekers.

Our next stop was Union Biblical Seminary (UBS), Pune. There we had a three-day workshop with 17 members of the UBS staff. Again we found participants enthusiastic over what we presented concerning learning styles and teaching methods.

Then it was on to New Delhi, India's capital. There we held two seminars -- one with secondary school teachers at Mt. Carmel School and another at the Green Park Free Church, where we had 24 participants. These were pastors, Sunday school teachers, and Child Evangelism Fellowship workers. Knowing that this group would be so very different from the usual, we went into this seminar with much fear. However, the Lord answered prayer in a wonderful way. We found it to be a very positive experience.

As we looked forward to our time in India, we thought we would miss Christmas celebrations. However, we attended at least four such events. An outstanding one was a multi-lingual Christmas concert sponsored by the Evangelical Fellowship of India and presented by the Delhi Music Association in aid of Uttarkashi earthquake relief.

On our Sunday in that city Earle preached at the St. James Church and in the afternoon we flew to the location of our last workshop at the Rajasthan Bible Institute, Jaipur. The State of Rajasthan received its name from the fact that before 1950 there were many small kingdoms with rajas, or kings, over each one. They are now all a part of India, and many of their palaces are now five star hotels.

We held a three-day seminar at the Rajasthan Bible Institute.

Again we met choice Indian believers. In Jaipur we were invited into the home of a young couple who work with university students. Again we thanked the Lord for our privilege to fellowship with his servants around the world.

We arrived back in the United States just before Christmas from what I like to think of as our *first missionary journey*. We had spent seven months working in the African countries of Nigeria, Rwanda and South Africa before our trip to India. When first called into this travelling ministry we were asked by one with whom we counseled, "Are you prepared to be nomads?" We thought we were, and this experience has taught us that God will go before us and prepare the way for anything to which he calls us. We are willing to go wherever we are needed, in a ministry that national leaders in both Africa and Asia see as meeting a vital need.

A Visit To Egypt

M. Doane Bonney
September/October 1994 p. 19

For a Westerner like me, Egypt is amazing -- even mind-boggling. "Do you suppose Moses visited this site?" I asked Pastor Gergis who had so kindly accompanied me to the pyramids just outside the city of Cairo.

"Oh yes," he replied. "These predate Moses. We can be sure he came this way."

Egypt is more than pyramids and ancient history. Skyscrapers line the Nile in Cairo. Subways tie the city together. Freeways and rails carry millions daily where camel caravans used to plod. Bishop Nathan Gindy arranged for me to stay in a hotel on Ramses Square in Cairo. The main train station was about a block away. The subway and freeways all converge there. It was a wonderful location from which to travel to any part of the city. Cairo never seemed to sleep. I awakened several times at two or three a.m. and looked out my eighth-story window. Thousands of people were still in the streets. Vendors still cried out their wares. Trucks, buses and cars still filled the highways.

In the midst of this bustling activity, the Free Methodist Church in Egypt proclaims Christ and ministers in his name. On Sunday morning I visited one of our 15 churches in Cairo. Pastor Mounir Hakim took me to his church on Kolali street about three blocks from Ramses Square. There 400 believers joyously worshipped God! The singing reminded me of my days in Latin America. God was present. The people went away blessed and encouraged in their walk with the Lord.

Bishop Gindy reported 100 Free Methodist congregations up and down the Nile with a membership of more than 17,000. The church operates medical clinics, retirement centers, book stores and an important school of theology for pastoral training. I returned home thanking God for the leaders and faithful members of our church in that dynamic country. Surely Egypt is strategically poised to play a leading role in continued outreach into the Arab world.

Please pray for our brothers and sisters in Egypt. Theirs is a great challenge. They need special divine assistance to love and lift up Christ in neighborhoods often hostile to them because of their faith.

Sketches Of Japan

Motoi Hatano
September/October 1992 pp. 1-3

In 1895, the Missionary Board of the Free Methodist Church of North America decided to carry the gospel into Japan and appointed a Japanese youth as a pioneer missionary. His name was Shoji Kakihara. He was a student at Greenville College and a faithful local preacher of the Illinois Conference. The next year, he left the United States for Japan.

Arriving at Yokohama, Kakihara went to a small fishing village named Fukura on a little island with a population of 2,000 inhabitants. One year later, the Reverend and Mrs. Teikichi Kawabe went to Awaji Island where they met Kakihara. Kawabe promised to work together with Kakihara, but soon after Kawabe began his work, Kakihara withdrew from our church. Today, Kawabe is usually recognized as the founder of the Free Methodist Church of Japan.

Kawabe moved to Osaka in 1903. Osaka was the largest city in the western area of mainland Honshu and a center of economic activities. The new Free Methodist Church in Osaka made splendid progress by his strenuous efforts, and Osaka Nipponbashi Church (one of the largest Free Methodist churches in Japan) was founded in 1903.

The mission board approved the organization of the Japan provisional conference in 1914 and the conference became a full conference in 1923. At the same time, Kawabe retired from the office of superintendent and devoted himself fully to preaching. Dr. Tetsuji Tsuchiyama who had returned from the United States was elected as superintendent of the Japan annual conference and was nominated as the principal of the seminary.

During the Second World War Christians all over Japan were persecuted under the pressure of authorities. The Japanese government ordered all Christian denominations to unify into one denomination. So the Free Methodist church was integrated into "The United Church of Christ of Japan."

When the war was over, the former Free Methodist churches came together to reorganize the denomination and established a fellowship named F. M. Kai, an association within the United Church of

Christ. In 1952, F. M. Kai left the United Church and reorganized the Free Methodist Church of Japan.

The Missionary Board recognized this reorganized denomination as a full annual conference. In 1960, according to the resolution of the General Conference of North America, it was recognized that this Japanese annual conference would establish a new general conference, "The Free Methodist General Conference of Japan." Rev. Kaneo Oda was elected as the first bishop of the Japan Free Methodist Church. Rev. Takesaburo Uzaki succeeded him as bishop in 1964. In 1984 Rev. Motoi Hatano was elected as the third bishop. In February of 1992, Rev. Hachiroemon Naiki was elected as the fourth bishop.

The Eastern Conference has six churches, each with its own building, and two evangelistic centers. These churches are scattered over a large area and work diligently to maintain fellowship among themselves.

The Central Conference has 14 churches, each with its own building, and one evangelistic center. Seven of these churches are situated in downtown Osaka. Now urban population is gradually decreasing, so it is not so easy for evangelism, which is centered on young people through gospel music meetings and camp meetings.

The Western Conference has six churches, each with its own building, and one evangelistic center. Last year, a new church was organized in a newly opened residential section of Kobe, and may become a model for urban evangelism.

The Japan church has a missions commitment as well. A world missions committee has been organized to raise support for evangelistic work among Japanese in New York and Argentina, and to support a Free Methodist Japanese missionary in the Philippines with Wycliff Bible Translators.

Osaka Christian College and seminary has 653 students. There are three departments: kindergarten teacher training, international culture, and church leadership training. A new headquarters building and chapel for the seminary were completed three years ago. The seminary has 53 students and offers two courses, a training course for ministers and one for layleaders.

The Japan church has plans to double in this decade. Goals are to train lay leaders, to obey the Great Commission, to grow in Christian perfection, and to have 5,000 full members by the year 2001.

DeShazer

C. Hoyt Watson
condensed by Daniel V. Runyon
September/October 1992 pp. 17-32

Introduction

Early on December 28, 1948, the world witnessed one of the greatest continuing miracles in modern missionary annals. The International Press was alerted. The Japanese Press waited. Photographers stood by. Military men, civil authorities, religious leaders, old men, young men, women, and children waited anxiously at the Yokohama dock for the arrival of a steamship from America. Why all the excitement? The Doolittle raider turned missionary was to arrive that morning.

Japan, a great nation, now defeated and disillusioned. What poverty! What spiritual hunger! And what an opportunity! Indeed, the Associated Press estimated the number of converts at 30,000 during DeShazer's first year in Japan. By his own report, 4,000 confessed and repented of their sins in one 15-day campaign. Many have been the instances when individual men have become heroic. Seldom, however, does a man reach the heights of public attention and world approbation merely by loving his enemies and acting accordingly.

1. The Western Frontier

Jacob DeShazer was born in Salem, Oregon, in 1912. His father worked on the farm during the week and preached on Sunday in the Church of God. Within two years of Jacob's birth his father died. After three years his mother married Mr. H.P. Andrus, and a new home was established in Madras, Oregon. In this windswept prairie town of some 300 people young DeShazer learned something of the necessity for work, the privilege of citizenship, and the meaning of community responsibility.

Math was his favorite subject in school. Although somewhat shy, he played baseball and football. On Sundays he went with his family to Sunday School at the local Free Methodist Church. If he stayed for the morning preaching service, he usually disappeared quickly after the benediction.

DeShazer did not openly rebel against his parents, but he smoked cigarettes and occasionally played hooky from school. He almost developed a habit of stealing, but this was nipped in the bud when he was caught red-handed after stealing a man's suitcase. His mother and stepfather prayed with him and for him, and then required that he make apology and restitution.

"It was hard to face my fine Christian parents and the neighbors after I had been reported as a thief," said DeShazer. "However, it was a very sure way to cure me of stealing."

Following his graduation from high school in 1931, DeShazer worked for one ranch neighbor, then another. Wages were a dollar a day and board. It seemed that the calls for money were beyond his resources. He found it impossible to save even a portion of his wages. After some years he heard about an opening for a camp tender for sheepherders on the California-Nevada border. It became his responsibility to carry supplies by pack-mule train into the mountains for the sheepherders. He remembers, "I enjoyed going to the mountains in the summer and back to the deserts of Nevada in winter." He did this healthful and vigorous work for two years, fairly living in the saddle.

With little opportunity to spend money, he accumulated $1,000 dollars, then felt ready to go into business. Not wanting to go back to his hometown, he located in Butte Falls, Oregon, to raise turkeys. He bought 500 day-old turkeys. Through the weeks he cared for them day and night. He watched them with great interest. Nothing was spared by way of providing correct food mixtures, proper shelter, and personal care.

By the holiday season his birds were ready for market. To his dismay, the price of turkeys took a sudden drop from 22¢ a pound to only 14¢ a pound. Reluctantly he marketed his birds. When all bills were paid, there was no profit. His entire $1,000 investment was gone. This experience satisfied DeShazer's urge to go into business for himself.

Meanwhile in Europe, World War II broke out. America tried to convince herself that she was safe, but at the same time the United States military leaders called for "peace-time conscription." The Army offered good pay. Then, too, as a single man DeShazer was most eligible for army service in the event of war. It was two years before Pearl Harbor when DeShazer enlisted and received basic training as an airplane mechanic and bombardier. For a full year he was located at the McChord Field near Tacoma, Washington.

2. Secret Mission

The United States and Japan were allies during World War I. Within a few years after the armistice of 1918, however, tensions mounted between the two countries. The United States objected to Japan's aggressive policy in China, and Japan openly violated various international treaties. When World War II broke out in Europe and Japan sided with Germany, it further shook diplomatic relations. Then came Pearl Harbor.

After Pearl Harbor came Wake, Guam, Manila, and the Java Straits, and then Bataan. These names became fixed in the American mind as defeats. The American people wondered whether news of something besides defeat would ever come. There was a pressing demand for military authorities to do something quickly and emphatically to jar the Japanese leaders.

Military authorities decided to make an unprecedented raid on the Japanese mainland. Perhaps our bombers could set the flimsy houses in Tokyo aflame and start a great conflagration, such as that which followed the earthquake of 1923. This possibility was calculated as being worth the risk, but to carry out such a raid meant much planning and intense training.

Army life for DeShazer before Pearl Harbor was routine, often dull. Two years of this produced the same effect on DeShazer as on most other careless-minded youths: "I associated with certain fellows and we went to dances and drinking places to pass the time. I feel ashamed of the events in my life during those years. There is really no reason why anyone should want to live such a life. It does not lead to happiness."

After Pearl Harbor, DeShazer was sent to the air base at Columbia, South Carolina, for further training as a bombardier. While on duty one day, word came for him to report to his captain. Being reprimanded was not an unknown experience to DeShazer. On this occasion he thought probably he was scheduled for some form of K.P. duty.

To his surprise he found 15 or 20 other fellows in the captain's office. Without any preliminary statement the captain asked whether they would volunteer for a dangerous mission. The whole thing was sudden. They hardly knew how to react. They began to question the nature of the mission, its destination, and purpose. The captain explained something of its danger and hazard but said it was so secret he could not provide details. The more he talked, however, the more the proposition sounded to the fellows like a great adventure. Everyone who reported to the captain's office volunteered.

Now DeShazer's life changed completely. Excitement ran high. Everything about the project was so mysterious and secret that it daily gathered glamour and interest. DeShazer was glad he had been chosen.

Within a few days the volunteers for this dangerous mission were sent to Eglin Field in Florida for intensive training in all types of air maneuvers. It was obvious the secret mission would require low flying and bombing. DeShazer's pilot, Lieutenant William Farrow, sometimes flew so low across fields that he had to rise to go over fences. At other times he flew along and inside a ditch so that the ditch banks were higher than the airplane. Hazards were numerous. Accidents were frequent.

General James Doolittle, at that time a lieutenant-colonel, was in charge of the expedition. He went to Washington to receive orders and special instructions. He was told he could have practically anything he felt necessary to carry out the mission. His requests were to have top priority. Cost was not to be a matter of consideration.

With the return of Doolittle from Washington, training greatly intensified. Airplanes were loaded with heavy dud bombs. Pilots tried to get the planes off the ground in very short distances. Training continued for a month. Then came the order to go to San Francisco. They turned the trip across the United States into a practice flight. Most of the way they flew very low. DeShazer says, "When we got to Texas and New Mexico, our pilots would fly low and frighten cattle in the fields. It was great sport to see them put their tails in the air and run for all they were worth."

On April 1, 1942, the 16 B-25 bombers were hoisted to the flight deck of the aircraft carrier, U.S.S. *Hornet*. DeShazer's plane was the last one, No. 16. It was anchored to the flight deck with a portion of the tail hanging over the stern. The next day the *Hornet* sailed out of the bay under the Golden Gate Bridge. It was high noon. Other ships joined the convoy until the Task Force consisted of 12 ships: the carrier *Hornet,* another aircraft carrier, the *Enterprise,* two cruisers, two tankers, and six destroyers.

About 10 miles offshore an announcement blared over the public address system of the *Hornet* describing the expedition. The objective was to bomb Japan. They would not stop at another port before the bombers would be launched for the raid. The 2,000 sailors and 160 Air Corps men aboard the *Hornet* began to cheer, not only because they were involved in a great adventure, but also because they felt bombing Japan would help bring to a halt the awful aggression of the Japanese.

"I sensed a fighting spirit among these men," DeShazer remembers. "We did not need speeches to point out what was wrong with Japan. Every person seemed to know that Japan was an outlaw and would have to be forced to surrender. The Japanese were taking things that didn't belong to them. They had started the war. These American men were ready to fight against such unrighteousness."

DeShazer had guard duty his first night on shipboard. About midnight when everything was dark, he apparently lost some of his courage. Even though he had a 45 pistol strapped to his side, he began to have strange feelings: "I began to wonder how many more days I was to spend in this world. Maybe I wasn't so fortunate after all to go on this trip. I tried to comfort myself with statistics which I could recall. I reminded myself that only 50,000 Americans had been killed in the first World War. I shuddered to think where I would go if I was to die."

During the day, things were different. Something exciting happened every hour. Seals swimming alongside the ship were of great interest. The albatross, particularly, drew DeShazer's attention: "The albatross followed us, flying on tireless wings. Each day I watched their graceful flying. It seemed strange that they could keep up to the aircraft carrier and never appear to move their wings. I studied aerodynamics in the army schools, but I did not understand the flying ease of the albatross. These strange birds didn't have to go to school to learn how to fly. They were shown the way to fly by their Creator."

Out on the great expanse of the continually moving blue water of the Pacific Ocean, DeShazer became meditative: "I felt a longing for something which is hard to describe. I did not know what that longing was. Job 12:9 tells us, *Which of all these does not know that the hand of the Lord has done this?* I longed for fellowship with the Creator of this great display of nature. I did not know how God would gladly fellowship with his creation. I did not realize that God would gladly fellowship with me, if I would meet the conditions written in the Bible."

Sunday, April 5, was Easter Sunday. An Easter service was held, and it was surprising how many men showed up. But DeShazer did not attend.

3. Alarm

On April 17 the commander of the Task Force announced to the other ships: "This Task Force has been directed to proceed to a position 400 miles east of Japan. The Army bombers will be launched from the

U.S.S. *Hornet*. They will bomb Tokyo."

Most of the men were seated at lunch when the announcement came. At first everyone seemed frozen to his seat. Then spirits brightened. On some ships gay little songs were cheerfully sung, such as, "Hi, ho, we're off to Tokyo. We will bomb and blast and come back fast."

Tension ran deep below the cheerful exteriors. A question arose in the mind of each one: How close to Tokyo can we get without being spotted?

The night was grim and silent as the ships, under forced draft, steamed westward. Zero hour was not far away. The sea was heavy. The sky was overcast. White-capped rollers flew over the tossing bows of battleships. Spray splashed over carrier flight decks. Lookouts were soaked in the driving rain. Men in the ward room of the *Hornet* spent most of their time looking at a big map on the wall. Few words were spoken. Finally, the men turned in -- most with their clothes on.

About 3:15 a.m. on Saturday, April 18, two Japanese surface craft were seen. It was believed they were part of a Japanese patrol. Immediately a General Quarters Alarm was given, a piercing "Clang! Clang! Clang!" calling all hands to battle stations. Men poured up through the hatches, covers came off guns, and ammunition was made ready. DeShazer and the Doolittle men were quickly up and waiting. The convoy was still nearly 900 miles east of Japan. Could they sail to within 400 miles of Japan before launching the airplanes?

Shortly after dawn, a Japanese fishing vessel was sighted, and low on the horizon were two ships which appeared to be Japanese destroyers. The commander of the Task Force now felt it was impossible to keep his presence unknown. These ships had no doubt seen the convoy and radioed its strength and position to Tokyo.

At about 8:00 a.m. the crisp order was given over the *Hornet*'s loudspeakers: "Army Personnel, man your planes." The pilot of DeShazer's plane was the six foot six inch tall Lieutenant William Farrow. The co-pilot was Lieutenant Hites, the navigator was Lieutenant Barr, and the rear gunner was Sergeant Spaatz. The bombardier was Sergeant Jacob DeShazer, at that time a corporal. These men became well acquainted during their intensive training. However, they did not realize how well they would become acquainted during the next three years -- they were busily scrambling to follow orders.

On the flight deck of the *Hornet* there was methodical movement. Pleasantries were exchanged. DeShazer's pilot came by and asked whether he knew how to row a boat. All realized that with 800 miles between them and any land at all – and that enemy land – a boat or some other device would be useful if they hoped to live out their natural lives.

Sergeant Spaatz filled gas tanks and made last minute checkups. DeShazer helped load bombs.

Everyone wondered how the airplanes would get into the air. All eyes were on General Doolittle, the first to take off. With 15 planes behind him, he had only about 450 feet for his takeoff. The shortest takeoff at any practice field had been about 700 feet. And this runway tossed up and down as the ship pitched in the water.

Doolittle's motors raced faster. The aircraft carrier cut into the waves at a speed seldom equaled in naval history. The wind almost blew a person off the deck. The airplane needed very little added speed before the air speed was enough to lift it.

As the forward part of the aircraft carrier went up, the navy man gave the signal. The brakes were released. The airplane fairly jumped into the air. When the *Hornet*'s bow came down, the airplane was seen in the air. Doolittle circled over the *Hornet* in a farewell salute. Cheers rose from the throats of those who watched.

Now it had been proven – a B-25 could take off from the deck of the *Hornet*. But there was no possible way for it to land back on the carrier.

Another plane took off, then another and another. One plane disappeared over the end of the deck. Gasps were heard from the spectators, but it came up toward the sky. Soon the sky was filled with planes – 15 of them.

DeShazer and comrades were in airplane 16. Because of the crowded conditions his plane was pushed to the stern of the deck, the tail actually hanging over. Just before they were ready to taxi into the takeoff position the nose of the airplane rose up off the deck. The tail went down. It looked as though the plane were about to drop into the sea. Sailors quickly tied lines to the nose of the plane, but these broke. Nothing but courage and man power would save the plane.

Every man who could get a handhold crowded in and hung on to the front end of the airplane. DeShazer himself tried to assist. By sheer grit, stamina, and human strength the plane was held on the deck. Lieutenant Farrow already had his motors going at fairly high speed and one sailor who backed into a spinning propeller quickly lost an arm. DeShazer helped others carry him to one side so the plane could take off.

Bombs had been loaded, but since the tail was sticking out so far, it had been impossible to load the crew's bags and other equipment. After the plane was in takeoff position, it was necessary to finish loading it – difficult because of the tremendous gale blowing across the deck.

When DeShazer finally got into position in the nose of the airplane, he found that something had broken the plane's plastic nose. Instead of being wind-tight and rounded, there was a jagged hole more than a foot in diameter just at the right of the gun mount. No one had noticed it before.

At that moment the pilot was speeding his engines for takeoff. The plane shook with the terrific speed of the motors. The Navy man was all set to give the signal for takeoff. Admiral Halsey had the *Hornet* headed straight into the wind. Further delay was impossible. An order had been received to push the plane overboard if it could not take off. DeShazer buckled his safety belt and tried to sit easy as the plane lurched forward. It was a perfect takeoff. The last plane, like the first, circled over the *Hornet* for a farewell salute.

Looking down, DeShazer saw that the *Hornet* already had changed course. With the other vessels of the convoy it had started back home. Its job was done. The "raiders" were off.

DeShazer told the pilot over the intercommunication phone about the big hole in the nose of the plane. Co-pilot Hite came forward and they tried putting a coat in the hole, but the wind took it away. They finally gave up. There was now nothing to do but try to reach Japan, drop their bombs, and then....

It was a dark hour. Their gas supply would be short at the very best. With this hole in the nose of the plane, the streamline effect of the B-25 was greatly reduced.

DeShazer's plane was one of three under the immediate command of Colonel John Hilger in plane 14. These three planes were supposed to fly in formation until they reached Japan. However, Hilger lost sight of plane 16 soon after takeoff when they passed through a rainstorm. Evidently the slow speed of Farrow's plane because of the broken nose was the reason for his failure to keep in formation.

4. Bombs Away

DeShazer's plane left the *Hornet* at 9:20 a.m. In spite of their slow speed they reached Japan about 1:00 p.m. The trip was uneventful. Very few airplanes were seen, and these apparently did not notice the American bomber. Much of the distance over open water was flown at a very low altitude, perhaps only 100 feet.

Upon reaching Japan they found high clouds. To get over the mountains it was necessary to fly up to 7,000 feet. To their surprise they found people living on these mountains. Much of the flying at this altitude was just above the treetops. DeShazer noticed an old gray-bearded gentleman with a cane walking along a mountain pathway. The old man threw himself flat on the ground as the plane rushed by only a few feet above him.

The target assigned to DeShazer was in Nagoya about 300 miles south of Tokyo. The day there was beautiful and the sun was shining as the pilot said, "Get set to drop bombs at 500 feet. There is the first target."

DeShazer looked straight ahead, saw some oil storage tanks, and let the incendiary bomb go. He tried to drop another bomb on another tank and then suddenly noticed that three bombs had been released instead of two. Here is DeShazer's own story.

We were making a complete turn, and I smelled smoke. I wanted to see how an oil refinery looked when on fire. To the left I saw where the first bombs dropped. There was fire all over the tank, but it had not blown up. What I smelled was powder of shells being shot at us instead of the bombs I had dropped.

We went over a big factory-looking building and dropped the last incendiary, then skimmed along down a valley on our way to the ocean. We flew along the coast intending to fly on the 13th parallel to Choo Chow Lishui, China. When night came, we saw dimly the coastline of China, but the fog was so thick we could not tell what part of China we were approaching. Our navigator said we should be over Choo Chow Lishui. The pilot circled, calling on the radio all the time. No answer came back. The fog cleared off a little. We could see a town below but no airfield.

We had gasoline enough for only one hour. We had to do something, and Lieutenant Farrow was anxious to save the B-25. With a hole in the nose it had already stayed in the air for more than 13 hours. By flying beyond Japanese-held territory we could get to Keyon in Free China, where more gasoline was stored. We might be able to see the airfield or get a response from the Chinese radio operator.

After we had flown for one hour, we saw a town. Our gasoline was nearly gone. We circled the town, calling and looking for lights from an airfield but to no avail. Finally Lieutenant Farrow said, "We gotta jump." We were at 3,000 feet when I jumped.

I lost my hat as the wind shrieked over me. When the plane had gone, I pulled the rip cord and felt a hard but welcome jerk as the parachute opened. I watched the light go out of sight from the opening in the fuselage of the plane. Soon the sound of the motors died out. Everywhere I looked it was dark. The fog was thick around me.

I had no feeling of falling since I could not see the ground and there was no sensation of wind with the parachute open. I began to wonder if I would have to sit up there all night. Suddenly I hit the earth with an awful jolt. I threw my arms around a mound of dirt and gave it a big hug, glad to be back on the ground even if it was a good long way from home. I saw several mounds of dirt and noticed that I was on a knoll. Then I realized it was a Chinese graveyard. All around were rice fields which were under water at that time of the year. I found out later that as I was coming down in the parachute my mother had awakened from her sleep and was praying for me.

DeShazer was too stunned to realize that some of his ribs were fractured in the landing. He was able, however, to move and to walk. He shot his pistol into the air several times, but there was no response. He then cut the parachute to pieces with his knife, used a portion of the silk to protect his head from the rain, and started walking until he came to a little brick building. Although it was very small, he was able to clear out enough space to get in and barely have room to sit. It was a shelter from the rain. Through sheer weariness he fell asleep and did not awaken until daylight.

Immediately he began to look for a road. After walking some distance, he came to a path. As he walked along this path, he began meeting people, but no one seemed interested, excited or suspicious. From time to time he stopped a man and tried to find out whether he was in Japanese territory. No one understood his questions, or perhaps they were unwilling to say.

The hours of walking gave DeShazer his first sight of the living conditions of the Chinese: "I could see inside their mud houses. Chicken, pigs, and children were wading around together in filthy mud inside the house. The people had heads about the size of a four-year-old child in America. The skin on their faces was wrinkled and old looking. I didn't expect to find anything to eat, although I was getting very hungry."

Eventually he came to a main road and a telephone line. He walked down the main road until he came to a house where he found two young soldiers playing with some Chinese children. He used the word *American* and pointed to himself. He then pointed to one of the soldiers and asked, "China or Japan?"

The soldier replied, "China," yet DeShazer had misgivings. Fear seemed to take possession of him. He fixed his 45 pistol so a bullet was in the chamber and the hammer was drawn back. He knew the pistol contained seven good bullets, and he was ready to shoot if they were Japanese.

As he stood there, he began to feel perhaps it was better for him to leave the house and go on his way. Just as he started to back away toward the door, to his consternation he found 10 soldiers, armed with bayonets, pistols, and swords, standing at the entrance. He yelled at them, "China or Japan?"

As he yelled, he was holding his hand on the pistol. Instantly, they hollered back, "China."

DeShazer says, "I didn't want to start shooting at the Chinese, so I let them come in."

The soldiers got him to shake hands, patted him on the back, and tried to act like old-time friends. They soon got him to go with them down the road to a camp. As they were walking along, they stopped for a moment, and to DeShazer's further consternation he found that a bayonet was against his back. Suddenly, guns were pointing at him from every direction. The leader of the group then reached over and took his pistol from the holster.

At the camp a fellow began asking questions. He knew English fairly well. It was now obvious to DeShazer that the men were Japanese, not Chinese. When this fact dawned upon him, he was completely discouraged. Nevertheless he tried to let on that he did not realize they were Japanese.

5. Inquisition in Tokyo

The Japanese gave DeShazer some hot cakes with a type of apple butter with an oriental tang. The tea and food made him feel a lot better. A short time later he was taken to another town where he learned that four of his comrades had also been picked up. They met for the first time the next morning and were photographed together on the front steps of the building. Later they were placed together in a transport plane and traveled a good share of the day before arriving in Nanking, China.

In the evening they were introduced to an oriental prison. The cells were made of wooden bars, placed straight up and down. The room was bare except for a wooden box for a toilet. Guards walked back and forth in front of the cell. Here someone took DeShazer's wristwatch, which he never saw again. A little later he was led into a room where a group of Japanese officers began questioning him:

One of the officers said I had better talk. He said they would torture me until I did talk. I was blindfolded as I had been most of the time for over 12 hours and hadn't eaten all day. I was asked questions at every opportunity, but I always told them I wouldn't talk. Sometimes they told me about places in America where Japan had bombed and taken possession of property; then they would come up very close to my face and open their mouths and laugh.

I was then led into a room, and the blindfold was removed. A little Japanese of stocky build stood behind a table, smoking a cigar, rubbing his hands together, and talking fast. Through an interpreter the man said, "I want to treat you real good. Everywhere I have the reputation of being the kindest judge in all China." We sat down and the judge looked at a paper.

Judge: "How do you pronounce H-O-R-N-E-T?"
DeShazer: "Hornet."
"Is this the aircraft carrier you flew off to bomb Japan?
"I won't talk,"
"Was Doolittle your commanding officer?
"I won't talk."

At this point the judge said in English, "Tomorrow morning at sunrise I'm going to have the honor of cutting off your head." In view of the tenseness of the situation and impending tragedy, one is amazed at DeShazer's answer. From his own account we read:

I told him I thought it would be a great honor to me if the kindest judge in China cut my head off. The judge and others laughed for the first time, and a little later I was taken to my cell.

I lay in the cell all night, blindfolded, handcuffed, without blankets. The next morning at sunrise I was led out of my cell. I had no breakfast. The blindfold was taken off, the handcuffs were removed. I looked around for the judge with his weapon of execution, but I saw a fellow with a camera, and everyone was smiling. After the picture was taken, I was loaded onto a Japanese two-motored transport. Again I was blindfolded, handcuffed, and tied with ropes. I could hear some of my companions talking, but I was not able to say anything to them. Soon after the plane took to the air, we were given some good ham sandwiches.

The flight carried them for several hours over water. In due time, they were again over land, and DeShazer heard the Japanese talking excitedly and, as is sometimes their custom, drawing air through their teeth. DeShazer peeked out through his blindfold and saw Mount Fuji. They landed and were taken by automobile to another prison. Again DeShazer and his comrades were subjected to questions.

The unexpected and bold attempt of the American airmen to bomb Japan was a great shock to General Headquarters at Tokyo. General Sugiyama, chief of the general staff, was greatly enraged and insisted upon the death penalty for DeShazer and seven other captured Doolittle raiders. General Tojo, who was the premier, felt the death penalty was too severe. However, Tojo quickly ordered the authorities to establish a law which would impose the death penalty in order to apply it if need be to the captured Doolittle flyers.

In the War Crimes Court in Tokyo, a statement was eventually made to the effect that the eight American flyers were "the unfortunate victims of war." Questioning and ill treatment continued for about two months. A memorandum found after the war in the diary of the minister of the imperial household, Mr. Kido, dated May 21, states: "Some military leaders came into my office to discuss the punishment of the captive flyers." Obviously, the matter had been reported to the Imperial Court officials. Whether the emperor took hand in the matter at this time, the record does not show. In any event the Japanese Army Headquarters in Tokyo finally decided to have the men tried by a court martial under the 13th Army at Shanghai.

6. Death Sentence

The return of the prisoners from Tokyo to Shanghai was not by airplane as they had come over some two months before. Instead, they went first by train to Nagasaki handcuffed, legcuffed, and rope tied. They had not had opportunity to bathe for 60 days, and the coal soot from the train ride did nothing to improve their looks.

At Nagasaki they were pushed into a cement prison cell. There were a few *tatami* (straw mats) on the floor. The conditions were unbearable and they suffered from dysentery, yet the captured flyers found some joy in this Nagasaki prison. For the first time they were able to talk without interference. DeShazer admits they almost forgot the filth and dirt while he and his four comrades from plane No. 16 swapped stories with the three men who survived plane No. 6 (the bombardier and rear gunner were lost in the crash landing at sea).

To their great relief, they spent but one night in this awful prison. The next morning they were put on a ship which took them, still handcuffed and tied, to Shanghai. They arrived on June 19, 1942.

If the previous 60 days had been a nightmare, the next 70 days were filled with stark horror. In Shanghai they were taken immediately to the "Bridge House," already greatly emaciated and barely able to move. They were placed in a 12 by 15 foot prison cell with 15 Chinese prisoners, two of them women. Food consisted of a cup of boiled rice soup for breakfast, four ounces of bread for lunch, and four ounces of bread again for dinner. Two quarts of water were given each day to the eight Americans.

The other prisoners were covered with scabs and old sores. There was not enough space for all to lie down at one time. Bedbugs, lice, and large rats were plentiful. The weather was hot and the water available was inadequate. When one of the Chinese women fell down and hurt her head, they laughed and said she was pretending to be sick. Guards hit her on the head with a stick. DeShazer recalls,

Sometimes they made us stand up during the night after they awakened us. They threatened to hit us with long clubs which they poked through the bars of the cell. It was the first time I had ever been in such a wicked environment. I could not help wondering why there was so much difference between America and the Orient. The bad in America did not begin to compare with that which we observed.

The truth was beginning to dawn upon me -- it is Christianity that makes the difference. Though Americans do not profess to be Christians, yet they follow the Christian ways. Christians have shown the rest of the world the right way to act. Christians are the light of the world. I had always tried to steer away from religion, but now I saw that Christianity is a great benefit to mankind. It is God's plan for mankind's happiness.

Along with the sickness, filth, and constant brutality was the ever-present suspense regarding their fate. Rumors were frequent that they were to be executed. From time to time they were subjected to further questionings. Whatever remained of morale was scarcely perceptible.

At one point the Americans were taken before Major-General Shoji Ito, chief justice officer of the Japanese 13th Army Military Court at Shanghai. The trial could scarcely be called one of justice, for personal word was already brought from Tokyo that General Sugiyama expected the death penalty. Therefore, the judges condemned all eight of the Americans to be executed. The verdict was promptly relayed to Tokyo. The American airmen, of course, were not informed.

Instead, they were moved to another prison near Shanghai, where solitary confinement began in earnest. Each man was placed in a 5 by 9 foot cell. Conditions were better, but there remained the haunting fear that at any time they might be called out to face a firing squad or something worse.

Meanwhile, jealousies and rivalries between top Japanese army leaders and officials in the War Cabinet played a part in the fate of the American flyers. The record of the Minister of the Imperial Household states that on October 3, 1942, "Premier Tojo came in at 11:30. He gave a detailed account of the capture of the flyers and the proposed punishment. I was requested to report it to the emperor. I was given an audience by the emperor from 1:05 to 1:15 P.M., and related Tojo's message to him." The record further shows that Kido, the Minister of the Imperial Household, told the emperor that Tojo was in favor of a more lenient punishment.

In the international Military Tribunal held in Tokyo after the war, testimony was given which shows considerable rivalry between General Sugiyama and General Tojo. Each wanted an audience with the emperor in advance of the other. If Sugiyama had talked with the emperor first, no doubt the prisoners would have been executed. Tojo, however, was able to reach the emperor first and make a request for leniency.

Of course, these military discussions were wholly unknown to the American flyers. About the middle of October, when for some time they had been in solitary confinement in individual cells and yet able to be together a few minutes each day, suddenly they found that three of the men did not appear, and were seen no more.

Soon thereafter the remaining five were taken into a courtroom. Knowing that three of their companions had disappeared, they were naturally worried. After a long statement was made in Japanese the prisoners were told they had been sentenced to be executed but that the emperor of Japan had changed the order and they were to receive life imprisonment.

DeShazer's reaction was this: "I expected to be executed from the way the Japanese acted. It was a relief to know they now planned to let us remain alive. I felt a strange sense of joy, even though solitary confinement and a long war deferred any chance of freedom. At the same time it seemed almost hopeless to think of ever being free again. The most probable thing was that we would be executed when America did win the war."

7. Solitary Confinement

It was now just six months since DeShazer and his four companions had taken off from the *Hornet* amidst the cheers of thousands of American soldiers and sailors. During this time they came to know something of suffering, fear, and almost death. Now as they looked to a future of solitary confinement and perhaps a long war, hopelessness took possession of them. Each was in a small cell with no windows except a small opening near the ceiling. Guards were in front of the door. There were no books, no radios, no newspapers, no play, no fellowship. No letters or Red Cross packages would be allowed.

They remembered how the hot summer had been. Now winter was not far away. If they had known then that there would be no heat, even during the coldest, freezing winter weather, their spirits would have dropped even lower. Also, the many hours in solitary confinement made it difficult to think normally. There was the constant problem of how to occupy their minds. By yelling they could hear one another from one cell to another. Yelling, however, attracted the guards and brought reprimand and punishment.

Climbing the walls was one alternative. Since the cell was only five feet wide, DeShazer found it was possible to put his hands on one wall and his feet on the other. By proper maneuvering he was able to climb in this fashion to the ceiling. It was about a 12-foot climb. Up near the ceiling, he could look out the little window and see the countryside for miles around. This was good exercise, and it was a real joy to look out on the scenery after the long hours of looking at four walls. He was never caught in this act by any guard.

When winter came they were given some additional clothing, but still there was much suffering. Lieutenant Hite became sick and suffered from the damp, cold cell for about three months. His conversation and actions became erratic and he did not return to normal until early spring.

In April 1943, one year after the Tokyo raid, DeShazer and his comrades were taken by airplane from Shanghai to Nanking. Such a move naturally aroused anticipation and excitement. They were particularly hoping for a nice courtyard in which they could move around. There was a perpetual dread in their minds of being all alone in a prison cell. There was also the dread of intense cold in the winter and extreme heat in the summer.

Upon arriving in Nanking, they were again placed in solitary confinement, but occasionally the guards in the Nanking prison showed some friendship. Being a guard in a prison was itself a somewhat lonesome business. These guards, even though ordered not to give out information, did occasionally talk to the prisoners. By piecing together scant bits of information they finally determined that the whole Japanese Navy had been sunk. At other times the guards would become abusive and cruel.

Each day for a few minutes DeShazer and his comrades were taken outside for exercise, and so their cells could be cleaned. The guards allowed them to say "Hello" to one another, but if they said much more the guards usually yelled, "Shut up!"

Hours were many and long. Days seemed unending. Week after week came and went. The hot summer of 1943 finally passed and once again there was the comfort of fall.

Frequently the prisoners were told there was no hope for them, that the war was going in Japan's favor. Then the guards would swing the conversation around and say, "Well, if Japan should lose and America should win, prisoners would all have their heads cut off." They insisted that the Japanese expected to fight until the last man died, and of course, they said the emperor of Japan would be the last one to die. Not once was a critical word spoken against the emperor.

Through such conversations DeShazer and his comrades came to know more of the Japanese worship of their emperor. The Japanese people believed the emperor was the representative on earth of deity. They also believed their emperor could not be wrong in any of his words or deeds. Since the emperor had asked them to fight for their country, it was their highest honor and joy to do so and, if need be, to die. DeShazer says:

They would tell us many fantastic tales of how God was on their side and how they were able to sink many ships with just one airplane. They said America had started the war. It was hard for us to understand how grown men could believe some of the things the Japanese government was telling their people. However, these men were convinced that they were in the right and that their country was going to win. They had unshakable confidence in a supernatural power. These bloody head-removers said they were in the right and that God was always on the side of righteousness.

Just about the time of the fall equinox in 1943, Lieutenant Meder took very sick with dysentery. His comrades had noticed that he was looking increasingly thin and weak. One day all five were in the yard together. It was a beautiful fall day, and they were allowed to run about a little. Lieutenant Meder was able to be out but was not able to exercise.

Weeks went by. Lieutenant Meder continued to grow worse and died December 1. His comrades would have helped him, but this was out of the question. He held the highest esteem of his comrades. In speaking of him DeShazer says:

Lieutenant Meder seemed to understand the Bible message well. He and I had a good talk one day while we were pulling weeds out in the yard. Meder told me that Jesus Christ is the Lord and coming King, that Jesus is God's Son and that God expects the nations and people to recognize Jesus as Lord and Savior. He said the war would last until Jesus Christ caused it to stop. I did not understand what he meant at the time, but I remembered his words later. Lieutenant Meder had a very brilliant mind. He was truly a gentleman in every way, and he was a prince of a fellow.

Meder's comrades did not know immediately of his death. Suddenly they were aware of considerable hammering out in the yard. They were making a large box. The next day DeShazer and the other three airmen, one at a time, were taken from their cells around into Meder's cell where they could take a last look. He was lying in the box with a nice wreath of flowers and the Bible on the lid. When back in their cells, they could tell by the sounds that the box with their comrade's body was being carried out. Later a small box was brought back, which the guard said contained Meder's ashes.

Evidently Meder's death brought about reprimands and a change in procedure. The captain of the prison came in to talk to the prisoners. He even asked what they would like to have. They wanted bread, butter, jam, steak, eggs, milk, and other American food. They knew that no Japanese official could provide such food, but almost 20 months on rations in an oriental prison made them long for American food.

The Japanese officials did arrange for them to have bread with their rice and soup, and they were fed three times, rather than twice each day. Soon both their health and their spirits greatly improved.

The airmen were also provided with a few books to read. Among these books was a Bible. DeShazer was the only man in the group who was not an officer. This meant that the other three men, being officers, had first choice with respect to reading. Not until the beginning of summer did DeShazer gain the privilege of having the Bible, and that for only three weeks.

Before getting the Bible DeShazer memorized portions from other books as indicated in a letter from another American prisoner, Captain

Nielson, who writes, "DeShazer was memorizing a very long poem, *The Pleasures of Hope,* from one of the few books we had. He would recite parts of it to us when we came together for our recreational period. Some of these lines will stay with me forever, such as:

Lo, Nature, Life and Liberty illume
The dim-eyed tenant of the dungeon gloom.
Truth shall pervade the unfathomed darkness there.
And light the dreadful features of despair."

8. Three Bible Weeks

Sometime in May 1944 in Nanking, China, a most significant event took place. There sat DeShazer in solitary confinement, homesick, hungry, discouraged, and almost hopeless. Throughout the dreary hours of more than two long years, he had been waiting. Waiting -- and thinking.

Now it was his turn to have the Bible. It was laid in his hands. With almost feverish grasp he seized the Bible and pressed it to his bosom. The Bible -- that Book he had heard read at the family altar years before near Madras, Oregon. That Book from which lessons had been studied in the Sunday school in the modest little Free Methodist Church. That Book he had long since lost interest in -- if, in truth, he ever had interest in it. Yes, the Bible, the very Word of God. This was the Book which fell into DeShazer's hands.

The light in DeShazer's cell was horribly dim, and the print was fairly small, but that did not matter. He opened the Book and began to read. From then on, there was little time to sleep. Warned that he could have the Book only three weeks, he read and read and read -- the entire Book through several times.

He read the Prophets through six times. Many hours were spent in memorizing. The entire Bible became alive. It appeared to be illuminated. Certain passages seemed to blaze forth with mysterious brightness. DeShazer had no one to guide him, but the Comforter, sent into the world to guide into all truth, was present to help the spiritually hungry young man.

As DeShazer read, new truths stared at him. He began looking for proof of the existence of God. He read Isaiah and came to this verse: "Surely he took up our infirmities and carried our sorrows, yet we considered him stricken by God, smitten by him, and afflicted. But he was pierced for our transgressions, he was crushed for our iniquities; the punishment that brought us peace was upon him, and by his wounds we are healed. We all, like sheep, have gone astray, each of us has turned to his own way; and the Lord has laid on him the iniquity of us all" (Isaiah 53:4-6).

DeShazer began to see how the prophecies in the Old Testament were revealed in the New. He became enamored with the supernatural. Having read the prophecy in Isaiah, he was greatly impressed when following the Gospel story to realize how the life and resurrection of Jesus was a complete fulfillment of prophecy. He was thinking, *Yes, Christ died for us; that is the message all the way through the Bible. Many different people were writing, but the same revelation of salvation was given to every one. The same thread of thought is carried from Genesis to Revelation. I've seen proof of it in my lifetime. I've seen the handiwork of God. God has shown himself to us.*

He was also charmed by the love of God and found himself thinking, *Jesus existed as God's Son before the world was created. When the time was right, nearly two thousand years ago, God sent His Son to take on the form of a human being. God foretold this event through prophecy. Now God gave the sign of miracles which Jesus performed. Jesus fulfilled every prophecy, and when he was crucified, he rose from the dead. Jesus died for us! We do not need to suffer the penalty for sin.*

It is difficult for us in normal situations to grasp what was going on in the soul of this prisoner as he tried to grasp the truth of the great Book. Over and over he turned the pages back to the prophet, then came again to the New Testament. Hour after hour he read. One reference after another was followed through. A miracle was taking place within his heart and mind. The light was shining brighter and brighter.

Perhaps the memory of boyhood days in Sunday school, long covered by the debris of careless thinking and worldly living, was being revived. Truths long forgotten were returning to mind. Certainly, the Spirit of God was making it possible for DeShazer to get a theological course unprecedented in scope and intensity. He was coming near to the inner revelation of God to himself.

As DeShazer eagerly read the Bible he more and more came to feel the message of the gospel was for him as an individual. He saw that all of these things were written, all of these events took place, so that he himself could have eternal life if he believed on Jesus Christ.

The desire grew in his heart to know pardon from his sins and the joy of forgiveness. He realized he was a sinner. He saw that God hates sin. He heard Jesus say, "Repent and believe the good news!" (Mark

1:15). The light finally broke, and DeShazer knew that salvation was his.

9. The Miracle

The prayers of DeShazer's parents followed him; prayers of old friends ascended to the throne of God. The word of God through the precious Book was illuminated by the Holy Spirit. The presence of Christ spoke to his inner consciousness and knocked at the door of his heart. But it was up to DeShazer to meet the conditions. This he did, on June 8, 1944.

DeShazer was reading Romans 10:9, "If you confess with your mouth, *Jesus is Lord,* and believe in your heart that God raised him from the dead, you will be saved." He had read those words before, but today it became a power in his life.

"Lord," he prayed, "though I am far from home and though I am in prison, I must have forgiveness." As he meditated and prayed along this line, there came into his soul a divine joy, a soul rest, an inner witness that God for Christ's sake had forgiven him.

There came over him a sense that God wanted obedience, yet there was little he could do to change his way of living. He was just simple enough to tell the Lord that he would obey. He yielded his spirit, his plans, his hopes, his aspirations. It was then he learned this truth: "Obedience to God is the way to eternal life."

He later wrote about this experience, *My heart was filled with joy. I wouldn't have traded places with anyone at that time. Oh, what a great joy it was to know that I was saved, that God had forgiven my sins, and that I had become partaker of the divine nature (II Peter 1:4). Though I was unworthy and sinful, I had redemption through his blood, the forgiveness of sins, according to the riches of his grace (Ephesians 1:7).*

Hunger, starvation, and a freezing cold prison cell no longer had horrors for me. They would be only for a passing moment. Even death held no threat when I knew that God had saved me. Death is just one more trial before I can enjoy the pleasures of eternal life. I had the promise of being like Jesus who is God's Son. In that day I will know all things, for I will then be a partaker of immortality.

The time drew near when DeShazer would have to give up the copy of the Bible. He memorized as much as possible. He had an amazing ability to memorize and held in his mind much Scripture for ready reference during his remaining 14 months in prison.

However, he was still in prison. Perhaps he would never get out.

He had the same guards, the same obligation to remain in solitary confinement, the same intolerable food, and the absence of fellowship. But he had believed on the Lord Jesus Christ. As a Christian he was now going to do his level best to live the way a Christian should.

As a child DeShazer was taught to love people and to be friendly to all. Seldom had he done this. But in the Bible he found much emphasis upon loving one another. He knew he had been disobedient to his parents and that throughout the years he had been disobedient to God and to his own conscience. Now through the grace of the Lord Jesus Christ he was forgiven for all those sins.

What he wanted now was divine strength. He wanted to strengthen his self-control and gain a new grip on his willpower. Many lessons were necessary for him to learn to trust the Lord. In John 1:12 he read, "As many as received him, to them gave he power to become the sons of God." It was that power which he needed and wanted.

He remembered wrong attitudes and feelings before his conversion. One day he had become very angry when he was supposed to be cleaning his cell. A guard came along and yelled, "Hurry up." Almost before he knew it, DeShazer told the guard in English, "Go jump in the lake." The guard didn't like this. DeShazer recalls, *Before I knew what was going to happen, the door was unlocked and the guard hit me on the head with his fist. I kicked him in the stomach with my bare foot, and he hit me with his steel scabbard. I picked up the dirty mop water I had been using and threw it on the guard. It cooled him off enough so that he didn't do any more than swear at me. It is strange that he didn't cut off my head. This was not the way that I had been taught to make friends.*

After DeShazer accepted the way of Christ his attitude changed. In due time his guards knew it, and so did his comrades. Even in prison, DeShazer realized, God expects us to keep his commandments: *The only way we know we are saved is to keep the commandments of Christ. God hates sin and disobedience. We cannot please God if we continue doing those things that we know are wrong. If we accept Jesus and continue to sin, we will be like the seed in the parable which fell on stony ground and when it sprung up, because it had no depth of soil, soon withered and died (Matthew 13:3-9).*

With his mind saturated with Scripture, DeShazer heard clearly the words of Jesus: "Not everyone who says to me, 'Lord, Lord,' will enter the kingdom of heaven, but only he who does the will of my Father who is in heaven" (Matthew 7:21).

DeShazer tells us, *When I memorized First John 2:3-6, I found it was necessary to be obedient. I wanted to know that I was a real Christian and not a hypocrite. These verses tell us we can know: "We know that we have come to know him if we obey his commands. The man who says, 'I know him,' but does not do what he commands is a liar, and the truth is not in him. But if anyone obeys his word, God's love is truly made complete in him. This is how we know we are in him: Whoever claims to live in him must walk as Jesus did."*

Submission to Jesus brings a wonderful peace. I realized my life would be more enjoyable if I were obedient. I found at first it was hard to do what I knew was right. I had much trouble for more than three weeks. The habits of swearing, thinking vulgar thoughts, and telling lies did not immediately leave me when I accepted Jesus. However, when the sin appeared I asked for forgiveness right away. The promise of I John 1:9 says, "If we confess our sins, he is faithful and just and will forgive us our sins and purify us from all unrighteousness." God always keeps his promises, and since I did my part all unrighteousness was taken away.

DeShazer felt the command of God was to love his fellowmen. Since the only individuals he met were guards, he waited for an opportunity to demonstrate love to them. An opportunity soon came. One day he was being taken back to his cell by one of the guards. For some reason the guard was in a special hurry, slapped DeShazer on the back with his hand and ordered, *Hiaku! hiaku!* (Hurry up! Hurry up!). When they came to the cell, he opened the door a little and shoved DeShazer inside. Before DeShazer could get through the door, the guard slammed it and caught DeShazer's foot. Instead of opening the door to release his foot, the guard began kicking DeShazer's bare foot with his hobnailed boots. Finally, DeShazer was able to push the door open and get his foot free. He jumped inside. DeShazer felt resentment and hatred for the guard until Matthew 5:44 came to mind in which Jesus said, "Love your enemies and pray for those who persecute you, that you may be sons of your Father in heaven."

DeShazer says: *Jesus' words were coming to my mind, but at first I wished that I couldn't remember them. But I had promised obedience if God showed me the way. God had helped me to memorize the Scripture and was now being faithful to show me the way. The only thing I could do was to submit and be obedient. Any other course would have meant God's displeasure, but by obedience God is pleased.*

Other Scripture also flooded DeShazer's mind, particularly chapter 13 of I Corinthians. This has become one of DeShazer's favorite passages which he now likes to quote from James Moffat's translation: "Love is very patient, very kind. Love knows no jealousy; love makes no parade, gives itself no airs, is never rude, never selfish, never irritated, never resentful; love is never glad when others go wrong, love is gladdened by goodness, always slow to expose, always eager to believe the best, always hopeful, always patient. Love never disappears."

The very next morning he had a chance to love an enemy -- the very guard who injured his foot the day before. As the guard came on duty, DeShazer moved toward the door of his cell and said, *Ohayoo Gozaimasu* (Good morning). The guard looked at DeShazer, puzzled and surprised. Perhaps he thought the prisoner had gone stark crazy, but he made no comment. Several mornings went by with DeShazer trying to be friendly.

One morning as the guard came on duty, he walked immediately over to DeShazer's cell and spoke to him through the door. He was smiling. DeShazer knew little Japanese, but he was able to talk to the guard enough to ask him how many brothers and sisters he had. This seemed to please the guard.

On another morning DeShazer saw the guard walking up and down the corridor with his hands in a prayerful attitude and his lips moving. After a while the guard came over to DeShazer's cell and said that he had been praying to his mother who had died when he was a small boy. This was in harmony with the guard's belief.

This guard became very friendly to DeShazer and from that time on did not shout at him nor treat him rudely. One day the guard slid back the little door and handed DeShazer a boiled sweet potato, a wonderful treat. DeShazer was already getting some payoff for being gracious to his enemies. Another time the guard gave him five figs and some candy. Again DeShazer was convinced that God's way is the best way.

Experiences of this type have convinced DeShazer, *God's way will work if we will try it out. Jesus was not an idealist whose ideals could not be realized. When he told us to love one another, he told us the best way to act, and it works -- better than any other way which could be tried, but people and nations still try some other way to their own confusion.*

10. Prison Extremes

When DeShazer accepted Christ it gave him inner spiritual fortitude, but did not rebuild his physical life. The summer of 1944 was extremely hot at Nanking. In the intense heat, the prison cells in the low wood frame buildings were almost unbearable in the daytime. Even at night it was sultry and difficult to rest. Conditions were further worsened by the doors, which were made of solid wood with no way to ventilate the cells.

Lieutenant Hite became very ill with an extremely high fever. When it became apparent that his life was in jeopardy, the guards replaced the solid wood door of his cell with a screen door. In spite of this, Hite's fever continued dangerously high. The Japanese officials took serious interest in his welfare and made an unusual effort to bring him back to health. A medical assistant was assigned to look after him. Apparently he was told to spare no effort to save him. The young physician actually moved into the prison himself to better care for Hite. Under the patient care of this young medical assistant and with the advent of cooler weather, Hite began to mend.

Throughout these unbearable days and nights DeShazer received unusual encouragement and strength because of his newfound love. Within himself he had the witness of the presence of the Lord. He had memorized all five chapters of the First Epistle of John and made special use of the teachings about abiding in the Lord. Again and again there recurred to his mind the importance of the commandments of God and the necessity of being *obedient*.

Even so, the hours and days dragged slowly. Finally, fall came with more moderate temperatures. Weeks passed, and then came the very cold winter of 1944-45. There was a heavy snowfall the first of December. From that time until the first of March there was snow in the prison yard. The guards brought heavier clothes, and, as the winter became more severe, finally returned to the men their old army clothes. These were put on over the Japanese garments.

Two or three weeks after the first heavy snowfall the prisoners were taken for exercise in the prison yard but were warned not to take off their slippers. The slippers were the loose Japanese kind, and it was difficult to run without losing them. They walked around the yard a few times but were eager to run in order to get warmed up. Finally they ignored the order, kicked off their slippers, and ran barefoot.

There was a penalty to pay! The guards ordered them back into their cells. The men started for the building expecting to go inside to wash their feet at the water hydrant. The guards, however, rushed them away and told them to go over to the snowbank and clean their feet in the snow.

The men said they would rather wash their feet at the water hydrant. The guards insisted that they use the snowbank. Lieutenant Barr, resenting their orders, tried to go inside. A guard grabbed him and tried to turn him around by taking hold of his coat sleeve. Barr jabbed his elbow into the guard's stomach.

After his comrades were taken to their cells, about 10 guards began beating Lieutenant Barr. Not disposed to submit willingly to a whipping, Barr gave the guards a rather rough time. Finally, they were able to shove him along and put him into his cell. Barr was then placed in a straitjacket, his arms tied behind his back, and ropes were drawn so tight that his shoulder nearly broke. His chest, too, was subjected to such awful tension by the ropes around his body that the pain was excruciating. To the other men it sounded as if Barr was being killed. He was certainly doing a good job of hollering.

The screaming had a wholesome effect on the prison official, who, according to DeShazer, "was really a kindhearted, tender-spirited man." One of the guards, Mr. Misaka, who had tried to be a gentleman and a good friend made an effort to persuade the others to release Barr. This they did after about one hour of torture. The guards seemed to feel rather virtuous, for they told Barr he was fortunate, since they tortured their own men by that means for four to six hours when they had occasion to discipline them.

The Barr incident once again brought dejection of spirit among the prisoners, but the mood changed on Christmas Day, 1944, with the appearance of American bombers in the skies over Nanking. The prisoners actually saw the dive bombers skimming over housetops, shooting as they came. Soon they heard bombs exploding and saw clouds of black smoke billowing skyward. Evidently some oil refineries and storage tanks had been the targets.

The satisfaction which came to the minds of the prisoners was inexpressible. For many months the guards had been telling them extreme stories regarding the losses of the United States and the successes of the Japanese. Repeatedly they claimed that Japan had taken possession of San Francisco and New York, and that Japanese soldiers were marching up and down the streets of these and other cities giving orders to the American people. Sometimes the prisoners wondered whether the stories told by the guards might be true.

The Japanese must have believed their own stories, for they were taken completely by surprise by the appearance of the American planes. But they quickly adjusted their stories and said the American planes had only dropped a few bombs in the rivers and killed a few fish. The thought of Japan ever having to surrender seemed completely foreign to their thinking.

The American planes, however, brought no relief to the intense cold inside the Japanese prison. The prisoners suffered constantly with colds. DeShazer began breaking out with large boils. Some boils appeared on the bottoms of his feet. These continued through the winter. When warmer weather came, the boils disappeared for a time but reappeared later in the summer.

It was the middle of June when one morning the prisoners were taken out of their cells, handcuffed and tied up in preparation for the move. It must have been interesting to see the guards shake hands with the men in this handcuffed position. Despite the fact that one group was guards, the other group prisoners, a real sense of friendship had developed. They had been together in the Nanking prison more than 26 months.

The prisoners rode by train in a northerly direction for more than 40 hours, not knowing their destination. They traveled through strange country and saw strange crowds. Their hands and legs were tied with their belts. Each man had a guard who hung on to the rope whether they were sitting or standing. Over each prisoner was a large green raincoat, and over each head was pulled a hat which had a mask for a face.

The train was crowded beyond description. Most of the passengers were soldiers. A few were civilians, and some were Red Cross workers. All of the women sat on the floor in the aisles or on some of the baggage. The men in the Japanese program are the ones who occupy the seats. High-ranking officers came into the car and ordered those of lower rank to get up and give them a place. Sometimes Chinese men or women tried to get through the car, but someone ordered them out, and, if they didn't understand, a slap of the hand convinced them that they were to stay out. The whole group, however, seemed to be a serious, tired-looking crowd of people.

DeShazer was not unmindful of his dedication to God while riding on that train: *I remembered the Bible message. I wondered what God would do with all of these people who had probably never heard of Him. I thanked God for his mercy to me, and I wished there was some way the people on the train could know about the salvation which God had provided for all people. What joy they would know if Jesus were dwelling in their hearts as he was dwelling in mine!*

After nearly three days they arrived in Peking. It was an extremely hot day. The prisoners were taken to the side of the station to wait in a shady place for a military truck.

People were everywhere. Many Chinese were lying in the shade of the railroad station. As the guards with their prisoners came near, these loafers were told to clear out. One old Chinese lady who had a great deal of baggage was unable to get out of the way rapidly enough. A Japanese officer screamed at the woman to hurry, but the poor woman was hurrying as fast as her age would allow. The officer slapped her on both sides of the face to make her really hurry. This treatment seemed to be common almost everywhere. DeShazer says, "It made me wish that they could be shown the way of love."

A truck eventually came and took the guards and prisoners to a large prison in Peking. Apparently it was a military prison with more than 1,000 Japanese prisoners receiving typical oriental punishment. Five or six Japanese soldier prisoners were placed in a cell together and for two hours were forced to kneel on the floor without changing position. After such a two hour period they were all supposed to sit on the floor, straight up, feet out in front, without any support for their backs.

The American prisoners were no longer to have the joy of even a prison courtyard. They were placed in the inner section of this military prison, each one in a solitary cell, and from that time on there was no more going outside for exercise. The only time they saw each other was once a week when they were allowed to get together for a bath.

The Americans frequently heard and occasionally saw the guards take soldiers out of their cells and beat them, apparently one of their chief methods of keeping discipline. It was difficult for DeShazer to think he was in a real world. There was so much cruelty and fear. He was constantly reminded that freedom is one of the great heritages in the United States not known in a non-Christian country.

11. Near Death

In the Peking Japanese prison, the Americans were forced to sit on the floor just as the other prisoners were. They were not accustomed to this, and the experience became so excruciating that the guards were finally persuaded to provide some relief. Each was given a little stool with a top made of a two by four, about eight inches long. Throughout the entire day each man was required to sit three feet from the wall and keep his face toward the rear wall. Evidently, the Japanese did not want the Americans to see some of the brutal treatment which their own soldiers received.

It is difficult to imagine the mental torment experienced by these men in this situation after 38 months of deprivation, hunger, sickness, and punishment. One month of this new treatment was all DeShazer could stand. Already weakened by severe attacks of dysentery, he was much emaciated. Boils appeared again, this time all over his body. He counted as many as 75 bad boils at one time. No longer able to sit on the little stool, he lay on his bed mat day after day.

After about three weeks he became delirious, but he does remember this: *I still kept going over the verses in the Bible that I had memorized. I thought it wouldn't be long before I would be in heaven with Lieutenant Meder. My heart was hurting, and I could remember how Lieutenant Meder said his heart had hurt before he died. Nanking prison guards told me the reason Meder died was that his heart had stopped. I thought I would probably die for the same reason.*

After several days, Matthew 17:20 came to mind. "If you have faith as small as a mustard seed, you can say to this mountain, 'Move from here to there' and it will move. Nothing will be impossible for you." He began to think about how small a mustard seed is, and then he thought, "Surely I have that much faith -- that God can make me well!"

DeShazer later described his thoughts and experience in this weakened condition: *Many times I had thanked God for faith to believe that I was saved. It now seemed that God wished for me to have the faith that he would heal me from my bad attack of dysentery. God had been such a good friend to me that I felt I could not act as a coward now. The only thing to do was to try it out and see if God was really talking to me.*

I got out of bed and sat on the little bench one morning after I had prayed it all out with God. I was so weak that my heart could have stopped very easily, but God knows how to keep a person's heart going. I didn't know what to expect. I just prayed that God would make me better. I made up my mind to sit there until I either passed out or God healed me.

It was not long before the voice of God broke into my thoughts, different from anything I had experienced before. I often wondered where a person's thoughts come from, and as I sat in prison I was conscious of the activity of my thoughts. Ordinarily, I had control over them, but now it was different. I still had control over my thoughts, yet I knew that I was being possessed by another power. I was sure I was not responsible for the thoughts coming to my mind. I had never dreamed of anything like this. It was hard for me to realize that I was experiencing such a glorious contact with God.

"It is the Holy Spirit who is speaking to you," the mysterious voice said. "The Holy Spirit has made you free." I immediately began to wonder if I was going to get out of prison. The voice said, "You are free to do as you please. You can go through the wall or jump over the wall. You are free." I couldn't figure that out, but I had only a desire to do what was pleasing to God. "The Holy Spirit has set you free from sin," I was told.

Free from sin! Yes, God's Word has said, "No one who lives in him keeps on sinning. No one who continues to sin has either seen him or known him." This was in the first Epistle of John that I had memorized. It was the third chapter and sixth verse.

I was free from any desire to do willful sin. If I knew something was wrong, I would put forth every effort I could not to do it any more. James 4:17 states, "Anyone who knows the good he ought to do and doesn't do it, sins." This is the kind of sin that God expects us to live above. The sin of ignorance spoken of in Leviticus is all taken care of by the blood of Jesus. We have been given power by Jesus to be free from willful, disobedient sin.

I was able to tell by this reasoning that the voice speaking to me agreed with the Bible. The Spirit and the Word agree. I was almost too happy for this world. I had been lonesome and sick, but now God spoke to me and filled my heart with an unearthly joy.

I found out that I could ask questions and I could receive answers right away. This was a big help in connection with my food. I was always hungry, but often, if I ate the food, I would become very sick. When the food came to the door, I would pray and ask if I should eat the food or should send it back. If the voice said, "Yes, yes," I would eat; but if the answer was, "No, no," I would send the food back. For two days I was not given permission to eat or drink. I was weak, but the sickness was leaving me.

I would not lie down in the daytime if I was not sure that it was permissible for me to do so. My body was tired and weak, but I wanted to be sure and show "faith as a grain of mustard seed." As I was sitting on the little seat facing the wall, I wondered if there wasn't some way that I could let the guards know about the wonderful spirit of Jesus which was so present with me. His power and life were throbbing with a thrilling consciousness to me at every heartbeat.

There didn't seem to be much that I could do, but I remembered the story about Daniel. I went down on my knees in front of the door, *folded my hands to pray, and I really did pray. The first guard came by, beat on the door with his sword and hollered at me to get back on my bench. It was against the rules for any prisoner even to look at the door. Japanese prisoners received a beating for such audacity, but I did not move when the guard shouted. I felt no fear since God had shown me what to do. I felt a great weight of joy.*

In a very short time the guard returned with several other guards. The door opened and the guards walked into my cell. They never hit me nor hollered at me. They acted a little awed. A medical man came to my cell, and I was picked up and laid down on a straw mat. The medical man rolled up my shirt sleeve and shot some medicine into my arm, after which I was left alone in my cell to thank Jesus who was close by my side.

When mealtime came, I was surprised to receive a nice pint of milk, boiled eggs, some good well-made bread, and some nice, nourishing soup. I couldn't help crying and laughing when I thought how beautifully and wonderfully God had worked all this out for me. From that time until we were released from prison, I received milk, eggs, bread, and good nourishing food. I stayed in bed because I thought God had indicated that this was the thing for me to do.

On August 10, 1945, when DeShazer first woke up in the morning he was told to "start praying. Pray for peace, and pray without ceasing." DeShazer remembers, *I started to pray for peace, although I had a very poor idea of what was taking place in the world at that time. I prayed that God would put a great desire in the hearts of the Japanese leaders for peace. I thought about the days of peace that would follow. Japanese people would no doubt be discouraged, and I felt sympathetic toward them. I prayed that God would not allow them to fall into persecution by the victorious armies.*

At two o'clock in the afternoon the Holy Spirit told me, "You don't need to pray anymore. The victory is won." I was amazed. I thought this was quicker and better than the regular method of receiving world news.

DeShazer had no radio and was not privileged for several days to get the news of that fateful tenth day of August 1945 when the first atomic bomb was dropped on Hiroshima. It was then that the Japanese leaders began to sue for peace.

During the next 10 days DeShazer "felt the love of God flooding my soul. Night and day a rapturous joy was being experienced. I felt certain that I was having a foretaste of heaven." At the same time new strength was coming to his weakened body. He was now receiving plenty of good food. Vitality was returning. It was almost sheer ecstasy as he lay on his straw mat to realize both the wonder of returning physical strength and the joy of the fullness of the Holy Spirit.

These thoughts poured through his mind: *I promised God I would make restitution for the things I had stolen. I felt certain I would return to the United States. I felt love toward the Japanese people and a deep interest in their welfare. How I wished I could tell the Japanese people about Jesus! I knew my Savior would be their Savior, too.*

One day soon after this experience he saw smoke and burnt paper rising up in the sky. The guards came on duty wearing new clothes. He saw them discarding old clothes and breaking into their supplies. He felt these were the first signs that the end had come. His heart beat faster and faster as he thought about the freedom that would soon be his.

Then his thoughts were directed to the Japanese: *I could not help wondering what would happen to Japan now. Their hopes had been set on victory. Defeat would be an awful blow. But, if the Japanese found out about Jesus, military defeat would in reality be a great victory. At this time the voice of the Holy Spirit spoke to me clearly: "You are called to teach the Japanese people and to go where I send you."*

12. Freedom

On August 20, 1945, after 40 months of imprisonment, a Japanese official announced to DeShazer, "The war is over. You can go home now." Those were wonderful words. The cells were opened. The men came out. All of them were very weak and thin, but there was a look of joy and happiness in their hollow eyes.

They were given their old army clothes – now more than three years old – which they had been wearing when they were captured. They were then loaded on a truck and taken to a big English hotel where, "We ate all of the Irish stew we could hold." The doctors gave them vitamin pills and shot vitamin fluid into their arms. The food they ate digested well and rapidly brought new strength.

They quickly digested war news along with their food. They heard about the atomic bomb. They learned that American parachute troops had flown in to rescue them, but were told by a Japanese official that all the Doolittle flyers had been executed.

It may never be known exactly how word got out that some Doolittle flyers were still alive. DeShazer thinks it may have been through some U. S. Marines in prison near them in Nanking. Soup was brought to them in aluminum teacups, and one day Lieutenant Nielson noticed that on the bottom of one teacup was scratched, "U. S. Marines."

Nielson told his comrades about it, they picked up nails in the yard, sharpened them on the cement walls, and corresponded with the marines by writing on the bottoms of the aluminum teacups. Their scratchings were not noticed by prison officials for about two months, and by then word had gone to the marines about the four Doolittle flyers in solitary confinement.

The Marines were captured at the very first of the war. After several months in a concentration camp, 10 of them tried to get away, but only three succeeded. The other seven were put in prison near the Doolittle men, and were the first to be released when the war ended. They were thus able to tell the American parachute officers that some of the Doolittle flyers were still alive.

On the third day, American B-24s landed on the airfield of the defeated Japanese, and the next day three of the flyers were flown to Chungking. Lieutenant Barr had to stay at Peking since his health would not permit an airplane trip. He later returned to America by steamship.

News of finding four Doolittle flyers was released to the world on August 20. The first word which came over the American radio did not give their names. For some hours the suspense in the heart of a little mother in Salem, Oregon, was indescribable. She had prayed and prayed. She had trusted the Lord continually, but still there was an inner longing for an outward evidence that her prayers were answered. Was it possible? Would it be true that one of the four would be her own Jake? Ears were glued to the radio anxiously waiting for further word. This further word came about noon when to the inexpressible joy of mother, stepfather, half sister, other relatives, and many, many friends, announcement was made that one of the four was Sergeant Jacob DeShazer.

Imagine the added joy to his mother's heart when word came over the airwaves that Jake had been converted while in prison but had decided to give his life to missionary work! The newspaper men seemed to think this was even greater news than his deliverance from prison. Pictures of DeShazer on his knees were radioed throughout the world. Some said the young man was only seeking the limelight. Others said it was undoubtedly a sincere statement but would be short-lived.

It was early September when the released flyers landed on American soil, where they were subjected to many interviews. DeShazer went to New York and spoke on "We the People" radio program where he received $400 for reading one sentence over the radio. He received $2,250 from a newspaper syndicate for his personal story, and was given back pay for the 40 months in prison which amounted to $5,600. He says, "I felt I was a very wealthy person when I boarded an airplane in Washington, D. C., to visit my parents in Salem, Oregon."

He finally reached home, where the Bible was read and prayer offered every morning since Jake had dropped out of sight. Now family prayer continued, with another member added. In that home there was much joy, a constant spirit of thanksgiving, and a desire to see Jake brought back to normal physical condition. Like any mother, Mrs. Andrus spent much time preparing good food. Nothing was spared in providing wholesome, appetizing, and enjoyable meals. The first 20 days out of prison Jake gained an average of one pound a day.

When Jake left home in 1940 for army service, his family lived in Madras, Oregon. In his absence they had retired from the farm and moved to Salem. Jake was anxious to visit his old hometown at Madras. He made such a trip, and great was the celebration held in his honor. He was given a watch and asked to make a speech. He says: *It was a good place to begin my speech making. I told as much as I could about the prison and about the salvation I received when I read the Bible. I ran out of wind pretty fast. I was sweating and working harder than I had ever worked in my life. It seems funny now, but I was nearly 33 years old, and this was my first public speech. In bed alone that night I prayed to God. I felt comfort from him and a promise of victory if I would continue to try.*

DeShazer was supposed to receive a 90-day leave from the Army. However, within two weeks after arriving home he received a telegram asking him to report to Santa Ana Air Base in California. After reporting there he immediately asked for a discharge from the Army. He was informed that it would be impossible to get out for some time since there was a large number of soldiers to be discharged.

With little to do and considerable freedom, Jake visited several relatives around Santa Ana. He was also called upon to speak at various church and youth services. At one church someone asked whether he had been baptized. He said yes, but not publicly. He recalled that while in prison he wished he could be baptized, so he went over to one side of his cell where the wind was blowing the water from the eaves through the window. DeShazer stood in this spattering rain and praised God for a water baptism.

While he was at Santa Ana, a military blunder by a leading

official received nationwide publicity. For no reason DeShazer was told to report for K. P. duty where he was assigned to cleaning dishes. A newspaper man came in and without authorization took DeShazer's picture as he, weak and emaciated, carried a large tray of dishes. This picture appeared in a leading Los Angeles paper and it aroused a great deal of public sentiment against the military authorities for putting DeShazer and other former prisoners of war at menial tasks.

The officials responsible were given a reprimand and DeShazer was sent immediately to a hospital for further observation and care. Just before he was sent to the hospital the commanding officer called him in and admitted that it was a great mistake for him to be put on K. P. duty. The commanding officer also told him he would do everything possible to help expedite DeShazer's request for discharge from the Army.

13. Re-Training Course

DeShazer's sister, Helen, was a student at Seattle Pacific College and secretary to President Watson. She went home to greet Jake, then on September 13, 1945, she wrote to President Watson: *My brother reached home about midnight last night. You can well imagine that there is not a happier home in the world than ours. He looks better than we had feared - has gained some fifteen pounds since being rescued. The most wonderful part of all, of course, is his experience with God and desire to return to Japan as a missionary after proper training. I am hoping that SPC will be his choice of a college....*

On September 20, President Charles Hoyt Watson of Seattle Pacific College wrote DeShazer in part: *Since Helen has been my secretary this summer, I have come to feel very close to you. We greatly appreciate what you and your comrades have done. I am sure God now has a plan whereby you can use the tragic experiences of the last 40 months for the uplift and salvation of many. I have just received a card from Helen indicating you are anxious to get started immediately with your school program. Be assured of our willingness and desire to cooperate in every way.*

DeShazer was not exactly sure what to do. Many calls were coming in for him to come as a speaker. One call was from the Reverend Mr. Finkbeiner, a good friend of DeShazer years before at Madras, Oregon. DeShazer accepted this invitation and while making the trip stopped off at Seattle Pacific College to visit his sister, who introduced him to the president. DeShazer describes this brief interview: *President*

Watson asked me when I was going to start to school. I said I didn't think I could go to school before the winter quarter, but he gave me a good chance to start immediately if I so desired. The result was that the next day I started college.

Think of it! Only three months before I started college I was seriously ill and thought I would die. God healed me from sickness, baptized me with the Holy Spirit, and provided everything I needed in preparing to become a missionary. How impossible it seemed to me, but all God asked me to do was to try, and then he worked. The government was paying my tuition and giving me subsistence money. I was free to give my full time to study.

It was a great change from a Japanese war prison. Everyone on the campus called me "Jake." They all knew me since my name and pictures had been in the papers. I tried to remember the other students' names, but it was difficult to remember all of them. However, they were all my friends, and I enjoyed their friendship.

As Jake's first year of school moved along he learned there would be a summer session. He made plans to complete his total four-year college course in three years. These plans, however, were intensified and given much more meaning after he began to share his desires and plans with a lovely young woman and fellow student.

14. Romance

Early in 1946 DeShazer went to a Youth for Christ service with Miss Florence Matheny. This young lady, a few years younger than DeShazer, was a junior in college. She had come to Seattle Pacific in the fall of 1945, from Toddville, Iowa, after completing her first two years in Lenox Junior College. Jake describes her: *She was a very attractive young lady, the most attractive young lady I had ever met, and she wanted to go into full-time work for the Lord. We both felt a oneness of purpose, and when I asked Miss Matheny if she would marry me, she said that she would. When we prayed to Jesus, we felt that he would be pleased to give us a life together.*

At the close of summer school in 1946, Jake and Florence went to Gresham, Oregon, where on August 29, they were married. The ceremony was performed by Florence's former pastor, the Reverend J. K. French. Jake and Florence felt God had directed them in finding one another. Now the two went forward together.

The calls for DeShazer to speak were just as numerous as ever.

Now Florence went along. The two young people seemed to get along in a wonderful way. Jake's message of love based upon his prison experiences and Florence's message of consecration to missionary endeavor seemed to touch the hearts and minds of every audience. People enjoyed having them in their homes. Youth groups enjoyed their testimonies. Many were the decisions for Christ, and many were the dedications to missionary service.

When at home, they read the Bible and prayed together at least twice every day. Over and over they emphasized the value of their little family altar. They said they had dedicated their time, their strength, and their possessions to the Lord.

On the last day of October 1947, Jake attended classes as usual, but seemed to be living out of this world. Other students greeted him with congratulations and asked, "Is it a boy or a girl?" It was not long, however, until everyone knew that the baby born that morning was a healthy boy in the very image of his mother. DeShazer announced that they would call the lad Paul Edward: "The Paul is after the apostle Paul, and I don't know where the Edward came from." The dad was rather free in the distribution of candy bars.

Florence stayed at home to take care of Paul for the remainder of the school year. She needed only eight credits more to finish her bachelor of arts degree. Since Jake would have to go to school the following summer, they agreed to finish their work together.

15. Back To Japan

Following college graduation, things moved very rapidly for the DeShazers. Already accepted as outgoing missionaries to Japan by the Missionary Board of the Free Methodist Church of North America, they took many calls to meet with various groups, and pondered plans for going to the Orient. The couple hoped to sail soon after the first of November. The maritime strike, however, made it impossible for them to sail until December 14.

For an eight-day period in September, Jake and Florence had charge of a booth at the Third World Missions Conference held at Seattle Pacific College. About 100 missionaries and 50 or 60 different missions participated in this conference. After the conference, the little family started on a speaking tour of the United States. On this trip Jake found there was great enthusiasm throughout America for promoting Christian missions in Japan. They toured east and then south and returned west to

Los Angeles and San Francisco.

Here they boarded the U.S.S. *General Meigs* and left San Francisco December 14, 1948, just six years and eight months after he had gone on the U.S.S. *Hornet* under the Golden Gate Bridge. The *General Meigs* was a rough-riding ship. There were 16 people in the cabin where Florence and Paul stayed. Most of them were missionaries, and one was Free Methodist missionary Miss Alice Fensome who was making her first trip to Japan [and who later became editor of *The Missionary Tidings*].

While making this two-week trip, DeShazer had many thoughts. Some of these he has written down: *This time I was not going as a bombardier, but as a missionary. Now I had love and good intentions toward Japan. How much better it is to go out to conquer evil with the gospel of peace! The strength and power must come from God, but God's promise is, "I have placed before you an open door that no man can shut" (Revelation 3:8). I have tried God's promises out in the past, and God always keeps his promises.*

My brave little wife was ready for the fight. There might be hardship and trouble, but there would be no turning back on her part. This is God's battle and God says, "Be not afraid nor dismayed by reason of this great multitude." To fight with God gives confidence and victory, and the victory will be glorious.

People who find Jesus are never sorry. Jesus gives a better life in this world and the sure promise of eternal joy in the next. We are going to Japan to tell about Jesus and show the way of peace and happiness. We hope to see Japan among the nations that have the joy of worshipping the true God.

16. Rookie Missionary

More than one million tracts concerning the Doolittle raider who turned missionary had been distributed throughout Japan. This tract in Japanese contained a blank to be signed by those who would accept Jesus Christ as their Savior. Many thousands of these were signed and returned. In view of this, the name *DeShazer* was known to many Japanese people.

So it was that on December 28, 1948, when DeShazer and his little family arrived in Yokohama docks, crowds were waiting to see him. Many wanted to know why a man who had been held for many months by the Japanese in a solitary cell could have a heart that overflowed with love for his persecutors.

As they pressed around DeShazer and asked many questions, he felt overwhelmed and reports, *By myself I was helpless. For flesh and blood cannot reveal the great spiritual truths. It is God that reveals and saves, and we must have God's forgiving, tender spirit in order for God to use us. If God will use us, even children can understand, and people who have put their trust in man-made idols will turn from idolatry and put their trust in the true and living God.*

Troubles and disappointment were not slow in coming. The DeShazers had been taken by friends to an American-style house, but there was little heat in the house. They felt damp and cold. The next day little Paul was ill with a bad cold. Jake had already accepted an appointment to speak at the Suginami Free Methodist Church in Tokyo on the next Sunday. The baby's cold became worse, and the house seemed to be extremely cold. By Saturday they began to look for a doctor. They finally learned that they could take Paul to an army hospital.

Here the doctor checked the baby carefully and said he should be left at the hospital where it was warmer and where he could be given medical care. This was a hard blow to Florence. How could she leave the little fellow in the hospital and not be near him for a week? They were able, however, to commit their situation to the Lord. DeShazer says: *It was good to know Jesus at that time and to realize that he knows all about us and our every problem. When we committed our lives to Jesus, we had given everything. The time of testing had come, but we must not turn back now.* "No man, having put his hand to the plow, and looking back, is fit for the kingdom of God" (Luke 9:62).

A week later Florence went back to the hospital and saw that Paul seemed to be improving. On this same Saturday, Jake visited two churches in Tokyo, the Suginami and the Oji. As an interpreter he had Dr. Kaneo Oda, also a graduate of Seattle Pacific College.

It was a great joy to DeShazer to preach the gospel in Japan. News concerning him spread everywhere. Churches and halls were filled to capacity. DeShazer used John 1:12 as a text many times. In this connection he asks people whether they are willing to receive Jesus. In response many hundreds are quick to indicate their decision to try out the promises of God in order that they may receive the gift of eternal life.

In due time, their overseas baggage arrived in Yokohama. A splendid gentleman, Mr. Yoshiki, arranged for them to live upstairs in his home. Here they set up a big oil stove which they had brought from America. They also dug out of their baggage cans of milk for baby Paul. Only a few days after having this proper food Paul was running about as if he had never been sick.

Florence started to hold Bible classes in her home. Many people came to see them, particularly in the evening, so both Jake and Florence held classes for instruction. This meant they needed an interpreter, for they were not yet able to converse readily in Japanese. They had a very faithful Christian interpreter, Mr. Nishidi, whose work during the day was interpreting for Japanese representatives of the U.S. Military Police. After about two months Florence took over all of the evening classes because Jake was out most of the time on speaking tours. Within a matter of weeks, five people from Mr. Yoshiki's home were baptized as Christians. Many others declared their intention of accepting Christ.

Within a few months after his arrival in Japan, DeShazer had spoken in nearly 200 places. Because it seemed almost impossible to get back immediately to the same place a second time, he made it a point always to call for decisions at his very first meeting.

Reports came to DeShazer in large numbers regarding the inspiration his messages brought and expressing a determination to live the Christian way. Here is a sample of such letters, received from a young lady: *On the 16th of May I received new life through your message which you gave. Thank you. While you were talking I cried very much. Through your prisoner-of-war life, you had a great deal of hatred toward the Japanese people. They were cruel. I know that some Japanese are very impolite and uncultivated. Please forgive us.*

However, you have forgiven us, and you came to Japan to save us. I cry to think of the love which God has put in your heart. I was a very sinful girl, but now I have repented. I worked as a factory girl, but I was very discouraged. I tried to kill myself three or four times, but without success. I just couldn't go through with suicide. I didn't have any affection toward Japan, and I had little interest.

I always hated God, and I had contracted the sickness of heart beriberi. I quit my work, but after a week I found a circular of your coming to our town to make a speech. I attended the meeting. And the 16th of May will always be a memorial and revolutionary day for me. By you I was reborn as a child is born on earth. I was now a child born in the heavenly kingdom. Now, "The Lord is my life and my salvation; whom shall I fear?"

Thank you very much for what you have done. I am full of optimism for the future.

In the spring of 1949, nearly four years after the war's end, one of the strangest meetings that has ever happened was DeShazer's happy experience at the O.S.S. Theatre in Osaka, Japan. By prearrangement many Japanese who lost loved ones during the war and as many prison guards as possible met on the platform of the big theater with Jake and Florence. An unusual spirit of forgiveness pervaded the place. DeShazer spoke to the large audience telling them about the message of forgiveness that Jesus preached. He told them that both they and he had been in the bitter anguish of the terrible war. "But now," he said, "we see the right thing to do is to forgive, to love one another, and to work together for one another's happiness."

He told about Jesus as God's Son and about the Holy Spirit who is able to bring light and truth. Two men, Mr. Aota and Mr. Misaka, DeShazer's prison guards, expressed their desire to become Christians. These men had been reading the Bible themselves and showing a very splendid attitude. DeShazer says, "We are praying, not only for my former guard, but for the Spirit of Christ to spread to all of the people in Japan so that the whole nation will become a Christian nation."

17. The 40-Day Fast

Early in 1950, DeShazer felt a burden for further self-analysis and Spirit-anointing if his ministry was to be highly effective. It seemed to him that the immediate evangelism of all Japan was so imperative it could not wait for the normal operations of the various missionary boards. So he entered upon a 40-day fast. He did not withdraw from active evangelistic work, nor did he stop his language study. During the entire period he ate practically nothing.

There was no thought on DeShazer's part of doing something spectacular. Rather, he felt a divine urge to pray for a spiritual awakening throughout all Japan. Many people were impressed by DeShazer's fast. A reporter for a leading Japanese newspaper told Bob Pierce, of Youth for Christ, that DeShazer's fast had produced a profound effect upon the Japanese people. DeShazer had already won the friendship of the Japanese by returning as a missionary; now he was even fasting for them! They were accustomed to the fastings of Buddhist priests but never knew of a foreign missionary fasting. The reporter said there were many things about Christianity the Japanese could not understand, but they understood DeShazer, and they liked him.

DeShazer reports that his fasting was a very rewarding experience. From that time on, God has been answering his prayer. One of the first evidences was the conversion on April 14, 1950, of Captain

Mitsuo Fuchida, commander of the 360 Japanese air squadron planes which bombed Pearl Harbor. Fuchida wrote the story of his conversion in tract form which has been distributed widely by the Pocket Testament League.

The tract tells about the unique manner in which God used DeShazer's testimony *I Was a Prisoner of Japan* (a tract published by the Bible Meditation League) to bring Fuchida under conviction. Within a month after conversion, he met DeShazer in a great mass meeting in the largest auditorium in Osaka, where both men gave their testimonies. At least 4,000 people crowded into the auditorium, and as many as 3,000 were outside unable to enter. At the close of the meeting some 500 individuals came down the aisles as seekers for the Christian way of life.

Soon after the conversion of Fuchida, DeShazer with his chief interpreter, the Reverend Dr. Kaneo Oda, began extensive evangelistic tours. They spent a month or more with the coal miners on Kyushu Island, holding two meetings a day with an average attendance of 1,000 or more. Opportunity was given for those interested to remain after each service for prayer. Many thus remained, the number in several instances reaching as high as 400. From Kyushu they went to Hiroshima, the city of the atom bomb, for a series of meetings.

Epilogue *by Leona K. Fear*

In following years Jake continued in a country-wide evangelism – from the northern island of Hokkaido to the southernmost island of Kyushu. Jake did not speak Japanese, but rather the language of love, a language readily understood by the Japanese people.

In 1951, the DeShazers asked for a miracle healing of their son, Paul, from encephalitis. Paul became critically ill and was taken to the army hospital where he slipped into a coma. Mrs. DeShazer says, "During those crisis hours the Lord sustained Jake and me in a wonderful way. Even as I prayed, the song came to me: 'Let all them that put their trust in thee rejoice, rejoice.'"

Paul wakened from the coma completely whole. Although everyone warned of possible brain damage, the doctors and nurses reported, "He is the worst case of sleeping sickness we have ever had, but he has made the quickest and most complete recovery." The DeShazers had come to expect miracles from God. God honored their simple faith.

Later, the DeShazer family moved into a new home near the site of Osaka Christian College. From this base DeShazer extended his ministry to the coal mines, factories, streets, theaters, and schools. In tent meetings, in their own home, and in churches DeShazer proclaimed God's love.

The rich and the poor, the high and the low, were touched by DeShazer. The maid in their home was converted. Those in the emperor's palace heard the story. At the invitation of the royal household DeShazer went to Tokyo and was received by Prince Takamatsu, brother of the emperor. DeShazer remembers, "I did not know what to do in the presence of royalty. I was with Colonel Hill, and I followed his example. He went in, shook the prince's hand, and said, 'How do you do?' We then sat down, and a servant brought tea and cakes. I was glad to give the message of Christian hope to the Prince. I also expressed thanks for the emperor's mercy in sparing my life during the war."

DeShazer was greatly concerned about the fate of Japanese war criminals and pleaded with American officials for mercy on their behalf, just as the emperor of Japan intervened for him when he was under the sentence of death. He wrote, "I owe the emperor of Japan an eternal debt of gratitude. I would have spent eternity in hell if I had been executed, for I was not a Christian. Our country was the first to drop the atomic bomb, now let us be the first to show mercy."

In October 1952, at the invitation of the United States Armed Forces, DeShazer held a two-week preaching mission among Air Force men in Korea. Special permission was given to visit some restricted war zones. He traveled 860 miles by jeep, truck, airplane, and helicopter. When not preaching, he chatted with the men, counseled them, and was popular with airmen everywhere. A high point of his Korean ministry was preaching to 1,000 people in a large Protestant church built by North Korean refugees.

The DeShazers had a great interest in Osaka Christian College. In March 1953, revival came in what DeShazer said was the greatest movement of the Spirit he had ever seen. "Sick are healed, demons cast out, storms stilled, people filled with the Holy Spirit, sins confessed, and the glory of the Lord manifested many times. Many people have been converted."

In April of that year DeShazer returned to the United States to meet for a reunion with the Doolittle flyers. He traveled extensively for a month, holding rallies in churches. As he brought news of revival in Japan, revival came to America. He spoke almost every night and often twice a day in college centers, churches, and interdenominational gatherings. Scores of young people were challenged and many opened their hearts to the Lord.

DeShazer decided in 1954 to launch a radio broadcast. From one station, in six months' time 291 enrolled in Bible correspondence courses. One station manager liked the program and sent it out on two other stations at no cost. The radio ministry penetrated even into Buddhist temples and reached young men who were training to be priests. At one time Jake turned over the remaining $2,000 of his prison pay and sold his camera to keep the program on the air, yet the ministry continued in financial straits and eventually was taken off the air.

At the close of 1954 the DeShazers had been in Japan for six years. The great interest in Christianity which had followed World War II was waning. Jake wrote, "We enroll many people in a Bible study course and it seems quite easy to win souls to the Lord, but the number of Christians in Japan does not increase very fast. The Japanese seem to enjoy Christianity for a while, but their family ties are strong, the Buddhist priests are powerful, and the government seems in favor of their old forms of worship. Then, too, the Japanese are very proud of their culture."

Yet in 1954 he reported more than 3,500 people had made decisions to accept Christ within the 12-month period. Typical of those persons responding was a young Japanese who was handed a tract on the street one day. As a result of that contact he came to the DeShazer home for Bible study. Soon afterwards he confessed Christ as Savior and began to lead others to Christ. He brought DeShazer to his high school and arranged for him to speak to about 400 students. As a result DeShazer was invited to begin a Bible class at the school.

In 1955 the DeShazers returned to the United States for furlough. Three more children had been born to them in Japan – John, Mark, and Carol. In the fall Jake enrolled at Asbury Theological Seminary in Wilmore, Kentucky, and three years later they returned to Japan. Their four older children and baby Ruth, just a few months old, accompanied them.

DeShazer now looked to the Japanese church leaders for guidance as to his future role in the church. Jake felt that his particular calling was to pioneer new churches. He planned to stay a year or two at a new location in order to start a church and then be ready to move on to another locality, leaving the new church in the capable hands of a Japanese pastor.

It was agreed that the family should locate in Nagoya, the city which Jake had helped to bomb. He wrote home to his mission board,

"Why should we not go out where we can work and others cannot? Nagoya is exactly the right place for us!"

To DeShazer it seemed like a dream come true to be able to move into the city he had once bombed to proclaim the love of God. In May of 1959 the DeShazer family were in their new home and ready to go to work. They began by making friends with their Japanese neighbors. They brought children into the home for Bible stories. They distributed Christian literature. They taught English Bible classes. In September when a typhoon hit the area they extended a helping hand to those who suffered the loss of loved ones and personal possessions.

In 1963, DeShazer wrote that four years of hard work and faithful sowing of the seed had come to fruition. With a growing congregation and a new building in place, the church was turned over to a Japanese pastor and the DeShazers returned to America for furlough.

Family needs and other circumstances kept the DeShazers at home for three and one-half years. In 1966 DeShazer wrote, "We are working on a film with Mitsuo Fuchida. I think the film will have great evangelistic possibilities. It would have more meaning for Japanese than for Americans."

Then in September of 1967 the DeShazers turned once more toward Japan where 20 new churches were established since his first coming as a missionary. The Evangelism Committee of the Japan Free Methodist Church assigned the DeShazers to work in the city of Katsuta, a new area designed for commuter homes about 100 miles from Tokyo and near to the great industrial city of Hitachi. With characteristic enthusiasm Jake conducted English Bible classes and Sunday services. DeShazer and the pastor visited homes, gave out tracts, and sold Bibles.

In October of 1971, DeShazer wrote, "Katsuta is planning to make a bigger building. I go to Katsuta once a month now to assist." Meanwhile, he was appointed superintendent of the eastern conference of the Japan General Church, a responsibility he was reluctant to assume. "Pray for me," he wrote. "I don't know how to be a superintendent."

In 1992, Jake and Florence DeShazer continue to travel and share the Christian gospel from their base in Salem, Oregon. Jacob writes:

We have had a home in Salem for 15 years. God has given us the joy of telling the good news of salvation at many places. Florence is accepted as a great Sunday school teacher. I have been to Japan four times and have found people who heard me from 1949-1955. It is heart warming to hear them say they have been going to church since hearing the gospel for the first time. I am glad that God gave me love through faith in Jesus Christ and taught me to "follow after love."

Five children were born to Florence and me and we have seven grandchildren and expect two more this year. God is good. I pray that many more people will read the Bible and believe it is the inerrant Word of God. God has watched over his Holy Word and even though heaven and earth will pass away, God's Word is forever. With this faith we can face eternity with joy unspeakable, for "The gift of God is eternal life in Jesus Christ our Lord" (Romans 6:23).

Land Of The Rising Sun

K. Lavern Snider
September/October 1992 p. 4-5

I sensed a call to missionary service when I was 15, and Lois after we began our courtship. In November 1957, after serving as teachers and principal for six years at Lorne Park College, the Japanese freighter *Settsu Maru* took us and our one-year-old daughter, Carol, on a 15-day journey across the Pacific to the Land of the Rising Sun. What an adventure these 35 years have been, living and working in such a beautiful, historic country.

When we first arrived, there remained little evidence of the war, although many cities had been devastated. The Free Methodist Church also suffered, but after the war made steady progress, though not without struggle. In the tumultuous decade of the 70s our denomination lost eight congregations reducing the number of churches to 30. Since that time two more churches have been established, and four church planting projects are currently underway.

Our new bishop, Hachiroemon Naiki (elected in February 1992), has announced that the church he pastors plans another church planting project in the immediate future. The Japan Free Methodist Church under the leadership of the evangelism committee is stretching to reach its goal to double church membership over the last decade of this century.

During the 1960s the desire of the Japanese to learn English became quite intense. We sensed here a door of opportunity -- English classes infused with Christian faith. Since 1971, when the program began, 93 VISA missionaries have gone to Japan to teach conversational English, hold Bible classes, and share their faith.

Our major activities in Japan have been teaching and administration in Osaka Christian College and Theological Seminary. I have taught a variety of subjects in the seminary while Lois has taught English as a Second Language in the teacher training department.

Today the Osaka Theological Seminary department with its 53 students, nine of whom are Free Methodists, boasts the largest enrollment in its history. Among the students are several Koreans who have come to assist in Japan's evangelization. Seminary graduates now serve Free

Methodist and other churches and provide administrative leadership in both college and seminary.

During our career missionary service God also gave us the privilege of planting a new church in the city of Nishinomiya where we lived for 18 years. This adventure began with neighbor ladies requesting Lois to teach western cooking. Cooking classes led to sharing the gospel on a personal basis followed by monthly Bible studies and then weekly Sunday services. Giving pastoral leadership at the present time are Canadian VISA missionaries Ron and Elaine Hobden.

Resistance Could Crumble

We are often asked why church growth in Japan is slow compared to some other countries. The reasons, I believe, are to be found in society and also in the church. Rather than curse the darkness, I felt that God was asking me to light some candles. This I endeavored to do through seminary classes, speaking engagements, and in writing books addressed to church leadership. I believe that if the church in Japan will pay the necessary price, impediments to progress such as ancestor worship and the common notion that to become a Christian is to become non-Japanese will shatter under the mighty power of God.

Other new developments could also break through the resistance. The Korean Provisional Conference of the Free Methodist Church (a new addition to our church family in November 1990) is offering to send missionary assistance to the Japan church.

Another point of progress is in Tokyo, where a separate cluster of Free Methodist churches pioneered by Mrs. Eva Millican from Seattle, has grown to nine congregations. Leaders of the two distinct Free Methodist denominations are discussing the possibilities of a merger.

We have now relinquished direct responsibility as missionaries among a great people to retire from career missionary service but we shall always love Japan and pray for the salvation of its people. We dare to believe that there will soon come spiritual renewal and vigorous evangelistic outreach in Japan which will result in a great spiritual harvest during the last years of this decade.

Welcome To Taiwan!

M. Doane Bonney
November/December 1992 pp. 1-2

Our church in Taiwan is vibrantly alive. Church planting and missions outreach overseas are actively being pursued. VISA and career missionaries are *all* involved in church planting along with their other regular activities. This is good!

Taiwan is making plans to evangelize and plant a church in Burma through the work of a graduate of Holy Light Seminary. And the eight-story Holy Light Seminary building is completed and paid for.

This June, Dr. Jonathan Lu, after 20 years of teaching and administration at the University of Northern Iowa, returned to Taiwan to become Holy Light's new president. This school year we have about 160 students with another 100 in TEE classes.

Is Taiwan Still A Mission Field?

The population of Taiwan presents an interesting mix, with three basic varieties of people. There are the aboriginals, or "mountain people." There are also the early invaders, the Minnan Chinese, who make up two-thirds of the population. And there are the ruling Mandarin-speaking, North Chinese who came to Taiwan in the World War II period.

Our work is mainly among the Mandarin Chinese, the governing, professional people. They tell me that David and Millie Samuelson (now living in McPherson, Kansas) were the only Free Methodist missionaries to learn the Taiwanese language. David reports that in 1967 when they went to Taiwan, this was important. It gave them an opening to large segments of the population.

Today, Mandarin is required in the schools. Only those outside the educational system cling to traditional languages. We must not overlook these unreached peoples, where language may be as different from Mandarin as German is from Italian.

Career And VISA Missionaries Needed

One-on-one evangelism is very productive. Rebecca Doyle, a VISA volunteer, won to Christ and discipled seven new believers in a 12-

month period. Veteran missionaries like the Bickslers, Wilma Kasten, Dorothy Raber and Susan Yu continue to make valuable contributions in preparing pastors and missionaries.

I believe Taiwan is a major key to evangelizing southeast Asia and the Chinese everywhere. The day will come when Mainland China will be wide open to the gospel – more than a *billion* people! We have sent the Petersons and Tim Kinkead to reinforce the mission team. But we ought to have 20 couples studying Chinese, gaining communication skills, and learning to depend on God. The door will open. The wall will come down. We must be prepared!

First-Hand Look

My recent visit to Taiwan was an eye-opener. Many churches are in high buildings where apartments are purchased and the walls rearranged to make suitable meeting places. A typical flat costs about $250,000. But salaries in Taiwan are high. One of our career missionaries, the Bickslers, are the lowest salaried couple in their church! Taxi drivers can make $2,000 a month. Mountain people recently arrived in cities make about $1,000 a month, and with that have difficulty making ends meet. Taiwan doesn't fit the *mud hut* concept of missions. It's a land of high rises and high tech. And it's the gateway to about 25% of the world's population.

Six Pieces Of Wood

James Wong & Dorothy Raber
November/December 1992 pp. 12-13

I am a Chinese Malaysian born in East Malaysia in the northern portion of the island of Borneo. My father moved there from mainland China and my mother was born there.

As in every typical Chinese family in those days, it was very important to have a son to carry on the name of the family. After giving birth to their first child, a daughter, Mom and Dad were working hard to get a boy. However, their second child was still a girl, as was their third, fourth, fifth, sixth and seventh! You can imagine how disappointed they were, but did they stop trying? Of course not.

Finally, I was born into that poor, non-Christian family. My birth brought joy and hope, for at last there was someone who could carry on the family name.

However, the joy was accompanied by deep sorrow and grief, for my father was suffering through the last stage of a terminal illness. When I was just three months old, he died.

My family was so poor that we couldn't afford to buy six pieces of the cheapest wood to put my father's body in. (Eventually, two of my sisters were given away and not one of my other five sisters completed senior high school. All of them had to work at an early age to support the family.)

I hated life in such an environment. I questioned God's love and justice -- if there was a God. I was pessimistic about my future. I feared death yet wished life would end soon.

Our family held heathen religious beliefs. When my father died, we did not have the money to bury him. It was then that the local church showed our family the love of Jesus Christ by buying the six pieces of wood for Dad's casket.

This demonstration of love made my mother sympathetic to Christianity and caused her to allow me to attend Sunday school when I was young -- I went to obtain candies and cookies!

As I grew up, I began to attend the junior youth fellowship

meetings. It was during those years that I learned more about Jesus Christ and accepted him as my personal Savior. He changed my life!

With Jesus in my heart I became more optimistic and positive. I began to realize there is more to life than just carrying on the family name. I discovered that life is more meaningful than just to have a better living. I came to understand that what matters most is having a correct attitude toward life situations, however difficult they may be.

These changes came to me after I accepted Jesus Christ as my personal Savior. Some came sooner, some came later. It was as Paul wrote in II Corinthians 5:17, *If anyone is in Christ, he is a new creation; the old has gone, the new has come!*

The Lord had a beautiful plan for my life. He called me into full time Christian service and upon the recommendation of a friend, I went to Taiwan to attend Holy Light Theological Seminary. There I received my B.Th. with honors and returned to Malaysia where I have pastored three different Methodist churches.

At the same time, Holy Light was making plans to train young men as future faculty. Because of my scholarly achievements, my burden for Holy Light, and my pastoral successes, I have been asked to join the faculty training program with the intention to return and teach. I am now finishing my second masters degree at Western Theological Seminary in Portland, Oregon. God has given me a loving wife and three beautiful children – first a girl and then – two boys!

Next summer we plan to return to Taiwan where I will teach New Testament and related courses at Holy Light Seminary. Please pray for us – and praise God for the Christians who were willing to buy six pieces of wood to bury my father.

40 Years In Hong Kong

Margaret Nelson
January/February 1993 pp. 6-7

Rooftop schools, squatter huts, refugees sleeping in the streets -- if you've been around our church for more than 10 years, a mention of Hong Kong may bring those images to mind, and with good reason.

When missionaries were forced out of China in 1949, mission boards turned to nearby countries populated by Chinese. In 1951, Rev. I.S.W. Ryding, a Free Methodist missionary evacuated from China, started a small chapel on Hong Kong Island (the Third Street Chapel, now Sai Ying Pun FMC). The same year, the Canadian Holiness Mission asked Mr. John T. Wang, to open a work in Hong Kong. The Alton Gould family arrived in 1954 to help the Wangs, and a chapel was opened in Kowloon (Cheung Wah Church). After Rev. Ryding's death in 1955, his small Free Methodist work was turned over to the Canadian Holiness Mission.

By 1959, when the Canadian Holiness Mission merged with the Free Methodist Church, a third church (Chuk Yuen, now Yan Sing or "Glad Blessings" FMC) had been started in the first rooftop school, and Cheung Wah church was researching the best spot to start a branch work in the New Territories. The Chuk Hong Chapel opened the end of that year (and 10 years later was moved to Kwai Chung).

In 1960, Hong Kong had a population of about three million people. About 10% lived in squatter villages, 10% were unemployed, and 50% lived at poverty level. Today, we have six million people, and the density has increased to nearly a half a million per square mile in some areas. Only 4.8% live in squatter huts, and unemployment has dropped to less than 3%. The standard of living has risen tremendously, and the Christian population has grown from 2% to 10%.

At the same time, our church grew from four small chapels to 14 churches. Rooftop schools have been replaced by the FM Bradbury Chun Lei Primary School. Refugee relief programs have been replaced by our study centers, nurseries, children and youth centers, and elderly centers to meet the needs of today's population.

By 1985, the Hong Kong Conference was self-supporting and no longer requests North American funds for national worker salaries or rent for churches. Originally a recipient of child sponsorship monies, we now sponsor 135 children around the world, and last year pledged $1 million (US $133,000) toward the *Home Free* campaign to pay the Indianapolis debt.

Our Hong Kong church also has a burden for evangelism. We still have four and a half years of known freedom to share the Gospel, and are doing all we can **now**. No one knows what will happen when the government of mainland China gains sovereignty over Hong Kong on July First of 1997. Many fear the worst and are moving to other countries. This includes Christians who want to live where they will be free to worship God openly.

Other Christians are committed to staying in Hong Kong no matter what happens, in order to witness to and encourage those who have no opportunity to leave, and to be a positive influence in society. Some are developing small groups that meet in homes -- groups which could keep on meeting even if visible places of worship are closed or harassed.

Over the past 40 years, the prayers of the world for mainland China resulted in tremendous church growth even while China was "closed" to the rest of the world. Now prayer for Hong Kong can make a difference in the future of the church here.

Leo Gives A Tour

Loren Van Tassel
January/February 1993 pp. 3-5

Note: *John Wesley was "the man who restored to a nation its soul" by his Gospel preaching and his tireless social action in 18th century England. And the 19th century missionary expansion included both preaching salvation and practical social improvement. During most of the 20th century evangelicals tended to neglect social concern, but in recent decades we are recovering that concern.*

It was Jesus himself who went about teaching and preaching, and who also "went about doing good and healing" (Acts 10:38). Our first priority should always be evangelism. We proclaim the Good News leading to eternal salvation by faith in Jesus Christ. But this immediately leads us into social concern, for the love of Jesus motivates us to care for others.

Our **Book of Discipline** *urges every conference to have a committee on social issues and ministries to meet the needs of people. The Hong Kong church demonstrates how this can be done, as Leonard explains to a visitor in the conversation below:*

VISITOR: Pleased to meet you, Leonard. Tell me about your church.
LEO: Call me *Leo!* Shatin Free Methodist is my church.
VISITOR: Very interesting! I attend a Free Methodist Church in North America. It's a lovely new building -- can seat 600 people. Nice soft seats. Central heating and cooling. Good acoustics. Big parking lot. Well landscaped.
LEO: That must be very nice.
VISITOR: May I take a picture of *your* church?
LEO: Uh, well... our church does not have a building...
VISITOR: What!? But a church *is* a building. How can I take a picture if you don't *have* a church?
LEO: I know we sometimes call a building a church. But my church is mainly a group of brothers and sisters who meet together every week. We enjoy the worship service, and sometimes we stay around for hours afterward doing things together.

VISITOR: I wish we did that. Within a few minutes after the benediction our building is empty. I wonder why we use our building for so little time each week? Anyway, if you don't have a building, where do you meet?
LEO: At the Study Center. I can show you the Study Center, but the brothers and sisters are not gathered there right now. Other people are using it.
VISITOR: What do you mean by *Study Center*?
LEO: It's a place where high school students come to study. It's just three rooms, each about 11 feet wide and 56 feet long.
VISITOR: I make my kids study at home. Why would high school kids want to drive all the way to your Study Center? Why don't their parents just send them off to their own bedroom to study?
LEO: The Study Center is located right inside the housing estate where the kids live. They can walk there in a matter of minutes. You asked, "Why don't they study in their homes?" Well, look up and down, look left to right. See those windows in that 30-story building? Each window is a different apartment. Each family lives in a flat about 15 feet wide and 20 feet deep. Let's go up the elevator and walk along the corridor inside an estate building.
VISITOR: Sounds exciting.
LEO: Here we are. We'll walk slowly along the corridor. Most people have their doors open to let the wind blow through their tiny flats. You can glance inside as we walk by.
VISITOR: Why do they have iron grating across each doorway?
LEO: For protection against intruders – thieves, and salesmen, and church visitation teams. Many times I've stood out here in the hall and chatted with a new church contact, while they stayed safely behind the locked iron grating. Of course, once they know us, on our second visit, they quickly invite us in for a cup of tea.
VISITOR: These flats *are* small. I see they have a fold-up dining table, a TV, and an electric wall fan.... What's that box with the red light, and the incense sticks burning, and the four oranges?
LEO: That's their worship center. They are offering food to the ancestors. But the gods they worship are dead. My wife's parents still pray to those paper idols. We're so thankful we've found the living God. Jesus rose victorious over death. Her parents have seen a big change in her during the past seven years since she gave her life to Christ. Sometimes her mom comes to church now, and she has two sisters who have learned to love Jesus.
VISITOR: Now I see that kids can't very well study in their own

bedrooms! Is that why you offer them a study center?
LEO: Correct. Now, look closely. See the little area enclosed by a wooden partition? Bunk beds are in there. And some of the kids sleep on the couch — it can fold out to be wide enough for two.
VISITOR: Sure is noisy in there! — TV blaring, people chatting....
LEO: Yes, and do you hear that constant clacking noise? Must be some housewives' afternoon ma-jong party. Many adults are addicted to playing ma-jong. This game uses plastic blocks that are moved around on the table top. Noisy. Now, let's go down to the Study Center on the third floor.
VISITOR: Why the third floor?
LEO: The ground floor is either a vegetable market or a parking garage. The second floor is for single elderly people. The third floor in this estate is where the shopping area is located. Next to the shopping areas are social service centers.
VISITOR: Oh yes, there's a clinic... and a youth center... and there is one that says it's for handicapped children. And a family planning center.
LEO: But no churches. The government allocates space for all kinds of human needs, and we really appreciate that. But our spiritual needs must be met in more creative ways. And government *does* allow us to do that if we want to.
VISITOR: Why don't you buy a space in the housing estate?
LEO: Some of our churches have done that in private apartment complexes. But in government housing estates no space can be *purchased* for any purpose — and about 25,000 people live just in this one estate.
VISITOR: That's the population of my entire town!
LEO: Across the street is another estate with 20,000 residents. Ours is the only government-sponsored Study Center for three estates in this district. That's why our limit of 400 members is filled up within a few days every September when we open up to new members. We can only seat 75-100 at one time. Of course, not everyone comes at one time, and the great pressure is during the spring just before the big end-of-school exams.
VISITOR: Couldn't you *rent* space here for a church? I see over there a watch and clock shop, and there's a pharmacy, and a stationery store, and an ice cream parlor...
LEO: And further on is a big supermarket, but the rent is **very** expensive. The **only** way churches can provide spiritual ministry to the thousands of people living in these estates is for the church to render social service.
VISITOR: How do you get permission to start a social service?
LEO: A couple times a year the government sends a list of spaces which

they plan to allocate for study centers, social centers for the elderly, children and youth centers, clinics, child-care centers (nurseries), kindergartens, and so forth. These are usually in new estates. Some of these spaces are small, others occupy an entire floor in a special building called an estate community center. And schools are very large 7-story buildings with at least 24 classrooms.

VISITOR: Who receives this list?

LEO: Voluntary agencies, such as Protestant and Catholic church groups, Buddhist organizations, non-religious special interest groups like those that serve the handicapped, boys and girls clubs, and so on.

VISITOR: How does our church decide what space to apply for?

LEO: Sometimes the Conference wants to plant a church in a certain district. So when we notice space coming up within a couple years in that district, we reply to the government announcement. In the case of this Study Center it's interesting what happened.

VISITOR: What happened?

LEO: This district of Shatin has grown from about 50,000 in 1970 to more than 500,000 today because the government developed this area as a housing district. Our missionaries, the Van Tassels, the Nelsons, and the Evoys live in rented apartments here. About 10 years ago Rev. Van Tassel would stand on his rooftop and look out across the valley and see one big building after another reaching completion, with other sites just in the beginning phase. One day he rode his motor scooter up on a hillside and took pictures when they were laying the foundations for this very estate. He didn't know that some day our church would meet in this estate, but he and his wife prayed for an opportunity to reach into this growing population with the good news of Jesus.

VISITOR: And then what happened?

LEO: In January 1982, they invited a group of Free Methodist members to meet in their living room. About 10 people committed themselves to assist this church-planting project. We applied to operate a Study Center, thinking it would give us a permanent church home.

VISITOR: And you did get the Study Center, right?

LEO: Yes! And then, amazingly, just a couple weeks later we were notified by another government department that we were **also** granted a new primary school! So we planted *two* churches within a mile of each other.

VISITOR: That's nice, but aren't they too close together?

LEO: Not when there are 40,000 people within a five minute walk of each church!

VISITOR: I guess you're right. Hey! I see your sign says *Shatin Free Methodist Church,* and it also says *Bradbury Shakok Study Center.* I insist! I want to take a picture!

LEO: Okay. Now that you understand what the word *church* means to us, you're welcome to take all the pictures you want.

Leprosy Care In China

Ruth Winslow
January/February 1993 pp. 30-32

Amy Carmichael, who worked with the poor in India for more than 50 years, said, "I cried because I had no shoes until I saw a man who had no feet." She was talking of those around her with leprosy, the poorest of the poor.

The poor are still with us. Mr. Kwok, living in a leprosy village in China, has just received his first pair of shoes. He cannot contain his joy. He has no hands, but because he has learned how to care for his own foot ulcers, he has been fitted with a pair of hard soled shoes into which a special insole has been placed. Now he won't lose his feet.

A person with leprosy, through lack of knowledge regarding his disease, usually has an ulcer form on the sole of his foot. Because he feels no pain, the ulcer will ultimately lead to the loss of his foot or leg.

The Truth About Leprosy

Contrary to most people's ideas about the disease, leprosy is the *least contagious* of all diseases. The bacilli are thought to be airborne and are not contracted through touch. Isolation is not necessary. Ninety percent of the world's population is immune.

Leprosy is found primarily in countries where there is extreme poverty and malnutrition. It affects the peripheral nerves in the hands, feet and face. Deformity and handicap to these areas is our primary concern in China.

In November of 1991 I participated as an instructor in a three-week workshop for 80 leprosy nurses representing 22 provinces in China. Eight minority groups were represented and two nurses were there from Xinjiang and Tibet. They learned about leprosy, the nurse's role in the prevention of handicaps, and took this information back to their own hospitals and out-patient clinics.

China has been an example to the world in eradicating leprosy. Now there are only 23,000 active cases compared to 400,000 in 1949. About 100,000 of these have died, 150,000 are cured and back in society, and 150,000 are cured but have handicaps and need rehabilitation. Of those who need rehabilitation, 40,000 are in Hong Kong's neighboring Guangdong province.

The leaders responsible for leprosy care and control in China know the importance of nurses being motivated to care for their own people. The doctors admit that one-third of the treatment is medicine; two-thirds is teaching preventive care by nurses and other health care workers.

Rehabilitation and prevention of new handicaps by the year 2000 is the target for every person suffering from leprosy. Moving them out of the leprosy villages and integrating them in society is the modern method of treatment. Guangdong Province has 65 leprosy villages with more than 5,000 patients, most of whom have second and third level disability. Most new cases, as well as those cured, are living at home with their families.

The India Model

Simple operations to correct deformity can be performed by well-trained doctors under local anesthesia. Several young doctors have been well-trained in reconstructive surgery in India's leprosy centers and have returned to China excited about the possibilities of rehabilitating their own handicapped people.

In a 1988 survey of 1,692 persons with leprosy in Guangdong Province, one-third suffered from lagophthalmos (inability to close the eye) and 50% of these have lost their eyesight. An eye doctor told me recently that he had operated, too late, on a woman who had saved $2 per month for two years to have surgery on her eye so she could close it. By the time she arrived it was too late -- she had already lost her eyesight.

For nurses to teach patients how to care for the feet, they need to teach them to use their hands. But the patient cannot remove the callus around the ulcers if they have a claw hand. By providing a simple operation in which a tendon is transferred to the fingers, these hands can be used again. After this operation, the nurses can do physiotherapy and teach them to care for their feet.

We also want to make sure they wear shoes to keep them from losing their feet (amputation is the last resort). In many parts of China the people with leprosy don't own shoes. They wear grass shoes which is the worst kind for an open ulcer.

People who suffer from leprosy are the poorest of the poor. It is extremely difficult for them to find the money for their operations. We are not speaking of beggars here, but rather people in the lowest income bracket. Still, most are involved in some kind of labor. We have begun making this operation possible by providing the financial assistance necessary for the operations. Payless Shoesource provided the first 250 pair of sneakers, and we are in the process of asking Nike for shoes to help meet this tremendous need.

Why Do I Care?

I have joyfully demonstrated hand and foot care in two leprosy villages. After a few months in the first village the results of teaching self-care on 38 patients were remarkable. Of the 88 ulcers treated, 48 were completely healed. These people were ready for protective shoes. Those needing prosthesis and crutches received them. More than 20 were admitted to the center for reconstructive surgery.

Knowing that healing and success is virtually guaranteed is highly rewarding, yet my motive runs deeper. "I try to give to the poor *for love* what the rich could get *for money*," said Mother Teresa. "No, I wouldn't touch a leper for a thousand pounds; yet I willingly cure him for the love of God."

The Amazing God Of China

Ming-Yau
July/August 1993 pp. 1-9

Never before, anywhere, at any time, have so many people in so short a period of time come to believe in Jesus Christ as in China today. China is the fastest-expanding nation for church growth ever in the history of the world.

In 1949, the year the Chinese Communist Party took over the government of China, there were 834,909 Protestant members. Today the estimate of some house church leaders inside China is that there are 70 million believers.

The Chinese Communist Party thinks that by closing church buildings, putting pastors in prison, and bringing intense pressure to bear on Christians to renounce their faith, they would destroy Christianity in China. They are finding out differently. They had left God out of the picture, and God had quite a different plan.

House Churches

The house churches of China today have their roots in the New Testament where the house church was the most common form of the church. The house churches grew by division. When the group of believers became too large to meet in one house, they divided and a new church was born. Evangelism took place spontaneously along the natural bridge of witnessing to one's relatives and close friends. Rapid growth was the result.

The same thing is happening in China today. After the People's Republic of China was born in 1949, the church was gradually squashed. Missionaries had to leave. All denominations were dissolved by 1958, and virtually all "churches" were closed. Out of this chaos, Christians began meeting in homes. As they prayed for one another, and for unsaved relatives and friends, the circle of believers grew. Class distinctions which had grown up in the institutional church were broken down.

Cultural Revolution

Bigger change came with the Cultural Revolution, from 1966 to 1976, when Mao inspired millions of Red Guard youth to destroy the *Four Olds* -- old thoughts, old ideas, old habits, and old customs (including religion). Anyone with thoughts different from Mao, "the Great Helmsman," was attacked.

The Red Guards were given free train passage, and eventually began to take over factories and even challenge municipal governments. Chaos was the result. Finally Mao had to bring back order by using the army to suppress the Red Guard!

The church suffered as the Red Guard called on all people to burn Bibles, destroy images and disperse religious associations. Many Christians lost Bibles and Christian books, were put into prison, or were made to do forced labor. Some were cruelly tortured.

The Cultural Revolution from 1966 to 1976 is one of those events by which people mark their lives -- "before" or "after" the Cultural Revolution. Extreme leftists thought they had utterly destroyed Christianity -- and institutional Christianity was indeed terminated. But the New Testament model of home meetings has spread widely and rapidly across China since 1976. To understand why this is happening it is necessary to see the amazing God of China at work. Therefore, I have collected these true stories of what God is doing **these days** in China.

This first story was first reported by Dr. Jonathan Chao in a church conference in Hong Kong in 1987.

Just Coincidence?

During the early 1980s an elder holding meetings was arrested by the local authorities. He was bound by the thumbs, extended from a beam, and beaten until blood ran down his body. He was then given a public trial to warn others not to preach the gospel. When the official told him not to preach anymore, he replied: "No matter what you are going to do, I am going to believe. When you release me, I am going to preach. This is my life, because I believe there is a God, and my God is a living God."

To this the cadre (government official) scoffed: "God? Is there a God? If there is a real living God like you said, then let your living God bring death to my family."

The elder prayed: "Lord, I hate to do this. I do not like harm to come to this man, but now that he has challenged You, and has demanded evidence, Lord, do unto him according to Your will."

When the official returned home he went to his outhouse. Suddenly he felt himself grow weak, and fell to his knees. He crawled back to the house and told his wife what happened and said, "You had better repent and believe right away. Tell all the town people to repent. That elder's God is real. I have sinned against Him." He then fell down and died. His wife believed, and told the town people. Fear struck them and many believed. The word spread to neighboring villages.

In one nearby village, another official said: "That is just a coincidence. If what this woman says is true, then let that God bring death to my family." When he returned home, he found his only son, an outstanding athlete who had just graduated first in his high school class, had dropped dead. The official's legs weakened, and falling down sick, he could not get up again. This is why in that area, 40,000 people believed.

God has not changed. He remains the same yesterday, today and forever. What God did through Jesus and the Apostles continues to happen today, with regularity. The signs and miracles which God performs are never done for man's curiosity. They are always done to manifest the Word, the Lord Jesus Christ, and are given to believers to establish their faith, and to non-believers to verify that Jesus is Lord.

House church Christians in China live with severe persecution. They have learned to depend constantly upon God. They have no one else to turn to. Over and over again God answers their earnest and trusting prayers with signs and miracles, which glorify himself and proclaim his mighty name. This is not strange or to be wondered at.

God In The Morgue

Jesus said in John 14:12: "I tell you the truth, anyone who has faith in Me will do what I have been doing. He will do even greater things than these, because I am going to the Father." Here are some examples of the fulfillment of this amazing promise:

A young brother, very faithful in his testimony for Christ, was taken by the authorities. They told him they had secretly sat in on some house church meetings and heard him speak about his all-powerful God. They then took him to the city morgue, pushed him into the cooler where the corpses lay, and said, "If your God is so great, He can deliver you."

The young Christian was dressed only in cotton trousers and top. It was pitch black, and he was trapped with many dead bodies. Within minutes he began to shiver and shake and realized he would soon die. He began to pray earnestly. The Spirit of God impressed on him that he should go and pray over one particular corpse. In the dark he felt over the tables where the bodies were and found the body. He laid his hands on the hands of the dead man. He began to pray again, and as he prayed he felt the fingers of the man's hand move. In a few minutes the dead man sat up. The Christian said to him, "If we don't get out of here we are both going to freeze to death!"

They beat on the door and began to yell. The guards heard two distinct voices, so they opened the door. The two men walked out and the Christian testified to what God had done. The guards and the man raised from the dead knelt down right there, and the Christian led them all to receive Jesus as their Savior.

Mother, I Am Hungry!

The 24-year old daughter of a cadre became ill with stomach pain. Her mother said they should pray. The father said this was superstition and took the daughter to the hospital. The doctor said they would need to operate immediately, so they did, but during the operation the daughter died. The doctor verified the death, sewed up the incision, and had her taken to the morgue. The mother followed along and insisted on staying by her daughter's corpse in the morgue.

The father began to hate his wife, thinking, "If instead of praying she had taken my daughter to the hospital earlier, probably she would have become well. The death of my daughter was all my wife's fault!" In his fierce anger, he decided to kill her.

The mother in the morgue continued to weep and pray for her daughter. For three days and nights she would not leave. Then, suddenly, the daughter sat up. She said, "Mother, I am hungry!" When the doctor examined her he found her illness was gone, so mother and daughter went home.

The husband was just then sharpening a knife. His plan was to kill his wife as soon as she entered the house. As she came in he raised the knife, but then he saw his daughter. The mother explained what happened, then the father knelt down and confessed, "The God you believe in is true. I also want to believe." As a result the Christian community in that village grew until there was one or more believers in every single home. People called it the "Gospel Village."

Playing Games With God

An older woman risked danger to let a group of Christians meet in her home. Her son was not a Christian and strongly opposed her. He even brought police so they could investigate, but each time they came, the service had already dismissed and no one was there.

The Christians were very troubled and prayed earnestly that the Lord would quickly save this son. One night, at the break of dawn, the son dreamed an angel, very beautiful and brightly shining, came into his room and said, "Little brother, you are very intelligent. Let's play a game together."

"Good," he said. "How do we play it?"

The angel took a rectangular sheet of paper, folded it three times, and with a pair of scissors cut it twice. It was then put on a table and the cut piece taken out. It was a cross. The angel asked, "Do you want this?"

He answered, "No, what good would it be to want a cross?"

The angel then took the leftover paper and arranged it into two characters, *szu wang* (to die). He asked, "How about *szu wang*? Do you want it?"

The son looked at this amazing arrangement of the paper and began to tremble. Why were there not any pieces left of the paper after these two characters were made? He replied, "*Szu wang*, of course I do not want it."

The angel took the paper which had made *szu wang*, and arranged it into the characters *yong sheng* (eternal life). He then asked, "*Yong sheng*, do you want it?"

The son answered, "*Yong sheng*, of course I want it."

The angel replied, "If one wants to have eternal life, he must go through the path of the cross. You must receive the Lord Jesus as your own personal Savior, then you will have eternal life." Then the angel left him.

The boy awoke, got out of bed, and found his mother having her devotions. He asked, "Is it true there are angels?"

"Yes, there are angels," she replied. "I told you before; Jehovah is the true God. Angels are sent by Jehovah."

He told his mother the dream. He then confessed his sins to God and received Jesus as his Savior. From that time on, he was very zealous in serving the Lord, and went out and preached the Gospel.

Arrested

A house church leader one day was walking down the road when looking behind her she saw Public Security men rapidly walking toward her. They had ropes to tie her hands when they arrested her. They would soon catch up to her. Just then she came to a railroad crossing and slipped across in front of a train. The train separated her from her pursuers, and she was able to get away safely.

But God's will is not always to deliver his children from the fiery furnace. This same leader was later arrested and spent many months in labor camps. In a short note written on a piece of toilet paper smuggled out, she said others were accepting Christ in prison, and if God wanted her to stay there the rest of her life, she was willing.

The PSB Is Angry

At a certain place new Christians are very bold in their public testimonies. This made the Public Security Bureau [PSB] official angry. He began to scream and yell at them about what would happen to them if they continued to tell others about Jesus. Suddenly, the official lost his voice. He felt invisible hands pressing at his neck.

His assistant asked the crowd, "What kind of a God are you people serving that would do this terrible thing?" Immediately the assistant's own two hands went together as though they were hand-cuffed. He could not get his wrists apart. Then his mouth slid over to the side of his face.

The crowd of believers told them both, "You must repent of your sins and accept Christ as your Lord and Savior. Then we will pray for God to release you."

They repented and accepted Christ. And as they did so, they returned to normal again. The rest of the PSB staff became frightened by what they saw and fled to their headquarters where the whole story was told. Thus the PSB in this area are afraid of these believers and will no longer go near them. And when the believers do see PSB officials on the street, they go up to them and say, "You must repent of your sins and accept Jesus Christ as your Lord and Savior."

The PSB official who felt hand-cuffed and whose mouth slid to the side of his face has become an evangelist!

Fed By Angels

It would be interesting to explore the entire Scriptures to find out how many miracles in the Bible have reoccurred within the last few decades in China. Surely the God of China is one and the same as the God of the Bible.

Consider the pastor's wife with several children, whose husband was in hard labor in Inner Mongolia for 20 years. Her home was stripped of everything, including furniture, bedding, and cooking utensils. How would she feed her children? "Divorce your husband and the state will care for you," was the advice given her.

"How can I divorce him? I love him and I know God will bring him back to me," was her answer. Food gone, with hungry and sick children, she poured her heart out to God. Before long she heard a knock at the door. There was a stranger with food, who said, "Someone told me to bring this to you." She tried to find out who he was but the only answer was, "Someone told me to bring this to you." This reoccurred continually, and in this way she was cared for over a 20-year period, until the return of her husband.

Gone Fishing

Here's a similar story. A man was sent to prison for his religious beliefs. He had a wife and four children who had no livelihood, and no food. In back of their little home was a small pond in a stream. No one had ever fished there before. The children first made a net and caught enough fish to feed the family. As time went on they got enough fish not only for their own needs, but enough to trade for the other necessities of life. Thirteen years later, the father returned from prison. There were no fish in the little stream from that day on.

Another Apostle Paul?

An elderly lady was praying that someone would come who could read the Bible and preach the gospel. One day a man came walking down the road when suddenly a loud sound came out of heaven -- so loud it gave him a terrible headache.

He asked this elderly woman to pray for his hurting head to be well.

She replied, "You are the preacher we have been looking for! We do not have a preacher. God has called you to preach for us!"

"I do not care about preaching," he answered. "Just pay attention and pray for my hurting head."

They both knelt down and she prayed. Like an electric shock, his headache immediately ceased. He came to know God, responded to God's call and became a preacher much used by God.

Heart Attack

A 70-year-old lady was the only one who had knowledge of the daily operations of her family and house church. She alone knew where the Bibles were, who the messengers were, who could or could not be trusted. Suddenly she died of a heart attack.

She had not been able to pass on her vital information. Her family felt lost. They began to pray, "Lord, restore our mother back to life." After being dead two days, she came back to life. She scolded her family for calling her back. They reasoned with her. They said they would pray that in two days she could return to the Lord. It would take that much time to set the matters straight.

After two days, the family and friends began to sing hymns and pray that the Lord would take her back. The mother's final words were, "They're coming. Two angels are coming." And she died again. This incident caused the entire village to repent.

Demon Possessed!

The following story shows the importance of living a holy life so that God's work will not be hindered. A Christian returned with his ox from the field and tied it to a post to feed it. Just then a man came running up saying, "A man is demon possessed! He is jumping around and shouting. Come quickly and help him! Drive the demon out."

When he heard this, his heart was anxious and he hurriedly gave some grass to feed the ox. He quickly ran to the village and there found the demon possessed man wildly jumping and shouting. He thought he would cast the demon out in the name of Jesus. But the demon spoke to him through the man possessed, saying "You yourself are a sinner! You do not have any authority to cast me out."

The brother answered, "What sin have I committed? I do not have sin. You quickly leave!"

To this the demon replied, "You are a sinner. Just now you took public grass to feed your ox. Is that not committing sin?"

It then dawned upon the brother what he had done. He thought to himself, "Yes, just before this, when my heart was anxious, I forgot that the grass to the side was public grass." He quickly ran back to his own house, got some grass and replaced the public grass. He then ran back to the village and found the man still wildly carrying on. He prayed, and in the name of Jesus commanded the demon to come out. This time the demon came out without a word. *How much sin is there in your life that must be fixed before you'll have that kind of authority?*

The Facts Of The Case

When questioned before the Sanhedrin Peter and the other apostles replied, *We must obey God rather than men* (Acts 5:29)! This was the same Sanhedrin which had recently condemned their Lord to death. The apostles were prepared to suffer for the Lord Jesus, if need be, but they were not going to be disobedient to God. Their mind was set. Peter later wrote to the early Christians, *Therefore, since Christ suffered in his body, arm yourselves also with the same attitude* (I Peter 4:1). Peter continues, *He who has suffered in his body is done with sin. As a result, he does not live the rest of his earthly life for evil human desires, but rather for the will of God* (I Peter 4:1-2).

Suffering for Christ purifies desires and straightens out priorities. Wang Mingdao was asked, soon after his release from prison in 1980, "What benefits have 30 years of suffering brought to the church in China?"

He replied, "There are great benefits. Through trials and sufferings those who did not truly believe in the Lord have been eliminated. The remnants remaining are all very strong ones. It has been a great purification."

For personal gain some people became informants to the government against earnest Christians in China. However, in many cases God has given his suffering children a spirit of wisdom and discernment in these matters and a close bond of unity, as the following story relates:

In 1974 people from other communes, and total strangers, were going to the house of an old man. Such gatherings were highly suspicious to the cadres, so they questioned the old man but got nowhere. They finally decided to find a Christian who could join the group and learn about things from the inside.

No one seemed willing to cooperate, so finally they enlisted the aid of a communist girl who was relieved of other duties for 10 weeks so she could attempt to join the fellowship. Individuals she knew who attended the meetings were glad to stop and talk about the Lord Jesus

Christ as the Savior from sin, but they never invited her to the meetings.

Sensing that for some reason she was not welcome, she cast aside all pretense and confronted the elderly gentleman himself. "Tell me, old comrade, why am I not welcome to come to your home when you have a worship service? Am I not as good as those other girls who attend? Is there something wrong with me?"

The old man smiled. "You have asked the right question this time. Now, take this Book and see for yourself. It says *All have sinned and come short of the glory of God! There is no one righteous, no, not one.* Those who come here know this about themselves, but they also know that Jesus has suffered in their place. When we gather we remember this in a dignified and quiet way. Tell me what purpose would be served if you came here to join us? Can you say, 'Thank You, Lord Jesus, for dying for me,' and really mean it?"

The girl reported to the authorities that she was making progress toward being allowed into the house when worship was going on. The cadres were pleased and encouraged her to make further effort. However, through the power of the Word, something occurred that *they* had not planned. A day came when the formerly enthusiastic young communist found she *could* say, "Thank You, Lord Jesus, for dying for me!" She told the old man what had happened, and he invited her to join the fellowship. She learned as much as she could in the following weeks and became a thoroughly convinced Christian. She received a New Testament of her own and read it faithfully each day.

When called by the cadres to give an account of her progress, she took her New Testament with her and presented the same texts that had led her to the Savior. Although the cadres refused to accept this for themselves, they could see the change in the girl and believed that she had found the "facts of the case."

A New God In China

David, king of Israel, earnestly desired to build a temple to the Lord his God, but that was not according to God's plan. Solomon, his son, would build it. David, instead, prepared lavish gifts for the building. He then prayed, *Yours, O Lord, is the greatness and the power and the glory and the majesty and the splendor, for everything in heaven and earth is yours. Yours, O Lord, is the kingdom* (I Chr. 29:11).

Many missionaries toiled long and faithfully in China, some sacrificing their lives to build the foundation of the Church, the Temple of the Living God. It was on this foundation that the house church of today has been erected.

The early missionaries, like David, did not live to see the temple in all of its glorious splendor. They planned for it, but God used their sons in the gospel to bring it to fruition. The church does not belong to any one denomination or group, it belongs to God. *Yours, O Lord, is the kingdom!*

After the temple is built, its light will permeate society. This is happening in China today, as shown in the following story:

While touring a Buddhist temple in southern China, a tourist fell into a discussion with his guide. The guide asked if the tourist believed in "this stuff," referring to the rituals of the temple. The tourist, a Christian, responded that he did not believe in Buddhism but that he did believe in God and proceeded to explain his faith.

The tourist then asked his guide what the religion is of New China. Thinking for a minute, the guide, a nonbeliever, responded that if New China has a religion, it is Christianity. When asked for an explanation, he said that Christians in China were "real" while what the people were doing in the Buddhist temple was all an act.

The Paradox of Pain

I have picked these stories from many that I have in order to show you God is enacting his plan for the evangelization of China. **What is his plan?** The plan for evangelizing lost persons first involved great suffering on his part, the ultimate sacrifice of his Son on the Cross. Now it involves suffering on the part of his children. It seems a paradox that Chinese believers should suffer as they do, and that the Church grow because of it. God's plan, however, is not our plan; His thoughts are not our thoughts, neither are His ways our ways.

A theology of success is fashionable in North America today. People think mainly of their own wants and needs. The notion that you must sacrifice or suffer for Christ receives little attention.

The opposite is true in the house church movement in China. One question often asked a new believer is simply: "Are you willing to suffer for Christ?"

Western Christians don't want to hear that. They want better food, nicer cars, larger homes, greater comfort, enhanced conveniences -- and you **will** have all those things -- but at what expense to the cause of Christ?

More Suffering, Not Less

"Are **you** willing to suffer for Christ?" This is the same question God has asked new believers from the beginning. Recall the words of God to Ananias about Paul: "I will show him how much he must suffer for my name."

Persecution of house church Christians has continued in China up to the present. In fact, it has increased since the "fall" of eastern Europe and the collapse of the Soviet Union. Chinese authorities blame the Christians for the fall of eastern Europe and are doing all they can to prevent a similar occurrence in China.

This incident took place in September 1991: Believers were conducting a meeting of about 2,000 people. Many new converts were to be baptized. These meetings have never been secret and never is anything said against the government.

During the meeting a large group of armed PSB policemen rushed in. Without saying anything they started firing wildly into the air, then rushed to the platform and began to viciously beat the preachers and assault them with electric cattle prods. The preachers were severely injured and several were arrested.

During the summer of 1991, China experienced devastating floods, the worst it has had in decades. The people of Hong Kong gave over $100 million (U.S.) for flood relief. But Christian flood victims have been discriminated against and persecuted, as you will see from this letter dated October 15, 1991: The Rural Government and the District Government has made a public declaration to the effect: "Any who believe in Jesus are not allowed to receive food relief and other material relief. Tell them to go to their God for food and clothes."

In the midst of suffering, God is building his church in China today. Because his children have learned to trust him, he answers their prayers with many miracles which verify Jesus is Lord. This is the heart of the gospel. Christ has suffered for you -- are you willing to suffer for him?

V. Europe

Page **Article**

309 Hungary: The Challenge To Go
312 Socialist Quest For The New Man
315 God In The Communist Bloc
319 A Prophetic Dream For Europe
321 Rock Music Paves The Way
323 Meet Our Hungarian Friends
326 Hungary In Context Of History
329 Haiti Invades France

STEPHANIE CROTHERS
Missionary to Europe

Hungary: The Challenge To Go

Interview with Stephanie Crothers
by Paula Innes
July/August, 1995

Hear the music on the subway, the street, and in the concert hall. See the colorful houses, vibrant embroidery, and bright costumes and festivals. Smell big city exhaust and fresh crops at harvest in rural areas. Touch the friendly hand outstretched in warm Christian friendship. **Experience** the people of Hungary. Like people anywhere, they have been through turmoil and political upheaval. They need time to heal the wounds of oppression. They are hungry for the love of God.

"I believe there is truth in the statement, 'the world is shrinking,'" Stephanie Crothers notes. "There are changes occurring with startling alacrity. People cannot afford to be uneducated about world events today. Now, more than ever, what happens across the oceans affects everyone."

Stephanie is preparing to minister to the people of Europe as European Missions Coordinator for Free Methodist World Missions. Stephanie will work alongside Tibor Ivanyi, president of the Hungarian Evangelical Fellowship (HEF). The HEF is very similar in its theology to the Free Methodist denomination and since 1991, our two churches have had a good partnership. Stephanie is ready to take that partnership into the future.

"When I was 13, our family went to Europe," says Stephanie. "I was enchanted with Europe, Europeans and the languages they spoke. I have since returned eight times and have lived in Europe for a total of almost three years."

The Beginning

Stephanie has been considering a missionary career from childhood: "My parents come from families that have been Free Methodists for generations. I can't remember a time that I didn't know Christ, but there have been times of great strengthening in my faith. I saw Christianity as the pursuit of closeness with Christ, rather than just a lifestyle. My relationship with God is my strength, comfort and the power behind my ministry."

The summer before her freshman year of college found Stephanie in West Germany as an exchange student. Her trip to the city of Berlin was a moving encounter. She remembers many sad stories about families separated from loved ones by the then-divided Germany. The questions and anger this situation brought encouraged Stephanie to want to travel in the east and see what was on the other side of the wall.

Stephanie had three majors in college. She earned a BA in humanities, history, and secondary education at Roberts Wesleyan College, Rochester, NY. Her background in literature, art and history helps Stephanie better understand the people she desires to work with. "It helps me talk with them on a human level. They like the fact that I appreciate what is important to them, whether or not they can relate to my Christianity."

During her last semester at Roberts, Stephanie took courses at the American College of Switzerland in international law and politics, global issues, international relations in the Middle East, and history of art. As part of this experience, Stephanie traveled to out-of-the-way places on weekends, which broadened her global perspective and opened her eyes to a more realistic picture of Europe. Stephanie roomed with a student from Abudhabi who had a mix of Christian and Muslim background.

The Confirmation

Bishop Gerald Bates encouraged Stephanie to consider a VISA (Volunteers In Service Abroad) term in Hungary after completing her bachelor's degree. She taught English to high school students in Nyiregyhaza, Hungary, from 1991-1993, and says this VISA term was the single most powerful event in confirmation of her choice to be a career missionary. "I was strengthened doubly for every demand put on me. I realized then that this really could be a career for me."

After her return to the United States, Stephanie was not sure what direction God wanted her to take. She sought guidance in prayer and counsel of others. "I was praying at the altar one Sunday night at a healing service with Dr. Don Demaray. The next day Kay Kline called and told me that Free Methodist World Missions was considering me for European Missions Coordinator. This was God's answer to many of my questions."

Stephanie completed her master's degree in education in May of 1995. She has been busy studying, working as a library assistant at a public library and speaking throughout the Genesee Conference. She has found it easy to keep actively involved in the work in Europe through letters received weekly from current VISA missionaries, contacts she has made through her travel in the conference, and reports from Hungary and from the missions office.

As European Missions Coordinator, Stephanie will work to develop three areas: ministry, academic training, and cooperation.

1. Ministry development will include church planting, sending short-term and long-term missionaries, and building relationships with the people. Stephanie says Eastern Europeans are so reserved, it can take up to two years to be on a first name basis with your neighbors. She added that our ministry will be cooperative rather than competitive. "We want to be sensitive to other churches already established," she explains.

2. Academic training will have the goal to equip pastors and lay leaders for ministry. Visiting professors will be needed to teach and hold conferences, develop curriculum, and provide seminary and pastoral training.

3. Building cooperation will require networking with Christians across Hungary and Europe, whether other mission groups or indigenous churches. With limited resources, it makes sense to link ministry groups and individuals through newsletters, conferences and the like to strengthen the Christian community.

Stephanie will also teach English part-time at John Wesley Bible Institute. "Teaching has been a goal of mine from the time I was a little girl. I would like to relay my passion for global perspectives to my future students."

"Therefore go and make disciples of all nations, baptizing them in the name of the Father and of the Son and of the Holy Spirit, and teaching them to obey everything I have commanded you. And surely I am with you always, to the very end of the age" (Matthew 28:19-20). This is the challenge to which Stephanie responds. She confesses it's hard to know if she's really prepared for the tasks before her in Hungary: "I have to go on faith that the Lord asked me to do this."

What started years ago as an interest in Europe has developed into a love for the people and an answer to God's challenging call.

Socialist Quest For The New Man

Josef Tson, Condensed by Dan Runyon
January/February 1991 p. 9

Marx, Lenin, and Stalin were deeply interested in religion in their youth. They studied it seriously and wrote about it sympathetically. What caused these men to turn against idealism in general and Christianity as such?

In England Marx encountered capitalist exploiters. The pattern of revolution he worked out to end this exploitation collided with the religious world outlook. When the working class believes in a better life in heaven and trusts in a God who punishes violence, there can be no revolution.

Religion was an obstacle on the road to revolution, and this led the Marxist teachers to fight against Christianity.

The New Man

The creators of Marxism-Leninism saw that for a man to take up arms in protest against "the crude and unjust system," he needed to be a desperate, bitter man without hope in an after life. Second, he had to be without scruples and untroubled by his conscience when faced with armed violence. They believed only atheism could produce such a man.

This desperate, unscrupulous man was essential to Communist revolution. But after the revolution he was dispensable. For the newly created society they introduced the concept of the "new man."

The new man resulting from a socialist system would not be alienated from the means of production. Therefore, he would be freed from corruption by the strength of the socialist system. He would handle goods honestly and distribute them freely, taking only as much as he needed so that enough remained for all his kinsmen.

This was the dream for the new man in socialism. Without this new man they clearly demonstrated that Communism would not be realized.

Today, many years after the revolution has passed, it is clear that socialist man's character has not changed. He remains as he was in the capitalist society: an egoist, full of vice, and devoid of uprightness. The creation of the new man still remains today a burden to be realized.

The Environmental Issue

Marxism teaches that man's character is the product of his environment. They believe a social system founded on justice and honor will produce a man of noble character, an honest, upright man.

Fundamental question: Is the character of man an automatic product of social forces, or is character shaped by the world outlook which inspires a man?

Modern Marxists who struggle with this problem conclude that the only way to inspire the giving of self for others is to claim that the pursuit of the common good means the realization of personal good. They acknowledge that this motivation fails when an individual realizes that the common good is only achieved slowly, probably over many generations. Socialist society desires a new man but offers no help or inspiration for achieving this noble character.

So, What <u>Does</u> Work?

What ideology is capable of producing the new man of high aspiration and noble character, one who will sacrifice himself for the common good and be absolutely upright in his behavior?

The only answer is Jesus Christ, who possessed the most noble character of all, who sacrificed himself for the good of his fellow men. For almost 2,000 years he has not ceased to produce the finest people who ever walked the earth.

Throughout history, wherever the spirit of Christ's teaching was accepted and assimilated, the result was a noble life put to the service of the common good, even at the cost of self-sacrifice.

When an individual accepts Christ he experiences fundamental change. Drunkards and adulterers forsake their ways. Those weak in character grow in strength and integrity. Drug addicts are delivered. One who trusts in Christ becomes a new creation, a **new man** after the likeness of Christ, who is the new man *par excellence*.

Why has Christianity in its 2,000 years not achieved the ideal Christian society? It became institutionalized and accepted as the state religion. Its original source of truth was neglected. Preference was given to thought-forms foreign to the Gospel. Institutionalized religion lost its revolutionary power.

Protestant Christianity [and the printing press] restored the Bible as central. The Bible was placed in the hands of people who could read it for themselves and develop their own spiritual lives.

Brought face to face with God, the individual became responsible, and this resulted in transformation of life. When this experience became general on a national scale, the improvement in societies like Sweden, Norway, Denmark, and England was immense.

Christ and Socialism

Religion did not vanish under socialism but rather grew in strength. This must cause, sooner or later, a revision of the Communist party's attitude toward this aspect of the individual and social life.

Socialism fights against its own interests when it maintains a war against religion. Socialism needs the new man, and only the spirit of Christ can transform and make man into a new kind of person.

Che Guevara, the passionate revolutionary, said, "If socialism does not mean the transformation of man's character, it does not interest me." Socialism has tried many ways to achieve this end. Why does it not allow Christ the opportunity to prove his power to transform men?

Jesus Christ is not the enemy of this society; he is its only chance. Let socialism give him a free hand to manifest his revolutionary and transforming power.

The divine task of the Christian living in a socialist country is to lead such a correct and beautiful life that he both demonstrates and convinces his society that he *is* the new man which socialism seeks.

God In The Communist Bloc

Daniel V. Runyon
January February 1991 pp. 1-4

On May 8, 1990, Free Methodist World Missions sponsored a seminar to consider our responsibility to reach into the Communist Bloc with the Gospel. Peter Deyneka, Jr., President of Slavic Gospel Association, Mark Elliot, a professor at Wheaton College, and other specialists on the Communist Bloc challenged our church to action.

In A Nutshell

Deyneka said we are seeing the demise of Communism and widespread revolt in the Union of Soviet Socialist Republics (U.S.S.R.) as people turn against all they have been taught in the last 72 years. Revolt is no cause for optimism in a land where consumer goods are scarce and people eat the same food daily. In their frustration with Marxism there is open talk of civil war.

"We are seeing the devastating results of Lenin's teaching that every mention of God is vile and man is useless to society as long as he believes in God," said Deyneka. "Stalin took Lenin's view one step farther by trying to eradicate the physical presence of the Church."

Turning Point

Early in Mikhail Gorbachev's leadership, Christians devoted one week to intense prayer during a 1988 celebration of 1,000 years of Christianity in the Soviet Union. The government did not intend to allow this celebration, but on March 23, 1988, Gorbachev made an about-face. He said it was no longer illegal to ship Bibles and Christian literature to his country.

"Before 1988 getting 100,000 Bibles and books a year into the U.S.S.R. was considered an excellent success," said Deyneka. "In 1988 Soviet citizens *openly* searched for Bibles but couldn't find them." Today 100,000 to 200,000 Bibles are being shipped to the Soviet Union each month – by the truckload. Others are mailed in, delivered by air freight, or shipped by railroad via Germany.

The interest is in *spirituality*, not necessarily in Christianity. They know nothing about Jesus or God, they just know they have been robbed of the spiritual dimension of life. "We are atheist *by education,*" they say, "*not by commitment.*"

Many non-Christian Party Members now say, "We need the Bible to counteract what has been done to our society. Can you give us 50 million Bibles?" Soviet socialists researching for the ideal value system have settled on The Ten Commandments as the best alternative!

"These 400 million people are the greatest mission challenge of the world today," Deyneka observed. "Sixty million people died as a result of Marxism. People have been lied to almost every moment of their lives. *Practically everyone* is interested in the spiritual dimension of life." The task is enormous. There is one Protestant church in Moscow for nine million people. The spiritual vacuum will be filled one way or another -- 30 sects have already registered with the government.

Is this spiritual interest merely the opening jaw of a Communist trap? "No," says Deyneka. "They did not develop this situation purposely. Nobody [in the West] realized how bad off the U.S.S.R. was until recently." Except for the military (25% of their Gross National Product is devoted to defense, compared to 6% in the U.S.) the U.S.S.R. fits Third World status.

"This is the people speaking out and has nothing to do with the Communist Party," Deyneka believes. But enemies of faith will exploit the situation. Deyneka advises us to remember that the KGB and the military are still in control. There is new opportunity here, but not freedom as we understand it. "In the past it was against the law to change another's way of thinking," said Deyneka. "New laws are being written, but there are really no laws governing what is happening now."

Seizing Opportunities

Practicing charity was not allowed under Communism (the government took care of every conceivable need). Now churches can enter *any* prisons to minister to inmates, and may be invited into schools, orphanages, psychiatric wards and hospitals. Christians visit patients and provide medicine and wheelchairs where possible. Football stadiums or other public places are sometimes used for evangelistic services. Christian films in Russian are being shown, and Campus Crusade's **Jesus** movie was shown on Russian television at Easter, reaching perhaps one half of the country!

Where Is Utopia?

Mark Elliott, Professor of History at Wheaton College (IL) and Director of the Institute for the Study of Christianity and Marxism, informed us that the word "Utopia" is Latin, and literally means "Nowhere." He said the U.S.S.R. has indeed achieved its utopian goals by going nowhere for 72 years.

"Russia is one of the wealthiest nations of the world as far as natural resources, but one of the poorest in standard of living," Elliott said. In spite of economic and political failure, he believes "educated folk in the Soviet Union are far more open to the claims of Christ than in North America. We are countries going in opposite directions...."

Elliott noted that Methodism in Eastern Europe was devastated in the World War II era when many Methodists fled to North America. As a result, the Methodist influence is less now than it was prior to the War. Yet (with the exception of Russia and Romania), there are still more Methodists than Baptists in Eastern Europe. Pentecostals are the fastest growing evangelical group.

No Bitterness

Elliot told of three Methodist pastors from Tallinn, Estonia. Pastor Alexander Kuum fought in World War II, spent four years in Siberia, and through his sufferings wants to "praise God for a chance to be brought closer to the Lord." He feels no bitterness.

In spite of deep hatred of Soviets, Pastor Olav Parnamets opened his church to services in both Russian and Estonian, and reports "no bitterness" toward those who oppressed his people.

Pastor Ullas Tonkler works with youth in Tallinn, having chosen this over finishing university training, and feels "no bitterness" toward a system that discriminates against Christians.

Concludes Elliot, "Every believer is God's gift to every other believer. We have a lot to learn as well as a lot to give" to our Christian brothers and sisters who suffered under Communism.

My Servant Gorby

Seminar speakers informed us that God raises up leaders to achieve his purposes, whether they know it or not, as in Romans 9:17 where it says concerning Pharaoh: "I raised you up..., that I might display my power in you and that my name might be proclaimed in all the earth." They believe Gorbachev was used of God in a similar way.

Formal Training Needed

We hear daily about the political and economic situation, but we know little about the people searching for answers. The question: "Can you tell me where to find God?" is now the underlying concern of the public. Because all religious training was stamped out under Communism, Protestants in the U.S.S.R. have no *formal* training programs.

Now weekend Bible schools are springing up and Theological Education by Extension (TEE) correspondence courses are being developed. Churches are also trying to start Sunday Schools but have no visual materials or methods for running such a program.

"I believe the largest church growth will go on around the kitchen table," Deyneka theorizes. In a land where fast food is not available and meals are still prepared from scratch, the kitchen is where much socializing and intellectual conversation takes place.

"Kitchen churches" already exist. Far East Broadcasting Corporation daily airs the Gospel in 115 languages and reports 39,750 "radio churches" in the Soviet Union. A healthy percentage of these radios are in the kitchen.

What Can Be Done?

In 1902 Lenin wrote *What Can Be Done?* and called for an elite group of leaders to pave the way for his revolution. Now it is time for Christians to ask, "What can be done?" and then begin doing it.

"They don't need traditional foreign missionaries," advises Deyneka. There is a severe lack of housing, and there are many lay leaders, local preachers, and evangelists, since no one travels great distances.

These individuals need to be equipped with Bibles and New Testaments for mass distribution, theological training materials, church libraries, and Sunday School literature.

"Teachers *are* needed," says Deyneka. But instead of establishing a Christian university he recommends the development of regional training centers to reach vastly more people in many locations throughout the area.

Statistics on the actual needs or possibilities are not available since that smacks of "intelligence gathering," an unwelcome activity in the former "Communist Bloc."

A Prophetic Dream For Europe

Gerald E. Bates
January/February 1991 p. 2

John 12:29 tells of the voice of God from heaven and the crowd that said it thundered. I wonder, in most of our lives, how many times God has spoken and we heard only thunder, or coincidence, or an echo ringing in our ears. How many times in history have miracles and extraordinary works of God been completely missed by those looking on?

I feel this is true of recent developments in Eastern Europe and the Soviet Union where God is speaking and newscasters say it thundered. In reality, God's arm, no doubt in response to decades of fervent prayers, has been bared and the empires of 40 to 70 years are toppling.

On a recent visit to Hungary we found that the staccato round of changes have burst so fast on the stage of history that even the Christians and churches most affected are blinking and startled in the light of new freedom. They are slowly gathering their forces and trying to adjust to the realities of a radically changed environment. An article in *Harvard Business Review* states flatly, "Four decades of socialist nightmare and Soviet domination have left a pitiful void in Hungarian society."

"This is no time to fumble around," roars Oswald Hoffman, longtime speaker of the Lutheran Hour, commenting on the Communist state of collapse in Eastern Europe and the Soviet Union, "This is the time for the church to get on her horse and RIDE!"

Free Methodists have some little-known historical connection with Eastern Europe. In the 1850s, founder B. T. Roberts felt a call to Bulgaria. The health of Mrs. Roberts prevented him from going (and, some will say humorously, he founded the Free Methodist Church instead!). In 1889, V. A. Dake of the Pentecost Bands organized a church in what is now East Germany. Dake died three years later and Roberts, who had supported him in his efforts, died a year after that. The fledgling church did not survive.

It may be now that God is giving the Free Methodists another chance. In fact, this conviction seized our delegation to Hungary. Here is a country bordered by Czechoslovakia, Romania, Yugoslavia, Austria and, as an entry to the Soviet Union, the Ukraine. We have the advantage of a close and open relationship with our sister church, the Hungarian Evangelical Fellowship. This connection brings with it an international network of churches over the borders in all directions, as well as an infrastructure on site which makes ministry immediately possible.

Do we have a prophetic dream for Europe? Of course we do. The Free Methodist World Fellowship is pursuing evangelization of Haitian communities in France with whom we have ties. The North Atlantic Area Fellowship linking Canada, the United Kingdom and the United States offers a ready vehicle to tie in European churches.

I can see, in a few years, a network of Free Methodist churches across Europe, and a Department of World Missions Secretary for Europe. I see these churches joining Canada, the U.K. and the United States in evangelizing the North Atlantic Area. I can see the Wesleyan doctrines of holy living and social holiness and service as very attractive to emergent Eastern Europe and the Soviet Union.

It is time, now, to live the dream, to get on our horse and ride! Read this issue of *Missionary Tidings* prayerfully, asking God what part of the dream he would have you fulfill.

Rock Music Paves The Way

Forest C. Bush
January/February 1991 p. 5

*Smack in the center of Eastern Europe is the country of Hungary. About the size of Indiana, Hungary is surrounded by Yugoslavia, Romania, Russia, Czechoslovakia, and Austria. With a population of just under 11 million people, Hungary is about 14% Atheist, 1% Jewish, 60% Roman Catholic or Orthodox, and 24% Protestant. Less than 4% of the Protestants are Evangelical (statistics from **Operation World**). For the Free Methodist Church, the open door into Eastern Europe is through Hungary. Our roots there are deep and well-watered.*

Scott Milliron was a member of a rock music group and assumed that Seattle's Eastside Free Methodist church sponsored dances for its youth. He met with youth director Patrick Vance in an effort to get his group hired to play for these imagined dances.

"Obviously, you don't know us very well," was Pat's response. It was time to get acquainted. Two and one-half hours later Scott was on his knees giving his life to Christ. That was in 1975. He became a very aggressive member of the youth group and brought others to church.

In 1980 Scott spent a summer in Europe with Eastern Europe Bible Mission. Based in Holland, this group ran VW vans equipped with secret compartments into East Bloc countries carrying Bibles and tracts to give away in public parks.

Scott was sent to Hungary where his contact person was Tibor Ivanyi, a man with churches sharing the doctrine and much of the history of the Free Methodist Church. When Scott returned to the U.S. he passed out cards with Tibor's address, asking people to write.

Pat Vance wrote to Tibor, and after a year of correspondence was invited to visit Hungary. Bishop Cryderman, then chairman of the Commission on Missions, encouraged Pat to make the trip, accompanied by Missions Secretary Charles Kirkpatrick.

The people of the Centralia, WA, church paid the $1,800 needed to send Vance to Hungary by way of England and Switzerland. Vance and

Kirkpatrick spent 12 days over Palm Sunday and Easter of 1982 with Tibor, who kept them busy speaking in one small church after another.

Victor Trinder's Dream

Within a year after the Vance and Kirkpatrick trip, Superintendent Victor Trinder of the United Kingdom went to Hungary. Tibor took him on an extensive tour of the Hungarian churches. In turn, Victor invited Tibor to England to visit Free Methodist churches.

Victor's dream was to establish a great European Free Methodist Church. He saw the Hungarian connection as the beginning of that development, and believed the British, as fellow Europeans, would be more likely than Americans to succeed in working with them. Trinder remained in continual contact with Tibor, but to date the European Church he envisioned has not been established. Victor died unexpectedly in 1988. Has his dream died with him?

The Upshot of 1989 General Conference

Tibor Ivanyi and his wife came from Hungary to the Seattle General Conference in 1989. By that time, political change in Hungary made it possible for Tibor to do more in the open. He told me, however, that during those many years when it was illegal to evangelize, his life was almost always on the line.

Secretly, Tibor translated and distributed important books. He would have been executed if caught. He and his wife lived in a large house to which individuals and groups came regularly for encouragement and training. Christian literature and supplies were also stored and distributed from the house.

Just before coming to General Conference the Ivanyis had a group of 16 people in their house for several days for training as Sunday School teachers.

Tibor told me the Hungarian race has 20 million people, but because of shifting borders, only 11 million actually live within Hungary. So groups belonging to his Fellowship are located inside Russia, Romania, and the former East Germany. As our ties are strengthened, we will have a remarkable opportunity to take the Gospel into East Bloc countries.

Meet Our Hungarian Friends

David M. Foster
January/February 1991 p. 6

Rev. Tibor Ivanyi is superintendent of about 180 congregations and fellowships that blanket Hungary. In his youth, Tibor was a Lutheran youth leader, although he said, "I was not truly a Christian at that time."

In 1945, a friend invited Tibor to a Methodist meeting. He refused several invitations, but finally went so as not to lose their friendship. At the meeting, he met a young Jewish man, also named Tibor, who took an immediate liking to him and very warmly received him.

During the meeting Tibor Ivanyi was strongly convinced by the message and soon surrendered his life to Jesus Christ. He said the lives of George Muller and James Hudson Taylor had greatly influenced him.

Tibor is a tall, pleasant, kindly, confident, comfortable looking man. His wife, Magda, is very pleasant, friendly, and hospitable. They have 11 children and 35 or so grandchildren. For more than 35 years, Tibor and Magda have trusted the Lord for their every need. "We do not beg from anyone," Tibor said, "but we tell the Lord our needs and he truly supplies them."

Hungarian Evangelical Fellowship

In 1976 there was a split in the Methodist Church. Politically, the church was encouraged to put out those who were conservative. When the bishop retired, instead of letting the church elect a new one, church leaders arbitrarily put in a very liberal man.

Tibor and about a dozen other pastors refused to accept this, believing it compromised the gospel. As a result, they were relieved of their pastoral positions and their licenses to preach. It was then illegal to be unemployed in Hungary, so these men and their families faced very difficult times.

Tibor was a recognized leader. It was felt that perhaps he would have been the next bishop. His expulsion in this time of turmoil led to the formation of the Hungarian Evangelical Fellowship (HEF). Today HEF includes 189 congregations in 113 population centers. Active membership stands at 2,269 with nine full-time pastors and three full-time lay workers.

"Umbrella" Churches

In those early days HEF members were threatened with persecution and jail, but in each case the Lord intervened. Put out of their churches by the government, they had to meet in homes. The people of one church in Budapest were locked out of their facilities. I asked the pastor, "What did you do then?"

The pastor replied, "We met out in a little strip of grass between the sidewalk and the street, and we nailed a cross to the tree. For almost four years we worshipped out between the sidewalk and the street."

"But this is Eastern Europe," I said to the pastor. "It gets cold. What did you do in the winter?"

"We swept the snow away and brought our chairs for worship. When it rained, we brought our umbrellas."

Today they are free and the government has given back their church. I was privileged to preach there. This house of worship gathers clothing for some of the neighboring countries that are less fortunate.

Pastoral Training

Pastors in Hungary must attend a university for three years and take an examination. They may at that time begin their ministry or go on for two or more years of study. Tibor really is a scholar, and if his personal library is any indication of his background, he is well trained. Books are everywhere. His office is lined with volumes in Hungarian, German, English, and perhaps other languages that I did not recognize.

Tibor says they have started a Bible school offering theological education for those who would like to prepare for ministry. In the past, very few had opportunity for training. Now, more than 20 students have started to prepare for ministry. This program needs our prayers.

Some pastors circulate among as many as 20 or 25 groups. Involved in services almost every night of the week, Hungarian pastors may have as many as two or three services in an evening, moving from one group to the next.

Church membership, in the past at least, has come at a dear price. You do not question the deep level of their commitment. I assume from what I saw that there are between five and six thousand people who on a weekly basis attend one of their churches or fellowship groups.

Missionaries To Gypsies

During my last visit of nine days in Hungary, I was involved in 11 different services in many areas of this country. A great deal of their work is done with the gypsy community. They consider the gypsies a mission field at home.

The HEF has a copy of our *Book of Discipline*, the book *From Age to Age* by Bishop Marston, and our new hymnal. They show deep appreciation for them, and showed me material from the 1979 *Book of Discipline* that was translated into Hungarian.

The Hungarian Evangelical Fellowship is indeed part of the true church. Their people are genuine in their relationship to God and their commitment to Wesleyan-Arminian theology. I have met most of their pastors and wives, and to meet them is to love them. They are warm, loving, sharp and committed. I was honored to worship and fellowship with them, and I am humbled at the price most of them pay to preach the gospel.

Hungary In Context Of History

Daniel V. Runyon
January/February 1991 p. 10

"To be or not to be.... Whether 'tis nobler in the mind to suffer the slings and arrows of outrageous fortune, or to take arms against a sea of troubles and by opposing, end them... that is the question."
— William Shakespeare, *Hamlet*

The church has suffered the slings and arrows of outrageous fortune for two thousand years. *Foxe Book of Martyrs* chronicles the lives of many who followed in the steps of Jesus and his apostles, who stood staunchly for truth, never compromising. They preached "in season and out of season," and paid with their lives.

We are learning through history. Modern historians deplore the Crusades, in which forces against Christianity were physically challenged in aggressive warfare. The war against Muslims today is fought with compassion. By loving our enemies we hope to introduce a few to the living God. How this can work is apparent in an appendix to Viggo Olsen's *Daktar II* (Moody Press, 1990, p. 575):

"If you are a Muslim, Hindu, or Buddhist person reading this book you will find it easy to follow — except for... calling God "Father." ...I have found this special title frequently in the Holy Bible and it is beautiful to me and full of deep meaning. He is like a human father in that He loves His own people, protects them, provides for them, disciplines them, cares for them, and guides them along life's pathway. I mention this because during my many years of living in Bangladesh I have observed that calling God "Father" sounds strange to most Bangladeshi ears. That is understandable, for the concept is not taught in Islam, Hinduism, or Buddhism."

Showing compassion does not guarantee that compassion will be offered in return. Thus, an unabridged *20th Century Book of Martyrs* would be a thick volume compared with a book chronicling those who gave their lives in previous centuries.

A Few Survivors

We know of Josef Tson (see his article on page 312) because he was faithful, and because he lived to tell his story. In 1973 as pastor of the largest Baptist church in Romania he published a document about government authorities illegally obstructing religious freedom. Indicted for "propaganda that endangers the security of the state," Tson was interrogated five days a week, sometimes up to 10 hours a day.

Tson told *Christian Herald* ("Thank You for the Beating," April, 1988), "The interrogator has his special tools: arrogance, mockery, threats, guile, lies and force." Believing those were Satan's tools, Tson instead used his Master's tools: "Trust in God, love, joy, truth, and self-sacrifice."

When threatened with torture and death, Tson replied, "Your supreme weapon is killing. My supreme weapon is dying. My sermons on tape have spread all over the country. If you kill me, these sermons will be sprinkled with my blood. Everyone will know I died for my preaching." Tson embodies **the new man** socialism was counting on. But for every succeeding reformer like Tson there are countless individuals who have sought reforms and have failed.

Soren In The Flesh

Consider Soren Kierkegaard of Denmark, remembered more for his philosophical contributions than for his influence in church reforms. In a March 26, 1855 newspaper article he observed that "Christianity does not exist," in his Lutheran Church in Denmark. He lamented, "We have a complete crew of bishops, deans, and priests; learned men, talented, gifted, humanly well-meaning,... but not one of them is in the character of the Christianity of the New Testament...."

Kierkegaard dedicated his life to reintroducing Christianity into Christendom, saying, "We have a complete inventory of churches: bells, organs, benches, alms-boxes, foot-warmers, tables, hearses, etc. But this inventory is likely to give rise to a false impression that when we have a complete Christian inventory we must of course have Christianity, too."

Kierkegaard viewed himself as a missionary, called by God to reach a "Christian" country, but his message went unheard. He died penniless at age 42, perhaps as much a martyr as those burned at the stake.

The Job For Us

Today, Eastern European evangelicals look to the similarly "Christian" country of the United States for answers. But much of what we offer is spiritually void, politically selfish, and likely to be of little help. It may be that persecuted Christians in the East have more to offer us than we have to offer them.

One thing we do have is money — 85% of all evangelical wealth is in North America. But only two percent of it is used for missions.

The Communist Bloc covers 13 time zones, 400 million people, speaking 140 languages. Will you help reach them for Christ? Communism is collapsing. The issue is, what is going to replace it?

To be the church or not to be... that is the question. The answer is that the church belongs to Jesus Christ. He is Lord and masterfully marches the church through history. It was without any brilliant intervention on our part that He — the Rock on which men stumble — broke the egg of socialism in Eastern Europe. He invites us, now, to work with him in Hungary. We must leap at this opportunity to spread the Good News. To do anything less is to be something other than the church.

Tentmaking Opportunities

Professors are needed who can teach ethics and morals in Hungarian universities. Certified teachers are needed to teach English in public schools (they **want** you to share your personal moral and religious values!). You can teach as a government employee and also work with church leaders in the Hungarian Evangelical Fellowship to fill the spiritual void in society.

Haiti Invades France!

M. Doane Bonney
November/December 1994 p. 17

Good news! There is now a Free Methodist presence in France! On Sunday, August 21, a group of 17 met in Josette Joseph's apartment in Saint-Gratien near Paris. There Pastor Benito Altidor (Florida) and missionary to Haiti, Warren Land, organized the first Free Methodist congregation in that country.

Missionary Land reported, "There was a keen sense that this service marked an important moment in the history of the Free Methodist Church and that it was the Lord who had opened the door and prepared the way."

Edgard Lambert, a 12-year resident in France, was installed as pastor with Jude Mervil as his assistant. Lambert has three years of training at the Free Methodist Bible School in Haiti and was Benito Altidor's assistant while both men were still pastoring in Haiti.

Land shared with me the excitement of seeing prayers answered, especially in regard to identifying the leaders God has raised up for this new church planting opportunity.

Pastor Lambert has a vision to open the church to all people in France -- Haitian, African, West Indians, as well as the French themselves. He envisions church plants all across that country.

Your prayers for this new congregation of believers in France and for Pastors Lambert and Mervil are urgently requested. Special gifts for this newest initiative on the continent of Europe may be sent to Free Methodist World Missions, marked "Project France."

VI. Latin America

Page	Article
333	Thompsons: Mission Driven In Latin America
343	Our Mission In The Caribbean
348	In the Dominican Republic
350	Glimpses Of Puerto Rico
352	My Mission To Samaria
354	Why Ivan Built A Church
356	In Ecuador
359	Costa Rica '92
363	From Costa Rica To Colombia
365	My Father: Leader Of The Church
367	Not In Kansas Anymore
369	In Perpetual Motion
373	Brazil
375	Busy People
379	Music Of Paraguay
381	Paraguay: A Concise History
383	How Our El Salvador Church Began
386	The Monk Who Lived Again [Condensed Book]

CLANCY and DORIS THOMPSON
LATIN AMERICA

Thompsons:
Mission Driven In Latin America

Interview by Daniel V. Runyon
January/February 1992 pp. 11-16

Tell about childhood experiences that shaped your life for missions work.

Clancy-- I grew up in Flint, Michigan, just a block from the Roosevelt Avenue Free Methodist Church. The "center of human warmth" was the bright, pleasant and good-smelling kitchen. I also fondly remember our living room where the family read together or listened to *The Green Hornet, Lone Ranger,* or *Amos and Andy* on the radio. This house sported hot water radiators for drying wet mittens and stocking caps. The furniture always stayed in the same place. Home was clean and orderly.

Mom always prayed with Dad before he left for work at Buick Motor where he was a tool and die maker. She prayed with my two older sisters when they went to school, and with my brother and me when we left. Sunday was family prayer time in the living room. We sang a hymn, read Scripture, and everyone knelt and prayed -- from Dad on down to the youngest. At church we had a family pew. It was the second row on the left for all six of us. Dad was song leader and Sunday school teacher. He and Mom were lay song evangelists.

Dad and Mom bought some lake property when I was four. We spent summers at the lake, and many Saturdays in the spring, fall and winter for ice skating, sliding downhill, swimming long hours, canoeing, fishing, hoeing the garden, mowing vast amounts of lawn, chopping firewood, and enjoying friends! Our pets were dogs. We went through several.

In town we played softball in the street using telephone poles and trees as the bases. Broken windows were the hazards, as well as the friendly police cruiser who occasionally interrupted our games. We also played kick-the-can games with neighborhood friends after dark.

On Monday nights Dad met with a group of boys and taught them how to use woodworking tools. We built hundreds of bird houses and sold them. We also went on camping trips, hikes, and toboggan runs together.

Tragedy came too. My second oldest sister, home for Christmas when a junior at Greenville College, drowned when she went through the ice while skating. Dad was killed in an auto accident and Mom was severely crippled but left alive. God was the center of our home and life, and at those moments he was our resource.

Doris-- I was born on a farm near Cedar Springs, Michigan (the Red Flannel Town), the last of four children, and the only girl. My mother died when I was three. My brother and I went to live with my aunt and uncle in Detroit who had six children.

I have happy memories of that time: picnics in the park, putting on plays, marching through the house as the lead person carrying a flag while my aunt played the piano, then on cue, marching up the stairs to bed.

After two years my aunt's health deteriorated, so my father hired a housekeeper and took us home to join my older brothers who had stayed with him. Shortly thereafter my father remarried and we moved to town.

When I was in the third grade my stepmother left, and arrangements were made for me to room and board with my girlfriend's family that lived around the corner. I later realized what a sacrifice that family made. They had a small house and three children of their own. Two months before my 12th birthday I moved to another neighbor's home, a couple with no children. I lived with them until I went to college.

As a child I loved to read. Anti-I-Over, roller skating and bike riding (after I saved enough money to buy a second-hand one), were favorite activities. My friend Glenna and I used to play jacks by the hour! And there were money-raising schemes, like the time we picked up angle worms in a neighbor's garden plot as it was being plowed. Then we went to the garage where he worked and sold him the worms!

I started working regularly as a babysitter when I was 12, and continued that even after I was hired to stock shelves in a local store after school. On Saturdays I was a bagger, and finally became a "checker." After graduation, I worked in the office of a milk company for a year and saved money for college. In the fall of 1948, I enrolled in Spring Arbor College and paid my own way with work and scholarships.

Do you remember any important childhood religious experiences?

Clancy— Sunday school, church, Bible school, children's meetings, and camp meetings were a significant part of life. So were my responses to invitations to ask forgiveness.

When I was about 12, on a Friday night, a youth evangelist and former sports writer spoke. That night as Dale Cryderman gave the invitation I went to the altar to pray and gave my heart to Christ. While at the altar, God asked me, "Will you be a missionary?" A quick, unmeasured, but definite "yes" was my response, and I told the church what had taken place.

Was I always faithful? No, and I marvel at God's patience, his mercy, and his protection!

Doris— The neighbors with whom I first lived were Free Methodists, so I went with them to church and there learned about sin and salvation. I invited Christ into my life during a vacation Bible school when I was eight or nine years old. I remember once when I was about 10 that the local Women's Missionary Society raised money and bought me some clothes so I could go to camp meeting and conference at Manton with a lady from the church.

My faith has made *all* the difference in my life. My father did not go to church, so neither did my brothers. I can only imagine what my life would have been had God not called me and so graciously guided me during those years!

Why are you a missionary?

Clancy— God spoke to me about missions when I was saved. His question was clear, direct and stabilizing. He has given me a heart for missions and actually designed me for this work. He provided me with a wife who has had the same calling and certainty of direction. He has given peace and assurance. Just as the stakes give stability to a tent, so the "Will you be a missionary?" question has been a stake in my life. It stabilizes; it is unequivocal.

Doris— While praying at the altar one Sunday night when I was around 12, I felt God asking me to be a missionary. And I felt prompted to tell the people about this during the testimony service that always followed an altar service. I remember the warm, supportive response to that testimony.

The conviction that this was God's plan for my life stayed with me through high school, but it was severely tested a month before I entered college. I had been told that if I didn't feel called to a specific place, it was doubtful I had been called. Also, I wasn't sure what course to pursue in preparation for missionary service. This resulted in confusion, uncertainty and questioning. After much prayer, I decided to walk by faith and leave the answers with God. My first step was to go to college.

Confirmation came through the husband God chose for me. After working through the doubts, then by going ahead without knowing anything – simply trusting – God prepared the way before me and I never doubted again.

Has there been any romance in your life?

Clancy– Once when I was a freshman at Spring Arbor Junior College, early in September I attended a prayer meeting night in the stone church. An attractive girl in the "Amen Corner" stood to give her testimony.

"Who is she?" I asked Bill Erickson. She happened to be from North Michigan, a friend of Bill's – Doris Towns! I requested an introduction later on and got it.

There was a problem – I was dating another girl. A couple of evenings later, my roommate wanted to double date, and to my dismay, he had a date with Doris! We wound up at the legendary ice cream "Parlor" in Jackson. Not just ice cream sent chills up and down my spine as I sat with Doris on one side of me, my date on the other. I knew before the evening was over that I was very much interested in Doris.

Doris and I dated throughout our two years at Spring Arbor, then on to Greenville. Some months after we started dating I discovered that she too had received a call from God for missionary service. We carefully built our friendship until I asked her to marry me. Our engagement became official in our junior year, and the following summer we were married. Our wedding took place in the Cedar Springs, Michigan, Free Methodist Church.

For our honeymoon, I borrowed my Dad's Buick for a trip to Cloyne, Ontario, to stay at my uncle's cottage on Marble Lake. On the way we stopped at Niagara Falls. Our honeymoon cost us $75 – all the money we had. After a great honeymoon we went back home and worked for the summer to earn money for our senior year at Greenville College.

The first day back from honeymoon, we borrowed $150 and purchased a 1934 Ford from a neighbor. When filling out the papers I was asked my age. "Twenty," was the response.

"You will have to have someone who is 21 or older to sign for you," I was told. So I went home and got Doris – she turned 21 the day before our wedding. Incidentally, we sold the car a couple of months later for $185!

I have a sense of completeness with Doris as my wife. There is the delight of being together, doing things together, getting things together, and planning the immediate future together. We worked together to get through college and then three years of seminary. Doris is the one human being whom I depend on continually. My ministry is always more effective when she is involved. Our marriage validates our ministry.

Doris– I met Clancy as a freshman at Spring Arbor. On our first date we attended a Marine Band Concert in Jackson. Dating was confined to Tuesday evening after dinner until study hour, Friday night, and Sunday after morning worship.

Clancy sang in a quartet which traveled almost every weekend, so our dating was mostly on campus. Not too long after we started going together I learned about his call to missions, so I decided to keep quiet about my call lest that become a factor before I knew him well. He did not necessarily have a "preacher" image on campus. Our relationship had its ups and downs, but by the middle of our junior year at Greenville, we announced our engagement and were married in June.

We had a very limited income ($19 a week minus tithe which was automatic with both of us) from Clancy's job at Joy's Annex. Our budget didn't allow for extras, but God miraculously provided extra money in two instances at the exact time of need – an emergency trip home because of Dad Thompson's death and Mom Thompson's critical condition, followed immediately by a trip to Kentucky to interview for a teaching position which was essential if Clancy was to go to seminary. God's provision in these and other experiences deepened our trust in God, and cemented our marriage by deepening our love and appreciation for one another.

Clancy complements me in so many ways. He is a decisive, take charge sort of person, while I ponder at length and have a hard time making decisions. I am more of a perfectionist, and a dedicated bargain hunter. And I have a deep need for security which comes from the lack of a permanent family structure as a child. Clancy and I are different, but I enjoy the "pizazz" he brings to our lives. Our relationship is a growing one because we are committed to working at the oneness God planned for marriage.

Is there anything you'd like to mention about your children?

Clancy– Our kids are our friends. We have great times together! Our first son, Kevin Dale, was stillborn in 1955, shortly after I graduated from seminary. Then Brian James was born in Flint on January 25, 1958. Mark Edward was born in Brazil on February 10, 1961. Our third son, Steven Michael, was born in Flint on May 20, 1971. All three are now adults, serving the Lord in their own ways.

Doris– Our children bring us great joy. We love being together. When we were asked to go back to Brazil in 1986, one of the first things we did was call the family together to talk it over, ask their counsel, and pray.

We try to keep current family prayer request lists. We have had two "dreaming prayer" (see *Adventures in Prayer* by Catherine Marshall, Chapter 3) experiences as a family, and God granted them both! It is a special joy to watch the married ones as parents. Being a grandparent is great! It's difficult to spoil grandchildren long-distance, though! We are extremely grateful to see them seek to know and follow God's will for their lives.

You've been many places. Do you have a favorite spot?

Clancy– We have enjoyed living in Michigan, Kentucky, Illinois, Oregon, Costa Rica and Brazil. We've been in Haiti, Dominican Republic, Paraguay, Chile, Ecuador, Venezuela, and Argentina. But Sao Paulo, Brazil is our home -- our place! Brazil is our choice for a field of service.

We enjoy being with family and home in Michigan, but we recognize that we are pilgrims. Life is a journey, not a destination. Therefore, moved by God's calling, we travel light and choose not to let things impede God's access to us and placement of us.

Doris– While we are in active ministry, we could only be happy where God wants us to be. Should we retire, we would like to be in a warm climate, but as close to our family as possible.

You have known many sorrows. What about disappointments in ministry? Anything you want to say about this?

Clancy— In 1970 I resigned from missionary appointment and traveled to Winona Lake to care for left-over details after 13 years of service. On my unwritten agenda I guess I wished to hear someone say, "Thanks Clancy, for giving 13 of the most vigorous years of your life to the church."

I didn't hear any such comments, and went away fuming inside. In white-hot internal indignation, I determined I would not set foot back in Winona Lake. So I fumed all the way back home – a five hour trip. As I drove into the city limits of Flint a voice suddenly asked me, "To whom did you give 13 years of missionary service?"

And then I understood. God called. My service is given to him -- through the agency of our church. This initial disappointment has made all the difference in my subsequent ministry -- a tremendously positive one!

Doris— The most disappointing thing in our career was the indication that the right thing to do in 1971 was to return to the States. We were called to be missionaries! Did God change His mind? However, God was still definitely leading us. He placed us in a challenging situation, surrounded us with loving people, and brought people into our lives from whom we learned and grew. He then gave us new ministries, some directly connected to missions, and always an awareness that our times were in his hands.

Clancy— One great encouragement to me is this: When thousands of miles from our children and family in service to God, to have the Lord call my attention to Isaiah 41:14 and be reminded that God is our *redeemer – the obligated protector of our family!* That is security!

What do you do for fun?

Clancy— Read, play table games with friends, go to the beach for swimming, and play tennis.

Doris— Reading, lap quilting (taken up during deputation travels), and ceramics.

Tell us about life in Latin America.

Clancy— Those who travel east and west have jet-lag to worry about. We don't, but when you travel north and south you must be prepared for both hot and cold weather. We live in a sub-tropic area.

Winter can mean a temperature plunge to 42 degrees. This sounds warm to people in Michigan, but it is difficult in buildings with no heat. The solution is to put on more clothing! Hug yourself!

The Latins are a warm, expressive people. They are a mixture of nationalities. In Brazil the mix is basically Indian, African and European/Portuguese — with a blend of Italian, German, and Oriental. They say the true Brazilian has not yet evolved!

My favorite Latin America foods are churrasco, virado a paulista, and feijoada. On a late Sunday evening after a long day I especially enjoy a plate of cucumber, sliced onion, tomato, palmito, oil/vinegar, cheese, a slice of toast, and good company.

Doris— I love Brazilian *Feijoada,* which is a pot of black beans in which is cooked a variety of meat — bacon, sausage, smoked fresh and salted pork, dried beef, and seasoned with garlic and onions, served over rice. Accompaniments: collards, toasted manioc flour, and oranges, or orange juice.

Also delicious is something the Japanese prepare called *Sukiyaki.* Thin slices of steak and a variety of bite-sized vegetables are cooked in special sauce in an electric pan on the table as you eat. This is served in a bowl with slightly beaten raw egg (I eat mine without the egg). The rice is in a separate bowl. This is a friendship dinner, meant to last a long time as you talk and fellowship together. I first ate it when Japanese pastors offered it for Bishop John and the missionaries.

What special needs do you face, and how can the North American church help?

Clancy and Doris— We must train and prepare people for both ministerial and lay leadership. We also need to create a support system for our national leaders.

Many of our Latin leaders are pioneers opening Free Methodist churches in their countries without adequate prayer backing. These people include Jorge Villacis in Ecuador, Sergio Loyola in Chile, Jorge Gomez in Costa Rica, and Abner Mieses in Puerto Rico. Without another brother who shares that "kindred spirit," these men experience unique loneliness.

The North American church can help:
1. Provide funds for educational purposes.
2. Create a "Task Force of Prayer" for these Latin brothers, carrying them daily before our Lord.

3. Send VISA teams to build schools, churches, clinics and housing, taking with them materials and equipment.
4. Help Latins achieve their dreams in creative ways which will be discovered through exposure to one another.

Suppose you get the help to meet these needs. What goals would be achieved as a result?

Clancy and Doris– The Latin America Free Methodist church has set a goal to establish a church in every Latin American country in the next eight years (by the year 2000). We want to see membership grow to a minimum of 50,000 Free Methodists in Latin America in the same eight years.

We also want to establish an International Training Task Force comprised of Latins and American missionaries functioning in every Latin American country. Latin America has a remarkable pool of youthful, gifted missionaries – the Dan Bonneys, Garry Cruces, Phil Gilmores, Tim Goodenoughs, Mike Henrys, Don Mercers, Dan Owsleys, and David Rollers. These young dynamos are backed by the mature and experienced Doug Smiths, all in the Spanish/Portuguese context.

(Haiti is a special situation, located in a Latin Caribe, but outside the Latin context. Our missionary team is a strong and efficient one – Warren Lands, Ken Harrises, Jerry Rushers and a highly qualified VISA team. Our Haitian church is one of our most rapidly growing churches.)

The increasing number of well-prepared and gifted Latin leaders creates much excitement and enthusiasm for the immediate future. It would be dangerous to formulate a list at this point, for I am not well acquainted with all of the countries. However, every one has at least one Latin leader who could easily contribute significantly to the Task Force.

These are realistic, yet challenging goals. We believe they will be achieved as we build "trust bonds" in relationships, develop vision and communicate the dreams. We must also work with Latin leaders to help them develop more financial self-sufficiency.

What advice would you give those thinking of becoming career missionaries?

Clancy– I know I should have been trained to better disciple men and women. A strong, consistent devotional life is also essential. And learn to be unafraid of "people closeness." In addition to traditional preparation, get specific training in administration, anthropology, guidance counseling, and financial management and accounting.

Doris– Be a growing Christian with a firm grasp of the Scriptural basis for our own doctrine. Gain as much Bible knowledge and tools for Bible study as possible.

And, develop helpful attitudes. The American way is not necessarily the right way of doing things, at least in other countries. Try to discover the difference between what is Christian and what is American. Be committed to teaching what is Christian, based on Scripture, and be willing to accept cultural differences.

You should also be dedicated to learning the language to the best of your ability. If married, have a growing marriage relationship. Other helpful experiences include training such as is given now in Missionary Internship, and previous cross-cultural experiences.

We're running out of space, but don't let me cut you off if there's something you want to add.

Clancy– If you were to ask what is the one foundational requirement for missionary service, my answer would be, "A well-established daily quiet time with God's Word, accompanied by a life-style of forgiveness."

Also, I want our readers to know that the Free Methodist Church has been started by Latin leaders in seven Latin American countries where we have no North American missionary presence. In all probability, this will be repeated in many other Latin countries during the decade of the 1990s.

I believe that the Latins now living in the United States could well help us launch an all-out drive to reach every Latin American country by the year 2,000. We must find a way to use every person and his or her gift in this mission!

Our Mission In The Caribbean

Wally Metts
September/October 1991 p. 1-6

A visitor to the Free Methodist missions in the Caribbean is struck by the texture of life in the Dominican Republic and Haiti.

Pastel greens and pinks are splashed against stucco walls and the market place is alive with bright oranges and reds in a moving, living fabric. The cloth is rougher; the roads are rougher, too.

The squeal of pigs and the chatter of people late into the night and the aroma of goat meat or pastries from the street vendors makes these cultures seem more vibrant than our own.

One also notices the measured leisurely pace of life set against the pulsating merengue of the Dominican Republic, the infectious rhythm heard on every street corner. Or against the music in the 200 Free Methodist churches or preaching points, clapping music, joyfully alive with the passion of faith. Or even against the haunting, pounding drums of a Haitian voodoo ceremony, tantalizing and mesmerizing late into the night.

These two cultures seem rich in sensory detail because ours is sensory poor, insulated as we are by technology. The smells of our lives are encased in plastic packages and the colors concentrated on a 24 inch screen. And their cultures are poor in other ways -- so the bright colors stand out against the black background of despair.

But given these textures and rhythms, it is easy to make two mistakes: The first is that these two cultures are the same, which is an error in perception. The second mistake is that our culture has the answers they need, which is an error in judgment.

One Island...

The Dominican Republic and Haiti share the same island, Hispaniola. They share some of the same foods-- rice and beans are staples, but they are seasoned differently. Tropical fruit abounds -- especially mangoes. And culturally they share an aversion to our clocks. Both are what first term missionary Paula Bonney calls "event oriented."

"I grew up in a family with a hard work ethic," she says. "I tend to be a perfectionist. I'm very time conscious. I always want to keep things moving. But the Latin American culture isn't like that. If church starts at 9 o'clock and no one is there until 10, big deal. I'm the only one who is upset."

These people are unaffected by our schedules and worksheets. Relationships are much more important than programs. Veteran missionary Warren Land says any tardiness in Haiti is forgiven with the explanation that you met someone and had to talk.

"It is easy to be friends here," says Phil Gilmore, a missionary kid raised in the Dominican Republic and now a career missionary there. "There is no suspicion about why you are friendly. Here it is normal. You are supposed to be someone's friend." But it is at this point of being friends that the differences between the two cultures begin to emerge.

Two Cultures

The Dominican Republic is a European culture. The people are descended from Spanish explorers. They assume they are your equal--and that you think so, too. In Haiti, an African culture, they are more suspicious. Maxine Riddle, a Free Methodist missionary in Haiti since the early 1950s, says Haitians "have a slave complex." Their country is the oldest black republic in the world, with a proud history dating back to 1804 when they overthrew the French slaveholders. But even now, Riddle says, "They are always watching you. They want to be a white person's friend, but they have to know it's on the same level."

These differences in history have created different problems. For example, the relational aspect of Dominican culture has given rise to institutionalized corruption. Paper work proceeds through the bureaucracy based on whom you know.

Policemen literally stop you on the street and ask for a bribe -- and you can hardly blame them in a culture where cops get paid about $200 a month and a steel claw hammer with a wooden handle costs $10.

Although there is little violent crime, petty theft is rampant. Yards are fenced and locked, windows barred. Missionaries have maids – not just to help with meals and the constant mopping of dust, but because there needs to be someone in the house all the time.

Graft at the higher levels has left the economy reeling. Triple digit inflation in just two years has resulted from stringent government policies to qualify for more international credit. School teachers and doctors in government hospitals have been on strike for several months. Unemployment is 30%.

Tensions rise from having a western culture, but without its benefits. Electricity is on a few hours a day, but no one knows which hours. Frustrating.

In Haiti, however, no one expects electricity. People are just surprised when it's there at all. Here an income of $200 *a year* is not uncommon. One baby in 10 dies within a year of its birth. Sixty percent of the people are illiterate. Two centuries of slash and burn agriculture have left the mountains of this land barren, even though it was once France's richest colony.

Corruption is also a problem in Haiti, but the more dominant problem is pervasive poverty which, combined with African fatalism, has created a downward spiral of dependency and despondency. One common mannerism is to alternately slap the back of one's own hands and shrug the shoulders. The meaning? "It's not my fault."

Haitians often add the expression "if God wishes" to the end of every statement, but it is not an expression of hope. The language (Creole) is full of proverbs which hint at the futility of life. One of the most common is "Daya mon gin mon." *Behind the mountains there are mountains.* The mountains are endless and insurmountable.

No easy answers

Given our own prosperity, it is easy to assume that what the people in these cultures need is to be more like us. If they just worked a little harder their life would eventually be a little easier.

The truth is, these people do work hard. Paula Bonney says the church in Santo Domingo (DR) is "the hardest working church I've ever been in. I don't know how it all comes together. There is a lot of lay involvement and lay initiative. It puts our churches back home to shame."

The same sort of energy is evidenced in their jobs. "They get up early and go to work. Then they come home and go to church or an activity almost every night. They get home about 11 o'clock and then get up early the next morning and go again. I don't know how they do it," says Dan Bonney.

In Haiti the pastors usually have jobs to support themselves and always have two or more churches or preaching points. Maxine Riddle says their churches don't support them. Rather, they have to support their churches. She often counsels pastors not to give all their money away.

The poverty which surrounds them is debilitating. "What their people do, doesn't produce," Riddle says. "The gardens don't grow. They work hard. It just doesn't do any good."

Looking Wistfully North

The result of endless and overwhelming difficulty is a dissatisfaction with the quality of life in both cultures, and they cast a wistful eye toward their more affluent neighbors to the north. Both countries are struggling with a "brain drain" as bright young professionals leave.

It isn't only those in the upper middle class who are trying to leave. More than a half million Haitians have fled through the mountains on foot to the Dominican Republic, only to become the outcasts of that society, eking out the barest of existences in crowded, unsanitary and primitive settlements near the sugar fields.

Meanwhile 50,000 poor Dominicans have tried to enter the U.S. illegally in the past 10 years, crossing the treacherous Mona Passage to Puerto Rico in small, crowded boats. Most are caught and returned by U.S. Customs officials. Some 6,000 have died in the attempt.

Those that do enter the United States legally often find that while the standard of living is higher, they become the objects of prejudice and discrimination. Some few eventually make it to the United States and eventually return, relatively rich, to their own land.

Tension

For those who remain in their native lands, the American missionary often represents the American dream. Phil Gilmore says the hardest part of his job in the Dominican Republic is saying no. Almost every pastor who talks with him asks for financial help. "People think we have infinite resources," he says.

In Haiti, with more missionaries per capita than any other country in the world, such largess may have backfired. According to VISA nurse Tanis Mealy in Dessalines, "People feel like they need someone to do it for them."

Combined with an historic suspicion of white domination, the situation is potentially explosive. The current Haitian president, leftist priest Jean-Betrand Aristride, was elected on a theme of "lavalas," a flood which will sweep aside the vestiges of oppression.

For some, waiting until someone gives it to them has been replaced with a desire to just reach out and take it. Tensions between the American and Haitian staff at the Free Methodist hospital in Dessalines have increased. The quarters built for missionary staff by Canadian donors seem almost opulent next to the squalid huts.

Personnel and discipline problems with nationals have increased in the current political climate.

"They see 'blancs' (whites) as coming with their own ideas, deriving their own benefit," says Mealy. This has created a need for new approaches and attitudes. "You don't have to go back to living in a grass hut to be a missionary," she explains. "But you can't put yourself so far above the people that you can't feel their needs."

A Better Objective

Free Methodist missions in both countries work against the temptation to put themselves "above the people." In the Dominican Republic, where the Free Methodist Church has been self reliant for a number of years, the missionaries serve at the invitation of the national church and work as assigned.

In Haiti, where the church is not strong enough to stand alone, there are serious efforts to build self sufficiency and ultimately the dignity which that culture requires. These include programs in agriculture and community development as well as the training of lay leaders and pastors.

Haitian pastor Noel Charite says "In the new day we want our church to have self-support. Some people think our church belongs to the white people. They believe the missionary must do everything. This is not true. In my vision, I want the church one day to have self support. If we have no missionary one day, the church will not fall down."

Mission director Warren Land came to Haiti after years of service in Africa. He says he remembers when the missionaries were expelled from Burundi in 1979. "When we were expelled, I remember thinking about the mimeograph machine. 'Who's going to run the mimeograph machine,' I thought. We've been here 20 years and there is no one who knows how to run the mimeograph machine."

It's a mistake he won't make twice.

"We are no longer the great white father," he says.

"We are not the church leaders here," explains Riddle. "The missionary task is more that of a friend or mentor."

"These people are not helpless," says Mealy. "We're just visitors. We should build each other up. And learn. We have a lot to learn."

About patience, perhaps. And about friendship. And about growth.

The object of Free Methodist missions in the Caribbean is not to teach people to be like us, after all.

But to learn together how to be like Christ.

In The Dominican Republic

by Arlene Gilmore
January/February 1992 pp. 27-28

In 1889 Samuel Mills, a Free Methodist pharmacist from Ashtabula, Ohio, felt called of God to move to the West Indies and begin missionary work. Perhaps no place in the Caribbean area had fewer missionaries than the Dominican Republic. Mills made his way north, locating first at Montecristi and later in Santiago. Great emphasis was placed upon the distribution of Scripture portions and home visitation. He sowed the seed and gathered together the nucleus of what later became the Dominican Republic Church.

Work in the Dominican Republic was organized differently from that on any other field. Samuel Mills went, with his wife and two children, as a self-supporting missionary with no financial ties to the home church. He later requested the missionary board to send Esther D. Clark, also from Ohio. The board appropriated money for her transportation and sent her out in 1893. In 1904, after serving 11 years, she was recognized as a Free Methodist missionary. She continued to be partially self-supporting, teaching English classes as many others did.

In 1907, on order of the director and in harmony with a request from Miss Clark, Missionary Secretary Winget went to the Dominican Republic to secure information regarding the country, the "Mills Mission," and to discover whether some cooperative program could be worked out with Mills.

Reaching The Spanish-speaking Population

Winget discovered that what little missionary work was being done was mostly concentrated on the south side of the island in and near the city of Santo Domingo. The largest mission was working primarily with English-speaking peoples. Winget found that about 150 people had been baptized by Mills and he himself baptized 16 during the trip. He learned also that Mills was favorable to Free Methodist missionaries coming. Miss Clark promised to give her house and several acres of land and join in the work if the Free Methodist Church opened this new field.

For a number of years only missionaries who could be self-supporting were appointed. As the need for workers grew, fully supported missionaries were also sent out. Samuel Mills continued in fellowship with our church until his death in 1913, although he never requested aid for himself from the Missionary Board. His son, George, and wife, Ruth, were appointed as Free Methodist missionaries in 1917 and continued until their retirement 40 years later.

Samuel Mills' faithful work cannot be overestimated. He labored seven years before there was a convert. Many of the early converts were persecuted. Some were put in jail, and at least one was killed.

They're Teaching *Girls*?

One method used to overcome opposition was to establish schools. At San Francisco de Macoris, east of Santiago and on the north part of the island, a school for girls was opened. Appreciative parents sent many daughters, paying fees for the privilege. Nursing in homes opened many other doors for testimony and personal evangelism. At Macoris the first Protestant church of the mission was built and dedicated in 1915.

Meanwhile, a seminary for young men was opened in Santiago. This was later merged with the Lincoln school for girls, and both were located on a site of 36 acres outside of Santiago. Suitable buildings were erected and a successful co-educational school was carried on.

Handing It Over To National Leaders

The organization of a provisional conference in 1930 placed new responsibility upon the native church. Pastors were ordained. Self-support increased. New churches were organized, new workers called out.

Sunday schools have done much to win adherents to the Protestant faith. At one time the largest Sunday school in Free Methodism was held in Santiago by having branch schools in different parts of the city, all going on at the same time, the teachers all trained in the main school, and all under one superintendent.

Because freedom of religion is fully guaranteed by the constitution, missionary work has reaped benefits. The Evangelical Institute has served children from some of the finest homes. Graduates now hold positions of influence throughout the island. Some may never become members of the church, but it will be hard for them to tolerate the throwing of rocks or the jailing of *convertidos*.

The climate is difficult, the people are poor, but the Mills' venture of 1889 laid the foundation of what today is a thriving church.

Glimpses Of Puerto Rico

Arturo Quinones
March/April 1992 p. 3-5

Last summer I felt God calling me to join the *Impacto '91* missionary group to Puerto Rico. I had doubts of doing so but felt convicted to send in my application anyway.

I thought, "What could I possibly contribute to the group? With my terribly crude Spanish, I'd probably make a fool of myself!" Little did I know the plans God had. Even though Spanish is my first language, I lost most of my ability to speak it.

To my surprise, I received a letter stating that I had been chosen for the team! God at that moment started to reveal his plans for me. Not only was I going with the team, but I felt convicted to go several days earlier and witness to my family on the island.

So I went early, only to find out that many had already committed themselves to Jesus! But I planted seeds in those who hadn't. After I witnessed to my relatives for about a week, the rest of the group arrived.

Two Big Mistakes

God worked in me several ways that week, but one is dear to me, performed just so that I may serve him better. You see, I was struggling to communicate with my crude Spanish. I was asked to give a testimony. In my panic I turned to my own strength and tried to memorize a few lines. BIG MISTAKE! I went up to the pulpit and did terribly.

Throughout the entire time prior to the testimony I felt God was convicting me to leave all my papers and tricks behind and go forth in faith. I ignored God [SECOND BIG MISTAKE!], and messed up. Afterwards I saw my problem and as soon as I let him, God overcame my problem for me.

At the end of the week I was asked once more to give a testimony. After all the things God had done through me that week, I was glad to! And this time I brought to the pulpit no stumbling blocks as I did before. This time I brought at my side the love of my triumphant Jesus.

When asked if I had prepared something to say I said I had nothing prepared. I was sure God would guide me to say what the church needed to hear.

After being introduced I went to the pulpit and at once felt God reassuring me and leading me. God did not want me to give a testimony. Rather, he delivered a *sermon* through *me* — the one who couldn't even say a few lines in front of church a week ago!

Never have I been more directly used to minister to a group of people. I managed to do the things God did through me, not by my power but by *His,* in whom I trust. I praise his name for allowing me to partake in his grace and majesty. I now realize that anything, *anything* is possible through God for the fulfillment of his will.

My Mission To Samaria

Edward Coleson, Ph.D.
March/April 1992 pp. 9

Just who are our Samaritans? Our Lord tells us in the great commission that we are to be witnesses unto him "in Jerusalem and in all Judea" (for us, the local and larger community), and "in Samaria" (an area close by where the people are of a different culture and language), and "unto the uttermost part of the earth" (Acts 1:8).

A century ago, C.I. Scofield, well known for his *Reference Bible,* noted that missionaries had been going "to the regions beyond" for many decades. Meanwhile, Central America, a short voyage from New Orleans, was being completely neglected. He said this was our Samaria, so he founded the Central American Mission to do something about this need. It seems it is easy to overlook opportunities for service which are near us.

My Adventure Begins

After teaching at Spring Arbor College for more than 20 years and now being partially retired, I became aware of a need in the Wesleyan Theological College in a suburb of San Juan, Puerto Rico. I would need Spanish, but I had already taken a year of it with the freshmen and had spent all my spare time thereafter studying the language.

I completed the first semester at Spring Arbor College in December of 1983. By January I was in another classroom more than 2,000 miles away with a group of students, most of whom did not speak English. I was now teaching pastors and preachers-to-be who were working toward ordination. Our classes were in the evening, since students had jobs during the day.

The hours were long, since each course met only one night a week. Those who have taken such courses know what it is like -- but pity the poor teacher, too! I had a good interpreter who was also a member of the class. This helped. We got along quite well.

Bi-lingual Prof

I could read the textbook and make up tests in Spanish and correct them, but I was not yet ready to lecture in the language. A couple years later it was a great day when I found I could get along without my interpreter.

When I was able to teach in Spanish, I saw an urgent need I could now do something about. We had some Free Methodist students in our little college who had been faithfully pursuing their programs and were almost finished, but they lacked Free Methodist History, a requirement for ordination.

I was familiar with that history and had about everything in print on the subject in my English library, but they knew only Spanish. With the help of David Roller I got a few copies of a slender book on Free Methodism which Burleigh Willard wrote in Spanish. And there was material in Spanish on the Reformation and rise of Methodism in England and America that I could photocopy. I also translated a few things, such as current statistics on world missions. It was a lot of work and fun.

For me the payoff came when Dr. Doane Bonney (then Latin America Area Director) made his quarterly visit at the end of the semester. He ordained three members of my class who finished their ministerial course: Samuel Diaz, Abner Mieses, and Rudy Ortiz. I am proud to have been the teacher of these three ministers, and I rejoiced with them and their families on the completion of their work.

Your Samaria

Your Samaria may not be 2,000 miles away from home, as mine is. When Rev. Scofield founded the Central American Mission a century ago, most North-American Spanish-speaking people lived in the southwest of the United States. Now millions of them are scattered across America, perhaps some of them next door to you.

We in our evangelical churches have not done very well relating to our minorities, but you and I can change that. We can go beyond our Jerusalem and Judea and find the neglected people between our home area and "the regions beyond."

Why Ivan Built A Church

Phil Gilmore
March/April 1992 p. 21, 25

Ivan and Yolanda Canot retired late one evening, satisfied. Their new mini-market was coming along fine. The forms were in place to begin pouring the concrete slab roof.

Yolanda, a Salvadoran, met her husband, a Dominican, in New York. She begged Ivan to build this mini-market to give her something to keep herself busy.

Ivan agreed. He was a successful businessman and community leader in the tourist town of Puerto Plata. He felt it would be a plus for the neighborhood, so he drew up plans for the facility.

The Canots were Christians but neglected church attendance. There was no church they particularly cared to attend. However, in the privacy of their home they regularly read their Bibles and prayed together.

Late that night Ivan was awakened by what seemed to be a strange dream. It was as if someone shook him and spoke to him saying, "The Lord does not want a mini-market — he wants a church."

Ivan, now completely awake, didn't know what to make of this dream. He got a glass of water, then went back to bed. An hour or so later he felt himself shaken again. This time the voice was much more insistent: "Listen to me. The Lord wants you to build a church!"

Now Ivan was frightened. Nothing like this had happened to him before. Yolanda, awakened by her husband's restlessness, asked what was wrong. Ivan did his best to ignore her questioning. He spent the remainder of the night thinking and reading his Bible.

In the morning Ivan skipped his customary breakfast and lunch. He spent the time in his upstairs bedroom. His wife knew something was very wrong but could not pry any information out of him.

At 2:00 p.m., Ivan felt suddenly very sleepy. He went to bed. No sooner had he fallen asleep then the strange messenger began shaking him violently, and forcefully said, "Pay attention to me! God does not want a mini-market. He wants you to build him a church!"

The shaking was so violent that Ivan fell out of bed and sprained his wrist.

Yolanda didn't know what to think when she heard Ivan's story. He was not given to wild tales. Either he had gone crazy or it was indeed the Lord speaking to him. She accepted the latter, believing that if it was the Lord speaking, the church project would prosper.

That same day Ivan spoke to the workers about changing the front of the mini-market to make it look like a church. A cross was added and the word *Iglesia* (church) was molded into the cement facade.

A few weeks earlier, Israel Brito, superintendent of the Dominican Free Methodist Church, sadly concluded that the church-planting project in Puerto Plata should be terminated. After 10 years of trying, no adequate location had been secured. No stable congregation had been established.

The Canots were obedient to the strange call. The mini-market was transformed into a sanctuary. The problem now was to find someone to take charge of the church. Who would see that the chapel was put to use? Various groups approached Ivan about the building, but he didn't feel good about turning it over to them.

A few weeks later in New York, Ivan met a young lady. She had visited a Free Methodist church in Santo Domingo and gave Ivan a telephone number to call. The number was incorrect, but after much searching, Ivan located Israel Brito. Within a week Brito, Ivan and Yolanda met to discuss the idea of turning the new facility over to the Free Methodists.

Ivan and Yolanda continue to invest their resources in the Puerto Plata church. Construction is underway to expand the sanctuary, and classrooms are being built so they can have a school.

The mini-market dream has not died. The money set aside to build and stock the market was used on the church, yet the Lord enabled Ivan and Yolanda to build and stock another market. Today the Canots have their mini-market and the Lord has his church.

In Ecuador

Jorge Villacis
May/June 1992 pp. 5-8

As a child I was raised in a very strong Catholic home. My parents were sincere, and Mother was especially devout. I studied in a Jesuit school and took part as an altar boy in the religious services. The very last thing I dreamed of was to be an evangelical.

As time passed I was really only a Catholic in name, and an acquaintance began to talk to me about the gospel. Although I didn't demonstrate much interest, still, I listened. I even attended some services, but I wasn't converted – I wanted someone to explain to me just how it could come about. Then my friend shared with me God's great plan of salvation and I understood that there was something very special in the gospel story. I wondered, is it possible? I am such a sinner. How is the Lord going to change me? How could he do such a great favor for me? But I opened my heart to him, and he saved me.

Years later when I was living in Massachusetts, some brothers from the church I was attending encouraged me to prepare myself for ministry. I had felt it was better for me to work in secular employment in order to support in a financial way the Lord's work. However, they continued to urge me, and I saw the obstacles which had impeded me gradually being removed.

Minister Without A Church

I attended for three years the Pentecostal Bible school of the area, where I was never convinced by nor comfortable with the enthusiasm they practiced. However, after pastoral training, the thought occurred to me that perhaps I should return to Ecuador, but not with any notion of assuming responsibility for a church.

I went back to work as a layman, but the Lord didn't leave me alone. Again, through influential brothers, I was led to attend Gordon Conwell Theological Seminary in Boston. On graduating, I was truly a minister without a church. During this time I did substitute preaching for vacationing or sick ministers.

One morning early, as I was praying, I seemed to hear a voice commanding me to get up, to go back [to Ecuador] and spread the gospel. I was amazed, but I was silent. I didn't tell anyone. Also, I didn't really believe in visions, so I was quite reserved in speaking of this experience. However, I was preoccupied about the incident and couldn't forget it.

A few days later at work, a Puerto Rican sat down beside me. We became acquainted and he invited me to his home in Lawrence, Mass. Because of his family's friendship and our spiritual fellowship, we also moved to Lawrence.

One day Isaac Brito, pastor of the local Free Methodist church, called to request that I fill his pulpit in his absence. It was truly a happy experience. I believe that the Lord led us to that church. I don't know, even yet, how Rev. Brito heard about me, but we felt at home with that congregation, and so continued to worship and work with them.

A Burden For My People

We became members of the Free Methodist Church. Still, I had no desire to become a pastor, though I continued to feel impressed that I should carry the good news to my people, and I began to sense a burden for them in Ecuador.

Rumors began to fly. People were interested in what I planned to do. I expressed my desire to return to Ecuador, even though I didn't know how I would support my wife and two daughters. Some thought that the Free Methodist Church would send me, but I had no information or security from the church. My answer was simply that I was so sure that God was sending me, that I didn't need to fear.

We came to Guayaquil and resettled here in the home which I had built before. We prepared the front part which opened on the busy sidewalk of the city for a chapel, and we occupied the house just back of it. We've been here since 1982, and truly the Lord has sustained us.

It was very difficult at first. Sometimes we just gathered in the church to fast and pray. Guayaquil had never heard of the Free Methodist Church. Some Protestant groups claimed we were heretics, similar to the cults. We felt the Lord leading us to go on the air with radio broadcasts, proclaiming Christ, and enlightening the public as to the people called Free Methodist. Some Christian brothers advised me to put out a sign calling the church *FM Pentecostal*. They assured me that if I did that, I would fill the pews! Many times I was tempted to give up, for I felt very alone. But the church in Lawrence had helped me initiate the radio programs, and I held on.

Help From DWM

About that time (in 1982), Mr. Doane Bonney (then Latin America Area Director) came to visit us. It was only a stop of a few hours, but in 1983 he returned for a longer time.

So it was through the Department of World Missions that we received financial help from the Light and Life Hour, and have been able to continue with the radio ministry. Many of our successful contacts have directly resulted from it, and people now in our congregation found us because of the radio program.

In 1984 we became a Mission District of the Free Methodist Church. By 1986 we had five places in the city where we have established congregations celebrating Sunday school, church worship service, and a weekday Bible study. They are: La Cuenca (the central and mother church), Mapasingue, La Treinta y cuatro (34), Goyena, and Gilgal.

We are projecting toward a new area, Santa Luncan, 40km southeast of Guayaquil.

Each of these points has a layman in charge of the work, and while my wife consistently attends the central church, I circulate to all of the areas, and also hold the week-night Bible study (one each night of the week).

Two of our young men spent 1985 at our Bible school in Hermosillo, Mexico, in theological studies. Also, we've had classes with visiting professors to give us intensive courses for pastoral preparation.

When I returned to Ecuador, I did so with the knowledge that within four years I would need to move again to the United States in order to keep my documents valid. For us Latin Americans, the permit to reside in the States is a very valuable official paper. It is our security for a better life.

In July of 1987, my four years were up. Knowing this, I had planned from the beginning to spend these four years here, and then go back and resume secular employment.

But it appears that the Lord had other plans. After wrestling in prayer and conversation with the mission, I felt that I could not abandon this work. Paula, my wife, and I have determined that we will remain here, for God's glory. The residence permit we leave in God's hands, and trust that if we need it again, it will be issued according to his will. I have been very joyful and filled with peace since making this decision.

Costa Rica '92

Jim Nelson
May/June 1992 pp. 10-12

There were 12 of us, 11 from Canada, led by Tom Mealey of the Calgary Free Methodist Church. Assistant pastor Lee Raine was our devotional leader. More than half of the team came from the Calgary congregation. I was the only real *gringo*.

The group assembled in Dallas. Frank and Gail Braun drove down from Ontario and I flew in from Seattle. What a strange thing it was to enter upon such a venture with a group of complete strangers. As I came into the terminal, however, there was no way to mistake all those smiling Canadian faces — they were holding a large sign with my name on it!

Later that night we worked our way through another terminal, this one in San José, Costa Rica, looking for yet another unknown face, that of Pastor Jorge Gómez of the *Iglesia Metodista Libre* of Alajuela, Costa Rica.

No hay problema

There really was no problem locating Pastor Jorge, getting our luggage loaded into three rented vehicles, and depositing ourselves at the rented house which would be our home for two weeks. The house was well-suited for our group, with just the right spaces for the married couple and the two single women, while the rest of us each claimed a spot with a cot. The living room was large enough for us all to sing choruses or play games in the evenings.

Meals were provided at the pastor's house each day starting at 7:00 a.m. It was a one mile walk to breakfast, but in a few days we were using taxis quite regularly at 75¢ per taxi load.

In charge of the kitchen were a wonderful couple from the congregation, Rolando and Urbelina Lazo. They were assisted by the pastor's wife, Mary, with two or three other women from the congregation, producing day after day many of the best foods and beverages in the Costa Rican culture.

During one evening meal Tom Mealey asked, "Am I just hungry

or is this food really this delicious?" We agreed we were getting a fantastic bargain — food and lodging for $15.00 per day. Best of all, the water and all the foods were agreeable to North American digestive systems!

Early our first day, we sat down with the pastor for our orientation to the work. The pastor spoke no English, and Tom Mealey spoke no Spanish, so it was my job to interpret.

We soon learned the scope of their need: finish the sanctuary (and add a second floor), finish the pastor's residence (it needed ceilings, wallboard, paint, wiring, and windows), construct a Sunday school unit so classes wouldn't have to meet in the pastor's home, and finish guest accommodations for future VISA teams and other visitors.

As soon as the pastor knew the total financial resources at the team's disposal, he was able to determine priorities. Our group was very quickly at work, divided between the pastor's house and the construction of the three room Sunday school unit.

It was great to see how the Lord blessed in the struggle to communicate across dialect and word usage difficulties. We were able to achieve a clear understanding of how the *ticos* (the Costa Rican's word for themselves — roughly equivalent to *gringo* or *canuck*) go about the business of building. It was very encouraging to see how smoothly we were able to adjust to helping the *ticos* do it their way.

Sacrifice Your Car?

As work progressed, I became more and more aware of what a great festival of giving I was a part of. The Canadians worked hard every day, from early until late. Work went steadily forward, all done by people paying for the privilege to do it! Each invested some personal funds as well as money contributed by the congregations involved.

By Wednesday, January 15, 1992, all the material purchased with team funds had been applied to the projects. The Sunday school building was roofed and usable, even though still without windows and doors. The pastor's house was much more liveable, with ceilings, wallboard and paint, and improved wiring. Our work wasn't measurable in project dollars, man-hours, or cubic yards. It was measured by gratitude.

There was deep gratitude. Pastor Jorge spoke of the encouragement by this visit — this *help* — this *life-touch*. He told how his people had invested themselves and their substance to the point of exhaustion over the past year.

We knew that the pastor himself had sold his car to buy building materials. Members had invested similar sacrifices. The pastor shared that with the congregation's current financial burden, it would have taken two years to add what the team accomplished in two weeks.

Cathedral Christianity

The real work being done in Alajuela is, of course, that of our Lord. He was attending the worship services in free-flowing anointing, loving his people as they poured out their praise and worship. He was in his Word, in the wonderful sermons, in the teaching and admonitions to true discipleship. Our Lord's presence transformed that half-finished, concrete block structure into a cathedral.

We witnessed a triumph of grace. Love, joy, and peace were in abundant evidence among our Costa Rican friends. The pastor, all the while, was keeping track of the details of the work, going for materials, on the phone, doing pastoral work, all with consistent witness of God's grace.

We on the team also knew a deep current of grace among us. There was no abrasiveness as one might expect in such close quarters. Looking back, I can't think of an awkward moment.

Tico Fellowship

The *tico* brothers and sisters gave us much in warm appreciation for our work. Their welcome to participate in worship activities was equally warm. Carlos, one of the worship leaders, and his wife, Victoria, had us all to their home on a Friday evening for a barbecue on the patio. Carlos and Victoria sang to us of their love for our Lord, in the rich ballad style of the Hispanic culture.

Rolando and Urbelina, after two weeks of operating the kitchen for all of us, had our group to their home for our last work day lunch -- only it wasn't a lunch but a feast!

Luis Plata, who spoke English well, took us on an excursion to a waterfall not far from town, showed younger team members around town, and gave us a mime performance. He is a member of a mime group which uses this form of acting as a means of witnessing Christ to the street kids of their city.

The pastor and his family, along with others of the congregation, spent a Saturday at the beach with us, and arranged that we see one of their volcanoes and a bit of their rain forest. Rolando and another brother also took us on a shopping tour of the capital, San José.

Thursday evening, just before our early Friday departure, the congregation gave us a farewell dinner. The meal featured fish prepared in unique Costa Rican fashion. Delicious! The table was set in the Sunday school unit under a roof just one day old.

After dinner Zinnia, representing the congregation, shared that in our two weeks away from home and family, in both our work and giving we were examples of obedience to Christ's command to go into the world and communicate the gospel.

By the time we left Costa Rica, we had mixed feelings about leaving. Breck Ritchie of our group expressed so well for all of us how we felt. He had been burned by tropical sun, bitten by swarms of gnats, sick with a bad cold, and even stolen from, but he wouldn't have missed this experience for anything!

From Costa Rica To Colombia

M. Doane Bonney
November/December 1993 p. 17

As soon as I met Jorge (*Hor-hay*) E. Gómez at the airport in Alajuela, Costa Rica, on September 18, I began to sense some of the excitement of being in the midst of a brand new, country-wide, Free Methodist movement.

Jorge lives and breathes a vision which doesn't stop at the borders of his country but moves out to include all of Central America and beyond. The Free Methodist Church is on the move in Costa Rica. Churches have been started in four key areas. Satellite church plants are planned around the hub, or central, church in each area. Eventually each area group of churches will become a district and the districts will become the annual conference of Costa Rica.

"Decentralization," says Superintendent Gómez, "is the key to expansion in Costa Rica."

Other Targets

The vision of Gómez, the four pastors, and about 400 church members goes beyond their small Central America country. A missionary effort into neighboring Nicaragua to the north is planned for this November. The goal is to leave a church plant in that country.

In December '93 this dynamic church is targeting Bogotá, capital of Colombia. Contacts are in place. The goal for Bogotá? The same as for Nicaragua -- to leave behind a Free Methodist Church. There is even talk of Cuba as a possible place God would be pleased to have a Free Methodist presence. Gómez feels the time to begin working in Cuba is *now* -- risk-taking at its best!

Gómez believes the recently formed church in Costa Rica must carry out a missionary vision. "We can't wait," he says, "until everything is in place *here*. Christ said *go* and I believe that means *now*."

Follow Up

Rev. Gómez is a Colombian and has been part of the evangelical scene in Costa Rica for nearly two decades. He tells me that the major shortcoming of most evangelistic outreach attempts in his adopted country is that they don't follow up. A big splash is made and then things fizzle out.

After decentralization and a missionary vision, Gómez says the three most important ingredients for the Free Methodist Church in Costa Rica are:

Discipleship,

Discipleship, and

Discipleship.

"The church is here for the long term," says Gómez. "Thus we must train, train, and train."

Let's welcome this new member country to the Free Methodist world family! And please remember that *family* prays for *family*.

My Father: Leader Of The Church

Karim Loyola
July/August 1992 p. 1-3

My father, at 46 years of age, has dedicated 17 years to the pastorate. In these years he has learned much from his own experiences and from what God has shown him in the moments of doubts. He is a man who gives everything to the work. He is not a person with limited focus. This has permitted him to get involved in many areas, including those which at one time he thought he would never take on.

His broad interests have served him well in the formation and the beginning of our church in Chile. Perhaps he lacked experience in many areas, but my father has known how to carry forward many projects.

His growth as a leader has been effective, thanks to the Lord, and he has not failed in any moment facing the problems that have presented themselves because he knows that God is with him.

At this time his main work is administrative. He carries out the responsibilities as president of the Free Methodist Church Corporation in Chile, and he is also pastor of the Iglesia Central Church.

He visits at least five to six times yearly the churches and their circuits, and oversees the management of each organization of the church such as: children's ministry, Bible school, ministry of communications (radio broadcasts and so on), youth organization, women's society, administrative sessions and many others.

He doesn't have a full-time assistant. His assistants are all the pastors, laymen, children, and especially his wife. We are all a large family, and we help one another.

Where The Land Ends The Church Begins

Chile is a long, narrow country on the west coast of South America. It stretches about 2,650 miles from Peru in the north to Cape Horn in the south. The rugged shore of the South Pacific Ocean forms the western border. The towering Andes Mountains to the east separate Chile from Argentina. Chile's name probably comes from an Indian word meaning *where the land ends*.

We have established 12 principal Free Methodist churches in our country, and other new works are targeted for Colton, El Carmen, and Comuna De Lagunillas. In addition, we have a missionary vision for neighboring countries. Our prayers continue for a missionary for La Paz, Bolivia. The contact is made, but a married couple is needed to establish the work and form a Missionary District. We also have plans to establish churches in the south of Argentina, by the frontier of Chile. We are aware that in Buenos Aires, the Free Methodist Church is established already with a work for the Japanese. But our intention is to open up even more of the country, and our first Chilean missionary has made a start across the frontier. We are also sending a missionary to Peru.

Not In Kansas Anymore

Rochelle Odermann
July/August 1992 pp. 8-9

Rochelle follows the yellow brick VISA road to six months of discovery in Chile.

As I lay under six blankets with my long-johns and sweat suit on, questions darted through my mind: *Is this really what God called me to do, or did I misinterpret the message somewhere along the line? Why can I see my breath? My family, my fiancé, my friends – how can I survive six months without them? I can't even speak Spanish and I'm the only missionary here – what have I gotten myself into?*

I pulled the covers over my head and curled up into the fetal position. The hot water bottle was doing its best to warm my double-socked feet. I gently breathed warm air on other body parts in an effort to keep from shivering. I drew a mental calendar to count the days until my return flight to the securities of Kansas.

How many more days? Lord, I can't do this on my own. I'm going to need your strength for every day. I know I'm here for you, and I want to do my best. Please don't let cold weather and a language barrier stifle my desire to show your love. I rocked back and forth to conserve what little warmth there was, determined to have a good stay in Chile.

Looking back on that first night, I smile to think how much I've learned. Before I came, I was aware that there would be hardships. Leaving mom and dad for this long hurts a girl who still cries every time she says good-bye. Not being able to share with my fiancé every day as usual is difficult when the wedding date is set for three months after I return. As far as Spanish is concerned, sure I studied how to conjugate the present tense verbs my freshman year in high school; but who would have thought I'd actually need it some day?

This was not just another short missions trip – this was my home for the next six months. In my insecurity I called on God who gave me strength for every situation and friendship to fill the emotional void.

Faster than I hoped, I began to fit in. The many different faces whose names I couldn't remember at first and whose mouths spoke funny words became close friends.

I learned, too. I learned simple things, like *always carry toilet paper*, and *never ask about food — just eat it!* I also learned more important lessons of living in another culture. It doesn't matter how they do it at home — when in Chile, do as the Chileans.

What impacted my life more than learning how to adapt culturally was the powerful Spirit of God that was working everywhere I turned. My life was enriched as I had more time for in-depth devotions and prayer than what my cluttered days of college had allowed. Going to worship services four or five times a week became a joy rather than something I just did.

Volunteers In Service Abroad (VISA) sent me here to work in communications. I wrote and helped film three videos on the work of our Free Methodist Church in Chile, I recorded a weekly program for a local Christian radio station, and I helped out in MICOM, the Free Methodist communications ministry.

Unexpected challenges rolled my way too — like teaching a course on communication and church growth in the seminary, and working with and doing my best to translate for groups that came from North America. Every day proved different, which was exciting, yet sometimes required a new perspective of the word *flexibility*.

I came to Chile ready to serve in whatever capacity needed. I came to give; yet I am amazed at how much more I have received. Just by observing and talking with my friends here, I've witnessed an attitude of love and sacrifice that carries an impact. I've seen this in the girl who took off the shirt she was wearing and gave it to me just because a few minutes earlier I had told her I liked it. I saw it in the pastor who walks three hours uphill to conduct a church service, then three hours back home. I saw it in two young Chilean missionaries — one in Peru and one in Argentina — who have no financial backing from the district mission committee, yet pursue their mission because God called them.

Living in Chile has broadened my awareness. I learned to drink hot tea and to endure cold showers. And something special has been planted in my heart. It's another dimension that only living abroad and relating to different people can give. I have fallen in love with my family and friends here. When I step on the plane that whisks me back to Kansas, part of me won't be making that trip. As before, I'm checking my mental calendar — only now I'm checking to see how long I have to wait before I can come back to Chile.

In Perpetual Motion

With Sergio Loyola
March/April 1995 pp. 6-10

The Free Methodist Church spreads steadily north and south along Chile's ribbon of fertile land between the mighty South Pacific and the towering Andes. The southern-most church is next door to Antarctica at Punta Arenas, a house church of about 25 adults started by the retired seminary professor of Superintendent Loyola.

What will become of the church when it becomes too large for the house? Loyola grins, plants his tongue firmly in both cheeks, and confides, "We don't want it to grow -- that only causes problems!"

There is historic truth behind Loyola's humor. A Pentecostal revival in 1909 with the Methodist Church gave birth to an indigenous movement with dynamic evangelistic zeal. About 25% of the population is now connected with an evangelical group, but the churches are plagued by division. One town of 30,000 boasts some 400 churches, each one claiming to be a separate denomination!

Multiplied, Not Divided

The growth of Free Methodism has been based on the cell model. Loyola's first house group in Chillan grew to seven groups, all of them led by the same person. This resulted in one worn out leader! So a new goal was adopted – to disciple leaders until each new congregation had its own pastor.

There are now 15 core groups in the city of Chillan. On Monday the 15 leaders meet with their leader, and on Tuesday these 15 pass on what they learned the previous day to their own group.

Two objectives of the Chillan congregations are to continue discipling those already in the church and to bring in new converts. Superintendent Loyola hopes this process, now in place in Chillan, can soon be duplicated in other locations throughout Chile.

Pastor Henry Agrees

Henry Riquelme has pastored several Chile Free Methodist Churches, most recently at the Loncoche facility built by a VISA team from Clarkston, Michigan.

Pastor Henry says in all his churches and preaching points the objective is always to train local leaders for ministry. This is often a long and difficult process. When working among the Mapuche Indians he uncovered traditional customs in direct conflict with his understanding of biblical teaching.

For example, Mapuche men believe their wives and children are their own personal property and therefore take whatever actions are necessary to get obedience. Careful and patient teaching is required to help these individuals learn to conduct themselves according to the relationship guidelines outlined in Scripture.

Some Sort Of Seminary

"As they say," Sergio wants to remind us before sharing much about the Bible Seminary in Chillan, "in a country of blind people, a fellow with one eye is king."

Feeling it is just as important to prepare people for leadership as to establish churches, the Chile Free Methodist Church launched its seminary program almost immediately. In January 1987, Sergio took on a heavy workload at the seminary, but there was no faculty, and he felt unprepared for the task.

"I was a one-eyed leader," admits Sergio, "but I did it." The building was constructed in 1989-90 and has the capacity for 20 students in dorms for one intensive week-long seminar per month.

Ambitious plans targeted to begin in 1996 were developed by a committee of administrators and faculty. The dual goal is to offer a two-year university-level program, and a three-year program resulting in a bachelor of theology degree. Those who have completed theological training would then qualify for a one-year school of missionary training, perhaps in cooperation with schools in Brazil or the Dominican Republic. Finally, week-long seminars on a monthly basis would be continued to train lay and pastoral leaders.

God At Work

Transcending formal structures, God continues to build the church in his usual informal and surprising ways. Miracles of healing are not uncommon. Financial miracles seem more frequent, such as the time in San Ignacio when Pastor Loyola was heard to say, "Let's buy the property from the Catholic Church to build a temple for our Free Methodist Church!"

"That is very difficult," replied Sister Graciela Bustamante. Along with her husband (when he was alive, and before her conversion), Graciela had donated a beautiful piece of land to the Catholic Church, but the Church never used it for anything.

"With God nothing is difficult," replied Loyola, who urgently needed land to establish a church and parsonage. Without a doubt, however, the Catholic Church would *never* sell one of its properties to a Protestant church, much less at a low price.

In light of this impossibility, Pastor Loyola proposed, "Sister, go to the priest and offer to buy back the property for $1,000 U.S."

She did as he suggested and the priest accepted the offer. When the land was legally hers, she sold it to our church for the same price.

More Than Buildings

Real estate miracles are helpful, but transformed hearts of people form the backbone of our church. One such change began in 1978 when Maria Loyola met a young couple in the city of Coelemu. Bernardo was attracted to the gospel but his wife, Miriam, was not. It took almost 10 years, but when Maria visited them in 1987, Bernardo and Miriam were ready to join the church and each had a Christian testimony.

A church was started and a simple chapel built. The group began to grow and a full time pastor was designated. The church suffered a blow when the last pastor decided to leave the ministry and there was no one to send in his place. It was then that the voice of Miriam was heard: "Brothers, this cannot be! We have to take up the weapons of faith and keep going."

Today the church is going well. Sister Miriam and other lay people do the hard work of ministry, with excellent results.

Air Time

Old fashioned relationships go far in building the church, and new technologies don't hurt. In 1987 Sergio Loyola, eager to establish a work in the central zone, managed to get five minutes of air time every Sunday on a secular radio station. He planned a micro-program consisting of a short introduction, part of a theme song, a brief Bible verse, and an invitation to write for free literature.

One young man requested literature and gave his home address. Loyola decided to go in person to deliver the material. In the little town bordering the mountains he encountered the young man's mother. After a friendly conversation he invited her to accept Christ as her Lord and

Savior. Loyola returned the following week when the young man was home. Their conversation ended with a prayer to accept Christ, and the meetings became a weekly event. Neighbors and relatives began to attend. Later, a Sunday school was started. Soon a neighbor offered a larger place without charge. Next came a decision to rent a building and install a pastor. The work expanded to include rural preaching points.

Property was purchased in San Ignacio. A VISA construction team came to remodel an old house and added to it for both a parsonage and a sanctuary. Today this church and its five rural chapels have a membership that borders on 100. They have a social work that benefits 50 under- privileged children. A Sunday school at each point of the circuit reaches about 100 children, another social program helps rural mothers, and the main church cares for a milk bar at the local hospital.

The mayor of San Ignacio recently presented Pastor Elias Sanchez an award in recognition of the church's work benefitting the community.

Team Players

Watching the perpetual motion in Chile -- both the man Sergio Loyola and the machine in his office -- you recognize an important difference between the two. The perpetual motion **machine** moves to no real purpose, while the perpetual motion **man** has a clearly defined goal: spiritual and numerical growth of the church to consolidate the work, establish a clear Free Methodist identity, and help people arrive at a place of commitment to achieve these goals. North American Free Methodists are privileged to participate by sending the occasional VISA team, by our modest financial support, and by our prayers.

Contributors to this article include Maria Salas Loyola (translation by Doris Thompson), Tim Shumaker, and Dan Runyon.

Brazil

Daniel V. Runyon
September/October 1994 pp. 1-3

The shopping mall a couple blocks from the home of Clancy and Doris Thompson in Sao Paulo, Brazil, is so huge that McDonald's has branch offices – they sell hamburgers in one place, ice cream in another. Meanwhile, up near Soledade (Solitary) in northeastern Brazil, the country is often best viewed from the back of a burro.

For most of its history the Free Methodist Church in Brazil has been largely urban. And the need is great in such places as Sao Paulo where 20 million people live in the thick of bus fumes, pornography and violence, or in Rio de Janeiro, one of the world's centers of moral decay and drug abuse.

Yet Brazil is a nation of 27 states covering half the continent of South America and containing more people than all the other South American nations combined. Our Brazilian Church has therefore set a goal to establish the church in *every* Brazilian state by the year 2,000. Currently we operate in just seven of the 27 states.

Both the Brazilian and Nikkei (Japanese) Annual Conferences of Brazil have dynamic and established leadership. All North American missionaries work alongside these leaders to achieve the evangelism, church planting, and education goals that the Brazilian church has set for itself.

Nikkei Conference

Superintendent Kodo Nakahara of the Japanese (Nikkei) Conference in Brazil was born in Tokyo, Japan. He emigrated to Brazil in 1976. Since World War II the conference has grown from three to 16 churches. The goal is to reach Japanese Brazilians with the gospel, so the greatest need is for more Portuguese-speakaing Japanese workers – we currently have more churches than ministers.

In 1928, Daniel Nishizumi, a graduate of the Osaka Free Methodist Seminary, Japan, emigrated to Brazil. The inaugural worship service of the Sao Paulo Free Methodist Church came a decade later on November 1, 1936. In 1938, Nishizumi visited General Missionary

Secretary Harry Johnson and Free Methodist churches in California to create the ministry link which continues today. This conference now has 21 ordained ministers, 1,602 members, and 16 churches.

Brazilian Conference

Superintendent Dorivaldo Puerta Mason of the Brazilian Conference reports on the *Brazil 2000* missions committee strategy: Plant churches in all 27 states using 42 workers, 10 of them ordained leaders and 32 lay evangelists and church planters. "Now is God's time for Brazil," says Dorivaldo. "Churches of all denominations are growing and sending out missionaries. We must also do this."

This work was begun in 1946 in Sao Paulo with Rev. Jose Emerenciamo and North American missionaries Helen Voller and Lucile Damon, who came at the invitation of the Japanese church to work among the Portuguese-speaking population of Brazil. This conference grew 300% in the decade of the 80s and has established mission points in central and northeastern Brazil. This conference now has 29 ordained ministers, 2,067 members, and 18 churches.

Busy People

A sampling of Brazilians who minister in Brazil.
September/October 1994 pp. 5-7

A Tribe That Had No Song
Dan Owsley

Motivated by a call to reach tribal groups in the Amazon, Lucilia Oliveira Maia was in the first group of missionary candidates trained by the Brazilian Conference in 1986. Her local church and conference supported her over the next five years as she ministered through Youth With A Mission (YWAM).

Lucilia learned the language and befriended Indians, but tough government regulations prohibiting open religious teaching thwarted her efforts.

Other opposition came when the electric company of the Amazon region insisted that the believers be removed when they learned that evangelical missionaries were helping in the health and educational areas of a government social program. The missionaries were banned and the program was discontinued.

The government Indian Affairs department aggressively *protects* Indian groups from missionaries. However, one such Indian group harvested brazil nuts along the great *Transamazonica Highway*. Lucilia befriended these Indians and met with them at the temporary camps set up near the highway.

When the harvest ended, contact with the tribal group was lost, but Lucilia continued reaching out to the many settlers who passed through.

Every year Lucilia attended the Brazilian Annual Conference meetings to report. Some leaders felt she should give up on the Indians and work among the settlers. Lucilia loved the settlers, but she was convinced of her calling to work among tribal groups.

In 1991, Lucilia moved to Porto Velho (Old Port), a river port city in the heart of the Amazon jungle. She did further studies at the mission where she lived and provided volunteer work at the Indian House, a government program to help tribal groups adjust to city life.

At the mission base Lucilia met fellow missionary Moises Viana.

Friendship grew. Life goals meshed. Mutual admiration was in evidence. They began dating seriously. A year later, in December 1992, Moises and Lucilia were married.

Just five months after the wedding, Moises and Lucilia were called to work with a very primitive tribal group in the deep jungle. The couple who had worked with the group for seven years needed a break, so on May 17, 1993, Moises and Lucilia boarded a small plane with six months' worth of supplies.

After flying for two hours over thick jungle they reached a landing strip near a river. Unloading their supplies into canoes, they went another 15 hours by water to reach a small house -- their base. From here they could walk the additional 12 hours to reach the tribal village.

Moises and Lucilia spent 40 days with the other missionary couple, learned to live in the primitive situation and made contacts with the tribal group. Then Moises and Lucilia remained alone to try to reach these people with the gospel.

When visiting the Indians, Moises and Lucilia took only the clothes on their backs. If they took more, they were obligated to give it away. That is the custom -- to share all you have, and the tribe has about 250 members.

The usual procedure is to live with the Indians in their long-houses for about two weeks at a time. These thatched roof communal houses for about 40 families are very basic and completely lacking in personal privacy, so Moises and Lucilia divide their time between the Indians and the private house on the river.

At base camp they dedicate time to devotions, study of the customs, culture and language, and the business of surviving. He hunts and fishes while she cleans, cooks, and washes clothes.

One cultural phenomenon of this tribe is death by suicide. The earlier missionaries noticed that the rate of suicide went way down whenever they were present. When missionaries were absent, suicides increased dramatically.

Strict government regulations prevent Moises and Lucilia to speak openly of their faith. So their strategy is to live with the Indians as much as possible, learn the language, and love them.

Moises and Lucilia also hold their own worship service between the two of them. Their singing is attractive to the Indians, who will gather around to listen, and then want to learn the songs.

For now, Moises and Lucilia see that singing is their best form of ministry. The tribe that had no song now has the music of heaven.

Peace Dwelling
Clancy Thompson

Emilia Marangon was very poor when she first dreamed of building an orphanage, for she grew up in an orphanage herself. She remembers, "I liked the orphanage better than my own home and have dreamed for a long time of providing such a home for others. I was in an institution just for girls, but my homes would be on a family model for both boys and girls."

Emilia was widowed with no children. She kept her vision for an orphanage alive through a business career, at one time owning several stores and eye clinics. She once traveled to the United States, felt useless there, and returned to Brazil.

A Free Methodist pastor in the Brazil Conference influenced Emilia to dedicate her life to Christ as an adult. She later became Child Care Director for Brazil, where 250 children are sponsored and 100 more await sponsors.

With the care of children uppermost in her mind, Emilia sold all her business interests except for one optical store where she stops in every day to handle the finances. She now plows her resources and energy into Peace Dwelling, a new orphanage in a home on 11 acres which she established with five children, ages 3, 4, 5, 6, and 8. The children were referred to Emilia by a judge at a government agency.

Launching Peace Dwelling has met with setbacks. In July 1993, six armed thieves entered the orphanage and threatened to kill Emilia. They stole many things by putting them in her truck and then stealing the truck. Military police later recovered the truck, and Emilia has recovered her courage. Her goal now is to establish three houses with 10 children and a set of "parents" in each house, thereby providing homes for 30 children.

I Just Pray
Dan Runyon

When native Brazilian José Emerenciamo became a Christian, his father gave him a choice — give up his faith or leave home.

José went to Rio where he found work as a carpenter, and was baptized in the Presbyterian Church. Later, a pastor arranged for him to study at a school in northern Brazil, doing janitor work to pay the bill. On weekends he traveled on horseback from farm to farm preaching the gospel.

After graduation José entered seminary in Recife, but lacked the funds to continue. However, Bishop Nakada, an evangelist from the Holiness Church in Japan, invited him to complete his studies at a seminary in Japan.

José did so, and two years later returned to Brazil as a pastor licensed by the Holiness Church of Japan. In 1935, he met Daniel Nishizumi who had come from Japan to plant the Free Methodist Church in Brazil. A close friendship developed because of their shared enthusiasm for the doctrine of sanctification.

When Americans visited Brazil (the Reverends E. E. Shelhamer, H. F. Johnson, and B. H. Pearson in 1940), José served as translator, for he spoke English as well as Portuguese and Japanese. Thus José became the link between the Japanese, Brazilians, and Americans in the beginning of the Free Methodist Church in Brazil.

In 1946, José pastored the first Portuguese-speaking Free Methodist Church at Mirandopolis, a section of Sao Paulo (the site today of the Mirandopolis Free Methodist Church and parsonage). As the Brazilian work grew, he pastored several of its churches, and also pastored one Japanese congregation for a year to meet an urgent need.

José credits his success in church planting to the Holiness Church philosophy of paying to train pastors, but not to support them after training: "This way we were forced to quickly establish churches that could support us."

At age 92, José is not without significant work. He explains, "Every day I pray for every Brazilian pastor, every Japanese pastor, and every American pastor and missionary in Brazil, as well as for all the countries in Latin America where there is a Free Methodist work. I pray for all the people I know, and for many that I don't know."

His daughter, Cleide, says he gets up at 7:30 a.m. to read the Bible, "then he prays all day long, sort of mumbling along out loud. He will say, 'What's the name of such and such a pastor or missionary?' -- because he is praying for them."

"I can no longer preach," says José, "I just pray."

Music Of Paraguay

Tim Goodenough
November/December 1994 pp. 1-3

Ask any group of Free Methodist pastors in Paraguay what they do exceptionally well. "We sing best," they are likely to say, then stand together and belt out a favorite hymn.

Free Methodists have been facing the music of Paraguay since 1946 with the arrival of missionaries Harold and Evalyn Ryckman. The work suffered a major decline in the late 1970s, when several churches closed. There were only two pastors and fewer than 100 members.

The music revived when God raised up superintendent Juan Monzón who challenged many young people to enter pastoral ministry. Phenomenal growth resulted. Today we have 18 churches and membership has passed the 600 mark.

Extension Prospects

Paraguay is divided into regional "departments," each with one or two leading cities. Our church has yet to penetrate these areas, including Alto Paraná, headed up by Paraguay's second-largest city, Ciudad del Este (City of the East). If the music of Paraguay is to become fully orchestrated, we must form new groups in these departmental capitals and reach out into the surrounding countryside.

In the Central Department (surrounding Asuncion), there are nine cities of 25,000 or more people each. The church must target these population centers and plant new works. We now have churches in three of these cities, and five in Asuncion, a city of one-half million people. Opportunities for extension are endless.

Equipping Leaders

The Paraguay church is young. Our rapid growth in the '80s means many leaders are recent converts. We must build a solid foundation for further growth. We missionaries are here to teach Bible, doctrine, and the practical skills of evangelism and making disciples.

The days when missionaries ran the show are long past. We don't want to impose North American church models on this rich Latin culture.

Our only hope is that the church will become fully Paraguayan. We want them to become mature, as Paul says in Ephesians 4, so that they will not be blown back and forth by every wind of doctrine. So the need to equip leaders is indeed great.

Teaching The Children

A final challenge is to establish Christian schools connected with churches. The first preschool and kindergarten opened this year at the Loma Pyta church. Opening this school has done more to raise the visibility of the Loma Pyta church than all the evangelistic campaigns they've held combined! Parents who never would have sent their kids to a Protestant church clamored to enroll them in our school. The children tell their parents about school on Sunday, and they want to come and bring their moms and dads along.

Our other churches see this response and want to open their own schools. It won't be easy – out of a membership of 600, we have only two certified teachers! Many lay leaders must finish their own basic education and take the two-year teacher-training course if the churches are to open more schools and have teachers to staff them.

But the opportunity is golden. Remember, we *sing* best. Through our symphony of extension, equipping, and teaching, we are trusting God to help us reach the people of Paraguay.

Paraguay: A Concise History

Esther Decoud
November/December 1994 p. 3

The Free Methodist work in Paraguay began in the years 1930-40 with the Penny-A-Day program in which every Free Methodist in the United States was asked to give one cent a day for missions. The money was used to open a mission in South America.

In 1940 three *spies*, Harry Johnson, B. H. Pearson and E. E. Shelhamer visited Paraguay and negotiated with independent missionary Ford Hendrickson to take over *Hogar Samaritano,* an orphanage for girls. However, World War II forced them to keep plans on hold until 1945.

On July 1, 1946, Harold and Evalyn Ryckman with their son, Don, arrived in Asuncion. Within the month Misses Ruth Foy (Carlson) and Esther Harris (Decoud) joined them. They cared for the girls of the orphanage, opened a clinic, and made contacts for evangelistic efforts. The first church was held at the orphanage using the garage for a place of worship. The first church building was dedicated February 5, 1950.

Although the Ryckmans were transferred to Brazil, Harold made periodic visits as superintendent of the Free Methodist work in South America. In 1950 a nurse, Elizabeth Reynolds, took over the duties of the orphanage and clinic.

Evangelistic missionaries Donald and Claris Vesey arrived in 1951, as did Wesley and Juanita Hankins, in charge of the Bible School. Ernest and Lucy Huston came in 1957. From 1951-58 preaching points were opened at Tablada and Loma Pyta, later combining to form the Cerrito church. The work at Sajonia was begun, the church at Emboscada was transferred to the Free Methodists by independent missionaries, and a preaching point at Loma Grande was started. The orphanage was gradually phased out as each missionary family took two or three girls into their homes.

The Japanese work began with the arrival of Minoru and Yoko Tsukamoto in 1962. They settled in Encarnacion and soon started five out-stations, including one at Posadas, Argentina.

The Portuguese work in Brazil and the Paraguay church made up the South American Provisional Conference until January 1966 when the

Paraguayan Provisional Conference was established. It had two districts, the Paraguayan and Japanese, with their respective superintendents: Ernest Huston and Minoru Tsukamoto. Career missionaries at this time were Tim and Phyllis Shumaker.

The 1970s saw a great exodus to Argentina as Paraguayans looked for employment or to escape the political situation. The Japanese section was hit the hardest with 60 families moving out. Only three churches in Asuncion and a struggling work in the Encarnacion area survived.

Our church began to revive in 1983 when a group of young people felt called into ministry. In 1986 the Light and Life Institute was organized with guidance from missionaries Garry and Patricia Cruce. One requisite for graduation, besides the academic subjects, was to plant a church. Each one did. The growth continues in the Paraguayan church today, and the Japanese work is supervised by the Nikkei Conference of Brazil.

How Our El Salvador Church Began

Clancy Thompson
January/February 1995 pp. 30-32

"Lord, is this for real? Can this deportation notice possibly be your will for our lives?" Jose Rauda, his wife Dolores, and infant son were being thrown out of Texas.

Seven years earlier the Rauda family left El Salvador to join Jose's eight brothers and their families who had established themselves in Texas. They planed to get green cards, settle down in their adopted country, and avoid further radical changes in their lives.

A Family Reborn

In Texas, through the faithful and persistent witness of a Free Methodist, Dolores gave her heart to God. Six months later, her husband was saved. His eight brothers and families were soon won to the Lord, and as faith grew and deepened, Jose felt the call of God to ministry. With guidance and encouragement from his pastor, Jose began to study for ordination.

In 1989, Jose was ordained Deacon in the Texas Conference and received his first appointment to a Spanish-speaking congregation.

Before Jose could assume his charge, terrible news arrived -- he and his family were being deported by the United States Government. Due to a change in government policy, his family could not legalize their documents as the other Rauda brothers had done under earlier regulations.

Return To Sender

Would God really let this happen? Had they not been called to minister to Hispanics in Texas? They now had a second son, American born. Didn't that count? To make matters worse, El Salvador was at war.

In October 1989, Jose, Dolores, Jaime and Edgar found themselves headed for El Salvador with some boxes and suitcases, but no house, no job, and no furniture awaiting them. They stayed with a friend in the town of Soyapango, but two weeks later rebel forces took over the area. Anguish and fear overtook them on November 11 – the most difficult moments of their lives – when a bomb fell in front of their house. They fled at midnight in spite of the risk of being shot.

With faith in an Almighty God, after praying, they left and in the name of the Lord began knocking on neighbors' doors, inviting them to come along to a safer place under the protection of God's angel. The power of God was evident to those neighbors when the shooting and bombing ceased until they were safely in another area.

Days later the situation improved so the family returned to their house. The doors, windows and roof were destroyed. A bullet had entered the open refrigerator without piercing the back. Enamel was missing, but it worked!

Bullets penetrated the boxes of clothing and exploded, but the cloth, though scorched, was not burned. It was as though someone had put out the fire. The Rauda family believes that was the work of God. They never tire of praising God for sparing their lives and salvaging many of their things.

Twice-Saved Neighbors

As the Rauda family searched for another place to live, God showed them that it was right there in Soyapango where he was opening doors to them – especially with the neighbors who accompanied them on the midnight flight from terror. They found a house just three doors down from their previous one!

With the help of a church in Texas, the Raudas rented the house and bought materials for benches and a pulpit. The great day arrived – March 18, 1990 – when the Free Methodist Church of El Salvador had its first service with neighbors attending.

That same year God gave the first converts. The baptismal service took place on August 4, 1990, and in September the first five preparatory members were received. A year later the owner sold the house. The church had to move to another one, small and narrow, but the work continued to grow. By November of 1991 a small official board was formed and the church had its first wedding.

Now almost five years old, the church is meeting in yet another location – still inadequate, but better than the last place. There are 27 members and a Sunday school attendance of 54, divided into four classes. There have been two more weddings, evangelistic campaigns, evangelistic film presentations, and the official board is complete.

It's Official

The Free Methodist work in El Salvador became an official mission district in October, 1994, by action of the Board of Administration of the Free Methodist Church of North America. World Missions is fully behind the work of the Rauda family, and the way is now clear to send VISA personnel to help the El Salvador church achieve its goals.

Today, this young church has definite goals: To sow God's Word, reach new neighborhoods, win more souls and have their own building, because with God all things are possible.

Dolores concludes, "God revealed his will. His servants obeyed. We praise God for this church he has raised up and know that he is able to keep it from failing."

It is our intention to plant the Free Methodist Church in every country in Latin America by the year 2000. The Rauda family models how this dream is being achieved.

The Monk Who Lived Again

B. H. Pearson. Condensed by Daniel V. Runyon
January/February 1995 pp. 8-13

North Americans who wish to understand the challenge of missions in Latin America have this to remember: While the United States was predominantly Protestant from its founding and actively persecuted Catholics, Catholicism has ruled for centuries south of the border. The gripping adventures of The Monk Who Lived Again portray the prejudices that are being overcome as revival and the simple Good News of Jesus Christ sweeps through Latin America.

1. Behind Closed Doors

The monastery of Santo Domingo was wrapped in the intense cold of early morning. Silence reigned within its black-gray walls which loomed above the city of Cuzco, Peru.

In the darkness of his cell Fray Luis stood motionless behind the door. This night had been an unending agony. At times there had come to him in startling vividness a vision of the time when he had consecrated himself upon the altars of the church -- the swelling organ music, the voices of the massed choir of monks, the clouds of incense.

What lay ahead now? Hatred of family and friends? Persecution? Death? Perhaps he was jumping headlong from one hell into a deeper one.

He remembered his father: scholar and gentleman, Regent of the University of Cochabamba. What would he say and do? And what of Uncle Eliodoro Villazon, former president of Bolivia?

What shame he was now bringing upon a family name which for 100 years and more had stood for all that was best in the life of the nation. Well, it was too late to think of that. Now he had nothing to lose but his life.

Fray Luis looked towards the wall where he knew Holy Mary, the Virgin of the Rosary, was hanging. Her fresh, rosy cheeks had been his companion for seven years. How often he felt her smile upon him. How often he had thrilled to her presence in the long hours of his loneliness. Yet she, too, had failed him.

A morning breeze, borne on the condor-inhabited heights of the Andes, sighed softly about the eves and swept a rustling murmur from the palms in the patio. It flashed through his mind that the monastery, as well as the towering Andes, formed parts of one great eternity. Through this eternity he stood in the darkness before a closed door that should never open.

All his life he had been locked behind doors. The doors of social caste and obligation bound him as a lad. The doors of religious pride and devotion locked him away from youth's usual pursuits. The doors of the monastery shut out the daylight of normal life.

So many locked doors, doors for which he could find no key. And outside those closed doors was the fear of excommunication, of the devil, and of hell.

Now he would push open all those doors at once. Dawn was coming over the Andes. The light grew brighter each moment. He felt sunup in his own soul. He would burst open the door of the monastery, defying priest, acolyte, cardinal and pope.

Fray Luis made the sign of the cross in blessing, and stepped out through the doorway into the chill air of the early dawn, escaping the monastery according to his carefully designed plan. The priests in the choir overhead were chanting, "My God! My God! Why hast Thou forsaken me? Why art Thou so far from helping me, and from the words of my roaring?"

As they chanted, Fray Luis hurried down Santo Domingo Street towards the great adventure of his life.

2. The Making Of A Monk

In the aristocratic suburb home of Dr. Montano, a four-year old boy placed his chubby hands upon the high cheekbones of an Indian servant girl and commanded autocratically, "Again! Again! Tell me *the* story!"

Using the Indian language was forbidden in the home lest the boy should fail to appreciate the beautiful cadences of Spanish. But the youth had already determined to favor the idiom which brought so many delightful tales of long-ago times, and in this he was aided by his brown-eyed nurse. The Indian girl began in the dialect of her own mountain highlands the tale her young charge had ordered:

When Manco Capac and Mama Ocllo came to Peru, these fathers of the Incas brought with them a wedge of purest gold. The sun-god had told them they must travel on and on until the magic, golden wedge should fly from their hands and bury itself in the earth -- there they should build the palace of our great Indian empire.

They came down the shore line of Peru where the mighty ocean is, but the magic, golden wedge did not move. They crossed the fertile plains beneath the mountains, and the golden magic wedge lay still in their hands. They started up the great Andean mountains on whose peaks the snow rests and at whose feet the rivers spring forth, but nothing happened.

One day they came to what we now call Cuzco. The magic, golden wedge stirred in their hands. They tried to hold it, but could not. It flew away and hovered for a moment in the air like a golden bird, then plunged down into the earth and disappeared.

Falling upon their knees they gave thanks to the great sun-god, and there they built the temple of the sun. It was a temple of purest gold -- Coricancha, the glory of the Indians -- for there it was the golden wedge revealed its magic.

"When I grow up," said the little master of the home in perfect Indian dialect, "I will find a magic, golden wedge. It will guide me, too, and I will build a royal city...."

"What is this, Maria?" came an angry cry in Spanish. "Have I not told you that filthy language of the mountains is forbidden in my home! Use Spanish or do not speak at all!"

"Don't say that, my stepmother!" cried the boy, sliding down off the Indian woman's knee. "This is an *Indian* story!"

The Spanish woman, with a contemptuous toss of her head, sent the boy into the garden patio to play. There, in the shade of a large cherimoya tree, sat a distinguished gentleman at a table, reading with deep absorption.

Young Walter Manuel walked toward the man. "Hello, daddy!"

Without lifting his eyes from the pages the father mechanically replied, "Yes, yes my son! How are you?"

"Daddy, I want to play!"

The father raised his eyes from his book, glanced swiftly at the titles of the volumes before him, and selected one for his son. "Take that," he directed, "this will be your play. You must read. You must study." With this the man turned back to his book. The lad carried off the heavy tome and announced gravely, "I wish I were an Indian!"

Not long afterward his father took him to the home of Father Ledezma, the leading Catholic authority of the district, a professor in the seminary, and Walter Manuel's uncle. "You must stay here, son," said the father. "You will be happier here. Your mother would wish it so if she could speak to us."

Walter's first duties in the priesthood were assigned him by Father Ledezma. Each afternoon the poor came to beg, and the boy was supplied with ten-cent pieces and given the duty of tossing one from the second-story balcony to all who might request aid.

One day he decided to hand the money to the needy rather than toss it through the air. Walter came down from the balcony and stood on the steps. It pleased him to have the beggars crowd around him, showering pretty names and titles upon him as he gave them coins.

When his uncle discovered the boy surrounded by beggars, he ordered, "Come here," in tones which scattered the group. "Gentlemen must not contaminate themselves by contact with low people," he explained. "They are but swine and beggars. You are a gentleman. Dios Mio, son! You were letting them *touch* you. Some of those dirty women were hugging you. Phih!"

One day when his father came to see him, love of home was too strong for little Walter. He threw his arms around his father's neck and refused to be separated from him.

"You will not be happy at home," said the man. "What will you do with the stepmother? She is a good woman, but she does not know children...."

But the lad clung desperately to him. he took the boy with him because he must, but to neither a home nor a mother. That is perhaps the reason for the choices which later shaped his strange destiny.

3. The Way Of Cain

As the years slipped by Walter Manuel grew into a very devout Catholic, carefully observing all the rituals and sacraments of the Church. But all was not going smoothly. One day at a chapel not far from his beautiful home he saw a vulgar attack by the sacristan on one of the parishioners. The sacristan came to blows from which the victim had to defend himself. As a witness to the roadside brawl, Walter was taken to the police station where he declared informally the guilt of the sacristan and was told to report back later at the time of the trial.

The local priest at once began a house-to-house campaign in an attempt to prove the innocence of the sacristan. Various persons were prepared to act as witnesses, even though they had not seen the fight. He visited Walter Manuel and insisted that he, too, should declare the guilty man's innocence.

"But I cannot do so, father," declared the boy. "The sacristan attacked the other man vilely. The sacristan is guilty."

"You are condemned to hell," said the priest, "unless you help establish the innocence of the sacristan."

So obstinate was Walter that parental authority had to be invoked in forcing the boy to testify as desired. His father declared, "The priest is right, of course. You must obey him."

At the trial Walter was placed upon the witness stand and asked, "Do you swear in the name of God and the holy Catholic religion to tell the truth?" He answered in the affirmative, then accused the innocent man and declared the guilty sacristan free from all blame.

4. Satan's Colporteur

Hypocrisy in his own life led Walter to suspect hypocrisy in others. One day this questioning youth saw a Catholic priest standing at the street corner talking to a group of boys. The priest's talk centered about the girls' school nearby. At times he laughed uproariously, looking about occasionally to make sure no lady passer-by was near. As the full force of the horrible suggestions began to dawn upon Walter he felt a fury. This man, a symbol of religion which pretended to be the arbiter of morals and the guide to heaven, now stood on the corner and poured into his ear filthy, lecherous plans.

A great volcano burst within his soul. He would believe their lies no longer. The next day Walter went to the largest bookstore in Cochabamba. "I want a book against God," he demanded boldly, and thus began The Student's Atheist Association. The work of this group was a great deal too successful as an obstacle to the advancement of the gospel.

One day as Walter sat in his study a question spoke itself to his mind. "*Why* are you an atheist?"

He knew all the arguments. He knew the attitude he felt toward the Church, but did he *know* there was no God? Was not his violent reaction to hypocrisy in the Church the result of a belief in a God of holiness, purity, and love? Was not his very atheism an expression of unguided loyalty to such a God?

"I cannot answer why I am an atheist," the young man finally replied to himself. "I cannot prove there is no God. To say the world made itself — that is folly. To say it always was is to make it God. Perhaps I have not gone far enough in religion to find Him. Because a few priests are evil and a few worshipers immoral — that is not to prove there is no

God. And to be an atheist, of course, is to be nothing." Walter concluded that he himself would become a priest!

5. A Renegade Atheist

"Good afternoon, Father. May I talk with you?" Walter ventured into his father's spacious library with its profusion of antique carvings, archeological findings, shelves of books, and rich rugs.

"Yes, yes, my son," the older man mechanically replied.

"Father, I have something important to say. I want to become a priest!"

"A priest?" he answered in amazement. "Hum-m-m-m! But you could never be a common priest – I would not permit that. You might, however, if you insist on this, become a monk."

After considering all their options, Walter and his father concluded that becoming a Dominican Friar (the wealthiest and most famous order of them all) was the place for Walter. Only a Dominican Friar might place "O.P." after his name signifying "Preaching Order."

At Lima, Peru, was one of the richest and most aristocratic monasteries of the Dominican Order in all Latin America. To be admitted there would be in keeping with the social prestige of the family.

In the Montano family various emotions prevailed. Political ambitions fanned by Uncle Eliodoro Villazon, former president of Bolivia, were forever ended. To the father it meant the loss of a son but the saving of the family name. The stepmother was relieved. To Walter it meant he could never marry or have a home of his own, but as he thought of his stepmother it seemed to him that this was no great sacrifice.

6. Walter Montano's Death

On February 9, 1920, at the age of 17, the journey began. At La Paz, the capital of Bolivia, a friend of the family acted as his companion and delivered him into the hands of Father Cristobal Vasquez, a Dominican monk and famed theologian.

Their course took them across Lake Titicaca, the highest navigable body of water in the world. And yet, so high did the Andes tower above it that Walter could scarcely believe he was more than two miles above sea level. On the Peruvian side of the lake they traveled by rail across the furnace-like desert to the Pacific Ocean. Here they embarked for Lima, Peru.

At the railway station in Lima Walter called a porter to carry his grips and valises. "No, you carry them," ordered the monk who had met him. With shame burning in his cheeks for the first time in his life he carried his own belongings. The negroes laughed to see a man whose derby hat indicated him to be of the better class carrying baggage through the streets.

They turned into the College of Saint Thomas Aquinas, connected with the monastery, and went on through the cloisters beyond, and Walter Manuel was formally delivered into the hands of the superior.

Walter and three other candidates prepared themselves with prayers, confessions, fasts, and the mass for entering upon their sacred duties. Upon completing their preparations, on March 25, Solemn Feast Day of the Virgin Mary, Walter and his companions were taken to the traditional altar inside the monastery, unseen save by the monks. Here, during an impressive ceremony, his outer garments were removed signifying the laying aside of his former life, and the black and white habit of a Dominican friar was blessed and placed upon him. Then he lay down in front of the altar while a burial ceremony was read over him. Thus did he die to the world, to live in the service of the church. Then, kneeling, he repeated the vow, "I, Walter Manuel Montano, promise to observe the vows of chastity, poverty, and obedience."

Walter Manuel Montano's name was changed to Fray Luis, after his patron saint Luis Beltrán, whose penance, preaching ability, and missionary zeal he earnestly desired to imitate.

7. The Life Of Fray Luis

The new life of Fray Luis consisted only of the living quarters and chapel of the novitiate. He had contact with none of the other monks except during the three daily prayer periods in the choir.

In addition, the novitiates had their own special prayers lasting about half an hour preceding breakfast, dinner, and bedtime. These exercises did not take the place of private devotions, which required up to an hour each day of repeating the Lord's Prayer and counting the beads of the rosary. There were also periods when they must lie down and concentrate their thought upon the passion of Christ and the sufferings of the Virgin Mary. While he had not yet come to a personal knowledge of God, Fray Luis was confident that he was drawing nearer to that revelation.

Day by day his devotion to the Virgin Mary increased. She listened to his every passing sorrow, forgave his sins, always smiled down upon him, and never chided him. He had never known a woman like that -- not since the age of three when his mother had wearily lain down to sleep the last long sleep of earth. He loved the Virgin as he felt he would have loved his mother had she lived.

8. A Deceptive Virgin

At the end of one year Fray Luis passed the examinations and was received into the Simple Profession. As in the novitiate, this group had a separate chapel of their own, but more liberty. Fray Luis raised ducks and chickens. In this way the loneliness became more bearable.

The liberalism of some of the teachers disturbed him. He was told of a chapel in the United States of America where the Catholics worshiped in the morning and the Protestants at night. The thought came to him that one group worshipped God and the other group worshipped the devil in the same place on the same day!

But asking questions was not encouraged, so Fray Luis devoted his mental and emotional energies toward the beautiful Virgin of the Rosary. She hung in his room and smiled upon him the first thing in the morning and the last thing at night. While he was denied a picture of his mother, still he wore pasted on the face of his watch the most bewitching face of the Virgin he was able to find.

Day by day his devotion to the Virgin grew greater. He read in the book *The Glories of the Rosary* that the Virgin would at times change the color of her face, thus expressing her anger or pleasure depending on the attentions which she received from the believers. It was nearing the time of the national election when one night as Fray Luis repeated the rosary he noticed that Mary's face was very pale. In fact, it had been growing whiter day by day.

After finishing prayers and while going to his room he suddenly remembered having left his cape in the priest's room. As he returned and stepped inside he noticed an unusual light in the chapel and the sound of movement. Cautiously Fray Luis stepped into the shadows. For a moment he was too astonished to believe his eyes. The devout woman in charge of the female saint's clothes and the Sacristan was busily engaged putting rouge upon the cheeks of the Virgin.

The next day the monks took part in a very solemn service in honor of the Virgin. The church was crowded. The sacristan preached a sermon extolling the administration of President Leguia. At the climax of the address he shouted, "You have seen the pallid cheeks of our Holy Mother recently. We have been asking for a sign so that we might know if our Virgin of the Rosary wished the re-election of President Leguia as president of this republic.

"See!" he cried pointing towards her. "Her pale cheeks are rosy once more. The Virgin has spoken. President Leguia must be re-elected in reverence, veneration, and devotion to our Most Holy Mother."

9. Within Monastery Walls

If there were disappointments in religion, there were compensating delights in studies. Fray Luis selected a Doctorate in Philosophy course. His degree would come from the San Marcos University of Lima, founded by the Dominican Order in 1551, the oldest institution of learning in the New World.

Fray Luis spent delightful hours studying church history, logic, commentaries on the Gospels, apologetics, proofs of Christianity, and Dominican constitutions. In reading Thomas Aquinas he found majesty, as of a universe built by a master mind. So swiftly that he himself could scarcely believe it, the three years of the Simple Profession were ended and he was recommended for the Solemn Profession.

As a fully accredited member of the Dominican community, for the first time Fray Luis discovered the real life of the priests. The routine now was entirely relaxed. He found himself free to break the rules as he pleased. Instead of a deeper holiness of life he found less. Instead of increased sincerity, he found cynicism.

One day as he prepared the bread and wine for the priest who would celebrate mass the priest said to him, "Do you believe this bread will actually become the body of Christ and this wine will become His blood?"

"Why, Father, of course!" exclaimed the astonished young monk of the Solemn Profession.

"Well, I do not."

"But then why do you celebrate mass?"

"Don't get excited," replied the older priest, "There are many things we do not believe which we teach the people. Transubstantiation is one of them."

Another day as Fray Luis was on his way to confession he met one of the order who had the reputation of not being a very moral priest. "Where are you going?" asked the latter.

"I am going to confess my sins, Father," returned Fray Luis.

"Foolish boy, do you still believe that the confessor can forgive your sins?"

"Why, yes, certainly!"

"You are a fool. When I used to hear confession I would go to sleep in the confession box and pay no attention to the silly things."

This was scarcely a spiritual preparation for the most solemn act of having one's sins dealt with in the only way which, according to the church, a holy God could accept. But even this was nothing as compared with the visit to the monastery of the canonical guest from Spain.

This man arrived for the purpose of making a spiritual and moral survey of all the friars, and Fray Luis was selected as secretary to this inquisitor. One by one, each priest was placed under a most sacred vow of obedience, and ordered to tell all he knew about the moral life of his companions. Fray Luis was obliged to write down page after page of matters relative to the secret lives of the priests, their follies and deceits, their betrayal of youthful innocence, their debaucheries and licentiousness.

Priests whom Fray Luis had looked upon as saints he now saw in the terrible light of reality. A sadness unutterable settled upon his soul to discover the depths of depravity to which they had sunk. The monastery appeared as a boat about to sink beneath the waves of sin.

In the Bible he read, "He that believeth on the Son hath eternal life." But according to the theology which he had memorized it was impossible for one ever to know that one's sins were forgiven. "No one can ever know that he is saved," remarked one of the professors. "Not even the pope knows whether he is saved until after he is dead."

10. "Little Hell" Points To Heaven

If there was one consuming passion in Fray Luis' life greater than religion it was literature. By age 23 he was an accomplished journalist and earned considerable money through his pen. Under the heading *The International Moment* he became a columnist for South American periodicals. Here he treated historical, patriotic, religious, and political subjects with vitality and passion.

A devotee of the library and by nature studious, Fray Luis was named head librarian of this place, the largest institution of its kind in South America. This gave him untrammeled opportunity to revel in the books of his choice, particularly the works of Saint Thomas Aquinas. Always before beginning his studies it was Fray Luis' custom to pray to Aquinas, and his triumphs in writing he attributed to the direct assistance which he thus received.

Perhaps there was prophecy in this, for many students affirm that had Protestantism been even humanly conceivable in the time of Aquinas he would probably have been one of the early reformers.

In his new office Fray Luis became responsible for "Little Hell," a room at the end of the main library filled with condemned religious books, particularly those of the Protestant sects. These volumes could only be consulted by special permission of the superior of the order. Not even the head librarian had any right so much as to open one of these volumes.

One day Fray Luis was overseeing the task of dusting "Little Hell." As he passed down the stacks his eye caught the title, "Nights with the Romanists." Intrigued, Fray Luis thrust the book under his monk's habit for later study. When he read about the Virgin Mary where it was explained that while evangelicals venerated her, they could not worship her, Fray Luis wanted to throw the volume out the window.

Another volume which fell into his hands was written "concerning the rights of priests and inveighing against the Roman Church." The pope had immediately excommunicated the author. But the doughty author wrote, "You may excommunicate me, but God does not excommunicate me." Such daring amazed Fray Luis.

One day Fray Luis acquired *The Salvation Army Song Book.* In his room he felt his soul truly stirred by the message of these simple gospel songs.

11. In The Temple Of The Son

Fray Luis asked for, and was granted, a transfer to Cuzco, ancient capital of the Incas. Here the monastery had been built upon the foundations of the Temple of the Sun. This was the scene of bygone glory when the Incas worshiped in their "Ingot of Gold," a building whose walls, columns and furniture were all of shining gold, and above whose altar hung an immense golden image of the sun just where the first rays of the dawn might fall upon it.

In Cuzco Fray Luis' religion was put to the test and seemed to fail. In Lima he had seen priests die. The mask of any seeming strength or consolation which religion might have afforded them was torn away. Death for them was a hideous, grudging surrender to the king of terrors. But now when Father Castro of Cuzco became ill, Fray Luis felt religion would be vindicated as victor over the last enemy. He regarded Father Castro as the most holy, saintly man he had ever met.

Such was not the case. This man was dying with the utter desperation of a condemned man who had no hope. His face was already like that of one damned. His room was terrible with nameless fear. It was something to be forgotten as quickly as possible. Religion did nothing for him when he needed it most.

After the death of his friend, Fray Luis began smoking as never before, lighting a fresh cigar with the dying embers of the one before. This brought a narcotic relief to his troubled soul, but could not resolve the uncertainty that filled his mind.

Another shocking experience in Cuzco happened one day as he was returning from a trip to the country where he had taken a group of students for recreation. They passed a small doorway above which was a sign reading, "Evangelical Mission." Fray Luis crossed himself devoutly to keep away any malevolent influence. He knew that these people were worshipers of the devil in person. He had preached this to large congregations. All good Catholics knew it to be so. This was the first time he had knowingly come so close to any such heretics.

12. The Monk Who Lived Again

Walter Manuel Montano was bound by the walls of social caste and traditional religion, from which, it seemed, there could never be escape. A thousand confused thoughts surged through his mind, but one became increasingly insistent: "Escape! Get out! Go! Run away! There is nothing here for you!"

The Protestants, he believed, worshiped the devil. But, what of it? Perhaps there was a joyous abandonment in giving oneself to the devil, though sold to him for eternity. Could it be worse than the living hell he now experienced? Suddenly the resolution formed in his mind. He would go to the Protestants. He would ask for an answer to life.

His plan was thoroughly thought out. The next morning he carried it swiftly into action. When he passed through the last of the closed doors to freedom the cold breeze from the Andes quickened him into action. In the gathering light of the dawn he started off rapidly down Santo Domingo Street.

The street door of the mission was shut. He pounded upon it. A gardener, early at his task, replied, "But Father, this is not a Catholic monastery. This is a Protestant mission."

"Yes, yes, I know. That is why I am here. Where is the chief of your order?"

Just then a young man of 35 put his head out the window above and shouted, "Wait a moment and I will be down." A few minutes later Rev. Charles A. Patton of the Evangelical Union of South America appeared on the steps of the parsonage. A tall, well-built man, he smiled kindly. There was a strange radiance and buoyancy about him, but the high altitude was already telling upon him. Within four-years' time he was destined to lay down his life in the depths of the Brazilian wilderness. But here he was this early dawn, landing in the gospel net a man who would shake Latin America with his God-given messages.

"For years," said Fray Luis, "I have desired to find peace and salvation. I have not found it, and now I have come to you. Please tell me whether you have peace in your heart. If you have it, tell me. If not, for God's sake tell me that."

"I cannot discuss theology with you," replied Patton, "but I can tell you that years ago I came to Christ Jesus with my heart burdened with sin and filled with unrest. I confessed all my sins to Jesus, and He forgave them every one. Now I have both peace and salvation. He will do the same for you."

It was 5:30 in the morning on January 3, 1927, when these two men knelt down before the living Savior. There was no argument. There were no long explanations. Protestant and Catholic apologetics had no place. They were praying — the one out of long years of fellowship with his Friend, His Guide, His Savior — the other beginning, stumblingly, falteringly, praying, really praying for the first time in his life.

From the broken depths of Fray Luis' heart there burst forth the confessions of one who finally saw himself in the clear light of God's holiness. The Spirit of the Living God was melting him, the fire of conviction was burning through his self-righteousness, sin was being brought to the light of his understanding that the blood of Christ might by faith cover his guilt once and for all by the divine High Priest.

The two men lost all count of time. But prayer was now ended. The answer had come. Fray Luis had indeed died, not upon the altars of a church building but upon Calvary with Christ. He now rose to newness of life through the power of the matchless life of One who had died but lived again.

The two men arose to their feet. It was 10:30 a.m. They had been on their knees five hours. The miracle had happened. Jesus had found another life in which to live incarnate. A new man could witness to Christ's victory. Instead of the devil, he was worshiping Christ, the living Christ, who now moved his heart to unspeakable joy.

Later at a meal together the former Fray Luis confessed, "I used to think you worshiped the devil in person. I thought you had a crucifix in the window pointing towards a river or perhaps a canal, and there you confessed your sins and blew them out the window hoping that the water would take them away. In fact, I brought a crucifix with me just in case I picture. Her words seemed those of some religious oracle.

Not long afterwards, seated in easy chairs on a veranda, they watched the brilliant gold of the evening sky turn to fire. Soon moon and stars would appear riding high above faraway mountains which lifted their fronded heights to the soft embrace of the night. Here the question of all questions was asked. The essential problem, after all, was this: Is it God's will? Together they faced all possibilities -- together they found the answer. "Yes."

On December 26, 1928, Walter Manuel and Esther were married. Dr. Montano was soon holding evangelistic campaigns throughout the nation and neighboring countries and working with the Evangelical Union of South America. He was later called to Lima where he superintended 160 self-supporting congregations, labored among the Indians, broadcast on the Radio Church of the Air, was responsible for the Evangelical Union periodical *Reborn,* helped establish a Bible institute, and was pastor of the First Peruvian Evangelical Church.

As we talk one afternoon with Dr. and Mrs. Montano, their daughter, Betty, six years of charm and mystery, bursts into the room and cries, "Oh, Mr. Pearson, I love you!"

"Junior," age four, looks on tolerantly, a bit of a smile tucking in the corners of his mouth in a way which causes ladies who know him well to take him and hug him in unseemly fashion.

Little Edmund nestles in his mother's arms, than which no better place was ever found for a young missionary of nine months.

Dr. Montano is showing pictures and curios from Mexico, where his work has been declared to be the outstanding religious event of the year.

This is home -- home like God meant it to be -- the Christian home of the monk who lived again.

Rev. B. H. Pearson, my sincere friend and brother, has written this book using my experiences in finding Christ. Since knowing the Savior I feel myself to be the happiest man in the world and also, on the other hand, I feel an agony for my people who cry for salvation.

Where are those who will reach out the arms of love to South America? This book has been a trumpet calling you to fight against the darkness and to win a victory through the cross of Christ. But we need more conquistadors. Who will reply?

-- Dr. Walter Manuel Montano

needed it in your worship."

Mr Patton smiled. There was no need to answer. Instead of being worshiped, the "Prince of this World" had been judged and cast out. Jesus, the Prince of Peace, had set up His kingdom in the heart of Fray Luis – Dr. Walter Manuel Montano, Protestant leader and preacher of the everlasting gospel.

13. Fires Of A Modern Inquisition

Almost immediately Walter Manuel began assisting Mr. Patton. Large numbers of Indians listened to his preaching. Thanks to his childhood Quechua Indian nurse he was able to preach to them in their own language. Many Indians believed as well as large numbers of the intellectuals and middle class, who also heard the Word gladly.

Dr. Montano extended his labors to an ever-widening circle of cities, convincing leaders of the Dominican Order that persuasion so far attempted could not stop him. A report against "the heretic" was submitted to the Vatican whereupon the sentence of excommunication issued by the pope himself fell upon the gospel crusader. But Christ was too real to him for this to cause even a ripple of fear.

There were threats on his life, and since the nation recognized only the Apostolic Roman Catholic Religion, becoming a Protestant in effect made Walter Manuel guilty of treason. He was tried, found guilty, and deported to Bolivia.

14. The Virgin's Rival

Increasing danger made it prudent to accept an invitation to visit the well-known Bible Institute in San Jose, Costa Rica. There he became grounded in Protestant theology and practice, served as a teacher, and met a young American lady, Miss Esther Piper.

Dr. Montano reached Costa Rica in September, 1927. In December of the same year Mrs. Lydia M. Piper came to see her daughter. She met Dr. Montano and, as a mother of her years has a right to do, fell in love with him. Walter Manuel called to see the mother and stayed to talk with Esther. He had little known a mother's love, and Mrs. Piper was kind and faithful to him as a spiritual guide and counselor. She became also a willing chaperon for her daughter.

Walter had often wondered what fellowship with pure and perfect womanhood might be. Well, here he was experiencing it. Here was an ideal made flesh and blood. In Esther's presence he felt caught up in living poetry, or art, as though he were standing before a sublime